Active Reading in the Arts and Sciences
Third Edition

Shirley Quinn
Educational and Reading Consultant

Susan Irvings
University of Massachusetts Boston

Allyn and Bacon
Boston • London • Toronto • Sydney • Tokyo • Singapore

Vice President, Publisher, Humanities: Joseph Opiela
Editorial Assistant: Kate Tolini
Marketing Manager: Karen Bowers
Editorial Production Service: Elm Street Publishing Services, Inc.
Manufacturing Buyer: Megan Cochran
Cover Administrator: Linda Knowles

Copyright © 1997, 1991 by Allyn & Bacon
A Viacom Company
160 Gould Street
Needham Heights, MA 02194

The first edition was published under the title *Active Reading: Reading Efficiently in the Arts and Sciences,* copyright © 1987 by Houghton Mifflin Company.

All rights reserved. No part of the material protected by this copyright notice may be reproduced or utilized in any form or by any means, electronic or mechanical, including photocopying, recording, or by any information storage and retrieval system, without written permission from the copyright holder.

Library of Congress Cataloging-in-Publication Data

Quinn, Shirley.
    Active reading in the arts and sciences / Shirley Quinn, Susan
Irvings. — 3rd ed.
      p.   cm.
    Includes index.
    ISBN 0-205-20047-8
    1. College readers.   I. Irvings, Susan.   II. Title.
PE1122.Q56   1997
428.4'3—dc20   96-20704
                                                                    CIP

Printed in the United States of America

10 9 8 7 6 5 4 3   01 00 99 98 97

Credits

Pages 19–22. Excerpt from *Understanding Psychology,* 5th edition, by Sandra Scarr and James Vander Zanden, copyright © 1987 by Random House, Inc. Reprinted by permission of McGraw-Hill Publishing Company.

Credits continued on page 469, which constitutes an extension of the copyright page.

To our parents

Contents

Preface ix
To the Student xiii

PART 1 Building the Foundation for Critical Reading 1

1 *Reading for Ideas* 3

   Making Connections 3
      Thinking and Reading 3
      What Is Reading 5
      Reading and You 6
   Questioning 10
      Defining Your Purpose 11
      Associating 13
      Predicting 14

2 *Previewing* 26

   Previewing a Course Syllabus 26
   Previewing a Textbook 31
   Previewing a Chapter 44
   Previewing an Article 48

3 *Developing Vocabulary: Connecting Words and Ideas* 59

   Words and Meaning 59
   General Vocabulary 60
      Using Context Clues 61
      Using Association Clues 66
      Using Word-part Clues 69

Academic Language 72
    General Words 73
    Same Words/Different Meanings 73
    Technical Words 73
Moving from a Passive to an Active Vocabulary 78

PART 2   Basic College Reading Skills   81

4   *Finding the Topic*   83

The Topic in Sentences 84
The Topic in Paragraphs 86
Topics and Subtopics in Longer Readings 90
Inferring the Topic from Clues 95

5   *Discovering the Key Idea*   100

The Key Idea of a Sentence 100
The Key Idea of Paragraphs 103
    Placement of the Key Idea 105
Inferred Key Ideas 110
Key Ideas of Longer Readings 113
Writing Summaries 124

6   *Identifying Supporting Ideas and Supporting Details*   128

Supporting Words and Phrases in Sentences 129
Supporting Ideas and Supporting Details in Paragraphs 132
Supporting Ideas and Supporting Details in Longer Readings 141

Mastery Exercise I   155

PART 3   Analytical and Critical Reading Skills   163

7   *Recognizing Basic Structure*   165

The Introduction 166
The Development of the Topic 167
The Conclusion 168
Signal Words for Basic Structure 171

8   *Analyzing Patterns of Organization*   179

List Pattern 181
    Signal Words for List Pattern 181
Order Pattern 183
    Chronological Order 183
    Process 183
    Size or Place 184

    Importance 185
    Signal Words for Order Pattern 186
   Compare/Contrast Pattern 186
    Signal Words for Compare/Contrast Pattern 188
   Cause-and-Effect Pattern 190
    Signal Words for Cause-and-Effect Pattern 191
   Problem-Solution Pattern 192

9 ***Becoming a Critical Reader: Determining the Author's Purpose* 207**

   Distinguishing between Informational Writing
    and Persuasive Writing 208
   Informational Writing 210
   Persuasive Writing 214

10 ***Becoming a Critical Reader: Evaluating Evidence and Reasoning* 226**

   The Author's Credibility and Bias 227
   Evidence 233
    Distinguishing between Fact and Opinion 233
    Evaluating Facts 236
   Reasoning 237
   Emotional Appeal 240
    Propaganda 241

11 ***Putting It Together: Flexible Reading and Active Learning* 245**

   The Three Approaches to Reading 246
   Reading Strategies 247
    Skimming 247
    Reading and Sectioning 266
    Studying and Organizing 277

   Mastery Exercise II 295

PART 4 **Critical Reading Skills Applied to Academic Fields**   **305**

12 ***Reading the Humanities*   307**

   The Nature of the Humanities 307
   Informational Writing 308
    Factual Writing 308
    Descriptive Writing 309
    Process Writing 309
    Patterns of Organization 312
   Imaginative Writing: Fiction 316
    Previewing Fiction 316
    Analytical and Critical Reading of Fiction 318

Persuasive Writing and Critical Reading 330
   Criticism 331
   Argument 338
Applications to Career Fields 345

13 *Reading the Natural Sciences* — 349

Characteristics of the Natural Sciences 349
Reading Mathematical and Scientific Material 350
   The Textbook 350
   Scientific Reports 359
Analytical and Critical Reading 363
   Patterns of Organization 368
   Organizing for Study 370
   Problem Solving 372
   Evaluation of Evidence 375
Applications to Career Fields 376

14 *Reading the Social Sciences and History* — 390

The Nature of the Social Sciences and History 390
   The Social Sciences 390
   History 392
Previewing 393
   Textbooks 393
   Nontextbook Material 393
Analytical and Critical Reading Skills 399
   Vocabulary 400
   Patterns of Organization 400
   Reading Graphic Aids 404
   The Research Report 412
   The Evaluation of Evidence 427
Applications to Career Fields 429
   Kinds of Reading 431
   Evaluation 432

Appendix A *List of Prefixes, Roots, and Suffixes* — 445

Appendix B *An Active Reader's Glossary* — 449

Appendix C *Answer Key* — 455

Index — 473

Preface

Active Reading in the Arts and Sciences was written to meet a need we recognized for a college reading text that would develop students' reading and critical thinking skills and teach them how to apply those skills to college texts and related readings. The very favorable response we had from instructors and students to our second edition, which represented a thorough revision of the first edition, has encouraged us to pursue, in this revision, our basic approach to the art of critical reading in the arts and sciences—that good thinking and good reading are based on good questioning. Previous users will note the major change: Many of the readings have been replaced by material of current interest. In addition, we have reorganized the flow of the book so that, for example, in line with our firm belief in the necessity of laying a solid foundation, previewing is included with other prereading tasks in Part 1, and previewing and reading graphics have been consolidated in Chapter 14.

An active reader is also an active learner who gains knowledge by looking for answers to questions. Questioning leads the reader to an awareness of the author's strategies of exposition; it enables the reader to extract the author's essential meanings, whether stated or implied, and to critically evaluate the author's ideas. The art of questioning, with explicit demonstrations of what questions to ask and what answers to look for, is the core of *Active Reading in the Arts and Sciences* because it leads to proficiency in both critical reading and critical thinking.

By the end of a course based on *Active Reading,* students can expect to have

1. mastered the fundamental cognitive and reading skills of building vocabulary in an academic context, reading for

stated and implied ideas, and recognizing the organization and hierarchy of ideas;
2. gained the ability to analyze the author's thinking as demonstrated in structure and patterns of organization;
3. learned how to apply critical thinking to the evaluation of the author's reasoning and use of evidence; and
4. transferred these skills and knowledge to reading and studying in the major academic fields.

At the same time, students will have learned how to look at their own thinking and reading processes by using such metacognitive skills as setting goals, monitoring progress toward those goals, and revising and modifying their reading strategies to achieve their goals.

Active Reading has four parts. Part 1 introduces the student to the ways a mature reader approaches reading and critical thinking through an understanding of the connections between thinking and reading, words and ideas, prereading and efficient reading, and vocabulary building and comprehension. Part 2 teaches the reading skills basic to college work, with emphasis on the ordering of ideas and discriminating between generalizations and supporting material. Part 3 moves the student, step-by-step, through the analytical reading skills of recognizing and working with the organization of material, to the critical reading skills of determining the author's intent and techniques and evaluating the author's evidence and reasoning. Part 3 ends with a chapter on such reading and studying strategies as flexible reading, skimming, marking up, note taking, outlining, and mapping. Part 4 consists of three chapters devoted to applying these skills and techniques to reading in specific academic fields—the humanities, the natural sciences, and the social sciences and history—and in so doing leads the student to an understanding of the roles of thought patterns and the rules of evidence in these disciplines. The concluding chapters also introduce material on reading fiction and criticism, on solving problems, and on reading graphics.

Three appendixes present (1) lists of word parts for use in building vocabulary; (2) a glossary of academic terms; and (3) answers for approximately half the exercises, to allow independent student work.

Eight features distinguish *Active Reading in the Arts and Sciences* as a comprehensive text for college students:

1. College-level readings, drawn from textbooks and other sources, on varied academic topics; on aspects of cognitive development, such as remembering and forgetting; and on thinking processes.

2. Many kinds of individual and group exercises to reinforce learning and give students practice in transferring active reading skills to the textbooks they use in other courses. Summary-writing exercises in most chapters and other questions provided in the instructor's manual emphasize the connection between reading and writing. Many exercises include marking up and diagraming to allow for a variety of learning styles.

3. Demonstrations of how to read, think, and learn in the various disciplines and a detailed examination—not generally found in reading texts—of the kinds of reading necessary to academic work, for example, the syllabus, case studies in the social sciences, problems in the natural sciences, and fiction, criticism, and argument in the humanities.

4. A chapter on vocabulary building that makes special references to inferring meaning from context, association, and word-part clues and to learning and using academic language.

5. Mastery exercises at the end of Parts 2 and 3 that allow the student and instructor to test and monitor understanding and application of skills.

6. Constant references to thinking skills, such as inference, generalization, recognition of hierarchical order, organizational patterns, and evaluation.

7. Sections on the application of active reading skills in the various academic disciplines to career fields.

8. A comprehensive instructor's manual, *Active Teaching*, that provides commentary, discussion questions, additional answers with explanations, essay questions, a three-hour reading workshop for students and a workshop for faculty colleagues on applying reading skills across the curriculum. The instructor's manual stresses ways in which the instructor can reinforce the development of critical and metacognitive thinking skills.

For their helpful suggestions about content and organization during the preparation of this book, we are grateful to the following reviewers: Pamela Leggat, Northern Virginia Community College; Roseanne Cook, Purdue University Calumet.

We would also like to thank Joe Opiela and the staffs of Allyn and Bacon and Elm Street Publishing Services, Inc. for their assistance, our colleagues and our students for their confidence and wisdom, and our families and friends for their continued encouragement and patience.

To the Student

Active Reading in the Arts and Sciences teaches you skills that are hard to acquire on your own. Through careful, step-by-step instruction you can gain a new understanding of the reading process. First, you are encouraged to think carefully about what reading is. What, for example, is the function of the words? What do authors want to accomplish when they write an article or a book? What do they expect your reaction to be? And what do you want to get out of a book or an article? By questioning your texts, you will discover the author's purpose in writing what you are reading; by questioning yourself, you will better understand why you are reading a particular book, chapter, article, or paragraph.

Next, you will see how words are arranged to help you grasp what you are reading and how ideas are structured in patterns to guide you from one set of ideas to the next. Posing questions and finding answers as you read will help you feel that you are having a conversation with the authors, a dialogue in which you are seeking to understand what they are saying. Understanding and thinking about your reading result in remembering.

If you carefully follow the principles of *Active Reading,* you will probably find that by the end of the course, you will have doubled your starting reading rate. And this increase in speed will have come about not at the expense of comprehension but because of improvement in understanding and efficient processing of the author's ideas.

This book is based primarily on the reading of nonfiction, such as textbooks, journal articles, and critical writing—the kind of prose you usually find in your academic work.

The table of contents provides an outline of the book and shows how its topics move from why and how you read for ideas, to how authors arrange those ideas into recognizable patterns, and finally to how you can apply these new strategies to your academic reading. Each chapter consists of a discussion explaining the concepts to be covered, examples illustrating those concepts, and reading selections and exercises to provide practice.

Through a variety of exercises you can apply the principles learned in this textbook to your other academic and daily work, such as note taking and writing. One particularly valuable skill is marking up a text. In *Active Reading* you will be asked quite often to show where a new principle applies by marking a passage in an exercise or by filling in a diagram. The mastery exercises at the ends of Parts 2 and 3 will help you judge how well you have understood and applied the concepts presented up to that point.

Also of value are Appendix A, a list of word parts for you to use in conjunction with vocabulary building; Appendix B, An Active Reader's Glossary, with definitions of useful academic terms and the words printed in boldface in the text; and Appendix C, answers to approximately every second exercise, to allow you to work independently.

Building the Foundation for Critical Reading

PART 1

Chapter 1

Reading for Ideas

In this chapter you will find answers to the following questions:

How are learning, thinking, and reading connected?
What is reading?
What are the different levels of reading comprehension?
Why is asking questions important?
How do associating and predicting help concentration?

Making Connections

Learning is making **connections** (associations, links, or bonds) between what is new and what you already know. Finding the connections between the new and the old makes the new familiar; once something has become familiar, you can understand it and use it. As you study and learn, your base of knowledge enlarges, to make connections and see relationships more easily. Thinking is the process by which you make these connections, and reading provides the new ideas that you will add to your store of knowledge. **Reading** is examining and understanding characters, words, or sentences.

Thinking and Reading

Each person is exposed to so many sensations every day that it is impossible to count them all. You get up in the morning and, depending on where you live, smell city or country smells, but unless you stop to think about them, those smells pass unnoticed. You see weather conditions, people, and things, but unless you stop to look, they too pass unnoticed. You hear the roar of traffic, the hum of insects, and the radio next door, but unless you stop to listen, those noises pass unnoticed. During the day you touch many objects, but unless you stop to feel them, they pass unnoticed. Life flows by you until you select certain sensations to be aware of: the smell of coffee, the sound of a friend's voice, the colors in a painting, the taste of an apple, the feel of a book page. **Thinking** is becoming aware and trying to connect yourself to what is going on around you. Thinking about meaning connects you to your reading.

Words used in the chapter titles and throughout *Active Reading*—words like *connecting, questioning, understanding, inferring, predicting, associating, developing, finding, discovering, identifying, recognizing, analyzing, determining, organizing, criticizing, judging, evaluating,* and *remembering*—and many others refer to active mental processes associated with thinking. Problem solving, decision making, and the processing and organizing of ideas are important thinking activities engaged in by every student.

Thinking is not a mystery; everyone does it all the time. But some people think more clearly and more systematically than others. The best way to sharpen your thinking is by being conscious of what, why, and how you and others think. The best means of achieving good analytical and critical thinking skills is through active, critical reading, where you think about the ideas of others and your reactions to those ideas. The psychologist E. L. Thorndike observes that reading is thinking, and the philosopher John Locke that "reading furnishes our minds only with material of knowledge; it is thinking [that] makes what we read ours." In both those views, reading and thinking are so closely connected that developing strength and efficiency in reading produces strength and efficiency in thinking, and vice versa.

Good reading and good thinking and studying depend on making the following connections:

- What you want from your reading and how you read
- What you know and what you want to know
- Your ideas and the author's ideas
- How ideas are stated and how they are applied
- The points authors make and the way they present them
- The general and the specific

What Is Reading?

You can read by looking at each letter in a word and at each word in a **sentence,** but unless you think about meaning, you won't comprehend the words or learn from them. Four levels of reading comprehension are reflected in the organization of *Active Reading:*

1. *Literal reading* is understanding what the actual words say. For instance, suppose you read, "Louisa is a student." The author's idea is plain and easily understood. Good literal reading is accomplished by learning what the words actually mean—that is, by improving your vocabulary—and by knowing how to read for the ideas set out in the written text. Chapters 3, 4, 5, and 6 provide you with these skills.

2. *Inferential reading* is figuring out what the author is implying but not actually stating. For instance, suppose you read, "Louisa's light is on, and it is way past midnight. She will certainly do well on the exam she has to take tomorrow." You infer that Louisa is studying and that she will do well on her exam because she is studying late. You **infer,** or guess, what the author is **implying,** or hinting at, by drawing conclusions from what has been said, based on your previous experience and knowledge. You will have many more occasions to work with **inference** throughout *Active Reading.*

3. *Analytical reading* is paying close attention to the ways in which authors organize their ideas. There is a basic **logic** (or relationship) in how authors structure their texts that becomes the introduction, the development of their ideas, and a conclusion. But beyond this fundamental structure are various patterns of thought that authors use as **patterns of organization,** such as comparing one thing with another or showing how some action causes a certain effect. Suppose you read, "Mike is a better student than Louisa for the following reasons." You know that the author is going to compare the two students' approaches to their work. Awareness of these patterns of organization leads to quicker and better understanding and improved retention. Chapters 7 and 8 deal specifically with how to read for structure and patterns of organization.

4. *Critical reading* starts with understanding the authors' purposes: why they wrote what you are reading and how they are achieving their aims. Are they writing to inform or to persuade? Are they using words to produce certain effects? What kinds of evidence support the arguments? Let us return to our examples about

Louisa. If the author wrote, "Mike is a better student and will do better on the exam than Louisa because he knows more and spends a longer time studying," the critical reader would question the author's assumptions that knowing more and studying longer necessarily result in better grades. Perhaps Louisa studies more efficiently and has a better sense of how to organize her thoughts when answering exam questions. More evidence is needed to prove that Mike is a better student. Critical readers think carefully about what authors have written by judging the authors' success in accomplishing their aims, by evaluating the evidence, and by agreeing or disagreeing with the authors' conclusions. Critical reading is taken up in Chapters 9 and 10.

Reading and You

By the time you complete *Active Reading*, you will have mastered these various types of reading. But first we will connect the topic of reading with you as an individual, by analyzing your current reading habits—such as where, when, and how you read. From this analysis you will see how you can read better, more attentively, and with greater comprehension over longer periods. The questions that follow will help you start thinking about the reading process. Although the answers to some of them may seem obvious, the **discussion** (examination in speech or writing) they provoke may encourage you to think more about reading and your role as a reader.

Exercise 1A

Circle the answer or answers that seem closest to what you think or feel, Most of these questions have more than one right answer, depending on individual responses.

Example:
What do I need to do to be a better reader?
(a.) improve my vocabulary
(b.) think more about what I'm reading
(c.) know what I want to get from reading
(d.) concentrate better

Most students would circle all the possible answers to this question.

1. What are words?
    a. the means of transmitting ideas
    b. symbols
    c. ideas
    d. meaningless series of letters
2. What is reading?
    a. looking at words
    b. sounding out letters
    c. translating written words into thoughts or ideas
    d. the opposite of writing
3. Why do people write?
    a. to organize their thoughts
    b. to communicate ideas
    c. to inform
    d. to learn
4. Why do people read?
    a. to learn
    b. to communicate
    c. to be informed
    d. to be amused
5. What is your attitude toward reading?
    a. Frankly, it bores me.
    b. I love to read.
    c. I'd sooner watch TV.
    d. I'd read more if I could read better.
6. What do you read mostly?
    a. textbooks
    b. novels
    c. magazines
    d. newspapers
    e. specialized journals

7. How do you read?
   a. I read word by word.
   b. I start at the beginning and read right through to the end.
   c. I read everything the same way and at the same speed.
   d. I look for the author's ideas.
   e. I lose my concentration and have to reread.
8. Where do you read?
   a. in a comfortable chair
   b. at my desk
   c. in the library
   d. always in the same place
   e. in a noisy room
9. When do you read?
   a. in the morning, when I'm most alert
   b. in the afternoon, when I'm most alert
   c. late at night
   d. when I can't think of anything else to do
10. How long should you read at a time?
    a. fifteen minutes
    b. two hours
    c. four hours
    d. It depends on the material.
11. Why are you taking this course?
    a. I want to read faster.
    b. I find it hard to concentrate when I read.
    c. I want to read with greater understanding.
    d. I want to better remember what I read.
    e. I want to find out how to get through all the reading I have to do for my courses.

In responding to these questions, you have been thinking about the kind of reading you do and why you do it. You probably found that you checked almost all the answers to question 11. Concentration is linked to greater understanding, which in turn leads to better retention of reading material. In the same way, reading faster so as to get through all the reading you have to do in college is connected to how well you understand and retain your reading. Through your answers you may have concluded that the prose on a printed page is a means of communicating ideas from author to reader and that these ideas are conveyed in words. These important **concepts,** or ideas, will be taken up in later chapters of *Active Reading.*

How and what you read are determined by why you read. Whereas you can relax in an easy chair and read a novel for enjoyment, you need to study attentively the information found in your physics assignment. When and where do you concentrate best and learn most? The evidence and your own experience suggest that there are a "better" time and a "better" place to read when concentration is your goal. Human beings are diurnal animals; that is, they operate best in the daylight hours. The mind, like the rest of the body, works best when it is fresh. Therefore, the best time for most people to take in and understand new ideas is in the morning, when the mind is ready for exercise. You can also help your concentration by finding a quiet place, like a particular spot in the library, to which you can go to read and study. Soon you will start associating that place with thinking, and you will find your concentration increases as distractions and interruptions decrease.

How long you read at a time depends again on what and when you read. It is wise, however, to begin by reading in fifteen-minute blocks or for as long as you can concentrate. If you start losing concentration, move to another task or assignment. Most people cannot concentrate on academic reading for much longer than an hour without taking a brief break. After several hours, you can take a longer break to relax a bit before resuming your studying.

Now, as you start this course, is a good time to adopt new habits, such as finding a reading place that is free of distractions and resolving to do more of your reading at the time of day when you are most alert. These are the first steps in gaining control over your reading. Questioning and setting the stage for good reading are taken up in the following sections.

Exercise 1B

In short but complete sentences, answer the following questions:

1. How are learning, thinking, and reading connected?

   _____

2. What is reading?

   _____

3. What are the different levels of reading comprehension?

   _____

Questioning

Defining purpose, associating what you are learning with what you already know, and anticipating what is to come through prediction—all are based on the answers to careful and precise questions. These conscious, thinking activities are key to the necessary activity of previewing and lay the groundwork for efficient reading.

Questioning is the foundation of all learning. As you read *Active Reading*, you will notice the emphasis on questions, starting with questions at the beginning of each chapter and continuing with questions related to each concept presented. When you ask a question, you are looking for an answer. Looking for answers gives you a focus and a purpose in reading that motivate you to continue with an assignment. Maintaining your interest and continuity of effort helps you concentrate and ultimately helps you remember. Questioning also leads to better comprehension through improved analytical and evaluative skills.

Asking questions helps you to sort information, to be precise about what you need to know, and to discriminate what is of value to you from what is not. Asking questions helps you understand what you are reading by probing deeper into the text—associating what you are learning with what you already know, and seeing how one aspect relates to another.

Asking questions sets your mind to looking actively for answers; by looking for an answer, you become actively involved with your reading material—your mind, not just your eyes, is working on it. Just as you can't learn how to ride a bicycle sitting by the side of the road and watching someone else struggle, you can't learn how to read efficiently without the active participation of your mind—and such participation is required when you ask and answer questions.

Exercise 1C

As you start Active Reading, *what are five questions that occur to you about reading?*

1. _____?

2. _____?

3. _____?

4. _____?

5. _____?

Defining Your Purpose

The lack of a well-thought-out objective can influence a person's motivation for the job at hand and may result in vague feelings about purpose. Think for a moment of the big decisions in your own life. Going to college is one. Do you know why you are attending college? Do you know why you chose the college you did? What do you hope to get out of your education? The answers to such questions may influence how you think about your college experience. If you haven't thought them through, you probably have no clear notion of why you are at college or what you hope to get from it. The resulting feelings of purposelessness will not produce your best performance. On the other hand, a clear notion of why you chose the college you did and what you want to get from your education will help you set your purpose and establish priorities.

Thinking about why you do anything forces you to articulate for yourself a **reason** (or basis) for doing it. Often, this thinking tells you how the current task fits into your larger scheme. For instance, suppose you chose the college you did because you wanted to major in business and, as a potential business major, you are now taking an accounting course. You read your accounting text both to learn how to do accounting and to pass the course; your immediate purpose in reading the accounting text is thus joined to your long-term goal of completing college and finding a place for yourself in the business world. This kind of thinking about your purpose and fitting it into your personal objectives can help motivate you to read more actively.

You can judge how to read an assignment when you know why you are reading it. If your purpose is to do a chemistry experiment or assemble apparatus for a physics problem, you will read the instructions about the procedure very carefully, for each step matters. If you are looking for a particular piece of information, you may have to **skim** (read or glance at quickly) through several publications to find it. If you are reading about the drought in Africa for a sociology course, your **principal** (or chief) interest will be how the drought affects the people: What are the mortality rates? What is happening to the family or tribal unit? On what basis is aid being distributed? And so on. If you read the same article for an economics course, your questions will have more to do with what caused the drought and with what effect the drought is having on the economy, the labor force, the balance of payments, and exports and imports. The difference in viewpoint produces a difference in emphasis and influences how each of two people reads the same article.

Efficient reading requires you to be active in both defining and pursuing your purpose. An efficient reader doesn't read every word of every book or article on a reading list. Knowing the demands on your time, instructors do not expect you to read each item on a reading list word by word, but they do expect you to read actively, with intelligence and discrimination. Selecting what is relevant to your task and letting go of what is irrelevant constitute the art of efficient reading.

Carefully and precisely defining your purpose in reading a text is an excellent way to improve concentration, and through concentration your understanding and retention of the material. Concentrating, reading with understanding, remembering, sorting the relevant from the irrelevant, and motivating yourself for the task all start with the question, *Why am I reading this?*

Exercise 1D

In this exercise you are to work with a partner. Each of you should choose a text that you are going to read either for a course or for personal interest. By asking and answering the following questions, try to help each other be as precise as possible about what your purpose in reading may be.

1. Why are you reading these texts?

   _____

2. Why have they been assigned? or Why do they interest you?

   _____

3. What do you want to get out of them?

   _____

4. How do they connect with other books you have been reading?

   _____

Associating

A story that is sometimes told about the nineteenth-century philosopher John Stuart Mill makes a relevant point. It seems that whenever Mill decided to read a book, he thought about its topic for several days, trying to remember everything he could about the subject; he then drew up questions based on what he did and did not know about the topic. The result of this practice was that when Mill started to read, his mind was totally engaged by the topic, his questions were ready, and he had a foundation for the new concepts or information he would get from his reading. Our minds are like a reef that has been built by the skeletons of tiny coral, each adding a minute layer to the base laid down by previous generations: The reef grows and grows and grows. You too can prepare for your reading by asking, *What do I already know about this topic?*

You learn new facts and new ideas from your own and others' experiences. The more you know, the more knowledge you have to relate to new information and new concepts. When you think about what you have learned about a topic, your mind is **associating,** or connecting, the topic with what you know about it. This process connects your purpose in reading something to what you already know about it, because your previous knowledge defines the questions you ask. Let's take a concrete example. If you know what a mammal is and you learn that a whale is a mammal, you can compare a whale with other mammals and know that a whale breathes air and produces live young, which it nurses. You can then contrast a whale with a fish, because you already know something about fish. Whales breathe air directly through blowholes; fish filter air from water by means of gills. With this knowledge as a base, you can ask other questions about the whale: How did a mammal end up in the ocean? How does the brain of a whale compare with that of other mammals and with that of fish? Thinking about the whale as a mammal, listing its attributes, and understanding the difference between a whale and a fish are far more likely to make this information stick in your mind than would be the case if you quickly read it in a book and thought no more about it.

When you consciously **refer** to your knowledge base, you can be prepared to receive new ideas and information and can make associations faster. Your art history course, for example, makes more sense and the material is easier to learn when you can connect its subject matter with what you learned in a history survey course; an American literature course is more meaningful when you know something about the authors and the setting in which they were writing; and the information in a personnel manual becomes clearer when you know some of the psychology on which it is based. You can gain a surer sense of purpose, make better predictions of what the author is going to say, and form more precise questions by asking, *What do I already know about this topic?*

Predicting

In a modern morality story, Jim Washington is a smart businessperson who thinks very carefully before he goes into an important meeting. He realizes that his job may depend on knowing not only what he himself is talking about but also what his associates will be talking about. He takes a good look at the agenda for the meeting so as to know what topic is coming up; then he tries to remember what he knows about that topic so as to be well prepared for the discussion. His thinking ahead may also reveal what he doesn't know about the topic and what he therefore needs to study. Jim tries to predict what to expect from the other people who will be at the meeting. What point of view will Sam Anderson have on this subject? Does Jim agree with him? Why or why not? How about the president of the company? What kind of information is she going to want—budget figures, production figures, sales figures, market forecasts? This kind of thinking puts Jim in a better position than Sam—who rushed into the meeting direct from a late lunch. Good predicting prepares you for what is to come and may even give you an edge over the competition.

With respect to reading assignments, **predicting** is based on questions that develop from the way you have prepared yourself by identifying the following:

- What your purpose is
- What you already know about the topic
- What you already know about the author
- What information you can get from such clues as chapter and section headings

The predictions you make may not always be correct. When you read, you might find that the author is treating the topic in a different way or introducing information you either did not think of or did not know about. The very act of checking your predictions, however, is another means of involving yourself in your reading and of improving your concentration and retention. Among the prediction questions you might ask are these:

- *What is the author going to discuss?*
- *Might the author have a point of view, or position, on the topic?*
- *What particular pieces of information will the author deal with?*
- *What kind of supporting information will the author use?*

For example, from looking at the title and first **paragraph** and knowing something about the authors, you can use these questions to make predictions about the following article, written by Jeff W. Garis and H. Richard Hess of the Career Development and Placement Center at Pennsylvania State University and Deborah J. Marron, a coordinator of career planning at Mount Vernon College.

For Liberal Arts Students Seeking Business Careers, Curriculum Counts

For some time now, career planning and placement offices nationwide have been aware of a common problem: Liberal arts graduates seeking entry-level professional positions in business and industry are having difficulty competing with business and technical majors. In recent decades, various journals have noted this trend, often followed by a cry from students, parents, and faculty that career planning and placement offices should do more to help liberal arts graduates find jobs.

The title provides a fairly detailed answer to the question: What is this reading about? It is about liberal arts students seeking business careers. The title also tells you that the discussion will deal with ways in which the curriculum, or courses that a student takes, may affect the possibility of a business career. Because all the authors are involved in career counseling and placement, they will undoubtedly discuss this issue from the viewpoint of student career planning. And because the first paragraph addresses the problem liberal arts graduates have in competing with business and technical majors for jobs, it is a good guess that the article will examine this issue, citing facts to support the authors' viewpoint and stating what can be done about the problem.

These questions help you set the foundation for reading "For Liberal Arts Students Seeking Business Careers, Curriculum Counts." They help you to start thinking about what you already know about the topic; you begin wondering what the authors will say. You then start reading the article actively, because you are testing your predictions and seeking answers to your further questions. You are concentrating, because you are actively engaged in reading. And you are more likely to remember what you have read because through associating and predicting you are involved in the process.

Exercise 1E

Imagine that you are expected to read articles or books on the topics that follow. Think about what you already know about these topics and then predict some things you think you might learn from your reading. Allow your mind to range freely, thinking about how, why, what, who, where, what kind, and when.

Example:
Topic: Relations between France and Germany from 1900 to 1925

  a. Some things I know about the topic: *France and Germany are two European countries. They were on opposite sides in World War I.*

  b. Some things I predict I will learn: *Why they were on opposite sides. Which side won the war. What the effect was on the other.*

1. Topic: The autobiography of Dwight Eisenhower

    a. Some things I know about the topic:

    _____

    _____

    _____

    b. Some things I predict I will learn:

    _____

    _____

    _____

2. Topic: The effect of acid rain on lakes and forests

    a. Some things I know about the topic:

    _____

    _____

    _____

    b. Some things I predict I will learn:

    _____

    _____

    _____

3. Topic: Minority rights in the workplace

    a. Some things I know about the topic:

    _____

b. Some things I predict I will learn:

4. Topic: The role of vitamins in good nutrition
   a. Some things I know about the topic:

   b. Some things I predict I will learn:

5. Topic: A comparison of automobile advertising on television and in magazines
   a. Some things I know about the topic:

   b. Some things I predict I will learn:

Exercise 1F

This exercise is designed to give you a sense of how you currently read. The reading selection is from a chapter in a psychology textbook. The subject matter—thought and thinking—builds on what we have been discussing in Chapter 1 and is highly relevant to your work as a student.

1. From looking at the article and at the information given above, predict three points that will be made in the selection.

    a. _____

    b. _____

    c. _____

2. Read the selection in your usual way and then complete the statements that come after it. You may find the following vocabulary useful:

    abstract: Considered apart from concrete existence, as when you think of "tables" in general rather than a specific "table," such as your kitchen table.

    attribute: A quality or characteristic of a person or thing, as in "Jay Leno's sense of humor is a useful attribute."

    stimulus: Something causing, or regarded as causing, a response, as in "The need for money is a stimulus for getting a job."

    domain: A sphere of activity, concern, or function, as in "the domain of history."

Thought

1 ...[H]uman beings are capable of doing things with information that make the most complex computer seem simple by comparison. They are capable of thought....

2 Our ability to engage in complex thought—to ponder matters, to reason about them logically, to engage in complicated problem solving, and to have sudden bursts of creative insight—is a vital component of humanness. Moreover, it has been and continues to be a primary mechanism by which people adapt to their environment. Human beings have learned to adjust to geographical and climatic environments

ranging from that experienced by Alaskan Eskimos to that of the nomads of the Sahara. Human civilization is a history of thought and problem solving, from the discovery of fire and the invention of the wheel to modern space travel.

Thinking

Thinking may be viewed as the process of changing and reorganizing the information stored in memory in order to create new information. For instance, by thinking, you are able to put together any combination of words from memory and create sentences never devised before (including this one). The processes of thought depend on several devices or units: images, symbols, concepts, and rules.

Units of Thought

...[H]uman beings possess a remarkable capacity for mental visualization. It is one of the primary means for channeling information into memory (Paivio, 1971; Nelson, Reed, and McEvoy, 1977).* Hence it is hardly surprising that imagery should play a central role in much of thinking activity. An *image*—a mental representation of a specific event or object—is the most primitive unit of thought. Evidence of mental operations using images abounds in everyday life. Consider this question. How do you get a card table through a narrow doorway without folding up the legs? Most people indicate that they first mentally envision the process of turning the table on its side, putting two legs through the opening, then rotating the table to get the other legs and top to pass through the doorway. Many scientists testify that their greatest achievements derived from imagined spatial relations and transformations. Albert Einstein's theory of relativity and James Watt's visualization of the mechanism for condensing steam in an engine were arrived at in this way (Cooper and Shepard, 1984).

A more abstract unit of thought is a *symbol,* a sound or design that stands for an object, event, or quality. The most common symbols in thinking are words: every word is a symbol that represents something other than itself. Symbols are arbitrary stand-ins for actual or imagined things. Although they stand for other things, symbols do not necessarily bear any relationship to them. For example, the word

---

*In this and other articles you read in this book, you will find references in parentheses. These references, giving a name and date, are to articles or books that the author uses to support his or her statements.

"small" is larger than the word "big," and on this page the symbol "yellow" appears just as black as the symbols "black" and "white." Whereas an image represents a specific sight or sound, a symbol may have a number of meanings. The fact that symbols differ from the things they represent enables you to think about things that are not present, to range over the past and future, to imagine things and situations that never were or will be. Numbers, letters, and punctuation marks are all familiar symbols of ideas that have no concrete existence.

When a symbol is used as a label for a class of objects or events with certain common attributes, or for the attributes themselves, it is called a *concept*. "Animals," "music," "liquid," and "beautiful people" are examples of concepts based on the common attributes of the objects and experiences belonging to each category. Thus the concept "animal" separates a group of organisms from such things as automobiles, carrots, and Roquefort cheese. Concepts enable you to chunk large amounts of information. You do not have to treat every new piece of information as unique, since you already know something about the class of objects or experiences to which the new item belongs. Thus by means of concepts you are able to sort large numbers of stimuli into manageable units and domains of related concepts. In this manner you reduce the complexity of your environment.

The fourth and most complex unit of thought is a *rule*, a statement of the relationship between two or more concepts. You do not live in a world characterized by just so many bits and pieces of information. Instead, some items are linked to other items in an orderly or recurrent manner. Examples of rules include "A person cannot be in two places at the same time" and "Mass remains constant despite changes in appearance."

Images, symbols, concepts, and rules are the building blocks of mental activity. They provide an economical and efficient way for people to represent reality, to manipulate and reorganize it, and to devise new ways of acting. A person can think about pursuing several different careers, weigh their pros and cons, and decide which to pursue without having to try them all....

Kinds of Thinking

People think in two distinct ways. The first, called *directed thinking*, is a systematic and logical attempt to reach a specific goal. This kind of thinking depends heavily on symbols, concepts, and rules. Directed thinking is deliberate and purposeful. Through directed thinking people solve problems, formulate and follow rules, and set, work toward, and achieve goals.

The other type of thinking, called *nondirected thinking*, consists of a free flow of thoughts through the mind, with no particular goal or plan, and depends more on images.... Nondirected thinking is usually rich in imagery and feelings. Daydreams, fantasies, and reveries are typical examples. People often engage in nondirected thought when they are relaxing or trying to escape from boredom or worry. This kind of thinking may provide unexpected insights into one's goals and beliefs. Scientists and artists say that some of their best ideas emerge from drifting thoughts that occur when they have set aside a problem for the moment. A number of psychologists (Osborn, 1963; Parnes, 1971) have promoted *brainstorming* as a technique for fostering nondirected thinking. It is a process by which a great many solutions to a problem are encouraged by thinking out loud and deferring judgment and evaluation. Freewheeling is welcomed, and individuals are urged to build on one another's ideas by improving on them or combining them in various ways with other ideas.

—Sandra Scarr and James Vander Zanden,
Understanding Psychology

A. *Circle the word or phrase that you think best completes the following statements.*

Example:
This article is about
a. remembering and forgetting.
b. reading.
c. writing.
(d.) thinking.

1. Thinking

   a. is done by computers.

   b. is done by animals.

   c. sets human beings apart from computers and nonhuman animals.

   d. is the same as feeling.

2. Thinking does *not*
    a. help us to adapt to our environment.
    b. play a part in invention and discovery.
    c. consist of changing and reorganizing information.
    d. make computers seem complex by comparison.
3. The process of thought depends on
    a. images, symbols, concepts, and rules.
    b. hearing, seeing, tasting, and smelling.
    c. feelings, sensations, attitudes, and impressions.
    d. opinions, facts, theories, and guesses.
4. An image is
    a. a mental representation of a specific event or object.
    b. a sound or design that stands for an object, event, or quality.
    c. more complex than a rule.
    d. used as a label for a class of objects or events with certain common attributes.
5. A symbol is
    a. a mental representation of a specific event or object.
    b. a sound or design that stands for an object, event, or quality.
    c. more complex than a rule.
    d. used as a label for a class of objects or events with certain common attributes.
6. Concepts make it possible to
    a. visualize something.
    b. distinguish one group of objects or events from another.
    c. treat every new piece of information as different from any other.
    d. make one's environment more complex.
7. Which of the following is *not* a rule?
    a. If you can't swim but you go into deep water without a life preserver, you will drown.

b. Good studying usually produces good grades.

c. Heat cooks.

d. All students get good grades.

8. To *chunk* probably means

   a. putting like things together into units.

   b. thinking about pieces of Roquefort cheese.

   c. separating units.

   d. the same as *symbol*.

9. People set their purposes and work toward goals by using

   a. nondirected thinking.

   b. directed thinking.

   c. chunking.

   d. their feelings.

10. People engage in nondirected thought when they

    a. daydream.

    b. plan ahead.

    c. make lists.

    d. follow rules.

11. Einstein

    a. lived in 1850.

    b. was a composer.

    c. is a chess champion.

    d. was a scientist.

12. This reading is

    a. based on facts.

    b. based on the author's opinion.

    c. probably written by a poet.

    d. based on a mixture of fact and opinion.

B. *Answer* yes *or* no *to these statements:*

1. I looked this reading over before I read it. _____

2. I tried to associate the topic with material I have been reading in Chapter 1. _____
3. I checked my predictions as I read. _____
4. My predictions were mostly right. _____
5. I found this passage easy to read. _____

Exercise 1G

In short but complete sentences, answer the following questions:

1. Why is asking questions important?

   _____

2. How do associating and predicting help concentration?

   _____

Chapter 2

Previewing

In this chapter you will find answers to these questions:

What are the benefits of previewing?
What questions do you ask when you preview?
What can you learn from a course syllabus?
Are books, chapters, and articles previewed in the same way?
How do you preview and read graphic aids?

Before you actually start reading something, you **preview** it to find out what it might include, why it was written, and how it is presented. Previewing textbooks and other course materials, such as a **syllabus,** or course outline, and supplementary readings, starts the process of understanding through active reading.

By taking just a few minutes to question and look over parts of the texts you are about to read, you can get a great deal of information that will help you ask more specific questions when you go back and actually read and study those texts. Your preview provides the broad picture and a context for the information you will read; your later reading will supply the supporting ideas and supporting details that answer your specific questions.

Previewing a Course Syllabus

Often the first piece of reading a student gets for a course is the course syllabus. If you examine this document thoughtfully, you can get much more from it than a list of assignments and the due dates of papers and exams.

The course syllabus can be a good guide to the development of the course and the place of the readings. This point applies particularly to courses for which no main textbook is assigned. On the first day of class you can preview the syllabus to determine what the course is about; what key idea about the topic the instructor is going to emphasize; how the course is organized; and how the various parts fit together. The syllabus thus provides a skeleton, or **outline,** of the course.

The excerpts, found on p. 28, from the syllabus of an introductory political science course illustrate several of these points. As you can see, the introduction to the syllabus furnishes an overview of the course. It delineates the structure of the course—where the course starts, where it ends, and what stages it goes through to get there. The introduction also indicates that the course is based on a comparative study of a variety of political systems, modern and ancient. It helps you discover the key idea: that the course will emphasize the similarities and differences in the fundamental conceptions of political leadership, political participation, social and political equality, and liberty of a group of countries. And from the portion of the syllabus on American democracy, you can see that most of the readings consist of book chapters, articles, or official documents.

Exercise 2A

Preview the following excerpts from a syllabus for an introductory course in a new technology studies program. Answer the questions with your predictions of what the course will cover.

Medical Technology and Critical Decisions Spring 1995

This course provides an examination of new options in medical diagnosis, treatment, and prevention and an analysis of methods for making decisions that can lead to informed choices by patients, doctors, and society. It will include the study of amniocentesis, and other issues of medical decision making, together with their economic and ethical aspects. The course is taught by Professors Ted Ducas (Physics) and Alan Shuchat (Mathematics).

Introduction to Politics

Tuesday, Thursday

Fall Semester

Political Science 101 is an introduction to the study of politics, political ideas, and political systems. The vehicle for our study will be the comparative examination of a variety of contrasting political systems: ancient Athens, Great Britain, the United States, Nazi Germany, and contemporary China. We will examine the philosophical foundations of each of these political systems, their major political institutions, and their characteristic political processes. In particular, we will attempt to understand these different forms of government by emphasizing the similarities and differences in their fundamental conceptions of political leadership, political participation, social and political equality, and liberty.

This course will begin with the study of ancient Greece, the focus of the great political philosophers, Plato and Aristotle. We will examine the classic responses these philosophers gave to the questions of the meaning of political life, the best organization of government, and who should rule and why. We will then compare the liberal democracies of Great Britain and the United States. We will next try to understand why liberal democracy failed in Weimar Germany and how Hitler came to power. Finally we will study Marxism and its distinctive application in contemporary China.

* * * *

PART III: AMERICAN DEMOCRACY

October 18   The Foundations of American Democracy

             The Articles of Confederation (skim)

             Declaration of Independence

             Alexander Hamilton and James Madison, *The Federalist Papers,* Numbers 10 and 51

             Constitution of the United States of America

October 23   American Democracy: Majorities and Minorities

             Alexis de Tocqueville, *Democracy in America,* Volume I, Chapters IV, XV, XVI; pp. 57–61, 264–297

October 25   American Politics: The Structure of Power

             Robert Ross, *American National Government,* Chapters 1–5, 7, 9, 10 (skim)

             Robert Dahl, "Power in New Haven: The Pluralist Thesis," in R. Gillam, *Power in Postwar America*

October 30   American Politics: Power, Elites, Classes, and Conflict

             Paul M. Sweezy, "The American Ruling Class," in R. Gillam, *Power in Postwar America*

             C. Wright Mills, "The Structure of Power in American Society," in R. Gillam, *Power in Postwar America*

November 1   Democracy and Empire

             Rachelle Marshall, *A Brief Account of Vietnam's Struggle for Independence*

             Leslie H. Gelb, "Vietnam: The System Worked"

—Lois Wasserspring

I. Introduction: *Overview of the course.*

Medical technology, risk, and decision making under certain conditions.

Focus on personal medical decisions such as amniocentesis.

Scientific and mathematical principles underlying the transmission of genetic defects, ultrasound technology, and decision making based on probabilities and personal values.

Fein, "Fetal Test Focuses the Health-Care Debate," *New York Times*, February 5, 1994. This article discusses the personal amniocentesis decision and its connection to larger-scale socioeconomic issues.

II. Representing Data: *Summarizing data numerically and graphically.*

Histograms, average, median, and standard deviation.

Freedman, *Statistics*, pp. 25–38, 48–57. Be prepared to discuss page 28, problem 8 in class.

Gould, "The Median Isn't the Message," *Discover*, June 1985, pp. 40–42.

The normal "bell" curve.

Freedman, *Statistics*, pp. 57–86. Be prepared to discuss page 64, problem 7 in class.

III. Probability: *Introduction to probabilistic reasoning.*

Elementary concepts and sources of probabilities.

Lab session on data and probability, probability trees.

Freedman, *Statistics*, pp. 203–222. To discuss in class: page 216, problem 5.

Murphy, "Quantitative concepts: What every doctor should know," SIAM News, March 1988, p. 6. To discuss in class: "Unlucky 13."

Conditional probabilities, testing, and diagnosis.

Weinstein, *Clinical Decision Analysis*, pp. 42–47, 79–99. Think about how the tables, Bayes' Formula, and the tree method are related.

Knox, "Who should be tested," *Boston Globe*, May 17, 1987, B14. To discuss in class: What are the conditional probabilities assumed in this article, and what would the tree structure be?

IV. Genetics: *How can we use biology and probability to make predictions about the next generation?*

    Molecular basis of genetics.

        Singer, *Human Genetics,* Chap. 3, pp. 53–79, Chap. 5, pp. 99–110.

    Generational analysis and genetically linked traits.

    Applications of probability to genetics; sex-linked traits, population genetics.

    The genetics and statistics of Down's syndrome.

    Ethical systems and reproductive issues.

        Singer, *Human Genetics,* Chap. 1, pp. 1–29, Chap. 6, pp. 121–136.

        Pauker, *Pregnancy after 30.*

        Francouer, *Biomedical Ethics,* Chap. 1.

V. Ultrasound and Other Imaging Technologies: *What information can be extracted using sound? How does this lessen the risk of amniocentesis and what new risks does it introduce?*

    The nature of sound.

    Imaging using sound as a non-invasive means of obtaining information.

    Other imaging techniques, such as X-rays, MRI, etc.

    Ultrasound in amniocentesis and the question of risk.

    Lab sessions on characteristics of sound.

        Powis, *Ultrasound.*

        Sochurek, "Medicine's New Vision," *National Geographic,* Jan. 1987, pp. 2–41.

    Take-home midterm exam

—Ted Ducas and Alan Shuchat

1. What is this course about?

    _____

    _____

2. What topics are covered in the first five sessions?

    _____

_____

_____

_____

_____

3. What example will probably be used as an application of the new technology?

_____

Previewing a Textbook

You preview a text by quickly looking for answers to several questions—some of which you were introduced to in Chapter 1 and others that will be dealt with in more detail in later chapters.

What is this reading about? (Chap. 4)
Who is the author?
When was the reading published?
What is the author's most important idea about the topic? (Chap. 5)
Why did the author write this text? (Chap. 9)
Why am I reading this text?
What do I already know about the topic?
How is the material presented?

As you learned in Chapter 1, the answers to some of these questions will help you set your purpose, decide on what you hope to gain from your reading, and relate what you are about to read to what you already know about the topic. The answer to these questions will also provide you with valuable insights on which to base your predictions of what the reading will contain and how the author will support his or her arguments. It is wise to take a few moments to preview everything you are about to read, because by doing so you ultimately will save time and gain understanding.

Most textbooks are organized so as to make previewing easy, and much information can be located quickly in parts of the text you may not ordinarily read. For instance, the **preface** (or introductory statement by the author) usually sets forth the key idea and organization of a book, and the table of contents helps you see how the author develops the material.

To give you a better sense of how to apply the preview questions to a textbook, let's use those questions in considering a book entitled *Environmental Science: Living Within the System of Nature,* by Charles E. Kupchella and Margaret C. Hyland, paying particular attention to the preface. (The authors have also written a note in their introductory material, "To the Student," which expands on the preface.)

1. *What is this textbook about?*
   The title provides the obvious answer: It's about environmental science. But the authors further define the topic by including a subtitle, "Living Within the System of Nature." Here is the first clue. The book is about environmental science in the context of how human beings live in and relate to the natural system.

2. *Who are the authors?*
   The title page provides the names of the authors and their academic affiliations. In this case, the introductory material includes a page titled "About the Authors." From this item you can learn that both authors have had a long history of work in the environmental field; Mr. Kupchella has specialized in the biological effects of environmental contaminants, and Ms. Hyland has worked on legislation dealing with issues of environmental and natural resources. Clearly, both authors are experts.

3. *When was it published?*
   The fact that the book is a third edition, published in 1993—as shown on the page following the title page—indicates that the material is relatively up to date. This aspect is more important in a book treating a new and changing field like environmental science than it would be in a book describing, say, the treasures of an art museum.

4. *What is the authors' most important idea about the topic?*
   For *Environmental Science,* as is true for most books, the answer to this question, and questions 5 and 8, can be found in the preface, or introduction. It is in the preface that authors state their **theses,** or propositions, **discuss,** or examine, the most important aspects of their books, and often speak directly and personally to the reader.

5. *Why did Kupchella and Hyland write this book?*
   In the preface and note to the student you can also expect to find a statement of what the authors hope to achieve by writing the book, why this book is different from other books in the field, what the authors emphasize, and how the book is organized. In addition, authors often use the preface to acknowledge people who have been helpful to them in the preparation of the manuscript.

Though usually not part of the required reading for a course, the preface and other introductory material are frequently some of the most valuable parts of a textbook. The marked-up preface to *Environmental Science* provides a good illustration of this point.

The first six paragraphs tell why Kupchella and Hyland wrote the book, the seventh paragraph spells out the audience they have in mind, and the eighth paragraph informs the reader that the authors' central concern is that "when the environment is harmed, humans are harmed." The authors go on to explain that they have based their textbook on ecological **principles** (the reader may not know exactly what these principles are; however, because of their importance you can predict that these principles will be dealt with early in the book) and that they will address the economic, social, political, ethical, and legal aspects of environmental problems.

Preface

1 In the not too distant future, the environment will be required subject matter for all college and university students. Knowing about the dependence of humans on a healthy environment is at least as important to all college graduates as knowing about history, science, math, language, or the arts.

2 Environmental issues are already so predominately important throughout the world—so critical to the future of human civilization, that we simply cannot have a world whose leaders are ignorant of the dynamics of the interaction between humans and the environment.

3 The governor of a western state told a group of us recently that about half the issues he deals with day to day are environmental issues. In Kentucky, the legislature met in special session in 1991 to deal mainly with a crisis in solid waste dis-

posal. Debris washing up on East Coast beaches illustrated the need to find better general ways of dealing with the solid waste problem. Air quality is a worsening problem throughout the world. Ozone in the ozone shield now appears to be decreasing even faster than originally feared. We face the threat of global warming as the levels of carbon dioxide and other "greenhouse" gases build up in the atmosphere. We continue to diminish our survival capital—fossil fuels, groundwater, and the earth's biodiversity. Each year the farmers of the world have to feed nearly 100 million more people on nearly 25 billion tons less topsoil.

Since our first edition was published, world population passed the five billion mark, an ozone hole was discovered, and there was a serious nuclear accident at Chernobyl in the Soviet Union. Tens of thousands of square miles of tropical rain forest continue to be cleared each year; wetlands continue to disappear at an alarming rate. Urban sprawl continues to overrun good farmland in the United States and our groundwater is becoming increasingly contaminated. Trees in Central Europe and in Eastern North America are dying; and lakes throughout the world are becoming afflicted by acid deposition.

Our prospects for dealing with these kinds of problems effectively are not good. Some of them are global problems whose solutions require unprecedented international cooperation. All of these are complex problems whose solutions will require people able to grasp the big picture, able to appreciate and deal with complex problems and able to support strategies having long-way off impacts. We don't have many of these kinds of people in the world; our schools must generate more of them. We wrote this book to help make this happen.

What

We wrote this book because we believe that the seriousness of our global ecological problems demands <u>a serious introductory environmental science textbook.</u> Many environmental science textbooks seem to assume that students of environmental science are uninterested in facts and substance, that they want to be told how to think and what to do, that they wish simply to be moved to indignation by pictures of sewers and smokestacks. Our book takes our readers beyond the superficial.

Who — This book is designed <u>to be used by students headed for leadership positions in business, science, law, government, education, engineering, agriculture,</u> and other fields, students who are taking their first environmental science course. Our book assumes no science background other than good secondary-level courses in biology and general science. [7]

Thesis — Our approach is <u>human-centered.</u> Our case for concern about the environment is that <u>when the environment is harmed, humans are harmed,</u> either now or in the future—or both. However, this book is based on the idea that the principles of ecology are the foundation upon which environmental science must be based. Our extended coverage of the interactions between humankind and the environment takes place on a solid framework of <u>ecological principles.</u> We also give <u>heavy emphasis to the economic, social, political, ethical, and legal aspects</u> of our environmental problems. All of these are important in environmental decision making. [8]

Objectives — There are no lists of simple solutions in this book. We want our readers to appreciate that most environmental problems are too complex for simple solutions. We have made every effort to present balanced, fair treatment of controversial topics, and we encourage our readers to formulate their own conclusions. <u>One of our main objectives is to provide facts that students can use in making their own reasoned decisions.</u> [9]

—Charles E. Kupchella and Margaret C. Hyland,
Environmental Science

The preface goes on to describe the organization and scope of the book. It also takes up study aids provided in the book such as mini-glossaries, enrichment boxes that contain interesting asides, outlines and discussion questions, references to further reading, and material on how to interpret tables and graphs. Finally, the authors acknowledge those people who have been helpful to them in preparing the manuscript.

6. *Why am I reading this book?*

This preview question will be answered somewhat differently by every reader. When the question is applied to reading a textbook, however, the assumption is that you are reading the text because you are taking a course and that you are taking the course because you want to learn about the topic or need to fulfill a requirement. Naturally, the reasons may go deeper. In the case at hand, the student might be concerned about the dangers to the planet or might want to understand better what steps are needed to improve the environment and why. Trying to state a reason for taking one course over other courses will help you set a purpose for your reading.

7. *What do I already know about the topic?*
The more you can apply your previous experience, knowledge, and even concerns to the reading at hand, the more relevant and interesting it will become. The more interesting your reading is, the more meaningful and unforgettable it will be.

8. *How is the material presented?*
Your answer to this question is important because it helps you orient yourself to a book by becoming acquainted with the flow of the author's ideas and seeing the book's physical layout. There are several places to look for the answer to this question:

> First, check the preface. On p. 35, we tell how the preface to *Environmental Science* gives information on the way the authors have organized their material and on the study aids provided in the text, such as outlines, summaries, discussion questions, glossaries, and other special features sometimes contained in appendixes.
>
> Second, read the table of contents. On p. 38 there is a brief table of contents taken from the much more detailed table of contents found in *Environmental Science*. This brief table of contents shows how the authors have divided the book into four parts, each treating a main aspect of the book. By looking at the titles of the parts and chapters, you can see that the book develops in a **logical** way: dealing first with ecology (it might help you, at this point, to look up *ecology* and learn that it is the branch of biology that deals with **relations** between living organisms and their environment); then how human beings fit into nature; next the effect of human beings on

nature; and finally some considerations of problems and a look to the future. You know that each chapter will have a topic and a key idea that are supported by the subtopics and supporting ideas taken up in the sections and subsections.

Third, look into the text itself to determine the physical organization of the book. From a quick survey of *Environmental Science,* you would discover that each part has an introduction, that the book has many helpful diagrams and charts, and that each chapter has a mini-glossary and ends with concepts to remember, discussion questions, and references for further reading.

You can **summarize** what you have learned in the short time it has taken to preview *Environmental Science* as follows:

Kupchella and Hyland are two experts who have written *Environmental Science* because environmental problems continue to grow and because they feel that "more than ever before, we need environmentally educated citizens." Their most important ideas are that what is bad for the environment is bad for human beings and that the more people know, the better their decisions. The book begins with the basic principles of ecology, takes up human beings in the scheme of nature, deals with the impact of human activities on health and the environment, and concludes with points of view. The book is clearly organized to reveal the main topics and has useful study aids, including interesting graphics.

This information is considerable. You have created a context for your reading, and you have knowledge on which to base your specific questions. You have a clear sense of what is important and will be able to follow these ideas through the book, relating them to what has come before and anticipating what is to follow.

Exercise 2B

Fill in the blanks in the following sentences.

Example:
One of the best places to find the topic of a book is <u>in the title or in the preface.</u>

Brief Contents

PART ONE
Basic Principles of Ecology 1

Chapter 1	The Framework of Ecology 2
Chapter 2	Energy in Ecosystems 20
Chapter 3	Material Cycles in Living Systems 44
Chapter 4	Populations and Communities 65
Chapter 5	Evolution and Ecology 94

PART TWO
Homo Sapiens in the Scheme of Natural Things 123

Chapter 6	Energy in Human Affairs 124
Chapter 7	Mineral and Water Resources 208
Chapter 8	Population, Food, and Hunger 241

PART THREE
The Impact of Human Activities on Health and the Environment 279

Chapter 9	Air Pollutants and Their Sources 280
Chapter 10	The Effects of Air Pollution 310
Chapter 11	Control of Air Pollution 354
Chapter 12	Water Pollution 386
Chapter 13	Land Use and Land Misuse 439
Chapter 14	Wildlife, Wilderness, and Other Biological Resources 470
Chapter 15	Noise as an Air Pollutant 495
Chapter 16	The Problem of Persistent Hazardous Material in the Ecosphere 576
Chapter 17	Waste Disposal in the Ecosphere 600
Chapter 18	Cancer and the Environment 627

PART FOUR
Points of View 657

| Chapter 19 | Human Institutions: Problems and Solutions   670 |
| Chapter 20 | From Problems to Promise: An Assessment   691 |

1. Knowing the author's _____, _____, and _____ can give you some idea of the author's emphasis in a book.

2. A book that is twenty years old is usually _____ than one published in the past three years.

3. An active reader can develop several specific questions about the topic after _____ a text.

4. A book's _____ is like an outline of the work.

5. A list of new words is often found in every chapter and _____, which appears in the back of the book.

6. The subtitle of a book often provides a strong clue to _____.

Exercise 2C

This exercise is to be done in pairs, using a textbook from one of your courses or using Active Reading. *Preview the textbook by answering the following questions; then discuss your answers with your partner.*

1. What is the topic of the textbook?

   _____

2. Where did you find this information?

   _____

3. When was the book published?

   _____

4. What do you think is the author's most important idea about the topic?

   _____

5. Where did you find this information?

   _____

6. Who is the author?

   _____

7. Why did the author write the book?

   _____

8. Does the book have any special features, like chapter summaries or a glossary? If so, what are they?

   _____

9. By looking at the table of contents, what subtopics do you think are emphasized?

   _____

   _____

10. What is your answer to the question, *Why am I reading this text?*

    _____

    _____

11. What do you already know about the topic?

    _____

    _____

    _____

Exercise 2D

Preview the Introduction, "For the Student," found in *Introductory Economics* and then answer the questions that follow.

Introduction

For the Student

You are beginning the study of a subject that surrounds your life. It is a subject of revolution. It helps to elect presidents, and it defeats them. It is a cause of wars, yet its main practitioners are not generals, diplomats, or leaders. Rather, the driving force for the subject originates with quiet professors. It is dry and dusty and has been called the "dismal science." Yet it is the cause of debates that border on violence. It has been important since the beginning of human activity and will be for all the foreseeable future. It is the frustrating and fascinating study of economics.

You will not be able to avoid the impact of economics even if you move to a remote wilderness area. Wherever you go, nature, for all its bounty, confronts you with one overwhelming truth: There is always something scarce. It is this scarcity that economics is about.

Economics is important. Economics is an essential part of your everyday living. Undoubtedly you will be affected by economic upheavals during your lifetime. Some industries may decline and lose their economic power. You may be unemployed. There may be rapid increase in inflation. Now is the time for you to learn about economics so that you can understand the economic events that go on around you. But how do you study economics?

There are two important points. First, the language of economics is important. You should be aware that an essential part of economics is its vocabulary. You will know that a term is being defined when it is in bold print in the text. These key concepts will be listed at the end of each chapter. A glossary of important terms is located at the end of the text. The terms must be understood. If you do not understand a term, you will not understand the discussion that uses the term. Economics is full of words, common to everyday speech, that have a special meaning to economists. You must carefully distinguish the common meaning from the economist's meaning, so be sure to learn the vocabulary.

The second important point is that economists have a fondness for asking "why?" We are not content to simply tell you that people buy more at a lower price. We want you to know why. So every chance we get, we are going to explain why something is true. You will want to pay attention to these explanations, as they are the heart of economics. At the end of each chapter, you will find questions for thought and discussion that will give you the opportunity to answer why.

So start by reading the text, and pay close attention to the definitions. Also note when the explanations are being given. You should do this before the class discussion. The class will be much clearer if you do. Do not be shy about rereading. You will be surprised at how much more you learn when you read the text again. You may also want to get out a pencil and some paper to work along with the text. While reading, stop and look at the tables and graphs that help to illustrate the point being made. They are not just there for beauty! Let the discussion in the text guide you through the illustrations. If you understand the aids, you will have a better understanding of economics.

This book has seven modules. Each of these modules has an introduction followed by the chapters. The module introduction provides an overview of the upcoming chapters and also explains the relationship between the modules. Each chapter is designed to cover one concept. Each chapter includes an introduction and a summary that will help you organize the material within the chapter and understand the connection between chapters. Economics is not just a collection of facts but a unified approach to thinking about the world. As you make your way through the text, you will develop this way of thinking.

We believe that hands-on experience is important. We have written a study guide to go along with the text. The study guide has questions to help you review the material in each chapter. We also include applications of concepts in the text to help you relate the material you are learning to the real world. You will have a better grasp of the material if you use the study guide, and we suggest that you ask your instructor about it if the study guide has not already been assigned.

What do we want you to be able to do when you are done with this book? Our main goal is for you to understand some basic economic concepts so that you can use economics to better understand the world around you. We believe that the economic principles you learn today will be just as applicable in four or even forty years.

It does not seem so long ago that we began our journey into economics, as you are doing now. One thing we remember about the start of that journey is the prospect of discovering new ideas and gaining a deeper understanding of the world. We hope that through this book we can share in your discovery.

—Arleen J. Hoag and John H. Hoag, *Introductory Economics*

1. Why was this book written? _____

2. Why do the authors think you should be interested in this subject? _____

3. What are the two main points made by the authors about the book? _____

4. What do the authors say about how the book is organized?
   _____

5. What do you think you will gain from having read the book?
   _____

Exercise 2E

Preview this table of contents and answer the questions that follow it.

Preface
Chapter 1   What Is Merchandising?
Chapter 2   How to Find Profit
Chapter 3   How to Find Markup
Chapter 4   How to Average Markup
Chapter 5   How to Plan Markup
Chapter 6   How to Plan Markdowns
Chapter 7   How to Price for Profit
Chapter 8   How to Use the Retail Method of Inventory
Chapter 9   How to Calculate Stock Turn
Chapter 10 How to Plan Sales and Stocks
Chapter 11 How to Plan Purchases and Open-to-Buy
Chapter 12 How to Plan and Control Fashion Merchandise
Chapter 13 How to Buy Foreign Merchandise
Chapter 14 How to Negotiate with Vendors
Chapter 15 Merchandising and the Computer
Appendix
Glossary of Merchandising Terms
Bibliography
Index

1. What is the topic of the book?

   _____

2. From the information given in the table of contents, what do you infer is the key idea?

   _____

   _____

3. If the book were divided into parts, what would the titles of two of them be?

   _____

   _____

4. Why do you think the author included a glossary?

   _____

_____

Previewing a Chapter

Just as it is important to preview a book in its entirety before reading any one part of it, so is it necessary to preview a chapter. But in this instance, instead of seeing the shape and theme of the whole work, you look at the way in which one part of a work fits into the larger whole and also how it stands alone.

Most textbook chapters are set up in a way that makes previewing easy. The topic is most often the title of the chapter. But if the topic is not readily apparent from the chapter title or from a survey of headings, or if there are no headings, then take a look at the introduction (the first four or five paragraphs) and the conclusion or summary. The author's most important or *key idea* may also be found in the introduction and in the conclusion or summary. Bear in mind that although some introductions contain a good preview of the author's topic and important ideas, others serve to provide background material, to create a setting, or simply to spark the reader's interest. Be careful not to infer the main idea too quickly; check your guess with a glance further on. (For training on discovering the author's *key idea*, see Chapter 5.) The concluding paragraph may also provide good clues, but again, don't depend on it. The last four or five paragraphs will certainly verify your guess.

You have seen from its table of contents how *Environmental Science* develops, with each part depending on the preceding part. Usually books also have detailed tables of contents that show how the authors' develop their thoughts within each chapter.

The detailed table of contents provides not only the title of a chapter but also the title of each of the chapter's sections. Each section discusses a particular aspect of the key idea of the chapter, as you can see in the table of contents for *Active Reading.* Such an organization makes the chapters easy to preview, because you can find most of what you need by carefully reading the table of contents. For instance, from the brief table of contents on p. 38 you know that the topic of Chapter 1 is probably about the nature of ecology. By looking at the section titles in the detailed table of contents, you would find the ideas that support this topic and possibly the key idea of the chapter. If there is not a clear statement of the key idea, you would have to make a guess based on clues derived from key words. In this instance from words like *framework, organization,* and *ecosystems,* you might infer that the key idea of Chapter 1 is something like "Ecology is organized into systems." You can check your notion of the key idea by looking at the following introduction to Chapter 1; here, you can expand on your notion of the key idea by adding, "Nature functions as one big system made up of countless smaller but similar systems."

The Framework of Ecology

At first glance, nature seems almost hopelessly complex. The webs that connect every living thing to every other living and nonliving element of our world are made of countless finely drawn and far-reaching threads. Everything is connected to everything else. The poet Francis Thompson went so far as to suggest that when one touches a flower, a star is disturbed. He was essentially correct.

Consider the task we would face if, in order to understand nature, we had to be familiar with *all* of its details. To completely appreciate how a rabbit relates to its world, for instance, we would have to take into account how each rabbit relates to other rabbits, and to owls, grass, and humans as well. We would also have to consider how physical and chemical environmental changes affect each rabbit relationship, subtle or dramatic, human-made or otherwise. To appreciate how the entire natural world functions, we would have to do this for the millions of species, subspecies, varieties, and subtypes of living and nonliving things—an impossible task.

Fortunately, there are patterns in nature. Nature functions as one big system made up of countless little systems, all with similar basic parts organized in the same basic patterns of interaction. The key to understanding the natural world is to recognize that the same types of activities go on everywhere in nature. The underlying plan will be our focus in Chapter 1. Our aim is to depict the living world in terms of its least common denominators, stripped of the differences that distinguish a desert from a jungle, an onion from a carrot, or a rabbit from a mouse.

Like that of most textbooks, the organization of *Environmental Science* is useful when it's time to start your actual reading, because by turning around the subheadings, you can ask precise questions about the text: *How do ecosystems function? What is the molecular basis of production and consumption?* And so forth. The subheadings are also clues to the *subtopics*—the topics or subjects of the various parts of the chapter. If a textbook has no headings, you will need to develop the subtopics and let them be the basis for your questions.

Exercise 2F

Fill in the blanks in the following sentences.

1. Background material, such as an explanation, some history, or general information, is usually found in _____ of a chapter.

2. Headings and subheadings provide clues to the _____ contained in a chapter.

3. Most textbooks include study aids, such as the following:

   _____

4. If you have been assigned a chapter in a textbook to read, it is a good idea to read _____ to see how the chapter fits into the rest of the book.

5. When you preview a chapter, you are most interested in discovering _____ .

Exercise 2G

This exercise should be done with a partner. Examine a chapter from one of your own textbooks, answer the following questions, and then discuss your answers with your partner.

1. What is the topic of the chapter?

   _____

2. What do you infer is the author's most important idea about the topic?

   _____

   _____

3. How is the chapter you selected connected to the chapters that precede and follow it?

   _____

   _____

4. Why would you read this chapter?

   _____

   _____

5. What do you already know about the topic?

   _____

   _____

6. What study aids are provided?

   _____

   _____

7. What two questions, based on headings or subheadings, can you form as a result of your preview?

_____

_____

Previewing an Article

Previewing articles assigned in courses differs little from previewing chapters, except that instead of seeing the material in the context of one larger whole, a book, you should consider how it fits into another larger whole, your course. You can ask yourself, *To what aspect of the course does this particular article relate? Why was it assigned?*

Because articles stand alone, how they relate to anything else is not made explicit in a table of contents. Therefore, the author often provides more clues to the topic and key idea in the form of illustrations, a subtitle, or an **abstract** (a brief summary of the contents of the article). An article's introductory paragraphs, or first two to three paragraphs, are more likely to provide background, hence less likely to contain the key ideas, than such paragraphs in chapters of textbooks are. Nevertheless, you will almost always find the key idea of an article stated in the first six to eight paragraphs and in the conclusion.

Exercise 2H

Preview the article below and answer the questions that follow it.

Adulthood and Aging

If you live for an average number of years, you will spend more than 70 percent of your life as an adult. (This assumes that the dividing line between adolescence and adulthood is about twenty years of age and that your life expectancy is greater than seventy years.) Will you continue to change during these long decades? By now, we're sure you know the answer: absolutely! Since human beings are affected by their experience, it could hardly be otherwise. Happy and unhappy love affairs, successes and failures in school or your career, marriage, divorce, parenthood: all these events leave their mark and assure that, in some ways, we *must* be different in our thirties than we were in our twenties, different in our forties than we were in our thirties, and so on....

Tasks and Stages of Adult Life

Many psychologists who study adult development have found it useful to divide this period of life into various stages. Some believe that entry into each of these stages is marked by definite, and sometimes stormy, transitions (Levinson, 1986). Others disagree and argue that unique, personal experiences are more important than age in determining adult behavior and lifestyles (Schlossberg, 1987). Both groups of researchers agree, however, that different periods in our lives are shaped by different tasks and activities.

The first question that arises about adult development is straightforward: when do we become adults? The answer seems to be: when we experience such important life events as graduation from school, taking a job, and setting up our own household (Levinson, 1986). These events usually take place in the years between our late teens and our middle twenties, depending on the career we have selected and the training it involves.

Early Adulthood: Getting Started

Once we are on our own, so to speak, we enter the period of *early adulthood*. This lasts through our twenties and thirties, and it is usually a very busy time of life. Careers are launched, most people marry, and many start families. Thus, responsibilities mount quickly, as individuals become full adult members of their society.

It is interesting to note that during recent decades, there have been important shifts in *when* individuals feel these key life events should take place.... [L]arge majorities now favor later marriage and parenthood and final selection of a career than was true earlier.

Middle Adulthood: Coming into One's Own

Sometime around age forty many persons seem to enter an important new period. During this *midlife transition* (Levinson, 1986) individuals begin to notice that their physical capabilities, while still adequate, are beginning to wane. At the same time, family obligations usually begin to decrease, as children near maturity. As a result, life becomes a bit less hectic, and many persons have more time to think about their lives, hopes, and goals. Many look back with satisfaction, pleased with what they have accomplished. But others must face the fact that some of their dreams will never be attained. The result, for some, is a *midlife crisis,* in which they experience emotional stress and ask themselves such questions as: "Has it all been worth it?" "Is this all there is?" We should hasten to note that many persons—perhaps most—do *not* experience such inner turmoil. They continue with their lives in much the same ways as before. But those who do sometimes react in ways that upset their families and friends. They may openly question the meaning of their lives, engage in numerous love affairs, or even quit their jobs and launch entirely new careers....

    For those who successfully traverse a midlife crisis, and for those who never experience one, the period of life that follows can be rewarding. Persons in their late forties and fifties tend to hold secure positions at work; indeed, they may fill top-level positions and have an important voice in key decisions. At the same time, family obligations decrease still further, thus allowing more time for hobbies, vacations, and the enjoyment of improved finances. For many, then, this is truly the "prime of life." [7]

    At this point, we should note that the pattern of development we have been discussing is based largely on research with men. Recent studies suggest that women may experience a somewhat different pattern. Thus, while many men in their forties and fifties become increasingly mellow and relaxed, women show a different pattern, becoming more ambitious, self-disciplined, and independent. This is not due simply to the fact that with children grown many return to the work force. In a careful longitudinal project, Helson and Moan (1987) studied a group of women from the time they were college seniors (in the late 1950s) until they were in their early forties (in 1981). They divided these subjects into three categories: women who were mainly family-oriented, women who were mainly career-oriented, and those who fit neither pattern (they did not have children but did not pursue active careers). Despite major differences in life experiences, all three groups showed the trends described above: they became more assertive, confident, and independent as they approached midlife. Clearly, such differences between the sexes should be taken into careful account in any conclusions about changes in our adult years. [8]

Late Adulthood: Winding Down

As individuals enter their sixties, many pass through another life transition. At this time, they must confront their coming retirement, an event many find disturbing. Further, family obligations, which have been low for years, often increase again as individuals find that they must take responsibility for their own aging parents. And when retirement actually occurs, it brings a mixed bag of gains and losses. Time for vacations, family visits, hobbies, and other leisure activities increases, but these pluses may be offset by a sharp drop in income, loss of contact with friends at work, and negative shifts in self-concept (from "I'm a useful member of society," to "I'm just a burden on others"). Thus, late adulthood, which has the potential to be one of the most enjoyable periods of life, becomes for some an unhappy prelude to despair.

—Robert A. Baron, *Psychology: The Essential Science*

1. What is the topic?

2. Why do you think the author wrote this article?

3. What are three things you already know about the topic?

4. From your answers to the preview questions and from the section headings, can you predict three questions this article might answer?

Exercise 2I

Preview the article titled "The Chicanos" by Tino Villanueva, a Chicano poet and professor, and answer the questions that follow it.

The Chicanos

The Mexican-American War (1846–1848) caught Mexico in complete prostration. She lost the war; and as a consequence of the Treaty of Guadalupe Hidalgo of February 2, 1848 received the sum of $15,000,000, but had to cede half her territory, the area which today makes up the five southwestern states—Texas, New Mexico, Colorado, Arizona and California, as well as Nevada and Utah.

February 2, 1848 constitutes, therefore, a turning point in Chicano history. From one day to the next Mexican citizens became American citizens. The Treaty carried provisions for a measure of protection for those Mexican citizens who wished to remain north of the Rio Grande (Article VIII: "Mexicans now established in territories previously belonging to Mexico...shall be free to continue where they now reside...retaining the property which they possess in the said territories...property of every kind, now established there, shall be inviolably respected"; Article IX: "Mexicans, in the territories aforesaid...shall...be admitted at the proper time...to the enjoyment of all the rights of citizens of the United States"; Article X, later deleted by President Polk and the Department of State: "All the land grants made by the Mexican government or by the competent authorities which pertained to Mexico in the past and which will remain in the future within the boundaries of the United States, will be respected as valid"). In reality these *de facto* American citizens ended up a defeated and colonized community. They were, as the renowned phrase goes, strangers in their own land. Many were cheated out of or were run off their legally-owned land under the threat of violence by Anglo settlers; the unskilled laborers in most cases became no more than virtual serfs for the new-landed Anglo Americans. When they were not *vaqueros* (cowboys) on cattle ranches and trails, sheep herders and shearers, copperminers, or livery-stable hands, Mexican Americans turned to being servants, laundresses, gardeners, cooks and seamstresses. In a large sense the Mexican American way of life paralleled the Black-

American way of life, although for the former there was no Emancipation Proclamation.

In the cities, and afterwards in the emerging towns, these new Americans became craftsmen in adobe-making, stonemasonery, furniture repair, plumbing, silversmithing, tinsmithing and blacksmithing. Others found employment as *arrieros* (mule and ox drivers) involved in the freight business, or as street vendors of consumable products (vegetables, goat meat, sun-dried beef, cakes, confectionery, Mexican food, arts and crafts and needlework). A significant though less numerous class included sheriffs, postmasters, policemen, newspaper editors, teachers, medical doctors, lawyers, druggists, and even clerks at the municipal and federal government administration level. Only a small class of property-owners and urban entrepreneurs were able to retain some semblance of their preconquest status. They were proprietors not only of farm land, livestock and real estate, but of retail stores, bakeries, restaurants, saloons, hotels, drug stores, barbershops and printshops as well.

Those who were not employed relied on seasonal migrant work (all the more so in the twentieth century), travelling around the Southwest, to the Midwest and East Coast as field hands and pickers, or as railroad construction workers, section hands and maintenance employees, occupations sometimes involving the whole family. Although many left for the cities when industry started up in this century (thus the beginnings of Mexican American communities in the Midwest, especially), agricultural work remained a source of employment for many, particularly for the new, unskilled immigrants from Mexico who began to flow across the border from the period of the Mexican Revolution (1910) to the present. Many chose to stay and become citizens; in this fashion they changed the demographics of Chicano communities throughout the United States.

As Anglo Americans settled the southwestern United States, the more contact Americans of Mexican descent had with the new socioeconomic, political and cultural order, with its particular brand of educational system and, most importantly, with the English language. Unskilled, uneducated, illiterate for the most part, and, at the outset, untutored in English, the Mexican American of the late nineteenth century became the easy target of discrimination for the Anglo American. The tradition of racial superiority and dominance also figured prominently in the patterns of prejudice against these new citizens, their language and Catholic religion, patterns which, to some extent, still survive albeit to a lesser degree. Assimilation into the mainstream society (always with limitations) does not begin to occur until the 1940s, after World War II, when Mexican American servicemen returned home with newly-acquired skills and with the sense that through education (and a solid foundation in the English language) they could improve themselves and the lot of their brethren, and, moreover, pursue their version of the American Dream, all of which signaled the emergence of a significant middle class.

In 1928 LULAC (League of United Latin American Citizens) became the first Mexican American organization to form itself to answer the needs of citizens of Mexican heritage, whereas before, only voluntary associations of the mutual benefit type had existed, among them *La Alianza Hispano Americana* (1894) and *La Sociedad Mutualista Mexicana* (1918). Organizing activity did not thrive until the post-World War II period. In 1947 the CSO (Community Service Organization) was established in California around civic issues as a conscious attempt at "Americanization" and "assimilation." But it was the G. I. Forum (1948) in Texas which began to make significant social reforms and political gains, challenging and, in some cases, striking down segregation policies against Mexican Americans in the public schools and successfully running candidates for local public office. In the 1950s other coalitions were formed, such as MAPA (Mexican American Political Association, 1958), while PASSO (Political Association of Spanish-Speaking Organizations) was formed in 1960.

Not until the mid-1960s, on the heels of the Black Civil Rights Movement, did Mexican Americans gain national and international attention, media coverage and a not insignificant measure of potential for political power. The series of farmworker strikes and lettuce and grape boycotts (begun in 1965) in California against long-standing unfair labor practices and general worker exploitation solidified into the United Farmworkers Union under the leadership of César Chávez. So significant were these developments that some referred to them as the second *Grito de Dolores*.

The labor movement, together with the land-grant movement in New Mexico headed by Reies López Tijerina (which exposed the violation of the 1848 Treaty of Guadalupe Hidalgo and demanded the restitution of stolen lands), urban mass demonstrations in the streets and electoral action, protests against the Vietnam War and similar activism by university students demanding more recruitment of Chicanos to the college ranks, financial aid, tutoring and support services and the establishment of Chicano Studies

Departments, proved once and for all that a neglected people had come of age, that it could assert itself in the interest of self-determination. Many organizations were formed by a new generation of grassroots and university-based activists, such as the Crusade for Justice (urban civil rights and cultural movement), La Raza Unida Political Party, MAYO (Mexican American Youth Organization) and MECHA (Movimiento Estudiantil Chicano de Aztlán). Community leaders and educators urged school boards to institute bilingual programs as a needed pedagogic tool to accelerate the learning capacity of students whose primary home-language had been Spanish, and to minimize the incidence of student frustration at the seemingly disdainful attitude of some teachers toward the Spanish language and Mexican culture, an attitude believed by some to be responsible for a disproportionately high dropout rate among Mexican Americans.

Concomitant with the Chicano Movement—known to some as *La Causa* (The Cause)—an attendant movement of arts and letters and intellectual activity flourished. Many painters (including muralists), writers of all genres and social scientists who made up the *Chicano Renaissance,* as it is known in academic circles, registered their psycho-social reality with penetrating testimonies and analyses about existence in America, acknowledged their pre-Columbian past and Indo-Hispanic (*mestizo*) history. In that process they prophesied the eventual liberation of Chicanos from the psychological bondage common to conquered and annexed people, subjugated in the aftermath of reconstruction. In their search for Chicano history, university students, artists and intellectuals were drawn to their pre-Hispanic past. In so doing, they no longer referred to the Southwest as such, but rather as Aztlán (Náhuatl for "land to the north," presumably the Southwest), that mythical ancestral home of the Aztecs before migrating south, where, in 1325 they settled on Lake Texcoco, the site of present-day Mexico City. The fundamental concept of Aztlán provided a geographical center, a political rallying point and the notion of a territorial base to be defended. This sense of belonging gave rise to ethno-cultural identity (something not felt toward mainstream Anglo America), inspired a new awareness of self and purpose, and became the source of much creative thinking.

Alongside the traditional, universal themes which were also evident in literature, these compelling self-reflections and life-concerns found a ready audience gathered around the many *barrio* and university tabloids, newspapers and literary and social science journals that suddenly sprang up, publications which writers, literary critics, sociologists and political scientists (not a few of them graduate students) greatly needed to display and convey their art and remarkable flurry of ideas....

The currency of the term *Chicano* itself grew out of and took hold in the mid-1960s on the University of California campuses and extended itself eastward to Texas. For all practical purposes it supplanted *Mexican American* (except among the older generations), and others which had preceded it, such as *Mexican, Latin American* and *Latin. Spanish American* and *Hispano,* terms peculiar to the Spanish-surnamed people of New Mexico and southern Colorado, more often than not held their own, except among some community members and college-age youth.

As an ethnic designation, *Chicano,* according to one commentator, has been around since the eighteenth century in the southwest and northern Mexico to refer to any invading foreigner from the south. As far as can be verified, the first time *Chicano* was recorded is on July 27, 1911 in a Laredo, Texas, newspaper to signify an (unskilled) Mexican national recently arrived in the United States, and therefore, naive about American customs or those of "Americanized Mexicans." Early twentieth century generations of Mexican Americans had a special aversion toward the label, as it connoted different nuances of "low-class." Teenagers in the 1950s, nonetheless, appropriated it as an in-group, positive self-designation to distinguish themselves from their elders' reference to their generation as *mexicanos,* which had the double application to a Mexican national or to an American of Mexican lineage.

When *Chicano* was brought into broader use in the 1960s by the more activist students, it came to mean, as it still does today, first, an act of defiance, then self-determination, ethnic pride and political consciousness. As such, the concept expressed by the word *Chicano* is not merely ethnic or racial, but also an historical position, and must be equated in spirit and substance with *Black,* which a few years earlier had replaced *Negro* as a consequence of Black consciousness grown out of similar socioeconomic conditions of Americans of African descent.

[As] to the elemental question of language: since 1848, Chicanos finding themselves within the borders of a newly expanded United States have experienced the superimposition of an alien language and culture. During these decades, the survival of Spanish amongst Mexican Americans is evidenced in varying degrees. Some families retained the sole usage of Spanish, while others adopted, either unwittingly or not, an ambience of bilingualism, the level of proficiency in either language having always depended upon the individual's generation, education, socioeconomic standing and, latterly, on ethnic pride and consciousness of the importance of bilingualism in the public schools and in public life, affirmations born of the 1960s. It is an irrefutable fact that adequate knowledge of and clear proficiency in the English language have, during the past decades, figured preeminently in the singlemost recognized area of success for Mexican Americans, i.e., the achievement of upward social mobility, gauged traditionally by educational and economic accomplishment.

Until recently then, the historical situation of the Chicano has served as a metaphor for victimization by conquest and colonialism, but since the decade of the 1960s serves more appropriately as a metaphor, at the least, for survival and at most, for growth and an increasing recognition of accomplishment and contribution.

—Tino Villanueva, "The Chicanos"

1. What is this article about?

2. What do you think is the most important idea the author has about the topic?

3. What do you think is the author's point of view about this topic? Why?

4. Do you predict Villanueva will use facts, illustrations, or examples to support his general statements?

5. How do you think the author will organize his material?

Summary Exercise

The following chart presents a summary of the material on previewing found in this chapter. Fill in the blanks, referring, if necessary, to the appropriate section within the chapter.

When You Read	You Will Discover
A course syllabus	The topic, key idea, and method of development of the course
A title and subtitles	The topic and subtopics
The author's name and affiliation	The author's point of view and area of expertise
The date of publication	a. _____
b. _____	An outline and organization of the book; special features
c. _____	The topic, key idea, author's purpose, explanation of the book, and emphasis
Introductory paragraphs or Chapter 1	d. _____ _____

Preview Questions

When you PREVIEW a text, ask:	You will DISCOVER
What is this text about?	The topic (Chap. 4)
What is the author's most important idea about the topic?	The key idea (Chap. 5)
Why am I reading this?	Your own purpose and reading strategies
What do I already know about the topic?	Associations or connections with your previous knowledge
What do I predict the author will say?	Insights into the topic

Chapter 3

Developing Vocabulary: Connecting Words and Ideas

In this chapter you will find answers to the following questions:

What are words?
What is the connection between words and ideas?
What should you do when you come across words you don't know in your reading?
Is academic vocabulary different from general vocabulary?
How can you increase your vocabulary?

Words and Meaning

A word is a mere sound or a few marks on a page. Taken by itself, it has no meaning. A word derives its meaning from the reader's previous experience with it and its associations. When you first learned the word *dog*, for example, you saw, or someone **described** for you, a furry four-legged animal with a long tongue and a wagging tail and that comes when it's called. As a small child you may have then called the neighbor's cat a dog until some differences were pointed out—a cat has claws and won't come when called. From then on, when you heard the word *dog* or *cat* these details flashed through your mind, and you knew what a dog or a cat was. You could even go on and perhaps by yourself distinguish a dog and a cat from a cow in the field.

Words have meaning only if everyone agrees on what they stand for or say. For example, if for you the word *bird* means a flying creature with wings but for someone else it means a flat surface with four legs, there can be no communication between you on the subject of "bird." Authors try to use words carefully to ensure that the words they use convey the authors' meanings accurately. Similarly, readers have the responsibility of searching for meaning in authors' words and of learning words that will increase their own ability to understand authors' messages.

Thinking and words are so closely related that for generations philosophers and psychologists have debated whether or not a person can think without words. One thing is clear, however: If you lack the words to formulate concepts and express your ideas, your ability to communicate with other people can be greatly hampered. Similarly, a limited vocabulary impedes your ability to understand other people's written or spoken ideas and explanations. A good vocabulary is fundamental to active reading and clear thinking.

General Vocabulary

The value of a strong vocabulary goes beyond the knowledge you gain now and the enjoyment such knowledge gives to life after college. Studies have shown that a large vocabulary is a key element of success for top-level executives and professionals.

You will learn most of the words that make up your vocabulary during your school and college years. Never again will you be so exposed to new words as you are now—they are the tools of new knowledge and the instruments of thought.

A good reader, a thinking reader, needs to possess a large vocabulary. If you believe you need to develop your vocabulary—and most of us do—you can take a vocabulary course or work on your own with one of the many books on vocabulary building that are available in your college learning center or bookstore. Meanwhile, though, there are ways to deal with unfamiliar words and ways to learn new words that will help you read more efficiently and increase your vocabulary. One way is to infer the meaning of a word from contextual clues; another is to infer the meaning of a word by associating it with words you already know; a third is to analyze a word by breaking it down into its components. In every case you are dealing with words as parts of whole sentences or paragraphs, not in isolation. The hardest way to learn new words is to try to memorize a list of unrelated words and their meanings.

Using Context Clues

Authors of nonfiction—that is, writing based on reality rather than imagination, the kind of writing found in textbooks, scholarly articles, and other academic work—are usually careful to provide clues to the meanings of words their readers may not know. These context clues tell the reader what the word means or give information on which the reader can base a correct inference, or educated guess.

The preceding paragraph includes several examples of context clues: *Nonfiction* is defined as "writing based on reality rather than imagination," and textbooks and scholarly articles are given as examples; a close synonym, "educated guess," is provided for the meaning of *inference;* and *context clues* are explained as elements that "tell the reader what the word means or give information on which the reader can base a correct inference, or educated guess."

An active reader can often determine the meaning of an unfamiliar word by noticing the **context** in which the word is used. That is, you can look at the other words in the sentence or paragraph for hints about the meaning of the unknown word. This is a direct and practical approach that will often serve you well.

Here are examples of words, phrases, and punctuation marks that commonly act as signals of context clues; that is, they indicate that an explanation of the word is coming.

1. Words or phrases:

is	to illustrate
are	rather than
or	not
that is	on the other hand
meaning	on the contrary
such as	however
including	but
for example	while
for instance	instead of
the opposite	

2. Punctuation marks used to set off words:

commas	dashes
parentheses	colons

Following are examples of five types of context clues: definition, explanation, example or illustration, logic, and contrast. As you read each example, watch for the signal that alerts you to the context clues. (In these examples, the words in question have been italicized.)

Definition. Sometimes a direct definition of the unknown word or a synonym—a word with a similar meaning—is provided in the sentence.

Examples
Justice Holmes was known as a man of great *erudition,* or knowledge. (Here *erudition* means knowledge. Signal: the word)
or
The man suffered from *monocular*—one-eyed—vision. (In this sentence *monocular* means one-eyed. Signal: dashes)

Explanation. Sometimes the other words in the sentence or paragraph provide an explanation of the unknown word.

Example:
An active reader can often determine the meaning of an unfamiliar word by noticing the *context* in which the word is used. That is, you can look at the other words in the sentence or paragraph for hints about the meaning of the unknown word. (Here it is explained that *context* means the other words in the sentence or paragraph. Signal: the phrase *that is*)

Example or illustration. Sometimes an author follows an unfamiliar word with an example, an illustration, or a list of similar words that leads you to its meaning.

Examples:
You can achieve *equilibrium* in an equation by balancing the two sides. For example, the equation $10 + 4 = 20 - 3$ does not balance. If you add 3 to $10 + 4$ you will balance the two sides: $10 + 4 + 3 = 20 - 3$. (The example of balancing the equation tells you that *equilibrium* means balance, or making two sides equal. Signal: the phrase *for example*)
Maria had a good stock of *cumin* on hand as well as nutmeg, cayenne pepper, cinnamon, and cloves. (Nutmeg, cayenne pepper, cinnamon, and cloves are all spices. Therefore, *cumin* is probably a spice too. Signal: a list of words)

Logic. Sometimes a sentence includes examples that provide the basis for inferring the meaning of an unknown word. Usually these clues are not accompanied by a signal; instead, you have to depend on your own awareness and common sense.

Example:
She decided to give up the luxuries of this world and live as a *penurious* student, with not enough money even to pay for her rent, meals, and books. (You can infer that *penurious* means poor, for giving up luxuries and not having enough money are both indications of poverty.)

Contrast. Sometimes a word is defined by a statement in the text that gives a meaning opposite to that of the one you are looking for.

Example:
Henry X was a *benign* king, very unlike Edward IX, who terrorized the peasants with his merciless behavior. (You can gather that *benign* means the opposite of *merciless* from the clue that Henry was unlike Edward. Signal: the word *unlike*—a term setting up the contrast)

Exercise 3A

Using the context clues of definition, explanation, example or illustration, logic, and contrast, write a synonym or an explanatory phrase that you think gives the meaning of the underlined words in the following sentences. For each sentence, indicate the type of context clue you used to obtain the word's meaning and state the signal that led you to the context clue.

Example:
Thinking and words are <u>inextricably</u> bound; that is, they cannot be untied or disentangled.
Inextricably means *tied together or knotted.*
The type of context clue is *explanation.*
Signal: *that is*

1. The <u>habitat</u> of a species is simply the place where that animal lives.

    Habitat means _____

    The type of context clue is _____

    Signal: _____

2. Many children seem to possess an <u>innate</u> ability to learn a foreign language—that is, nobody teaches them; they pick it up by themselves.

   Innate means _____

   The type of context clue is _____

   Signal: _____

3. If all the cars in this country were made by one company and that company could charge as much as it wanted to because there was no competition, you would say that company has a <u>monopoly</u>.

   Monopoly means _____

   The type of context clue is _____

   Signal: _____

4. The symptoms of <u>anorexia nervosa</u> are exactly the opposite of those of obesity, which is a condition of overweight that occurs when a person eats more than his or her system can transfer into energy or muscle.

   Anorexia nervosa means _____

   The type of context clue is _____

   Signal: _____

5. Lee found himself facing the difficult <u>dilemma</u> of having to choose between spending the reward money on a new television set, which would provide hours of amusement for him and his friends, or spending it on a computer, which would greatly aid his course work.

   Dilemma means _____

   The type of context clue is _____

   Signal: _____

6. The raucous noises of screaming brakes, howling sirens, and shouting people slowly evaporated from the block where the accident had occurred.

   Raucous means _____

   The type of context clue is _____

   Signal: _____

7. By enabling us to know and master relevant information, information having to do with the task at hand, reading can lead to success in our jobs.

   Relevant means _____

   The type of context clue is _____

   Signal: _____

8. Insulin is a hormone that enables glucose, or blood sugar, to be used as an energy source by the body.

   Glucose means _____

   The type of context clue is _____

   Signal: _____

9. When they gazed out on the harbor in the morning, they saw one lonely destroyer instead of the armada of ships they had expected.

   Armada means _____

   The type of context clue is _____

   Signal: _____

10. The two professors worked out a paradigm, or model, to explain how the tension between the two opposing forces would eventually lead to war.

    Paradigm means _____

The type of context clue is _____

Signal: _____

Using Association Clues

We all work with two types of vocabulary: (1) passive, those words we recognize but seldom, if ever, use, and (2) active, those words we use in speaking or writing. A reader's vocabulary is based mainly on passive vocabulary. As a student, though, you will need to greatly increase your active use of academic vocabulary so that you can speak and write about topics in particular fields. The average first-year college student has a reading vocabulary of about ten thousand words. That's a lot of words. Nevertheless, by the time you finish college your reading vocabulary will probably be at least double that number, and many of the ten thousand words now in your passive vocabulary will have become active.

These ten thousand words provide a good foundation of knowledge on which to base your predictions of what the new words you encounter in your reading might mean. By paying attention to each new word and either looking for context clues or breaking down the word to find its familiar parts, you may come close to its meaning. For example, if you didn't know the word *familiar*, its spelling might remind you of *family*; because you know that a family is an intimate group, its members well known to one another, you might guess that *familiar* has something to do with being well known to the speaker. Analyzing the word *microphone* tells you that it has something to do with *micro* (which you can associate with *microbe* and *microscope*, words having to do with smallness) and *phone* (which reminds you of *telephone* and *phonics*, words having to do with sound); thus, you could infer that *microphone* involves small sound—the context might tell you that *microphone* means an instrument that makes a small sound bigger. In this way you are inferring the meaning by associating the new word with other items from your knowledge of language.

Exercise 3B

In the sentences below, circle the answer that best conveys the meaning of the underlined word. Write the word you used as an association.

Example:
The article was nothing more than an <u>enumeration</u> of the steps needed to perform the new laboratory procedures.

a. collection

(b.) numbered list

c. review

d. numbness

Word used: *number*

1. <u>Sociology</u> is an academic department found in most liberal arts colleges.

    a. study of thinking

    b. study of soil science

    c. study of groups of people

    d. study of the individual

    Word used: _____

2. The <u>importation</u> of cocaine has been prohibited by law.

    a. bringing in

    b. carrying out

    c. taking of

    d. selling

    Word used: _____

3. It took them three hours to cover twenty miles because they took a <u>circuitous</u> route.

    a. recommended

    b. bumpy

    c. beautiful

d. roundabout

Word used: _____

4. The prince tried the slipper on Cinderella's <u>diminutive</u> foot.
   a. narrow
   b. smelly
   c. tiny
   d. muscular

   Word used: _____

5. His actions were the <u>antithesis</u> of what she had expected.
   a. hypothesis
   b. result
   c. essence
   d. opposite

   Word used: _____

6. The lawyer contested the <u>validity</u> of Norma's argument.
   a. reasonableness
   b. strength
   c. meaning
   d. fairness

   Word used: _____

7. The combining of two bland chemicals often produces a <u>malodorous</u> result.
   a. successful
   b. not fragrant
   c. unsuccessful
   d. unexpected

   Word used: _____

8. Many of the former Yugoslavia's troubles stemmed from the struggle of the Serbs and Croats for <u>autonomy</u>.

   a. land

   b. an auto industry

   c. victory

   d. self-rule

   Word used: _____

9. The initial agreement to ban the use of <u>pesticides</u> was limited to crops being planted the following spring.

   a. insect killers

   b. ploughs

   c. imported seeds

   d. poppies

   Word used: _____

10. The play's <u>prologue</u> clarified what might have been a confusing production by explaining some of the action and characters.

    a. main character

    b. playwright

    c. introduction

    d. final act

    Word used: _____

Using Word-part Clues

Another way to make an educated guess about the meanings of words you meet in your reading is to become familiar with some elements of the English language. Because so many of our words, nontechnical as well as technical, originated in or were derived from Latin and Greek, even slight knowledge of some of the more usual word parts can be useful to college students in recognizing words and building vocabulary.

Prefixes, found at the beginnings of words, are indications of time (*pre-,* as in *preview*—seeing before), position (*sub-,* as in *submarine*—under sea), quality and condition (*un-,* as in *unjust*—not just), or number and amount (*bi-,* as in *bicycle*—two wheels). The **root,** also known as the stem, is the most important element of the word, because it carries most of the meaning (like *dict,* meaning "say," in *predict* or *dictionary*). And the **suffix,** which comes at the end of the word, usually indicates the word's grammatical function (like *-or,* meaning "the person who," in *professor*). Take the complicated and probably unfamiliar word *prestidigitator.* You can unravel its meaning if you know that *presti* comes from *presto,* meaning "quickly"; *digita* means "finger" (*digit*); and *or* makes the word a noun and means "the person who." Together, these word parts mean "a person who moves his or her fingers quickly," hence a magician or sleight-of-hand artist.

Some of the word parts used most often in English are listed in Appendix A (an **appendix** is additional material found at the back of a book). You can refer to them as a first step when you find you cannot infer the meaning of a word you come upon in the readings in this book.

Exercise 3C

Using the list of word parts in Appendix A, break down the underlined words in the following sentences. (Some may have prefix and root, others root and suffix, and still others all three.) Write out what you think is the meaning of each word.

Example:
You could tell that her <u>contradiction</u> of the president influenced the thinking of many people.

Prefix: *contra-* Meaning: against
Root: *dict*   Meaning: speak or say
Suffix: *-ion*   Meaning: the act of or state of being

Contradiction means the act of speaking against.

1. Gangs have become completely <u>antisocial</u> in their behavior.

    Prefix: Meaning:

Root: Meaning:
Suffix: Meaning:

Antisocial means _____

2. When Columbus sailed from Spain he thought he was going to <u>circumnavigate</u> the world.
   Prefix: Meaning:
   Root: Meaning:
   Suffix: Meaning:

   Circumnavigate means _____

3. It is the nature of human beings to think of themselves as <u>immortal</u>.
   Prefix: Meaning:
   Root: Meaning:
   Suffix: Meaning:

   Immortal means _____

4. Juan Carlos was <u>omnipotent</u> in the small community outside Santa Cruz.
   Prefix: Meaning:
   Root: Meaning:
   Suffix: Meaning:

   Omnipotent means _____

5. The letter was <u>transmitted</u> on the fax to the corporate headquarters in Tokyo.
   Prefix: Meaning:
   Root: Meaning:
   Suffix: Meaning:

   Transmitted means _____

6. That people will eventually make their homes on the moon seems <u>incredible</u> at this time.
   Prefix: Meaning:
   Root: Meaning:
   Suffix: Meaning:

   Incredible means _____

7. Swans are known to be <u>monogamous</u> for life.
   Prefix: Meaning:
   Root: Meaning:
   Suffix: Meaning:

   Monogamous means_____

8. The <u>infrastructure</u> of our cities is becoming worn out and needs attention.
   Prefix: Meaning:
   Root: Meaning:
   Suffix: Meaning:

   Infrastructure means_____

9. A 20-<u>kilometer</u> run is good training for a marathon.
   Prefix: Meaning:
   Root: Meaning:

   Kilometer means_____

10. The lives of Martin Luther King, Jr., and Mohandas K. Gandhi have served as <u>inspirations</u> for many Americans.
    Prefix: Meaning:
    Root: Meaning:
    Suffix: Meaning:

    Inspirations means_____

Academic Language

It is generally true that in the academic world, ideas, rather than words, are valued. But this situation does not mean that words are unimportant in the academic environment. To understand ideas, it is necessary to understand the words that convey them. Chapters 12 through 14 take up the specific vocabulary of a number of disciplines; here we offer a few observations that apply to all academic language. Academic language consists of (1) words that you use every day, (2) words that are familiar to you but are used in specialized ways in different academic disciplines, and (3) words that have been coined, or made up, because of the need for a new, precise word to **explain** a new concept in a specific discipline. A casual guess by the reader as to the meaning of academic language words is not enough. You need to know the exact meaning of each word; otherwise you are unlikely to understand a vital idea that is being explained. To make sure students are learning the language of the discipline, faculty members frequently include questions on word meanings in tests and exams.

General Words

General words are words that have the same meaning whenever they are used but are often found in particular disciplines; examples are *rationalize* (to excuse) and *repress* (to prevent the expression of), which are used in psychology. Other general words are words that originated in one field of study and have now become part of our general language, such as *ego* (self) from psychology, *congenital* (resulting from one's heredity or prenatal development) from biology, and *ethnic* (describing a minority or national group that is part of a larger community) from anthropology. The preceding sections on general vocabulary have dealt with ways to think about words you are unfamiliar with, and these general academic words fall into that group.

Same Words/Different Meanings

As you are introduced to the vocabulary of the various fields you are studying, you will find that you seem to know many of the words used. It is possible, however, that a word has a special meaning when used by professionals in a field. For instance, *tone* means one thing in literature, another thing in music; *organic* means one thing in chemistry, another thing in medicine; and *work* means one thing in physics, another thing in business. Therefore, you cannot depend on being able to understand a concept by inferring or guessing at the meaning of words used to explain it. It's a good idea to check your prediction of what a word means by referring to a dictionary or to a **glossary**—that is, a listing of specialized terms and their meanings as used in a particular subject. Many textbooks include a glossary at the back of the book.

Technical Words

Words that are specific to a field of study—like *magma* (molten rock) in geology, *multiplicand* (the number to be multiplied by another) in mathematics, and *sanctions* (punitive measures taken by one nation against another) in political science—often seem the most difficult because learning them is like learning a foreign language. Understanding the technical terms of a field is fundamental to knowledge of that field. Here you have to depend on the author of your textbook—and often on a good dictionary as well—for an explanation.

Using a Dictionary

There are several important considerations to remember when using a dictionary.

1. Although a pocket dictionary is convenient to carry around, be aware that the smaller the dictionary, the fewer the words, definitions, and examples it contains. Every college student should own, if possible, a full-size collegiate dictionary and should locate unabridged dictionaries and specialized dictionaries in the library reference room.

2. Read the introductory material in your dictionary to understand the meaning of the diacritical marks (marks showing how to pronounce a word) and, most important, to learn how the definitions are ordered. Some dictionaries give the most common use of a word first; others start with the oldest use of the word.

3. Most words have more than one definition. Test the various definitions in the context of your reading and choose the appropriate one.

4. Always look at how the word is broken down into prefix, root, and suffix, paying close attention to the meaning of the root. Awareness of a word's etymology (its origin and development—from *etmos*, meaning "true," and *logos*, meaning "description") can often lead you to whole families of words—for instance, *describe, ascribe, prescribe, circumscribe, proscribe.*

As an example, notice this entry from *Webster's New World Dictionary:*

pro·scribe (prō skrīb′) *vt.* **-scribed′, -scrib′ing** [ME *proscriben* < L *proscribere* < *pro-*, PRO-² + *scribere*, to write: see SCRIBE] **1** in ancient Rome, to publish the name of (a person) condemned to death, banishment, etc.   **2** to deprive of the protection of the law; outlaw   **3** to banish; exile   **4** to denounce or forbid the practice, use, etc. of; interdict — **pros·crib′er** *n.*

Textbook Aids

Textbooks usually contain definitions of new words and phrases. Customarily, new technical terms are printed in boldface when first used and defined. Often you will find a list of new terms at the beginning or end of a chapter. And again, at the back of most textbooks is a glossary (Appendix B of *Active Reading* is an example).

Classroom Aids

It is helpful to listen carefully for the ways in which your instructors deal with new terms and to underline or circle these words in your class notes. Most likely, the instructor will define or explain such terms both orally and on the board. These terms are obviously the ones the instructor thinks are important to your learning. If you don't understand the meaning in class, ask the instructor or teaching assistant (TA) to define the word for you, and make sure you can use it yourself.

Symbols, notations, and abbreviations are increasingly important parts of a technical vocabulary. Here again you need to be precise. Symbols, notations, and abbreviations don't mean "something like"; they mean exactly what they say they mean—nothing more and nothing less. Try to translate every symbol and abbreviation into words. For instance,

$$\frac{3 + 3^3}{\sqrt{25}} = \frac{30}{5} = 6$$

translates into "If I take the square root of 25 and divide it into the result of 3 added to 3 cubed, or taken to the third power, I will get a result of 6."

Exercise 3D

For the sentences below, write what you think each underlined word means, using either the context and associational clues outlined in this chapter or the word parts listed in Appendix A. Check your guess in the dictionary; then write the appropriate dictionary definition.

Example:
An amoeba is a <u>microscopic,</u> one-celled animal.
My definition: *Microscopic means very small.*

Dictionary definition: *very small; visible only with the aid of a microscope.*

1. "The <u>delirious</u> person has trouble 'thinking' straight, may be unable to focus on a conversation or other environmental events, and may appear confused."

   —Bernstein et al.

   My definition: _____

   Dictionary definition: _____

2. "When two goods are typically used together (bread and butter, tape players and cassettes, automobiles and gasoline, or gin and vermouth) such that an increase in the price of one causes a decline in the demand for the other, we call them <u>complements</u>."

   —Fleisher, Ray, and Kniesner

   My definition: _____

   Dictionary definition: _____

3. The computer instructor told the students to make sure they had a <u>backup</u> of all their input to date.

   My definition: _____

   Dictionary definition: _____

4. By putting together the information from the two sources, the historian was able to come up with a good <u>synthesis</u> of the argument.

   My definition: _____

   Dictionary definition: _____

5. Linda's stand on gun control was <u>equivocal</u>. She hated guns but felt she needed to be able to protect herself.

   My definition: _____

1 / Building the Foundation for Critical Reading

Dictionary definition: _____

6. "Molecules have both <u>kinetic</u> energy, or energy of motion, and internal energy, the potential energy of vibrations of atoms and bonds within the molecules."

   —Fessenden and Fessenden

   My definition: _____

   Dictionary definition: _____

7. The painted <u>frieze</u> surrounding the Great Hall depicted the stages of the hunt.

   My definition: _____

   Dictionary definition: _____

8. As you walked by the classroom, you could hear the <u>metronomes</u> clicking while the students learned the rhythms of the new dance step.

   My definition: _____

   Dictionary definition: _____

9. Although they apparently made an effort to straighten up, wash up, and pick up, their room was far from <u>impeccable</u>.

   My definition: _____

   Dictionary definition: _____

10. "The developed countries, with less than a quarter of the people in the world and an average <u>per capita</u> income of more than $9,000, control some 80 percent of the global economy. In stark contrast, the less developed countries, with an average per capita income of less than $1,000, control only about 17.6 percent of that economy. Further, the developed countries consume about 80 percent of the total world supply of energy, the less developed countries about 12 percent. And as a final <u>index</u> to the <u>disproportionate</u> distribution of wealth, the consumption of iron, copper and aluminum by developed

countries ranges from 86 to 92 percent, by the less developed countries, even including China, from 8 to 14 percent."

—Peter H. Raven, "Third World in the Global Future"

a. My definition of *per capita:* _____

   Dictionary definition: _____

b. My definition of *index:* _____

   Dictionary definition: _____

c. My definition of *disproportionate:* _____

   Dictionary definition: _____

Moving from a Passive to an Active Vocabulary

Here are several steps you can take to learn new words while reading:

1. Notice the new words. Don't simply skip over a word because you don't know what it means and hope it doesn't matter. It may be important. Be aware of words you don't understand.

2. Look for ways to figure out the meaning of a word from the context clues.

3. See if you can work out a probable meaning of the word by associating it with words you already know—looking especially at the prefix, root, and suffix.

4. Circle the word.

5. After you have finished reading—or while you are reading, if the exact meaning of the word is essential to understanding the material—check what you think the word means by referring to a good dictionary.

6. Start your own vocabulary list by using index cards. On one side, write the word; on the other, write its dictionary definition and a sentence using the word. Carry the cards in your pocket and study them whenever you have the opportunity.

7. Make the word a part of your active vocabulary by using it as soon and as often as you can, either in writing or in speaking, and preferably in both. Some say that if you use a word three times it becomes part of your active vocabulary.

Exercise 3E

In this exercise, use one of your own textbooks to increase your passive vocabulary and to incorporate new words into your active vocabulary.

1. Find six new words.
2. See if you can work out the meanings of each new word from the context of the reading or by association.
3. Look up each new word in the dictionary.
4. Notice whether the word is a general word that is new to you, a word that you think you know but one that seems to be used in a special way, or a technical term.
5. Write each word on one side of an index card and, on the other side of the card, write the dictionary definition and a sentence using the word.
6. Use the word in conversation at your next opportunity.

Basic College Reading Skills

PART 2

Chapter 4

Finding the Topic

In this chapter you will find answers to the following questions:

What is meant by the term topic?
How do you find the topic?
Do you find the topic of a sentence and the topic of a paragraph in the same way?
Can two paragraphs of a reading have the same topic?
What is a subtopic?
Why is finding the topic an important part of previewing?

The **topic** of whatever you are reading—a book, chapter, section, paragraph, or sentence—is the person, place, thing, or idea that starts the action or that is most often mentioned or referred to. The best way to identify the topic is to ask, *Who or what is this about?* The following sentence can be used as an illustration:

> Rising from the ranks of the common man, Benjamin Franklin achieved success in everything he tried, whether it was running a Philadelphia newspaper in his youth or wooing the ladies of Paris in his old age.
>
> —John M. Blum et al.

In this sentence, Franklin starts the action and is referred to most often—Franklin rose from the ranks; Franklin achieved success; he ran a newspaper; he wooed the ladies. There is little doubt about the answer to *Who or what is this about?* Franklin is the topic.

As you learned in Chapter 2 on Previewing, the first and most fundamental question that naturally comes to mind when you preview or start to read something is, *Who or what is this about?* This question becomes important because it can help you to decide whether or not you want or need to read the material, as well as to get an idea of what your **purpose** in reading it is.

Although the notion of finding the topic seems simple, the task becomes more difficult and complex when applied to college-level reading. Finding the topic is the first step in actively reading for ideas. Attempting to answer *Who or what is this about?* sets your mind to work and begins the process of thinking about the author's ideas. You are starting to *associate* what you already know about the topic with what the author might be saying about it. You begin to wonder about what ideas the passage might contain. Referring to the preceding example, you begin to think about Franklin and his importance in the early days of this country. What was his influence? What else was he successful in? What was his role in France? You and the author have started your dialogue, and you are beginning to define your purpose in reading this passage.

The Topic in Sentences

In reading a sentence, ordinarily it is not hard to find the answer to *Who or what is this sentence about?* The person, place, thing, or idea that is central to the sentence's meaning or that forms the basis for action is usually the subject of the verb. In our example, the noun *Franklin* is the subject of the verb *achieved*.

Exercise 4A

In the following sentences, circle the correct answer to the question, Who or what is this sentence about?

Example:
The batter hit the ball out of the park.

a. the ball
b. the park
c. the batter ⭕
d. hit

1. By 1913, Henry Ford had turned out the Model T at prodigious rates and put America on wheels.

    a. the Model T

    b. Henry Ford

    c. America

    d. 1913

2. No matter how hard he tried to forget, Paul continued to be haunted by the memory of that disastrous decision.

    a. Paul

    b. memory

    c. decision

    d. to forget

3. Mary Anderson's testimony was crucial to the prosecutor's case.

    a. the case

    b. the testimony

    c. Mary Anderson

    d. the prosecutor

4. It was not an easy task to condense the story into 150 words.

    a. the story

    b. it

    c. task

    d. words

5. Condensing the story into 150 words was not an easy task.

    a. task

    b. the story

    c. condensing

    d. condensing and task

Exercise 4B

In the following sentences, find the topic wherever it appears by circling the answer to Who or what is this sentence about?

Example:
For a number of years, (Joan Benoit) won every marathon (she) entered.

1. Columbus's theory that the world was round was believed only by his crew and Queen Isabella.

2. The ships sailed out of sight, but they did not fall off the edge of the world.

3. A real question facing the Supreme Court today is, When does life begin?

4. The experiments on nuclear fusion are being seriously questioned by many famous scientists.

5. Although he really couldn't afford it, the store owner decided to sell the new dresses at 10 percent above cost.

The Topic in Paragraphs

Paragraphs usually consist of several sentences dealing with a central topic. The answer to *Who or what is this about?* is no longer the subject of a sentence but the topic of the whole paragraph. To find the topic of a paragraph, first ask, *What is "the" person, place, thing, or idea that starts the action or is most often mentioned in the paragraph?* Then ask, *What word or short phrase would be the best general statement of the content of the passage?* Your answer to these questions is a statement of the topic, and it is the topic that provides a focus for your thinking about the reading.

For example, what general phrase best describes what the following paragraph is about?

> In San Francisco, where 3rd meets Mission, an odd building rises amid the flatness of parking lots and construction pits. Granite-faced and about ten stories tall, it has the look of a building that somehow escaped the wrecker's ball, hunched and apprehensive despite its height.
>
> —Andrew Quinn

Both sentences describe a building in San Francisco. The building is the focus of the writing and is therefore the general topic that is described by specific details, such as "odd," "granite-faced," "tall," and "hunched."

Sometimes it is harder to locate the topic of a passage because it is buried in the paragraph. Here is an example:

> Suppose that a man holds down two jobs, consistently turns down friends' invitations to the movies, wears old clothes, drives an old car, eats food left behind from other people's lunches, refuses to give to charity, and keeps the furnace set at sixty degrees in the dead of winter. Why? Possibly he does so because he likes to work hard, hates movies, fears new clothes and new cars, enjoys other people's cold leftovers, does not care about the poor and likes cold air. This set of statements certainly covers all of this man's behaviors. But a far simpler way of accounting for those behaviors is to suggest that the man is trying to save as much money as possible. In other words, by suggesting a motive, a reason or purpose for a person's behavior, you can find unity beneath the apparent diversity of many behaviors.
>
> —Douglas A. Bernstein et al., *Psychology*

Here, it may be a little harder to discover the answer to *Who or what is this paragraph about?* The paragraph starts with many details and a question about a man. But do the details and the question refer to the man, to his behavior, or to both? As you keep reading, you see that your question is answered. The focus, the topic of the paragraph, is "the man's behavior." The beginning is an example of behavior, and the second half is an attempt to explain that behavior. Opening a paragraph with an introduction that gives one or more illustrations, followed by a definition or explanation, is not an unusual way of presenting a topic. In this example, it would be incorrect to say that the topic is simply "behavior," because there are different kinds of behavior—animal behavior, the behavior of the stars, and so on. Specifying "a person's behavior" or "the man's behavior" gives precision to the topic.

Exercise 4C

In the following passages, circle what you think is the correct answer to Who or what is this paragraph about?

1. ... The modern conception of childhood is a product of the sixteenth century, as Philippe Ariès has documented in his *The Centuries of Childhood.* Prior to that century, children as young as six and seven were treated in all important respects as if they were adults. Their language, their dress, their legal status, their responsibilities, their labor, were much the same as those of adults. The concept of childhood as an identifiable stage in human growth began to develop in the sixteenth century and has continued into our own times. However, with the emergence of electronic media of communication a reversal of this trend seems to be taking place.... Television, in itself, may bring an end to childhood. In truth, there is no such thing as "children's programming," at least not for children over the age of eight or nine. Everyone sees and hears the same things. We have already reached a point where crimes of youth are indistinguishable from those of adults, and we may soon reach a point where the punishments will be the same.

   —Neil Postman, *Teaching as a Conserving Activity*

   a. television
   b. childhood
   c. the sixteenth century
   d. juvenile crime

2. A territory is a defended space. In the broadest sense, there are three kinds of human territory: tribal, family, and personal. It is rare for people to be driven to physical fighting in defense of these "owned" spaces, but fight they will, if pushed to the limit. The invading army encroaching on national territory, the gang moving into a rival district, the trespasser climbing into an orchard, the burglar breaking into a house, the bully pushing to the front of a queue, the driver trying to steal a parking space, all of these intruders are liable to be met with resistance varying from the vigorous to the savagely violent. Even if the law is on the side of the intruder, the urge to protect a territory may be so strong that otherwise peaceful citizens abandon all their usual controls and inhibitions. Attempts to evict families from their homes, no matter how

socially valid the reasons, can lead to siege conditions reminiscent of the defense of a medieval fortress.

—Desmond Morris, *Manwatching*

   a. gangs

   b. evicting families

   c. protecting territory

   d. trespassers and intruders

Exercise 4D

Circle the topic wherever it appears in the following paragraphs.

1. Stephen King has become a household name in at least three senses. He is a writer pretty much everyone in the English-speaking world has heard of, if they have heard of writers at all. He is regularly read by many people who don't read many other writers. And, along with Danielle Steel and a few others, he is taken to represent everything that is wrong with contemporary publishing, that engine of junk pushing serious literature out of our minds and our bookstores. The English writer Clive Barker has said, "There are apparently two books in every American household—one of them is the Bible and the other one is probably by Stephen King."

   —Michael Wood, "Horror of Horrors"

2. When a dog bites a man, that's not news. When man bites dog, that is news. This old cliché has been told and retold to every aspiring journalist. What it says is that to be news, a story has to be something out of the ordinary.

3. Any physical theory is always provisional, in the sense that it is only a hypothesis: you can never prove it. No matter how many times the results of experiments agree with some theory, you can never be sure that the next time the result will not contradict the theory. On the other hand, you can disprove a theory by finding even a single observation that disagrees with the predictions of the theory.... Each time new experiments are observed to agree with the predictions the theory survives, and our confidence in it is increased; but if ever a new observation is found to disagree, we have to aban-

don or modify the theory. At least that is what is supposed to happen, but you can always question the competence of the person who carried out the observation.

—Stephen W. Hawking, *A Brief History of Time*

Topics and Subtopics in Longer Readings

Every part of a reading is about something. The word *topic* refers to the subject of the *entire reading*. The word **subtopic** is used to refer to the topics or subjects of the various *parts* that make up the entire reading, such as the units and chapters of a book or the paragraphs of an article. These parts are different aspects, or features, of the topic.

Thus, the topic of this book is "active reading"; a subtopic of active reading and also the topic of Chapter 1 is "reading for ideas"; another subtopic, "developing vocabulary," is the topic of Chapter 3; and still another subtopic, "finding the topic," is the topic of this chapter.

Take a look at the following reading to see whether you can identify the topic of the passage and the subtopics found in each paragraph, by asking, *Who or what is this about?*

> ***Infectious Mononucleosis*** This affliction of college-aged students is often jokingly referred to as the "kissing disease." The symptoms of mononucleosis, or "mono," include sore throat, fever, headache, nausea, chills, and a pervasive weakness or tiredness in the initial stages. As the disease progresses, lymph nodes may become increasingly enlarged, and jaundice, spleen enlargement, aching joints, and body rashes may occur.
>
> Theories on the transmission and treatment of mononucleosis are highly controversial. Caused by the *Epstein-Barr virus*, mononucleosis is readily detected through a *monospot test*, a blood test that measures the percentage of specific forms of white blood cells. Because many viruses are caused by transmission of body fluids, many people once believed that young people passed the disease on by kissing. Although this is still considered a possible cause, mononucleosis is not believed to be highly contagious. It does not appear to be easily contracted through normal, everyday personal contact. Multiple cases among family members are rare, as are cases between intimate partners.
>
> Treatment of mononucleosis is often a lengthy process that involves bed rest, balanced nutrition, and medications

to control the symptoms of the disease. Gradually, the body develops a form of immunity to the disease and the person returns to normal activity levels.

—Rebecca J. Donatelle and Lorraine G. Davis, *Health: The Basics*

The topic of paragraph 1 seems to be symptoms of mononucleosis. The topic of paragraph 2 is causes of mononucleosis, and that of paragraph 3 is treatment. As you can see in the diagram (Figure 4.1), each of these subtopics follows logically from the topic of the entire reading: mononucleosis.

Sometimes an author will devote more than one paragraph to a single topic, to provide more detail—an example or illustration of a particular aspect of the topic—as in the following passage:

> It started by mistake in a New Haven laboratory, and turned into a bonanza by sheer chance on New York's Fifth Avenue. There has never been a more accidental toy.
>
> Maybe it had to be. Who could have sat down and deliberately designed a piece of pink goo that stretches like taffy, shatters when struck sharply with a hammer, picks up newsprint and photos in color, molds like clay, flows like molasses, and—when rolled into a ball—bounces like mad?... The prodigy is Silly Putty, still as unique and popular today as it was almost twenty-five years ago, when it was accidentally developed in a General Electric research lab.
>
> —Marvin Kaye, *The Story of Monopoly, Silly Putty, Bingo, Twister, Frisbee, Scrabble, Etc.*

In paragraph 1, "accidental toy" is the answer to *Who or what is this about?* Paragraph 2 then describes the accidental toy and gives it a name, Silly Putty, which proves to be the topic of the paragraph. Both *accidental toy* and *Silly Putty* refer to the same thing; therefore, the topic of both paragraphs and of the whole reading is Silly Putty.

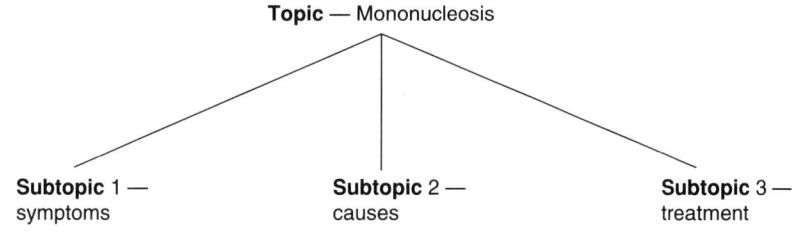

Figure 4.1

Exercise 4E

In the following paragraphs, circle the letter of the choice that best answers the question, Who or what is this about?

1. For people under tension, an ordinary work load can seem unbearable. Remember that this is a temporary condition. You can work your way out of it. How? By tackling a few of the most urgent tasks one at a time. Once you take care of the first few items, you'll see that the rest can also be done....

    Consider this story of a father, in Italy, who tied a bundle of small sticks together with a strand of twine. Handing the bundle to his son, he said, "Here break these sticks in half." Using his hands, knees, and feet, and try as he might, the son could not snap a single stick. Tired and sad, the boy said, "Father, take back the bundle, I cannot break it." Without a word, the father untied the twine and, using only his fingers, snapped each stick, one by one.

    —Walter Pauk, *How to Study in College*

    a. tension

    b. an Italian father

    c. working without tension

    d. the work load

2. Young people should have the right to control and direct their own learning, that is, to decide what they want to learn, and when, where, how, how much, how fast, and with what help they want to learn it. To be still more specific, I want them to have the right to decide whether they want to learn in a school and if so which one and for how much of the time.

    No human right, except the right to life itself, is more fundamental than this. A person's freedom of learning is part of his freedom of thought, even more basic than his freedom of speech. If we take from someone his right to decide what he will be curious about, we destroy his freedom of thought. We say, in effect, you must think not about what interests and concerns you, but about what interests and concerns us.

    —John Holt, *Escape from Childhood*

a. young people

b. learning

c. freedom

d. freedom of learning

e. freedom of thought

Exercise 4F

Read the following passages and answer the questions that follow. You may need to identify the subtopics before you can be sure of the topic.

1. Proteins perform a great variety of functions in our bodies. They protect us against disease, help our blood clot, and form the membranes, muscles, and connective tissues that build our bodies.

    Proteins are very large molecules made up of carbon, oxygen, hydrogen, nitrogen, and sometimes sulfur, iodine, iron, or phosphorus. They are formed when molecules called amino acids link together in special arrangements (peptide linkages)....

    Foods with all the essential amino acids are said to contain complete proteins: these include eggs, meat, milk, and fish. Foods that do not contain all the essential amino acids are said to be incomplete; such foods include nuts and cereals....

    Proteins are the main constituents of all the cells in the body. Protein molecules are needed to build new cells, to maintain existing cells, and to replace old, wornout cells. The chemicals that take part in body reactions and those that help control the rates at which body reactions occur (such as enzymes and hormones) are made of protein molecules. In addition, the all-important molecules that carry our genetic information are made of proteins.

    —Alan Sherman et al., *Basic Concepts of Chemistry*

    a. What is the topic of the entire reading?

b. What is the subtopic found in paragraph 1?

_____

c. What is the subtopic found in paragraph 2?

_____

d. What is the subtopic found in paragraph 3?

_____

e. What is the subtopic found in paragraph 4?

_____

2. It is not only Americans who have wrestled with the problems of creating a government to meet their needs. In 1789, cries of "Liberty, Equality, and Fraternity" rang out in France as members of the working class, inspired by the American Revolution, rose up against King Louis XVI. The king, members of his family, and many French aristocrats were executed. Civil unrest continued and mobs controlled Paris until order was restored through the creation of a provisional government.

In the early 1900s in Russia, the radical Bolshevik Party mobilized citizens who were demoralized by war and who were without jobs or food, to overthrow and ultimately execute Czar Nicholas II and his family. The Bolshevik Revolution was followed by a period of civil war, and the Union of Soviet Socialist Republics was created from the ruins of the Russian Empire. Inspired by the Bolshevik model, Chinese communists similarly established a communist government in the late 1940s after a prolonged period of civil war.

More recently, these once revolutionary communist governments have themselves been faced with revolutionary discontent. In 1989, Chinese students demonstrated for democracy in Tienanmen Square, but to little avail. The communist rulers responded with a massive and bloody show of force that left many dead or injured. These events caused little political change in China. The early 1990s, however, saw the breakup of the Soviet Union. Most of this breakup was spurred by citizen demands, particularly in Eastern Europe, for democratization. In one new Eastern European state after another, citizens have gone to the polls to elect new leaders. Some of the changes have occurred with relatively little violence; others, such as the carving out of Bosnia-Herzogovenia from the former Yugoslavia, have produced all-out war and tremendous personal tragedy.

In each of these situations, whether peaceful or not, men and women have attempted to create new political systems to resolve the classic, age-old question of politics: Who gets what, when, and how? 4

—Karen O'Connor and Larry J. Sabato, *American Government*

a. What is the topic of the entire reading?

_____

b. What is the subtopic found in paragraph 1?

_____

c. What is the subtopic found in paragraph 2?

_____

d. What is the subtopic found in paragraph 3?

_____

e. What is the subtopic found in paragraph 4?

_____

Inferring the Topic from Clues

Quite often, just a little reading can produce the answer to the question, *Who or what is this about?* But when the answer to that question is not so obvious, an active reader looks for clues provided by the author—a title, a subtitle, a headline, or a picture. Proper attention to these aids can quickly suggest to you the topic of what you are about to read.

Thinking about not only the title but also the subtitle tells you that *The Personnel Management Process: Cases in Human*

Resources Administration is about how managers or administrators can most effectively use the people (that is, human resources) available to them and that much of the book will deal with actual personnel problems in various businesses or industries.

Looking at chapter titles and headings will also help you to find and to see the importance of connections between the topic and subtopics of chapters in a textbook. For example, the textbook *Economics* by Martin Bronfenbrenner, Werner Sichel, and Wayland Gardner includes a chapter entitled "The Private Sector: Households and Business Firms." This title gives you the major topic of the chapter. A quick look at the headings and subheadings produces the following, which tells you a good deal more:

> Households
>   Population and Age Groups
>   Changes in the Family
>   Sources of Income
>   Distribution of Income
>   Household Expenditures
> Business Firms
>   Forms of Business Organization
>   Corporations in the United States
>   Multinational Corporations
>   Business Accounting

These headings and subheadings clearly and concisely answer the question, *Who or what is this chapter about?* Before reading a word of text, you are thus firmly oriented to the content and are ready to ask specific questions based on the headings, such as, *Which population and age-groups are being discussed?* or *What are the sources of income?*

If the title of a book or article does not provide you with a clear idea of the topic, you may have to look further. The topic is normally stated near the beginning of a book or article. If you had to guess at the topic from the clues, the first few paragraphs of an article and the introduction or first chapter of a book would either confirm your guess or give you the correct answer.

The answer to *Who or what is this chapter about?* will do the following:

- Tell you what person, place, thing, or idea is the topic of the reading;
- Help you decide whether you have an interest in or need to read the material;

- Start you thinking about the topic and associating what you already know with what you are about to read;
- Enable you to base questions on your predictions of what the author will say.

Exercise 4G

From the clues provided in the following opening paragraphs of two articles, circle the correct answer to Who or what is this article about?

1. **Beer Ads and Gutter Talk** The primary function of language is to communicate ideas. Although proper grammar, spelling, and punctuation do not guarantee accurate communication, they increase the likelihood that the message intended by the sender is the one that will be understood by the receiver.

   —Lawrence Casler, President of the Society for the Advancement of Good English

   a. beer ads

   b. language and communication

   c. language and advertising

   d. proper grammar

2. Economic boycotts occupy an important and honored place in the long history of protest movements. They have an advantage over other forms of protest in that they can be conducted in a legal and nonviolent fashion, a fact which no doubt explains their continued popularity in the face of a high rate of failure. Seeking their objectives primarily through a disruption of certain vital services, economic boycotts are usually not allowed to proceed to a point where they can wreak devastation on an economy. At the same time, the inconvenience and hardship that they cause provide strong financial incentives for evasion, among both supporters and opponents. Once substantial evasion occurs, the collapse of the boycott becomes a matter of time. Another reason for the failure of boycotts is that their success can only be guaranteed by a sustained stand by the masses, and this is exceedingly difficult to achieve.

The Bugandan trade boycott of 1959 was an attempt to achieve certain political and economic goals through a boycott of alien traders. Its study provides an illuminating lesson on the strength and limitations of the boycott as a medium of protest.

—Dharam P. Ghai, *Protest and Power in Black Africa*

a. protest movements

b. the Bugandan trade boycott

c. economic boycotts

d. political goals

Exercise 4H

Chapter 10 of a book entitled Broadcasting in America, *by Sydney Head and Christopher Sterling, has these headings. What do you think is the topic of the chapter?*

Why Public Broadcasting?
Rise of Educational Broadcasting
National Organization
Types of Public Broadcasting Stations
The Search for Funding
Programming for Public Broadcasting
Children and Classrooms
The Influence of Public Broadcasting
The Outlook

The topic of the chapter is _____

Exercise 4I

Following are the beginnings of two articles from the Boston Globe, *each representing a different point of view in a dialogue. What is the topic of the dialogue?*

Malpractice Costs Hurt All

The cost of malpractice insurance is soaring out of control in Massachusetts, and what, at first, seems only a problem for physicians quickly becomes everybody's problem.

—Frederick J. Duncan, Jr., and Barbara Rockett

Blame Negligent Doctors, Not Insurance

Doctors claim a crisis in malpractice insurance and are pushing the Legislature to adopt a package of bills to immunize the medical profession from responsibility for damage done by their negligence at the expense of innocent victims.

—David J. Sargent

The topic of the dialogue is _____

Summary Exercise

In two or three complete sentences, write your answer to these questions:

What is the topic of Chapter 3?
What is one of the subtopics of Chapter 3?
How did you find the topic and the subtopic?

Preview Questions

What is this text about?
Why am I reading it?
What do I already know about the topic?
What do I predict the author will say?

Chapter 5

Discovering the Key Idea

In this chapter you will find answers to these questions:

What is a key idea?
How do you find the key idea of a sentence?
What is the difference between the topic and the key idea?
Do you find the key idea of a sentence and of a paragraph in the same way?
What is an inferred key idea?
Why is finding the key idea an important part of previewing?

The **key idea** of a sentence, paragraph, chapter, or book is the main thought or principal idea about the topic that the author wants to communicate to the reader. The key idea is the most important idea you get from your reading or the thought you most want to remember. Another way of thinking of the key idea is to view it as a statement about the topic that everything else in the reading supports. Discovering the key idea unlocks the meaning of the passage and is your key to understanding. You can find the key idea by asking, *What is the author's most important idea about the topic?*

The Key Idea of a Sentence

The key idea of a sentence is expressed in the subject, verb, and object of the sentence. The rest of the words in the sentence explain, support, or develop the key idea. Recognizing the words that carry most of the meaning will help you to grasp more quickly what the author is saying. The first step in identifying the key idea is to **analyze,** or break down, a sentence. Then you can see how the words in the sentence are arranged into phrases that support the key idea by connecting thoughts or by describing, explaining, or developing the author's key ideas. The following sentence from Chapter 4 can be used as an illustration:

> Rising from the ranks of the common man, Benjamin Franklin achieved success in everything he tried, whether it was running a Philadelphia newspaper in his youth or wooing the ladies of Paris in his old age.
>
> —John M. Blum et al.

Here, Franklin is referred to most often and takes the action. The answer to *Who or what is this about?* is "Franklin." To find the key idea you can now ask, *What is the author's most important idea about Franklin?* The answer to this question is that Franklin achieved success in everything he tried.

Let's look at another example.

> In all matters, before beginning, a diligent preparation should be made.
>
> —Cicero

This sentence is about preparation (preparation is the subject). But another question is needed. What *about* the preparation? *What is the author's most important idea about preparation?* It should be made (made is the main verb). Thus, the key idea is that preparation should be made.

Exercise 5A

Identify the topic in each of the following sentences. Then answer the question, What is the author's most important idea about the topic? *Underline the key idea in each of the following sentences.*

Example:
The <u>batter hit the ball</u> out of the park.
Topic: batter
Key idea: batter hit the ball

1. Vaccination can prevent influenza.

   a. Topic: _____

   b. Key idea: _____

2. The guidelines will extend the eligibility for state financial assistance.

   a. Topic: _____

   b. Key idea: _____

3. Calico-coated, small-bodied, with delicate legs and pink faces in which their mismatched eyes rolled wild and subdued, they huddled, gaudy, motionless and alert, wild as deer, deadly as rattlesnakes, quiet as doves.

   —William Faulkner

   a. Topic: _____

   b. Key idea: _____

4. Whatever the assigned function of social institutions, their psychological function is to protect the citizen against the irrational, incalculable forces that hover about the edges of human life like cosmic destruction lurking within an atomic stockpile.

   —Ralph Ellison

   a. Topic: _____

   b. Key idea: _____

5. Joad's lips stretched tight over his long teeth for a moment, and he licked his lips, like a dog, two licks, one in each direction from the middle.

   —John Steinbeck

   a. Topic: _____

   b. Key idea: _____

The Key Idea of Paragraphs

An author writes to convey an idea, or a message, to an audience. When you have found the answer to *Who or what is this about?* you know the topic of the message, but you don't know anything about why the author thinks the topic is important or what direction the author's thoughts will take. The answer to *What is the author's most important idea about the topic?* gives you the key idea. It tells you what is important and gives you a sense of what aspect of the topic the author is going to discuss. In a paragraph, as well as in longer readings, the key idea is usually a general statement, expressed as a sentence rather than in a few words.

Let's use the following example to demonstrate how to find the key idea in a paragraph.

> Earthquakes can cause enormous destruction, particularly in areas that are heavily populated. Buildings are toppled. Thousands of people lose their lives. Others are severely injured. Fires are started by broken electric power lines. Damaged water mains hinder efforts to combat the flames.

Who or what is the paragraph about? The topic of the paragraph is earthquakes. *What is the author's most important idea about earthquakes?* Earthquakes can cause enormous destruction. This point must be the key idea, because the sentences that follow this general idea support it by providing specific information that explains the ways earthquakes can cause enormous destruction—by toppling buildings, killing people, starting fires, and damaging water mains.

Exercise 5B

Determine whether each of the following phrases or sentences is a topic or a key idea. Write T on the line if it is a topic; write KI if it is a key idea.

Examples:
T: College life
KI: College life is busy.

1. ____ Paragraph structure

2. ____ No-fault auto insurance increases efficiency in handling claims.

3. _____ A reporter's education

4. _____ Acquiring skills

5. _____ Environmental conditions vary among geographic areas.

6. _____ Emerging from depression

7. _____ Drug use has increased.

8. _____ Word-processing programs are excellent tools.

Exercise 5C

Write a key idea for each of these topics by answering the question, What is the author's most important idea about the topic?

Example:
T: Pencils
KI: The pencils have disappeared.

1. T: College

   KI: _____

2. T: Photography

   KI: _____

3. T: The movements of a dancer

   KI: _____

4. T: Reading comprehension

   KI: _____

5. T: Freedom

   KI: _____

Placement of the Key Idea

The Key Idea in the First Sentence of a Paragraph

You may find the key idea stated anywhere in a paragraph; however, the most common placement of the key idea is in the first sentence. The author presents the key idea and then explains or supports it throughout the rest of the paragraph.

Here is an example of a paragraph whose key idea is stated in the first sentence:

> *Reading is both a necessity and a pleasure.* By enabling us to know and master relevant information, reading can lead to success in our jobs. At the same time, reading can provide relief from the stresses of daily life by taking us into a variety of worlds and situations.

The Key Idea in the Last Sentence of a Paragraph

Presenting the key idea in the last sentence of a paragraph is the next most common placement of the key idea. When authors wait until the final sentence to state the key idea, they lead up to this statement by providing supporting information first. The first several sentences are the basis for the key idea that follows in the last sentence.

Here is an example of a paragraph in which the key idea is stated in the last sentence:

> Ninety women and children crowded the eight-bedroom Victorian house. But the air was electric with excitement. Even the disorder instilled confidence that if this chaos could be managed, anything could. That night, armed with wallpaper, basic tools, and portable toilets, *a group of women "liberated" an abandoned railroad hotel.*
>
> —Evan Stark and Anne Flitcraft

The Key Idea in the Middle of a Paragraph

You may also find the key idea in the middle of a paragraph. In this case, the first few sentences may introduce the topic or lead up to the key idea and the sentences after the key idea explain or support the key idea. Here is an example:

> There is one key idea which contains, in itself, the very essence of effective reading, and on which the improvement of reading depends: *Reading is reasoning.* When you read properly, you are not merely assimilating. You are not automati-

cally transferring into your head what your eyes pick up on the page. What you see on the page sets your mind at work, collating, criticizing, interpreting, questioning, comprehending, comparing. When this process goes on well, you read well. When it goes on ill, you read badly.

—James Mursell, *Using Your Mind Effectively*

The Key Idea in the First and Last Sentences of a Paragraph

Sometimes authors state the key idea twice in the same paragraph. In such instances, authors usually present the key idea in the first and last sentences of the paragraph. The first sentence states the key idea, the next sentences support it, and the final sentence restates the key idea in different words. Here is an example:

> *Comic performers are very distinctive.* They have distinctive faces, mannerisms, or ways of speaking that set them off entirely. More strongly than any other kind of performer, they maintain the ancient concept of the *mask:* the stylized covering which sets dramatic actors aside from reality. The Keystone comics, the Marx brothers, and the Three Stooges have masks only slightly less exaggerated than those of *commedia dell'arte* [comedy developed in Italy in the sixteenth century]. Chaplin and Keaton kept clown-like masks even in realistic feature films. Later comedians from Eddie Bracken to Jerry Lewis to Woody Allen lost the clown look but exploited funny faces and mannerisms. The same is true of minor comedians, some of whom appear as comic relief in melodramas: *they stand apart,* thanks to this power of the comic mask.
>
> —George Wead and George Lellis, *Film: Form and Function*

Exercise 5D

Read each of the following paragraphs and answer the question, What is this about? *Then circle the letter of the sentence that best states the key idea by answering the question,* What is the author's most important idea about the topic?

Example:
Generally, the distinction between divorce and annulment revolves around the time of the cause or the time in which certain actions occurred. Divorce generally involves an action that occurred *after* the date of marriage—adultery, incompatibility, cruelty, desertion, nonsupport, alcoholism, and the like. Annulment generally

involves an action that occurred *before* the date of marriage—being under age, another existing marriage, incurable impotence, incestuous relationship, and the like.

—J. Ross Eshleman, *The Family*

a. Divorce involves an action that occurred after the marriage.

b. Divorce and annulment are two ways to end a marriage.

c. Annulment involves an action that occurred before the marriage.

(d.) The difference between divorce and annulment concerns the time of the cause or the time in which certain actions occurred.

1. Most upper elementary-grade children are still concrete thinkers and they may feel obliged to make up a separate rule for every contingency. A fifth-grade teacher encountered this problem when he asked his pupils to propose class rules. Within twenty minutes over fifty rules had been proposed and when the teacher ran out of blackboard space, he had to call a halt. The major reason for this profusion of regulations was that a separate rule was suggested for variations of a particular type of behavior. For example, there was a rule "Don't run in the hall," followed by another rule, "Don't run in the class room," followed by yet another rule, "Don't run on the way to the boys' room," and so on.

—Richard A. Ripple et al., *Human Development*

a. The children made up many rules.

b. A fifth-grade teacher had a problem.

c. Upper elementary-grade children are still concrete thinkers.

d. There was a rule "Don't run in the classroom" and another rule "Don't run on the way to the boys' room."

2. In order to make students more active and more intelligent learners, it is necessary to change the traditional roles of both student and teacher. One approach that has proved effective is pair problem solving. In it, students work together in pairs on sets of specially designed problems. Each member of the pair has a distinct and well-defined role. One partner reads and thinks aloud, while the other listens. On subsequent problems the partners change roles, taking turns as problem solver and listener.

—Jack Lochhead, "Teaching Analytical Reasoning Skills through Pair Problem Solving"

a. Pair problem solving involves students working together in pairs.

b. Pair problem solving is an effective approach to helping students become more active and more intelligent learners.

c. Partners take turns as problem solver and listener when they are doing pair problem solving.

d. Each member of the team has a distinct and well-defined role.

3. Two methods of measuring temperature are Fahrenheit and Celsius. Some people refer to Celsius as centigrade. Most countries use Celsius—we are beginning to hear more about this method in the United States. In the United States, temperature is usually expressed in terms of Fahrenheit, and so it is the method most familiar to us. When the radio announcer says it is 95 degrees, we assume that the reference is to Fahrenheit, and we recognize that it is a very warm day. On the Fahrenheit scale, the number used to express the temperature for freezing water is 32, and the number for boiling is 212. In Celsius, the number used to express the temperature for freezing water is 0, and the number for boiling water is 100.

—Linda Falstein, *Basic Mathematics for College Students*

a. Celsius is based on a system of measuring temperature on a scale from 0 to 100.

b. On the Fahrenheit scale, the number used to express the temperature for freezing water is 32, and the number for boiling is 212.

c. In the United States, temperature is usually expressed in terms of Fahrenheit, and so it is the method most familiar to us.

d. Two methods of measuring temperature are Fahrenheit and Celsius.

Exercise 5E

Read the following paragraphs and ask the question, What is the author's most important idea about the topic? *Then underline the key idea in each paragraph. Remember first to find the topic by asking,* Who or what is this paragraph about?

Example:
Cave drawings tell us of prehistoric man's taste for honey, figs, and dates. The beekeeping practices of Egyptians are depicted in the artwork in tombs dating around 2600 B.C. The Bible tells us that the "promised land" flowed with milk and honey. It turned into a flood once sugar cane was discovered. In the writings of an obscure officer in Alexander's army during its invasion of India, one finds the first written mention of sugar cane. That was around 25 B.C. Yet, despite this long history, <u>the use of sugar in the diet has become a controversial issue</u> in recent years that has involved doctors, scientists, nutritionists, private citizens, the Government, and the industry itself.

—Chris W. Lecos, "Sugar: How Sweet It Is—And Isn't"

1. What we perceive also depends on our past experience in terms of how "educated" our eyes are. Take the case of two people who are watching a football game. One person, who has very little understanding of football, sees merely a bunch of grown men hitting each other for no apparent reason. The other person, who loves football, sees complex play patterns, daring coaching strategies, effective blocking and tackling techniques, and zone defenses with "seams" that the receivers are trying to "split." Both persons have their eyes glued to the same event, but they are perceiving two entirely different situations. The perceptions differ because each person is actively selecting, organizing, and interpreting the available stimuli in different ways.

—John Chaffee, *Thinking Critically*

2. The study of human ecology leaves no doubt that people are the most influential organisms in the biosphere, in that they can raise crops, control infectious diseases, and alter any ecosystem to meet their needs. Yet in a very real sense, people are themselves ecosystems because the existence of all human beings depends on the presence of bacteria that live on or in our bodies. Madison Avenue notwithstanding, human well-being is highly dependent on contact with environmental microbes. Within our guts bacteria recycle metabolic products from the liver and thereby enable us to digest fats. Gut bacteria probably also supply us with at least some of our daily requirements of vitamins, and skin microbes prevent the colonization of your body surfaces by potentially pathogenic [disease causing] organisms. From the outmost reaches of the biosphere to the very center of our guts, we people are not alone on Earth, nor are our lives isolated from those of other living things.

—Sam Singer and Henry Hilgard, *The Biology of People*

3. Conscious of grounding their literature firmly in their history as a people, many contemporary black women writers turn to the past. Alice Walker looks to Zora Neale Hurston for her inspiration and for folk sources to inform "The Revenge of Hannah Kemhuff." Lucille Clifton records the oral histories of her family in *Generations*. Toni Morrison examines the history that links together three generations of women in *Sula*. Sherley Williams writes a series of poems entitled "Generations," and Yvonne sketches poetic portraits of her female ancestors. All of the writers create a sense of community that implicitly connects the individual to her history.

—Dexter Fisher, *The Third Woman: Minority Women Writers of the United States*

4. It is difficult to live in today's society without having had some contact with computers. Computers are used to provide instructional material in some schools, print transcripts, send out bills, reserve airline and concert tickets, play games, and even help authors write books.

—Elliot B. Koffman, *Problem Solving and Structured Programming in Pascal*

5. According to ancient legend, the Greek goddess Thetis heard a prophecy that her son, Achilles, would die in battle. To protect him, she attempted what might be called the first inoculation by dipping him head first into the magical River Styx. This made him invulnerable—except for the part of his body that Thetis held onto, his heel. Thus, we get the colorful phrase "Achilles heel" for a weak point in an otherwise strong person. In terms of an invasion route for many bacteria and viruses, our Achilles heel is located at the other end of the anatomy, the respiratory tract: the nose, throat, windpipe, bronchial tubes and lungs.

—Tim Larkin, "Flu/Cold—Never the Strain Shall Meet"

Inferred Key Ideas

In the examples and exercises so far, you have been finding stated, or expressed, key ideas—that is, key ideas that are directly stated somewhere in the paragraph. Sometimes the key idea is not

explicitly stated in the passage. When the key idea is not directly expressed, you have to infer it from what the author implies. That is, you try to think of one key idea or general statement that all the sentences would support. You may have to read through the entire piece before you have enough evidence to infer the key idea, as in the following passage:

> I lay rigid in my bed with every muscle from the top of my head to the end of my toes taut and straining. My breathing had stopped. My total being was centered on my ears, which were listening for that creak on the stairs, that slight rustle of clothes, that indrawn breath which would betray the presence of someone.

What is this paragraph about? The topic is fear. The answer to the question, *What is the most important thing the author is saying about the topic?* is "I was afraid." Although it is not stated explicitly, the author gives you evidence of the physical symptoms of fear—rigid muscles, halted breathing, intense listening. From this evidence the reader can gather that the writer was experiencing fear. All the symptoms relate to experiencing fear.

Exercise 5F

None of the following paragraphs contain expressed key ideas. First, find the topic of each paragraph. Next, determine the inferred key idea of each paragraph by asking the question, What is the author's most important idea about the topic? *Then write the topic and key idea of each paragraph on the lines that follow.*

Example:
When people first planted their fields to grain, they harvested by pulling the heads off the stalks by hand. Then someone introduced the use of a knife, by which several heads could be reaped at once. The knife blade developed a curve that became a sickle, and the sickle grew to a scythe, with corresponding increases in efficiency. Finally, the modern age brought the harvesting machine, which reaps many acres of grain a day.
Topic: *Harvesting tools*
Key idea: *The tools used for harvesting have undergone a gradual development.*

1. Frazier walked to the front of the class and dramatically pulled a two-foot papier-mâché model of a cockroach out of a sack. He attached a string to the "bug" and suspended it from the ceiling. Then he began his speech about how to rid a home of pests. The trouble was, no one listened to Frazier's message. His audience was obsessed with the creature dangling in midair.

    —Steven A. Beebee and Susan J. Beebee, *Public Speaking*

    a. Topic: _____

    b. Key idea: _____

2. A 32-year-old middle-class female, poly-drug abuser for fifteen years, is a prostitute and involved in numerous abusive relationships with men. She denies the risks of her sexual and substance abuse behavior and continues to engage in them despite several health problems. Her father was physically abusive and her mother is an alcoholic with whom she has had no contact in the last two years. She describes herself as a loner with no female friends; she primarily spends time with a live-in boyfriend who periodically beats her. She views herself as "too dumb" to complete high school and "too stupid" to stop "hooking."

    —Thomas Mieczkowski, *Drugs, Crime, and Social Policy*

    a. Topic: _____

    b. Key idea: _____

3. Further diagnosis, based on angiography, a detailed X-ray study of the circulatory system, showed the tumor to be about two inches in diameter and supplied by many small blood vessels. It rested beneath the brain, just above the pituitary gland, stretching the optic nerves to either side and intimately close to the major blood vessels supplying the brain. Removing it would pose many technical problems. Probably benign and slow-growing, it may have been present for several years. If left alone it would continue to grow and produce blindness and might become impossible to remove completely. Removing it, however, might not improve the patient's vision and could make it worse. A major blood vessel could be damaged, causing a stroke. Damage to the undersurface of the brain could cause impairment of memory and changes in mood and

personality. The hypothalamus, a most important structure of the brain, could be injured.

—Roy C. Selby, Jr., "A Delicate Operation"

a. Topic: _____

b. Key idea: _____

4. When you walk, you don't think about the placement of your legs but of where you wish to go. Flying an airplane or driving an automobile is done in that same way by the skilled performer. When you learned to drive, you concentrated on how to move your arms and legs. Then you worried about the smoothness of your activities. Eventually you reached the point where you simply thought of turning and your actions took care of themselves. But even that phase changed. The skilled driver simply goes somewhere—to the store, home, to the bank. The skilled airplane pilot no longer manipulates controls and watches instruments, but simply flies—not "flies the plane," but "flies." The person is flying or driving or going. The plane or the automobile or the legs are incidental tools to the activity.

—Donald A. Norman, *Learning and Memory*

a. Topic: _____

b. Key idea: _____

Key Ideas of Longer Readings

Just as a paragraph has a key idea that expands on the topic and that the rest of the paragraph develops, a longer selection has one key idea that tells you the author's most important idea about the topic. The entire selection explains or supports this key idea. The key idea may be stated in the first paragraph of the selection, as in the following example:

One of the most popular variations of permanent part-time employment is job sharing. Here a full-time position is divided into two part-time positions, and the duties and responsibilities of the job are assigned to two separate employees. In some cases the job functions of the two individuals may be distinctly different, since each may be responsible for sepa-

1

rate activities. Accountability for the total job may be divided between the two sharers, or both may assume equal and full accountability. Job sharing usually involves a splitting of the responsibilities and the accountability between the sharers. When both part-time employees are held responsible for the whole job it is sometimes called "job pairing."

The initial interest in job sharing was expressed by female professionals who were interested in maintaining a better balance between their career and family responsibilities. Two successful job sharing experiments in the mid-1960s—one with social workers and the other with teachers—stimulated considerable interest in this work arrangement. Approximately 80 percent of the job sharers are females.

An example of job sharing is the case of a husband and wife who share one teaching position in the history department of a university. He teaches American history classes, his speciality, and she teaches Asian history classes, her speciality. Together their combined teaching loads, committee assignments, and salary are equivalent to one position.

Job sharing has been tried successfully among many different employees, including clerical and office workers, elementary school teachers, district attorneys, librarians, and various production-level workers. In most instances job sharing has been initiated by two individuals who submitted a proposal to split a job in response to a job opening.

—David J. Cherrington, *Organizational Behavior: The Management of Individual and Organizational Performance*

The topic of this selection is job sharing. *What is the author's most important idea about job sharing?* Job sharing is one of the most popular variations of permanent part-time employment. This idea is stated in the first sentence of the passage. The entire selection supports this key idea.

Alternatively, the key idea may be a general statement that you infer from the key ideas of all the paragraphs. You may have to add up the key ideas of all the paragraphs to figure out the key idea of the whole selection. The paragraphs are linked together by one key idea that answers the question, *What is the author's most important idea about the topic?*

The passage about revolution from the previous chapter is an example of a longer selection whose key idea is inferred by putting together the key ideas of each paragraph:

It is not only Americans who have wrestled with the problems of creating a government to meet their needs. In 1789, cries of "Liberty, Equality, and Fraternity" rang out in France as members of the working class, inspired by the

American Revolution, rose up against King Louis XVI. The king, members of his family, and many French aristocrats were executed. Civil unrest continued and mobs controlled Paris until order was restored through the creation of a provisional government.

In the early 1900s in Russia, the radical Bolshevik Party mobilized citizens who were demoralized by war and who were without jobs or food, to overthrow and ultimately execute Czar Nicholas II and his family. The Bolshevik Revolution was followed by a period of civil war, and the Union of Soviet Socialist Republics was created from the ruins of the Russian Empire. Inspired by the Bolshevik model, Chinese communists similarly established a communist government in the late 1940s after a prolonged period of civil war.

More recently, these once revolutionary communist governments have themselves been faced with revolutionary discontent. In 1989, Chinese students demonstrated for democracy in Tienanmen Square, but to little avail. The communist rulers responded with a massive and bloody show of force that left many dead or injured. These events caused little political change in China. The early 1990s, however, saw the breakup of the Soviet Union. Most of this breakup was spurred by citizen demands, particularly in Eastern Europe, for democratization. In one new Eastern European state after another, citizens have gone to the polls to elect new leaders. Some of the changes have occurred with relatively little violence; others, such as the carving out of Bosnia-Herzogovenia from the former Yugoslavia, have produced all-out war and tremendous personal tragedy.

In each of these situations, whether peaceful or not, men and women have attempted to create new political systems to resolve the classic, age-old question of politics: Who gets what, when, and how?

—Karen O'Connor and Larry J. Sabato, *American Government*

As you learned in Chapter 4, the topic of this passage is revolution. The first subtopic, found in paragraph 1, is the French Revolution. The author's most important idea about the French Revolution is that the French participated in a revolution to create a new government. The second subtopic, found in paragraph 2, is the Communist revolutions. The key idea of this paragraph is that the Communists in Russia and China overthrew their governments. The third subtopic, found in paragraph 3 is revolutions in Communist countries. The key idea of this paragraph is that revolutions for democracy have occurred in Communist countries. If you combine these three key ideas, you will discover that the key idea of the entire selection is that revolutions are part of the struggle for new political systems.

Exercise 5G

Read each of the following passages, looking for the topic and the key idea. Then answer the questions that follow.

Example:

How does one frame a question? The logical method is: Think through your question plan, just as a quarterback or a coach plans the game strategy prior to the playing of the game. As a teacher, you establish goals with objectives to be met and the appropriate questioning strategy to reach those goals. Once the initial preparation has been accomplished, then it becomes a matter of implementation: Ask the question and elicit an appropriate response. 1

The basic rule for framing a question is: Ask the question; pause, then call on a student. This rule is grounded in the psychological principle that when a question is asked and then followed by a short pause, all students will "attend" to the communication. The nonverbal message (pause) communicates that any student in the class may be selected for a response. Thus, the attention level of the class remains high. 2

If the teacher reverses this pattern by requesting a particular student to respond prior to asking the question, then all those students who are not involved have the opportunity "not to attend" to the communication between teacher and student. 3

—Donald C. Orlich et al., *Teaching Strategies*

Circle the letter beside the phrase that best answers the question, What is this about?

a. Teaching

b. Quarterbacks and coaches

(c.) Asking questions appropriately

d. Pausing

Circle the letter beside the sentence that best answers the question, What is the author's most important idea about the topic?

a. If teachers follow the rules, they will reach their goals.

b. Quarterbacks and coaches plan strategies before a game.

(c.) The rule for posing a question is based on a psychological principle.

d. Teachers establish goals.

1. ...[S]ome people learn to cope with numbers in interesting and sometimes extraordinary ways. They know they have gaps in their knowledge, but they are sufficiently confident and familiar with the way their minds work to reconstruct problems and solve them.

   In a session for a mixed group of adults, Knowles Dougherty, a specialist in teaching the math disabled, demonstrated this phenomenon. He began by asking the group to do a simple subtraction problem in their heads.

   "A woman is 38 years old. It is now 1993. In what year was she born?"

   "Don't tell me the answer," he said. "But as I go around the room, do tell me how you worked out the solution." The methods were astonishingly varied. One male adult said, "I had that certain feeling I had to get to the nearest ten. So I added two to 38 to get 40 and then subtracted 40 from 93 and then added two to the answer." Another person reported that she had adjusted the problem to her own age. Starting with her own year of birth, she added and subtracted until she got 1955 (the correct answer).

   Each adult was a little ashamed of his system. Everyone assumed that just as there was only one right answer to math problems, there was probably only one right way to subtract. But Dougherty reassured them the systems they were using were legitimate algorithms (an algorithm being just a system for getting an answer). If you have to get to the nearest ten, then get there. If you have some personal reference point, use it. The fact that most people had not used the method they had been taught in school indicated that they had probably learned a fair amount of mathematics on their own since second grade.

   Many adults know all this intuitively and develop ways to work out number problems that make sense to them. In Washington, D.C., a professional woman receives bimonthly account records from her bookkeeper. She can make no sense at all of what they show until she goes off by herself and reorganizes the data. She turns columns into rows and rows into boxes, adjusting the numerical information to fit her thinking style. Then she returns to the discussion with her bookkeeper, facts in hand. Some people need to draw pictures. Some have to speak the numbers or the problems out loud.

—Sheila Tobias, *Overcoming Math Anxiety*

Circle the letter beside the phrase that best answers the question, What is this about?

a. Mathematics

b. Coping strategies

c. Knowles Dougherty, a specialist in teaching mathematics

d. Coping strategies for doing mathematics

Circle the letter beside the sentence that best answers the question, What is the author's most important idea about the topic?

a. The woman in the example was born in 1955.

b. People work out their own ways of doing mathematics.

c. A professional woman needs to rework her bookkeeper's account records.

d. Everyone in the group thought there was only one way to do a mathematics problem.

2. The frog is a "cold-blooded" vertebrate, as are the fishes and the reptiles. This does not mean that the blood of these animals is always cold. It means that their body temperatures vary with the temperature of the surroundings. Man maintains a constant average body temperature of about 98.6°F through the regulation of the rate of food oxidation and resulting heat release in the tissues as well as of heat loss from the body surface. The coldblooded vertebrates carry on much slower oxidation and do not maintain relatively constant body temperatures.

With the coming of fall and the seasonal lowering of temperature, the body temperature of the frog drops to the point where the frog can no longer be very active. It buries itself in the mud at the bottom of a pond or finds shelter in some other protected place in the water. Heart action slows down to a point at which blood hardly circulates in the vessels. The greatly reduced amount of oxygen necessary for life is supplied through the moist surface of the skin. The tissues are kept alive by the slow oxidation of food stored in the liver and in the fat bodies attached above the kidneys in most frogs. Nervous activity almost ceases, and the frog lies in a stupor. This is the condition of the frog during hibernation, or winter rest. With the coming of spring the warm days speed up body activity, and the frog gradually resumes the physiological and functional activities of normal life.

The hot summer months bring other problems. Lacking a device for cooling the body, the frog must escape from the extreme heat. It may lie quietly in deep, cool water or bury itself in the mud at the bottom of a pond. This condition of summer activity is called estivation. Many smaller ponds dry up during midsummer, and the frogs and other cold-blooded animals only survive by burying themselves in the mud and estivating. With the coming of cooler weather and the return of water to the pond, they come out of estivation and continue normal activity until hibernation.

—James H. Otto and A. Towle, *Modern Biology*

Circle the letter beside the phrase that best answers the question, What is this about?

a. Frogs

b. Summer and winter

c. Estivation

d. Hibernation

Circle the letter beside the sentence that best answers the question, What is the author's most important idea about the topic?

a. Frogs hibernate in the winter.

b. Frogs' activities depend on the weather.

c. Frogs estivate in the summer.

d. Frogs are cold-blooded vertebrates.

Exercise 5H

Preview and read the following passages and determine the topic, the subtopics, the key idea of each paragraph, and the key idea of the entire selection. Write these elements on the lines that follow.

1. One of the most vivid of the mythical episodes added to the history of the Celtic captain, Arthur, is that deed by which he was disclosed to be the predestined king. His father, Uther Pendragon, had died, and the powerful lords of the kingdom were all grasping for the crown. By Merlin's advice and counsel it was finally decided that the supernatural powers should be left to determine the troubled issue. Before the greatest church in London a stone had appeared in which a sword was buried; and letters of gold were to be seen on the stone around the sword to the effect that the one who could draw the blade should be recognized as king. Many tried in vain. Then, at last, this unknown youth, Arthur, who had been reared secretly under the guardianship of Merlin, rode up to the church, and ignorant of the magic of his deed, pulled out the sword.

    This striking symbol of the hero's election and sacred power is derived from the prehistoric period at the close of the Age of Stone. Swords were not made until after the discovery of bronze and iron: before that time there were only spears and arrows and axes. And so, who is the one who frees the metal from the stone? The culture-hero: the magic smith, who released the world from the Stone Age and taught mankind the art of smelting bronze and iron from the ore. The hero who can draw the iron sword from the stone is not necessarily a great warrior, but always a powerful magician, lord over spiritual and material things: a seer comparable, in terms of the Iron Age, to the modern inventor, chemist or engineer, who creates new weapons for his people. And just as today we live in awe—and some fear—of the man of science, so it is only natural that the folk of that faraway other day should have thought of the one who freed for them metal from stone as the chosen master of the secrets of existence.

    —Heinrich Zimmer, *The King and the Corpse*

a. Topic: _____

   b. Subtopic found in paragraph 1: _____

   c. Key idea of paragraph 1: _____

   d. Subtopic found in paragraph 2: _____

   e. Key idea of paragraph 2: _____

   f. Key idea of entire selection: _____

2. Does the moon exert an effect upon human behavior? Many people believe it does. In fact, in a recent survey (Rotton & Kelly, 1985) almost half of the undergraduates polled reported their belief that at least some people act strangely when the moon is full! Given the plots of many Hollywood epics, this is hardly surprising. After all, most persons have seen actors or actresses turn into frightening monsters under the influence of lunar rays. Is there any basis to such beliefs? Do people actually enter an altered state of consciousness when the moon is full? A major study conducted by Rotton and Kelly (1985) casts serious doubt on this possibility.

   These researchers subjected the results of all the research conducted on this topic—some thirty-seven separate studies dealing with "moon madness"—to highly sophisticated statistical analysis. The analyses performed were complex, but the purpose was straightforward: to determine whether any evidence was provided for the occurrence of lunar effects. In their investigation Rotton and Kelly examined the potential impact of phases of the moon on a wide range of behaviors—admissions to mental hospitals, calls to crisis centers, suicides and other types of self-harm, homicides, and other criminal offenses. Although they did not specifically examine altered states of consciousness, it seems reasonable to suggest that many of the behaviors included in their study would be preceded by such shifts. For example, many persons who commit homicide report, later, that they were "not themselves" when they carried out this violent crime.

   The results of the project were both clear and conclusive: little, if any, evidence was found for an impact of the moon on human behavior. While there were slightly more criminal actions when the moon was full than when it was in other phases, this trend was not statistically significant. Further, the incidence of "lunar madness" was not higher when the moon was close to the earth than when it was farthest away, and the incidence of such behaviors was not higher near the equator than farther away from it. (The distance between the moon and the earth is slightly less at the equator than elsewhere.) Moreover, in examining the findings of all thirty-seven previous studies, Rotton and Kelly (1985) found that some reported a higher incidence of behaviors linked to "lunar madness" when the moon was full, while others reported a lower incidence of these behaviors at such times.

On the basis of these negative results, Rotton and Kelly conclude there are no scientific grounds for the contention that the moon influences human behavior or human consciousness. In fact, at the end of their article they break with the strong tradition in psychology of calling for additional research. Instead, they express the hope that their paper will put an end to further studies of "lunar madness," for in their view, at least, such research has been "much ado about nothing!"

—Robert A. Baron, "Lunar Madness:
The 'Transylvanian Effect' Revisited," *Psychology*

a. Topic: _____

b. Subtopic found in paragraph 1: _____

c. Key idea of paragraph 1: _____

d. Subtopic found in paragraph 2: _____

e. Key idea of paragraph 2: _____

f. Subtopic found in paragraph 3: _____

g. Key idea of paragraph 3: _____

h. Subtopic found in paragraph 4: _____

i. Key idea of paragraph 4: _____

j. Key idea of entire selection: _____

3. The most significant and widespread area of discontent and protest in the post–Civil War period was agrarian in origin and orientation, and the American farmer seemed determined to steer a middle course between "goo-goos" [good government leaders] and radicals. Like the civil service reformer, the farmer avoided long-range considerations of social planning and control, and he had no direct purpose to abandon free enterprise capitalism. Like his radical contemporaries, however, he was fully prepared to attain immediate objectives through State action, and throughout the period his angry cries for governmental intervention to secure economic and political reform seriously threatened and frightened the industrial ruling class.

Nor were the farmer's demands for reform without cause. Constantly subjected to the vicissitudes of drought and storm—and market—in many ways the farm population was even more deprived than the propertyless workers who crowded into the city. For as the farmer continued his barren, isolated, and culturally impoverished life, rural areas lagged far behind in the enjoyment of a higher standard of living, and the benefits of the industrial revolution seemed largely confined to the rapidly growing cities. Agriculture suffered a particularly severe depression during the thirty years before 1897, and the farmer's economic situation had grown increasingly more desperate as his costs mounted and prices for farm products tumbled. Cotton that cost 6 or 7 cents per pound to produce sold for 4 or 5 cents, while wheat that had brought $1.45 per bushel at the end of the Civil War brought 49 cents thirty years later, and corn that sold for 75 cents in 1869 fell to 28 cents in 1889. Crushed between minimal farm prices and the intolerable burden of debts assumed in prosperous, expansive years, it was the oppressed and disgruntled farmer who spearheaded America's crusade for reform.

Fundamentally, declining farm prices and income were due to a vastly increased competition of farm products on the world market and to the overexpansion of agriculture that had taken place during the Civil War. In assaying his plight, however, the farmer almost invariably attributed hard times to an inadequate money supply and to the immediate, tangible abuses he suffered at the hands of his economic masters, the railroads and the banks. Against the railroads his grievances were real enough. The carriers not only charged the farmer exorbitant rates that frequently took the value of one bushel of wheat or corn to pay the freight on another, but through rebates and other secret agreements they viciously discriminated against him in favor of larger and wealthier shippers. The bankers, too, as money became scarcer, as interest rates on loans and mortgages soared, and as foreclosures multiplied, seemed the farmer's mortal enemies. As one Nebraska farm editor lamented, "We have three crops—corn, freight rates, and interest. The farmers farm the land, and the businessmen farm the farmers."

—Richard D. Heffner, *A Documentary History of the United States*

a. Topic: _____

b. Subtopic found in paragraph 1: _____

c. Key idea of paragraph 1: _____

d. Subtopic found in paragraph 2: _____

e. Key idea of paragraph 2: _____

f. Subtopic found in paragraph 3: _____

g. Key idea of paragraph 3: _____

h. Key idea of entire selection: _____

Exercise 5I

With a partner, select a three- to five-paragraph passage from one of your textbooks and determine the topic, subtopics, and key idea of the reading.

Writing Summaries

A **summary** is the condensation of a larger work. In the summary exercise at the end of most chapters in *Active Reading*, you will be asked to write a short paragraph (three to four sentences) stating briefly what was in the lesson. By thinking about the work you have just done and then writing down your thoughts in full sentences, you can become a more active learner. You will begin to see how ideas are related. Consciously and systematically reviewing the main points made in each lesson will imprint those points on your mind. Memory experts state that it is through such conscious effort that people put what they have learned into their short-term memory. Later repetition and review will transfer the information to long-term memory. The process is like remembering a dream. If you wake to the distracting sound of an alarm and then jump out of bed thinking about the tasks of the day ahead, you probably won't remember the dream you know you had. If, however, you have some time to lie there thinking about your dream, you probably will remember it and will continue to remember it later, when you tell one of your classmates about it.

Another benefit of writing a summary is that doing so prevents you from having hazy, half-formed, or semiunderstood ideas about what you have read. Writing in sentences exposes the gaps in your comprehension. You will also find that this immediate review and summary will help you review for exams.

The following points will help you focus your thoughts when you write a summary:

1. Think about the entire text you have been asked to summarize.
2. Find the topic by asking, *What is this about?*
3. Identify the key idea by asking, *What is the author's most important idea about the topic?*
4. Look for the subtopics by asking of each paragraph or section, *Who or what is this about?*
5. Find the key ideas of the subtopics by asking, *What is the author's most important idea about this subtopic?*
6. Put the topic, subtopics, and key ideas together in sentences, the number of which will depend on the length of the text you are summarizing.

In writing a summary, it is important to try to be **objective.** You are dealing only with the author's ideas and words, and not with your personal views about what is good or bad or right or wrong. You are trying to make the summary shorter than the reading selection without changing the author's ideas or the emphasis given them. You identify what is important and state it essentially in your own words. You do not need to include examples or other illustrative materials unless they are necessary to the author's point. You can include some of the author's words in your summary, particularly those terms or phrases which convey the author's basic notion, but usually you should not quote complete sentences or paragraphs. If you do, you should always put such material in quotation marks so as to give the original author credit for the idea.

A summary of the passage on mononucleosis (p. 90) could be worked out like this:

Topic: mononucleosis

Subtopic, paragraph 1: who gets it and symptoms
Key idea, paragraph 1: Mononucleosis, an affliction of college-aged students, will produce many symptoms.

Subtopic, paragraph 2: causes
Key idea, paragraph 2: Causes of mononucleosis are not certain.

Subtopic, paragraph 3: treatment
Key idea, paragraph 3: Treatment of mononucleosis often takes a long time.

Summary: Mononucleosis, an affliction of college-aged students, is a disease of uncertain causes that takes a long time to cure.

A summary of the article on the frog (p. 118) might read as follows:

> Frogs are cold-blooded animals, meaning that their body temperature reflects the temperature of the world around them. Therefore, the frog has to adapt to changes in temperature. When it gets cold in the wintertime, the frog's bodily functions slow down; it buries itself in the bottom of the pond and hibernates over the winter. In summer it again buries itself as protection against the heat; this process is called estivation.

You can also apply the technique of summarizing to your other courses. At the end of a class, take a few minutes to write a summary of the topic, subtopics, and key ideas of the class, asking, *What was this class about?* and *What were the instructor's most important ideas about the topic and subtopics?* In doing so, you will improve not only your comprehension but also your writing.

Summary Exercise

Think about the chapter you have just completed, Chapter 5. Then write a short paragraph summarizing what it is about and what the authors' most important idea about that topic is.

Preview Questions

What is this text about?
What is the author's most important idea about the topic?
Why am I reading this?
What do I already know about the topic?
What do I predict the author will say?

Chapter 6

Identifying Supporting Ideas and Supporting Details

In this chapter you will find answers to the following questions:

What are supporting ideas?

What are supporting details?

How do supporting ideas differ from supporting details?

How do supporting ideas and supporting details relate to the key idea?

Why is it important to be able to identify supporting ideas and supporting details?

Thus far you have learned two fundamental reading questions: *Who or what is this about?* and *What is the author's most important idea about the topic?* The answers to these questions give you, respectively, the topic and the key idea. Sometimes the topic and the key idea will be all you need to get from your reading. More often, though, if you are to understand your texts fully you will need to ask further questions. These additional questions are what lead you to supporting ideas and supporting details.

Supporting ideas and **supporting details** are provided by authors to develop and explain their key ideas. By asking specific questions—such as *What? Why? How? Who? Which? What kind? Where?* and *When?*—you challenge the authors to reveal the facts and opinions that back up the assertions made in their key ideas.

Supporting Words and Phrases in Sentences

At the sentence level, an author's **key words**—the nouns and verbs—provide the key idea and are supported by words and phrases that connect, describe, or explain the various elements of the sentence. These words and phrases answer questions like the following:

- *Why* did it happen? *Why* will it happen? *Why* is it important?
- *What* is happening? *What* caused the action? *What* resulted?
- *What kind* of person, thing, or idea is it?
- *How* did it happen? *How* does it work?
- *Who* did it? *Who* thought it? *Who* was it? *Who* was involved?
- *Which* is it? *Which* was it?
- *Where* did it happen?
- *When* will it happen?

Applying such questions to an example will make these concepts clearer:

The library committee was pleased to see the newly acquired shelves filled with the hundreds of books that last month had been heaped on the floor.

Who or what is this sentence about?
The answer gives you the topic: the library committee.

What is the author's most important idea about the committee?
The answer gives you the key idea: The committee was pleased to see the shelves.

Which shelves?
The newly acquired shelves.

Why?
Because the shelves were filled with books.

Which books?
The books that had been heaped.

Where?
On the floor.

When?
Last month.

The answers to these questions show us how the words and phrases in the sentence are connected to the topic, to the key words and the key idea, and to one another. These words and phrases convey the ideas and details that tell us more about the key words in the sentence.

Exercise 6A

Fill in the blanks after each sentence.

Example:
After the accident, the nurse assisted the doctor by tying the ligature around the boy's arm.
Who or what is this sentence about? (Topic) *the nurse.*
What is the author's most important idea about the topic? (Key idea) *The nurse assisted the doctor.*
   How? *by tying the ligature* _____
   Where? *around the boy's arm* _____
   When? *after the accident* _____

1. In many parts of the United States, fast-walking has become the favorite exercise for people of all ages because, in a brief period, without fancy apparatus or clothing, the walker can improve his or her heart rate, muscle tone, and general health.

    a. Topic: _____

    b. Key idea: _____

    c. Where? _____

    d. For whom? _____

    e. Why? _____

2. Light and shadow are the most primary of television's implements since without light, we could have no picture.

    —Peter B. Orlik

a. Topic: _____

   b. Key idea: _____

   c. Why? _____

3. Four score and seven years ago our fathers brought forth on this continent, a new nation, conceived in Liberty, and dedicated to the proposition that all men are created equal.

   —Abraham Lincoln

   a. Topic: _____

   b. Key idea: _____

   c. What word does the phrase "conceived in Liberty" support? _____

   d. What question does the phrase "conceived in Liberty" answer? _____

4. Last week stock market observers were surprised that the third quarter report of dismal earnings by National Tractor did not affect the sale of its stock.

   a. Topic: _____

   b. Key Idea: _____

   c. Why? _____

   d. What should have affected the sale? _____

   e. When? _____

5. In psychological terms, professionals frequently describe motivation as wanting or intending to do well.

   a. Topic: _____

   b. Key idea: _____

   c. How is motivation described? _____

   d. When is motivation described? _____

Supporting Ideas and Supporting Details in Paragraphs

Just as it is necessary to understand how the words and phrases in a sentence connect and convey the author's thoughts, so it is important to analyze how the sentences in a paragraph work together to support the author's key idea.

Paragraphs consist of several sentences, one of which is usually the **generalization**—a statement that includes or implies the key idea. The other sentences are more specific and expand or clarify the key idea by defining, describing, explaining, and illustrating it.

When you are dealing with paragraphs, it is best to think of three levels, moving from general to more specific:

- *Level 1* is the key idea. The key idea is usually a general statement that conveys the author's most important idea about the topic.
- *Level 2* consists of the supporting ideas. The supporting ideas are more specific statements that define, describe, explain, and illustrate (to clarify by the use of examples) the key idea. Supporting ideas may be facts or opinions.
- *Level 3* consists of the supporting details. The supporting details are even more specific sentences, phrases, and words that define, describe, explain, and illustrate the supporting ideas. Supporting details are the most concrete elements of a passage, facts as opposed to opinions or ideas.

Both supporting ideas and supporting details answer the questions, *Who? How? Why? Where? When? What? Which?* and *What kind?* Both elaborate or amplify, clarify, and explain or modify, and both take various forms: illustrations, examples, verifying statistics, reasons, definitions, and descriptions. The important distinctions are that <u>a supporting idea (Level 2) directly relates to the key idea (Level 1) and a supporting detail (Level 3) is more specific and directly relates to a supporting idea (Level 2)</u>. This relationship is illustrated in the **analysis** and diagram (Figure 6.1) of the following example:

> The plays of Shakespeare are universally admired. Most serious students of drama claim that Shakespeare's tragedies and comedies are timeless classics. *King Lear* moved audiences to tears in the seventeenth century just as it does now.

The topic is the plays of Shakespeare. Level 1, the key idea, is that the plays of Shakespeare are universally admired. Level 2 is

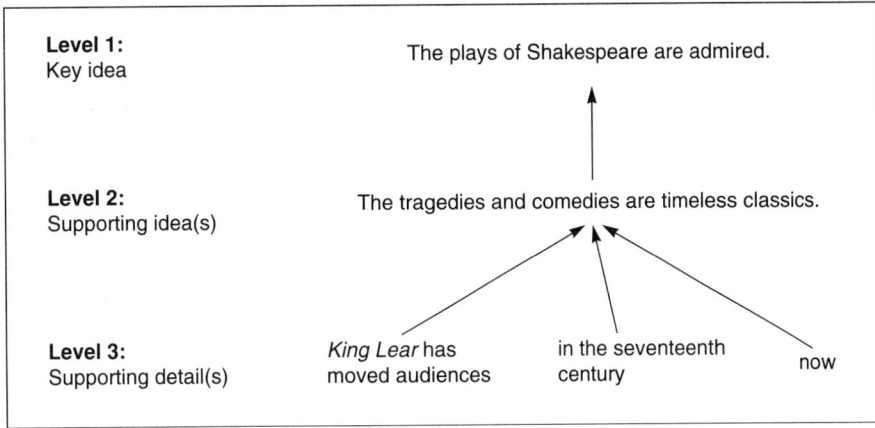

Figure 6.1 Relationship of key idea, supporting idea(s), and supporting details

the supporting idea that answers the question, *Why?* Here the answer is that Shakespeare's plays are admired because they are timeless classics. This statement supports the key idea. Level 3 is a supporting detail answering the question, *How do you know?* The answer to this question is that you know the plays are timeless classics because you are given the example of people having been moved by *King Lear* in the seventeenth century just as audiences are today. This sentence gives you more specific information about the supporting idea.

Often an author will provide more than one supporting idea for the key idea. The following example has been marked up by noting the topic (T)—reading—in the margin, by underlining the key idea, and by bracketing the supporting ideas.

T: Reading
<u>Reading is both a necessity and a pleasure</u>. By enabling us to know and master relevant information, [reading can lead to success in our jobs.] At the same time, [reading can provide relief from the stresses of daily life] by taking us into a variety of worlds and situations.

This paragraph is about reading, and the key idea, Level 1, is that reading is both a necessity and a pleasure. At Level 2 are two supporting ideas: "Reading can lead to success" and "reading can provide relief." These ideas answer the question, *Why is reading both a necessity and a pleasure?* You can find the supporting details, Level 3, by asking and answering the following questions:

Where does reading lead to success?
   In our jobs.

How does reading lead to success in our jobs?
   By enabling us to know and master relevant information.

What does reading provide relief from?
   The stresses of daily life.

How does reading provide relief from life's daily stresses?
   By taking us into a variety of worlds and situations.

Exercise 6B

Read each of the following paragraphs. To gain practice in marking up paragraphs, write the topic in the margin, underline the key idea, and bracket the supporting ideas. Then fill in the blanks that follow each passage.

Example:

T: Am. government

<u>The American government works through an intricate system of checks and balances</u>. In an effort to divide the power, the responsibility, and the oversight, [the founders established three federal branches through which the people could exercise their collective will—the executive, the legislative, and the judicial.] The executive power resides in the president and his cabinet, the legislative in the Congress, and the judicial in the Supreme Court.
Topic: *the American government*
Key idea (Level 1): *The American government works through an intricate system of checks and balances.*
One supporting idea (Level 2): *The founders established three federal branches through which the people could exercise their will—the executive, the legislative, and the judicial.*
Two supporting details (Level 3): *the president and his cabinet; Congress*
What question do the supporting details answer?
   Where do the different kinds of power reside?
Are the supporting details definitions, descriptions, explanations, or illustrations? *Illustrations.*

1. When they went ashore the animals that took up a land life carried with them a part of the sea in their bodies, a heritage which they passed on to their children and which even today links each land animal with its origin in the ancient sea. Fish, amphibian, and reptile, warm-blooded bird and mammal—each of us carries in our veins a salty stream in which the elements of sodium, potassium, and calcium are combined in almost the same proportions as in sea water. This is our inheritance from the day, untold millions of years ago, when a remote ancestor, having progressed from the one-celled to the many-celled stage, first developed a circulatory system in which the fluid was merely the water of the sea.

    —Rachel Carson, *The Sea Around Us*

    a. Topic: _____

    b. Key idea (Level 1): _____
    _____

    c. Which supporting idea (Level 2) develops the key idea?
    _____

    d. What question does this supporting idea answer?
    _____

    e. What supporting details (Level 3) illustrate the idea of land animals?
    _____

2. El Niño and La Niña

    The tropical Pacific Ocean is thought to have a significant impact on short-term climatic changes. You will from time to time hear reference to El Niño and La Niña to explain some abnormal weather occurrence. El Niño refers to a large mass of exceptionally warm water that occurs in the eastern Pacific at the equator near the coast of South America. This strip of warm water shows up periodically and has a counterpart with which it alternates—an exceptionally cold equatorial strip of water referred to as La Niña. These two phenomena alternate every three to six years, resulting in worldwide weather changes. The atmospheric changes that result from this periodic shift in temperature are called the *southern oscillation.* The impetus for the occurrence of El Niño or La Niña is the trade winds. Strong trade winds tend to blow warm surface waters toward the western Pacific, causing cooler waters to prevail in the eastern Pacific and bringing on the cold phase. In the spring, trade winds tend to be weaker, and warmer surface waters prevail. This change in oceanic temperatures causes heavy storms and atmospheric disturbances. These atmospheric disturbances can in turn affect rainfall patterns and temperatures worldwide. El Niño in 1982–1983 caused droughts in India and Australia and heavy rains on the western coast of South America. La Niña on the heels of El Niño in the spring of 1988 resulted in extremely cold temperatures in Alaska and Canada the following winter.

—Charles E. Kupchella and Margaret C. Hyland,
Environmental Science

a. What is the key idea (Level 1)? _____

_____

b. What are two supporting ideas (Level 2)? _____

_____

c. Provide four supporting details (Level 3) and indicate which supporting idea each relates to. _____

_____

_____

3. Zinnias, marigolds, petunias, red salvia, ageratum, coleus, etc., in character mostly busy, scentless and brilliantly colored, owe their success to improved greenhouse construction about the middle of the nineteenth century and new techniques of mass production that made it possible to market them on a huge scale. Victorian taste did the rest and they quickly became the basis for the only really hideous gardening style on record. In England it was called carpet-bedding because the low-growing plants could be packed into patterns like those of an Oriental rug—but also be made to spell out mottoes, depict clocks and maps, even the human face.... Examples survive at

Balmoral, the Boston Public Garden and in many a municipal planting.... Communist regimes...are also partial to carpet-bedding, which I am distressed to read now figures prominently in Peking's [Beijing's] once elegant parks.

—Eleanor Perenyi, *Green Thoughts*

a. Topic: _____

b. Key idea (Level 1): _____
_____

c. What is one supporting idea (Level 2)? _____
_____

d. What question does the supporting idea answer? _____
_____

e. What are two supporting details (Level 3)? _____
_____

f. To which supporting idea do those supporting details relate? _____

4. Scarcity is a relationship between how much there is of something and how much of it is wanted. Resources are scarce compared to all of the uses we have for them. If we want to use more than there is of an item, it is scarce. Note that this meaning is different from the usual meaning of scarce, which is "rarely found in nature." How are they different? Consider this example. Is water scarce? How could anyone argue that water is scarce in the usual sense? Water covers nearly two-thirds of the earth's surface. Yet an economist would say that water is scarce. Why? The reason is that there are so many competing uses for water that more water is wanted than is available. If you find this hard to believe, ask farmers and ranchers in the West, where water rights are jealously guarded. As soon as someone is willing to pay for a good, or a resource, it is scarce by the economist's definition.

—Arleen J. Hoag and John H. Hoag, *Introductory Economics*

a. What are two supporting ideas (Level 2) contained in this reading? _____

_____

b. What are three supporting details (Level 3) related to one of these supporting ideas? _____

_____

5. The group dynamics approach is based on the working assumption that the members of policy-making groups, no matter how mindful they may be of their exalted national status and of their heavy responsibilities, are subjected to the pressures widely observed in groups of ordinary citizens. In my earlier research on group dynamics, I was impressed by repeated manifestations of the effects—both unfavorable and favorable—of the social pressures that typically develop in cohesive groups—in infantry platoons, air crews, therapy groups, seminars, and self-study or encounter groups of executives receiving leadership training. In all these groups, just as in the industrial work groups described by other investigators, members tend to evolve informal norms to preserve friendly intragroup relations and these become part of the hidden agenda at their meetings. When conducting research on groups of heavy smokers at a clinic set up to help people stop smoking, I noticed a seemingly irrational tendency for the members to exert pressure on each other to increase their smoking as the time for the final meeting approached. This appeared to be a collusive effort to display mutual dependence and resistance to the termination of the group sessions.

—Irving L. Janis, *Groupthink*

a. Topic: _____

b. Key idea (Level 1):

_____

c. What are two supporting ideas (Level 2)?

_____

d. What are two supporting details (Level 3)?

_____

_____

From the context, what do you think are the meanings of the following words?

e. manifestation _____

f. cohesive _____

g. collusive _____

Exercise 6C

Read the following paragraphs and fill in the relevant blanks in each diagram (Figures 6.2, and 6.3).

Example:
   The innovations and alterations in economic life in this century, and more especially since the beginning of World War II, have, by any calculation, been great. The most visible has been the application of increasingly intricate and sophisticated technology to the production of things. Machines have continued to replace crude

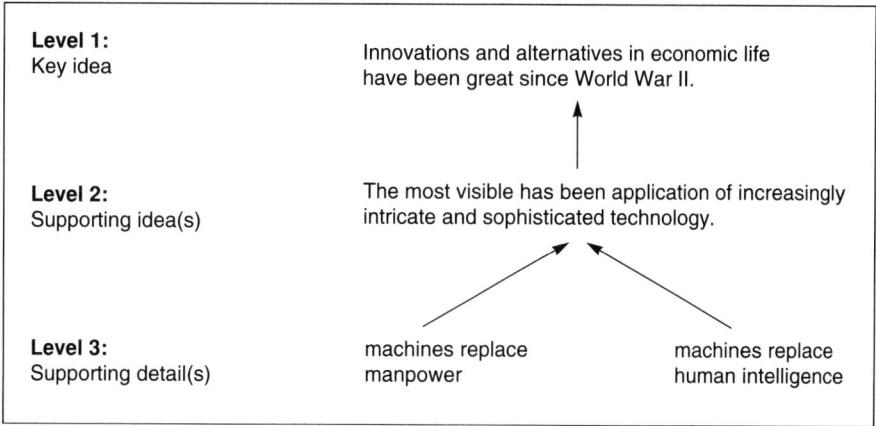

Relationship of key idea, supporting idea(s), and supporting details manpower. And increasingly, as they are used to instruct other machines, they replace the cruder forms of human intelligence.

—J. K. Galbraith, *The New Industrial State*

1. True believers among social planners and research and development innovators envision the day when all the many bits and pieces of communications technology now on the market or projected for the near future will coalesce into a single, multipurpose home communications center. In contrast to the earlier trend toward miniaturized, personalized, highly portable units, the home center would be an elaborate and permanent installation. It would probably require setting aside an entire room primarily for the reception, recording, storage, playback, and initiation of communications. There the television screen, like a queen bee glowing in the center of an electronic hive, would be fed by an army of working inputs—disc and tape recorders and players, cable and over-the-air program suppliers, teletext reception capable of making hard-copy printouts as required, direct broadcast satellite relays picked up by rooftop dish antennas, two-way communication circuits, and so on.

—Sydney Head and Christopher Sterling, *Broadcasting in America*

2. ...However complex and solid civilisation seems, it is actually quite fragile. It can be destroyed: What are its enemies? Well, first of all fear—fear of war, fear of invasion, fear of plague and famine, that make it simply not worthwhile con-

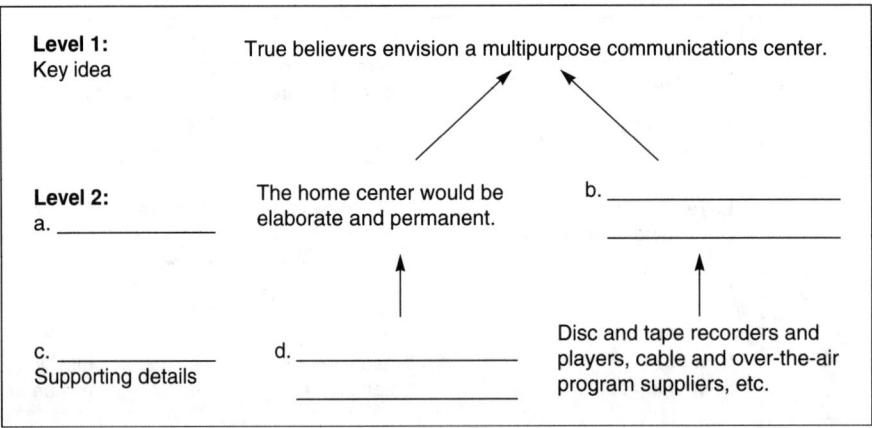

Figure 6.2 Relationship of key idea, supporting idea(s), and supporting details

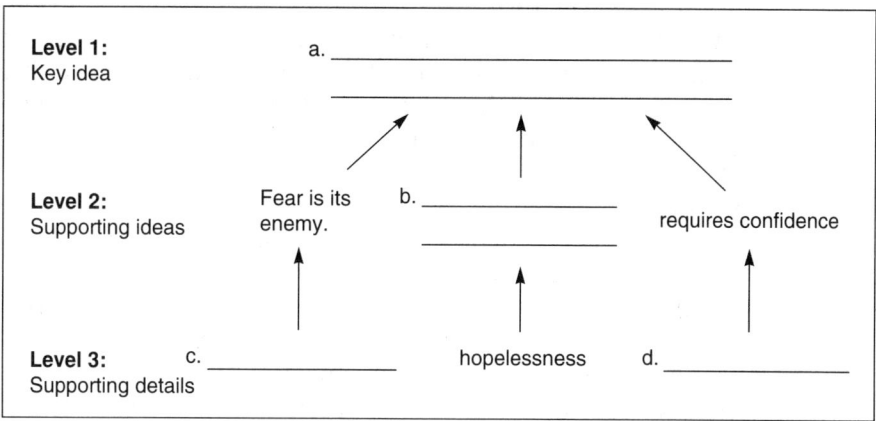

Figure 6.3 Relationship of key idea, supporting idea(s), and supporting details

structing things, or planting trees or even planning next year's crops. And fear of the supernatural, which means that you daren't question anything or change anything. The late antique world was full of meaningless rituals, mystery religions, that destroyed self-confidence. And then exhaustion, the feeling of hopelessness which can overtake people even with a high degree of material prosperity....Of course, civilisation requires a modicum of material prosperity—enough to provide a little leisure. But, far more, it requires confidence—confidence in the society in which one lives, belief in its philosophy, belief in its laws, and confidence in one's own mental powers....Vigor, energy, vitality: all the great civilisations—or civilising epochs—have had a weight of energy behind them. People sometimes think that civilisation consists in fine sensibilities and good conversation and all that. These can be among the agreeable results of civilisation, but they are not what make a civilisation, and a society can have these amenities and yet be dead and rigid. (Note the British spelling of "civilisation.")

—Kenneth Clark, *Civilisation*

Supporting Ideas and Supporting Details in Longer Readings

The concept of the three levels is easily transferred from the reading of single paragraphs to the reading of passages containing two or more paragraphs—in fact, to the reading of sections, chapters, and entire books.

But as you move from reading paragraphs to reading longer material, you must address an important element: the notion of topics and subtopics, outlined in Chapters 4 and 5. You will remember that in a longer reading, the word *topic* refers to the subject of the entire reading, and the word *subtopics* refers to the subjects of the various parts that treat different aspects of the entire reading. Just as the entire reading has a key idea (Level 1), so, too, does each subtopic have a key idea. A key idea in this position is called a supporting idea (Level 2), because it supports the key idea of the entire reading. In longer readings, as in paragraphs, the supporting details (Level 3) are the details, or facts and opinions, that back up the supporting ideas by providing more specific information, such as definitions, descriptions, explanations, and illustrations.

Figure 6.4 illustrates an example from biology. The circulatory, digestive, reproductive, and respiratory systems contribute to the total functioning of the body. The key idea here is that the body depends on many systems. One supporting idea would be

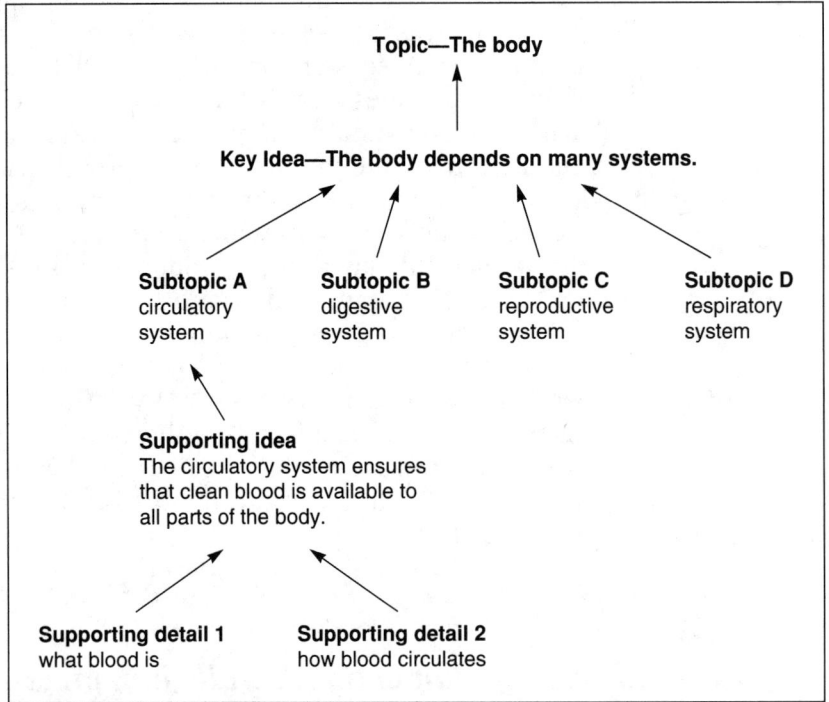

Figure 6.4 Relationship between the topic and subtopic, between the key idea and supporting idea, and between the supporting idea(s) and supporting details

that the circulatory system ensures that clean blood is available to all parts of the body; another supporting idea would be that the digestive system maintains the body. Both these ideas answer the question, *How?* and support the key idea, not each other. Supporting details that answer the questions, *What?* and *How?* define and tell us how the circulatory system works.

By analyzing a text, you can see the relationships between the topic and subtopics, between the key idea and supporting ideas, and between the supporting ideas and supporting details. When you know the roles of the various parts of a reading, you can discriminate the important from the unimportant and can distinguish what you need to know from what you don't need to know. Many instructors report that students who do well in courses can see how the ideas presented in a reading relate to one another and can recognize the levels of these ideas—moving from general ideas to specific details. Less successful students focus on the details being presented, because specific facts are easier to remember than general concepts. It's the old business of the forest and the trees: If you get too involved in trying to describe each tree, you will see neither the shape of the forest nor how the forest fits into the landscape. It is therefore essential for a reader to know which is the forest and which are the trees—that is, to be able to discriminate the key and supporting ideas from the supporting details and to see how they relate.

If you are having trouble identifying the topic or key idea of a paragraph or an article, try first to find the supporting ideas. Let's use the passage on the frog, from an exercise you did in Chapter 5, as an example. As you reread it now, bracket the supporting ideas.

> The frog is a "cold-blooded" vertebrate, as are the fishes and the reptiles. This does not mean that the blood of these animals is always cold. It means that their body temperatures vary with the temperature of the surroundings. Man maintains a constant average body temperature of about 98.6° F through the regulation of the rate of food oxidation and resulting heat release in the tissues as well as of heat loss from the body surface. The cold-blooded vertebrates carry on much slower oxidation and do not maintain relatively constant body temperatures.   1
>
> With the coming of fall and the seasonal lowering of temperature, the body temperature of the frog drops to the point where the frog can no longer be very active. It buries itself in the mud at the bottom of a pond or finds shelter in some other protected place in the water. Heart action slows   2

down to a point at which blood hardly circulates in the vessels. The greatly reduced amount of oxygen necessary for life is supplied through the moist surface of the skin. The tissues are kept alive by the slow oxidation of food stored in the liver and in the fat bodies attached above the kidneys in most frogs. Nervous activity almost ceases, and the frog lies in a stupor. This is the condition of the frog during hibernation, or winter rest. With the coming of spring the warm days speed up body activity, and the frog gradually resumes the physiological and functional activities of normal life.

The hot summer months bring other problems. Lacking a device for cooling the body, the frog must escape from the extreme heat. It may lie quietly in deep, cool water or bury itself in the mud at the bottom of a pond. This condition of summer inactivity is called estivation. Many smaller ponds dry up during midsummer, and the frogs and other cold-blooded animals only survive by burying themselves in the mud and estivating. With the coming of cooler weather and the return of water to the pond, they come out of estivation and continue normal activity until hibernation. 3

—James H. Otto and A. Towle, *Modern Biology*

You may have found earlier that the key idea was not readily apparent. The supporting ideas that emerge from your reading of the individual paragraphs tell you that the frog (1) is a cold-blooded vertebrate that slows down its body functions in winter as a protection against cold and (2) is inactive in summer to escape the heat. These ideas support the key idea of the entire reading: that frogs have to adapt to changes in temperature. Supporting details, providing such facts as the definition of *cold-blooded*, the way in which the frog is kept alive during hibernation, and the way in which it keeps cool in the summer, elaborate on the supporting ideas.

Exercise 6D

Write the topic (T) and subtopics (ST) of the following passages in the margin, remembering that two or more paragraphs in a reading may have the same subtopics. Then fill in the blanks that come after each reading.

Example:

The Pueblos of New Mexico

T: The Pueblo Indians

The Pueblo Indians of the Southwest are one of the most widely known primitive peoples in Western civilization. They live in the midst of America, within easy reach of any transcontinental traveller. And they are living after the old native fashion. Their culture has not disintegrated like that of all the Indian communities outside of Arizona and New Mexico. Month by month and year by year, the old dances of the gods are danced in their stone villages, life follows essentially the old routines, and what they have taken from our civilization they have remodelled and subordinated to their own attitudes.

They have a romantic history. All through that part of America which they still inhabit are found the homes of their cultural ancestors, the cliff-dwellings and great planned valley cities of the golden age of the Pueblos. Their unbelievably numerous cities were built in the twelfth and thirteenth centuries, but we can follow their history much further back to its simple beginnings in one-room stone houses to each of which an underground ceremonial chamber was attached....

ST: One-room stone houses

ST: Cliff dwellings

The Pueblo culture flourished greatly after it had settled upon its arid plateau. It had brought with it the bow and arrow, a knowledge of stone architecture, and a diversified agriculture. Why it chose for the site of its greatest development the inhospitable, almost waterless valley of the San Juan, which flows into the Colorado River from the north, no one ventures to explain. It seems one of the most forbidding regions in the whole of what is now the United States, yet it was here that there grew up the greatest Indian cities north of Mexico. These were of two kinds, and they seem to have been built by the same civilization at the same period: the cliff-dwellings, and the semicircular valley citadels. The cliff-dwellings dug into the sheer face of the precipice, or built on a ledge hundreds of feet from the valley floor, are some of the most romantic habitations of mankind. We cannot guess what the circumstances were that led to the construction of these homes, far from the cornfields and far from any water supply, which must have been serious if they were planned as fortifications, but some of the ruins enduringly challenge our admiration of ingenuity and beauty. One thing is never omitted in them, no matter how solid the rock ledge upon which the pueblo is built: the underground ceremonial chamber, the kiva, is hewn out to accommodate a man

ST: Valley citadels

upright, and is large enough to serve as a gathering-room. It is entered by a ladder through a hatchway.

The other type of dwelling was a prototype of the modern planned city: a semicircular sweep of wall that rose three stories at the fortified exterior and was terraced inward as it approached the underground kivas that clustered in the embrace of the great masonry arms. Some of the great valley cities of this type have not only the small kivas, but one great additional temple similarly sunk into the earth and of the most finished and perfect masonry.

—Ruth Benedict, *Patterns of Culture*

a. What is the topic of the reading?

The Pueblo Indians

b. What is the key idea of the reading?

The Pueblo Indians had three types of homes.

c. What is the key idea of subtopic 1, or a supporting idea that backs up the key idea of the entire reading?

The early buildings were one-room stone houses.

d. What is the key idea of subtopic 2 that also supports the key idea of the entire reading?

The cliff-dwellings were among the most romantic habitations of mankind.

e. What is the key idea of subtopic 3 that also supports the key idea of the entire reading?

The semicircular citadels were a prototype of the modern planned city.

f. What are three supporting details that back up the second supporting idea?

Built on a ledge. They are beautiful. The kiva can hold a man upright and can serve as a meeting room.

T:

ST:

1. Two kinds of logic are used [in motorcycle maintenance], inductive and deductive. Inductive inferences start with observations of the machine and arrive at general conclusions. For example, if the cycle goes over a bump and the engine misfires, and then goes over another bump and the

ST.: engine misfires, and then goes over another bump and the engine misfires, and then goes over a long smooth stretch of road and there is no misfiring, and then goes over a fourth bump and the engine misfires again, one can logically conclude that the misfiring is caused by the bumps. That is induction: reasoning from particular experiences to general truths.

Deductive inferences do the reverse. They start with general knowledge and predict a specific observation. For example, if, from reading the hierarchy of facts about the machine, the mechanic knows the horn of the cycle is powered exclusively by electricity from the battery, then he can logically infer that if the battery is dead the horn will not work. That is deduction.

—Robert Pirsig, *Zen and the Art of Motorcycle Maintenance*

a. What is the key idea?

___

b. What is one idea that supports the first subtopic?

___

c. What is one detail that supports the supporting idea?

___

d. What is one idea that supports the second subtopic?

___

e. What is one detail that supports the supporting idea?

___

T:
ST: 2. A solitary ant, afield, cannot be considered to have much of anything on his mind; indeed, with only a few neurons strung together by fibers, he can't be imagined to have a mind at all, much less a thought. He is more like a ganglion on legs. Four ants together, or ten, encircling a dead moth on a path, begin to look more like an idea. They

ST: fumble and shove, gradually moving the food toward the Hill, but as though by blind chance. It is only when you watch the dense mass of thousands of ants, crowded together around the Hill, blackening the ground, that you begin to see the whole beast, and now you observe it thinking, planning, calculating. It is an intelligence, a kind of live computer, with crawling bits for its wits.

2 At a stage in the construction, twigs of a certain size are needed, and all the members forage obsessively for twigs of just this size. Later, when outer walls are to be finished, thatched, the size must change, and as though given new orders by telephone, all the workers shift the search to the new twigs. If you disturb the arrangement of a part of the Hill, hundreds of ants will set it vibrating, shifting, until it is put right again. Distant sources of food are somehow sensed, and long lines, like tentacles, reach out over the ground, up over the walls, behind boulders, to fetch it in.

—Lewis Thomas, *The Lives of a Cell*

a. What is the key idea?

_____

b. What is the subtopic found in paragraph 1?

_____

c. What is the subtopic found in paragraph 2?

_____

d. What is the function of paragraph 2?

_____

T:
ST: 3. A central quest in American life is for pure motion, movement either for its own sake or as a means of freeing oneself from a prior mode of existence. A relatively new and chronically rootless society, America has always set an unusually

1

high premium on mobility. It is not surprising, therefore, that American literature is densely populated with heroes who try "to find in motion what was lost in space," fundamentally restless people in search of settings which are fluid enough to accommodate their passion for radical forms of freedom and independence. Cooper's West, Melville's ocean, Whitman's open road, and Twain's river are the mythic spaces Americans yearn for. As John Steinbeck observed of his own travels late in his career, nearly every American has a "burning desire to go, to move, to get under way, any place, away from any Here."

ST: Although American and Afro-American literary traditions differ in many important ways, they are in essential agreement on this way of imagining movement. The journey motif, which is central to both traditions, is often aggressively nonteleological; that is, it nearly always resists being directed toward a particular place and instead exults in movement through indefinite space. Unlike representative journey books from English and European traditions, American and Afro-American classics are typically open-ended in nature. They view movement and change as intrinsically valuable—a process of endless becoming rather than progress culminating in a state of completed being. As such, these journeys are a compelling metaphor of the American desire for the "new life," consisting of unlimited personal development.

ST: Whereas, for example, Odysseus travels home to a place in a hierarchical society, Huck Finn heads vaguely West toward a socially open world, attracted, as Ralph Ellison would later be, by the "magical fluidity and freedom" of American life (*Shadow and Act* 113). In the same way, representative slave narratives usually conclude with the hero pointed "North"—a state of human liberation rather than a particular place. Tom Jones, Joseph Andrews, and even Robinson Crusoe see their movements as a necessary evil as they look for a stable world which will provide them the definite values they need for a secure identity, but Jack Kerouac longs simply to be on the road itself, intoxicated by its continual novelty and escape from a restrictive society. In a comparable way, the typical blues singer often yearns for open motion as a release from troubles, even though fully aware that the place up ahead is not likely to be very different from previous places. As a result, the blues are saturated with bittersweet images of movement—traveling down an endless highway, leaving town on a fast Greyhound bus, and hopping real freights destined for a mythic North.

—Robert James Butler, "Making a Way Out of No Way: The Open Journey in Alice Walker's *The Third Life of Grange Copeland*"

a. What is the key idea?

___

b. What is one supporting idea found in paragraph 1?

___

c. What is one supporting detail found in paragraph 1?

___

d. What is one supporting idea found in paragraph 2?

___

e. What is one supporting detail found in paragraph 2?

___

f. What is one supporting idea found in paragraph 3?

___

g. What is one supporting detail found in paragraph 3?

___

Exercise 6E

Read the following passages and fill in the blanks in the appropriate diagrams (Figures 6.5 and 6.6).

1. Three passions, simple but overwhelmingly strong, have governed my life: the longing for love, the search for knowledge, and unbearable pity for the suffering of mankind. These passions, like great winds, have blown me hither and thither, in a wayward course, over a deep ocean of anguish, reaching to the very verge of despair.

   I have sought love, first, because it brings ecstasy—ecstasy so great that I would often have sacrificed all the rest of life for a few hours of this joy. I have sought it, next,

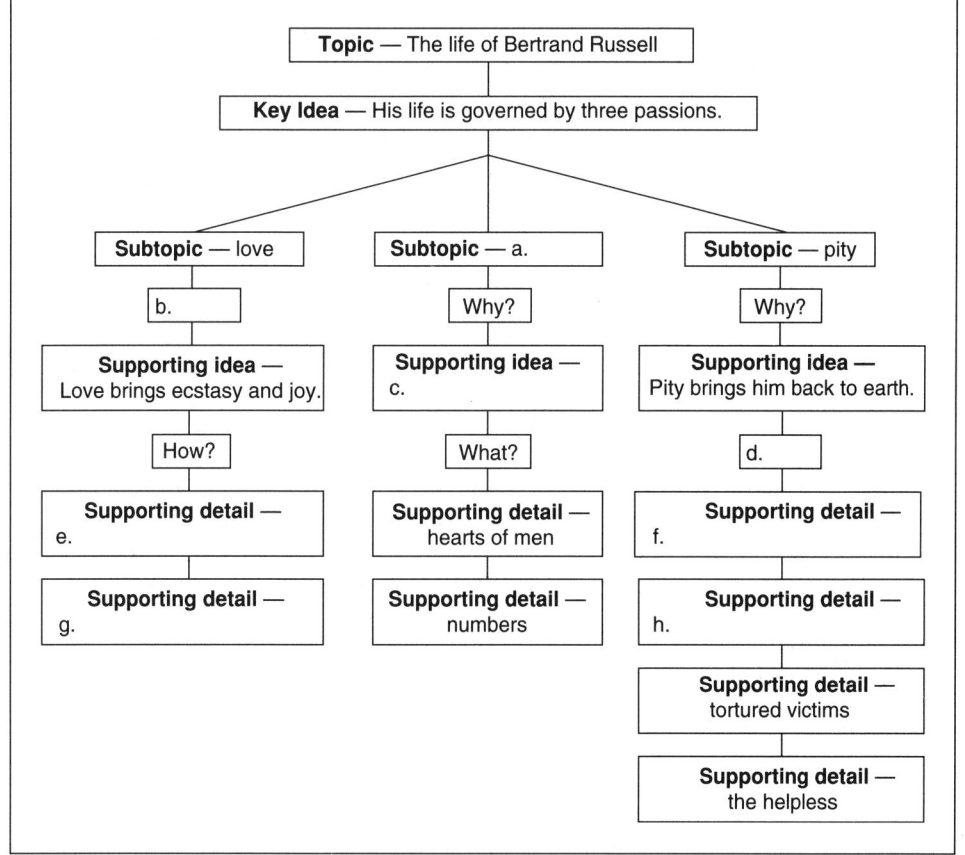

Figure 6.5

6 / *Identifying Supporting Ideas and Supporting Details*

because it relieves loneliness—that terrible loneliness in which one shivering consciousness looks over the rim of the world into the cold unfathomable lifeless abyss. I have sought it, finally, because in the union of love I have seen, in a mystic miniature, the prefiguring vision of the heaven that saints and poets have imagined. This is what I sought, and though it might seem too good for human life, this is what—at last—I have found.

With equal passion I have sought knowledge. I have wished to understand the hearts of men. I have wished to know why the stars shine. And I have tried to apprehend the Pythagorean power by which number holds sway above the flux. A little of this, but not much, I have achieved.

Love and knowledge, so far as they were possible, led upward toward the heavens. But always pity brought me back to earth. Echoes of cries of pain reverberate in my heart. Children in famine, victims tortured by oppressors, helpless old people a hated burden to their sons, and the whole world of loneliness, poverty, and pain make a mockery of what human life should be. I long to alleviate the evil, but I cannot, and I too suffer.

—Bertrand Russell, *The Autobiography of Bertrand Russell*

2. Julius Caesar reportedly barred chariots from certain parts of Rome during certain hours of the day and most of the night. Chariot wheels on cobblestones must have made quite a racket. Although there are other such references to noise throughout ancient literature, noise, like other pollution problems, is by and large a modern problem. In our stampede for bigger and better we have literally set the environment vibrating with misspent energy.

Although estimates vary, some say that background noise levels have been increasing for decades by as much as 1 decibel per year. There is general agreement among the experts that background noise long ago passed the point of causing significant harm. We have jackhammers, power mowers, demolition equipment, air compressors, generators, cars and trucks (including some without mufflers), aircraft, washing machines, dishwashers, food processors, stereos, meat grinders, chain saws, and much, much more. Most of these are associated with urban life, but even in what used to be secluded, quiet areas we have minibikes, snowmobiles, and other appliances that disturb the serenity of the outdoors and damage the hearing of operators.

```
                         Topic—Noise

Level 1:
Key idea:            a. _____

Subtopics:           background noise    b. _____

Level 2:
Supporting ideas:    c. _____   There are three negative effects.
                     _____

                     How much?           d. _____ ?      Which?

Level 3:
Supporting details:  e. _____  urban noise       impair hearing
                     passed point of                       physiological effects
                     significant harm    f. _____
                                                           g. _____
```

Figure 6.6

    We do know that very loud sounds and unwanted sounds affect humans in three general negative ways. First and foremost, loud sound can impair hearing and thus interfere with the functioning of our bodies and in this general respect is not unlike ozone. Second, very loud sounds and unwanted sounds can also have other negative physiological effects—for example, change in blood vessel diameter, heart rate, and blood pressure. Third, unwanted or startling sounds can affect humans psychologically.

—Charles E. Kupchella and Margaret C. Hyland,
Environmental Science

Exercise 6F

Make up a topic that has three subtopics, two supporting ideas for each subtopic and as many supporting details as you need. Diagram it, following the pattern used in Exercise 6E. Samples of topics are "My Neighborhood," "My College," or "Sports."

Summary Exercise

Write a summary of this chapter. Include in your summary a discussion of how a reading's topic, key idea, supporting ideas, and supporting details are related to one another. To make your point, you will probably need to include a brief example as well. (Refer to p. 124 if you need more information on writing summaries.)

Mastery Exercise I

This mastery exercise provides an opportunity for you to review the basic skills presented in Chapters 1 through 6—questioning; defining a purpose, associating, and predicting; finding topics and subtopics; previewing; reading for the key idea, supporting ideas, and supporting details. You will apply these skills to an article on memory, by following the instructions outlined below.

A. Preview the article and answer questions 1 through 7.

Remembering and Forgetting

1. Do you have a hard time remembering where you parked your car, recalling what book you read last week, recollecting a dentist appointment, or memorizing simple words like *uta, hio, wai, dah, oma, ineo, hio?*

2. Some aspects of memory are a mystery and perhaps always will be. Although scientists are still debating the difference between the mind and the brain and precisely where in the brain memory resides, progress has been made recently in understanding how memory works. Just as diagnosis of a disease leads to correct treatment of the disease, knowledge of how memory works enables a person to start improving his or her memory.

3. Our understanding of memory owes much to the computer, because computers illustrate how memory operates. Computers store information and then later, when asked the right questions, retrieve it. Similarly, an efficient memory is based on good storage and good retrieval.

Storing

4. Would you be surprised to know that the human mind contains five hundred times the information contained in the *Encyclopaedia Britannica?* For a start, there's language and many of you know at least two languages—informal and formal English and a language like Spanish or Italian that perhaps you speak at home. When you then add in all the experiences you have had and all the concepts and information you have learned that make up your understanding of yourselves and the world around you, you can begin to comprehend the extraordinary amount of information you're already remembering. Thus, when your head seems full with the grocery list, the errands to be done, and the studying

required for an exam, is it any wonder that you sometimes have difficulty remembering where you parked the car?

How does the mind deal with new information? It has to choose what it wants to remember and then decide how to store it through three processes: encoding, short-term memory, and long-term memory.

Encoding

You are surrounded by things that maybe you want to remember and maybe you don't. Do you try to remember everything you read in the daily newspaper? Of course not; you couldn't even if you wanted to. Fortunately, not everything in the newspaper is equally interesting or important to you, and so you don't need to remember it all. Now think of yourself in a bookstore, glancing at shelves full of new books: Your eyes run over them, skipping by most of them until one draws your attention, perhaps because of its title, author, or cover. Somewhere, however, a decision is made—the book is insufficiently interesting to pick up, and so you let it lie. On another shelf you see a book that really appeals to you. This one you take from the shelf and look over; you read the blurb on the cover; and you say to yourself, *I must remember to put this book on my birthday list.*

You and your mind have gone through a process of selection. Based on the stimulus of seeing many books, you have chosen one and decided to try to remember it—a process called encoding.

Short-term Memory

The facts about the chosen book now pass into your short-term memory, where another sorting process takes place. Short-term memory is very limited in its capacity for retention. It lasts only for the several seconds it takes to remember a telephone number or to decide to put this book rather than that shirt on your birthday list, but if the information involves something you think you need to know both now and in the future, it passes to long-term memory.

Long-term Memory

Long-term memory is your operating base. Everything you know—from physical acts like how to drive a car to exotic trivia like the names of the kings of Denmark—is there. Long-term memory is organized into what amounts to complex filing cabinets in which the information that is put in is stored under headings—sometimes under many headings; sometimes under only one. Your sister, for instance, may be filed under "women," "relatives," "pests," and/or "role models," whereas the geological term *magma* is filed under only one heading—"igneous rock." You can see that your chances of finding your way to what is filed is better with a variety of different files than with only one file. As everyone discovers at one time or another, it does no good to "know you know" something or to "know you did know" something if you can't use it when you need it. The necessary keys are (1) not forgetting, (2) remembering, and (3) retrieval.

Forgetting

The main reason you forget something is that you never had it in the first place—it never made it from short-term to long-term memory. Maybe you didn't understand it, as in the nonsense words at the beginning of this article. Or maybe something interfered with what you were trying to remember, such as that chat you had with a friend you met in the parking lot on the way into the market, a conversation that distracted you from thinking about where you just parked the car. Or maybe you didn't want to remember, as with that dentist appointment. Or maybe over time you have so seldom used the information that your mind can't trace the file.

Let's go back to that book you picked out. You get home and are ready to jot down the title, but—horrors!—the name has escaped you. It's a new bit of information; you wanted to remember it; nobody interfered in the process. Something must have gone wrong with the filing system, and now you have to return to the store to check the title. But wait. Is there a way to remember the title?

Remembering

Now that you know something about how memory works, you can examine the various steps involved to see where you can improve your input so as to get the output you want.

1. When you are encoding, do the following:
   - Intend to remember.
   - Define your purpose by telling yourself why you want to remember.
   - Don't let yourself be distracted.
2. When you are storing by moving from short-term to long-term memory, do the following:
   - Associate the new with the old by making connections.

- Review or rehearse immediately by making notes, writing summaries, or talking about what you want to remember.
- Think about what you want to remember—preview it, make predictions based on it, organize it into lists, find similarities and differences, look for sequences and patterns of organization. In short, make associations.
- Use what you want to remember—apply it to something, make mental images, think of examples and, if possible, associations.
- Use a variety of sensory modes—write it, draw it, imagine it, feel it, listen to it, smell it.
- Put yourself in the picture. What do you think of it? How can you use it? How does it affect you?

13   The object is to try to provide as many clues as possible that will lead to the right file or files. Returning to the example of the book, let us assume that the reason you didn't remember the title is that you can't find your way to the file. How can you retrieve it?

Retrieving

14   The word that comes up repeatedly is *association*. The more things you can associate with what you want to remember, the easier it is to find the file. Let's create a scenario to see how the procedure might have worked with the book you noticed in the bookstore and wanted to remember: Say that the book was The *Name of the Rose,* by Umberto Eco. Clue 1: history class—the reason you wanted to read the book was that it had been mentioned in an interesting way in your medieval history class. Clue 2: the sound of the author's name—you noticed that the book was written by someone with an Italian name that sounded like a sound, "echo." Clue 3: the cover illustration of a large red rose—you thought about how a rose smells, looks, and feels. Had you made these associations, is there any way you would not have remembered the name of the book when you got home?

15   Like learning a new skill, remembering takes practice. But the task is almost impossible unless what you are trying to remember makes sense to you. Look again at those nonsense words at the beginning of this article. You might remember that the second and the last words were the same—*hoi*—but that's probably as far as you got. Now try again: *Utah, Iowa, Idaho, Maine, Ohio.* Easier? Remembering and learning begin with understanding and associating. You can train yourself to be a good "rememberer" by reading

for meaning and by being a good "associator." Your memory is there, ready and waiting.

1. What is the reading about?

   _____

2. Why might you want to read about this topic?

   _____

   _____

3. What do you think is the author's most important idea about the topic?

   _____

   _____

4. How many subtopics are there altogether? _____
   List the four main subtopics:

   _____

   _____

   _____

   _____

5. What three statements, based on what you already know, come to mind when you think about remembering and forgetting?

   _____

   _____

   _____

6. What are three points you predict the author will make?

   _____

   _____

   _____

7. What are three questions you have on this topic?

   _____

   _____

   _____

B. Now read and study the article; then complete the following tasks.

   1. Diagram the section entitled "Storing" (paragraphs 4–9), indicating topic, subtopics, supporting ideas, and supporting details. (You may want to refer to the diagrams in Chapter 6, pp. 151 and 153.)

      Topic:

      Level 1

      Key idea:

      Subtopics:

      Level 2

      Supporting ideas:

      Level 3

      Supporting details:

   2. Write the answers you found to the questions you asked in part A, item 7.

      _____

      _____

      _____

   3. Following are words whose meanings you may have had to guess at. Circle the letter that indicates what you think is the correct meaning for each word, using, where possible, context, association, and word-part clues.

      encode

      a. to put in short-term memory

b. to put in long-term memory

   c. to forget

   d. to write

retrieval

   a. going forward

   b. resuming

   c. throwing

   d. getting back

sensory

   a. nonsensical

   b. correct

   c. pertaining to the senses

   d. pertaining to the census

4. Look up the following words in a dictionary and write the definitions in the spaces provided.

   stimulus: _____

   diagnosis: _____

5. Complete the following questions related to comprehension by circling the appropriate answer.

Another name for this article might be

   a. "How Memory Works."

   b. "Why the Brain Is Like a Computer."

   c. "Nine Ways to Remember."

   d. "Encoding and Decoding."

The best statement of the key idea is as follows:

   a. Memory is very complex.

   b. Everyone forgets.

   c. A person can improve his or her memory.

   d. A person doesn't have to understand something in order to remember it.

Short-term memory and long-term memory are
- a. supporting details.
- b. the topic of the article.
- c. subtopics.
- d. supporting ideas.

The main reason people forget is that
- a. they get interrupted.
- b. they do not understand the information.
- c. they do not want to remember it.
- d. they never had it to start with.

Short-term memory lasts for several
- a. days.
- b. seconds.
- c. hours.
- d. minutes.

According to the article, the keys to remembering are understanding and
- a. reading.
- b. reviewing.
- c. associating.
- d. defining.

This article is meant to
- a. discourage the reader.
- b. encourage the reader.
- c. amuse the reader.
- d. scare the reader.

6. Write a summary of the article.

Analytical and Critical Reading Skills

PART 3

Chapter 7

Recognizing Basic Structure

In this chapter you will find answers to these questions:

What three parts make up the basic structure of a reading selection?

What parts do you read when you preview?

What purposes may the introduction of a reading selection serve?

What is included in the development section of a reading selection?

What questions do the introduction and the conclusion of a reading selection answer?

What are the differences between a summary and a commentary?

Letters make up words, words form sentences, and sentences and paragraphs develop topics. Letters must appear in a specific order for you to understand the word being formed. Words in sentences must also have an order. Sentences must have an appropriate beginning, middle, and end so as to be clearly understood. Reading selections, too, are structured with a beginning, middle, and end: an **introduction, development,** and **conclusion.**

Authors use the basic structure of introduction, development, and conclusion to connect their ideas. Discovering the way a reading selection is organized—seeing how the topic, key idea, subtopics, supporting ideas, and supporting details are presented and connected through this interdependent structure—will help you understand and remember what you read.

The Introduction

Every book, chapter, and article has an introduction. Although the introduction is not always labeled and may vary in length from only the first paragraph to the first several paragraphs of a passage, it is easy to recognize. It is always located at the beginning of each book, chapter, or article section. What other common traits does an introduction have? It usually provides the reader with the key idea that will be explained further in the development of the reading. Frequently, the introduction also contains the subtopics, in the order in which the author will present them, as a preview of the major points that will be discussed in the development of the passage. The introduction gives clues to help you predict what the reading will include.

In addition to, or instead of, being a plan of the reading, the introduction may serve two other purposes. First, it may provide background information about the topic and give a context for the reading selection. Second, it may explain the importance or relevance of the key idea by stating how the key idea applies to you or why you should know about it; this involvement helps you focus on why you are reading a particular selection. But regardless of the specific function of the introduction, it must attract your attention and convince you that the passage is worth reading. Occasionally, to arouse your interest the author may begin a selection by describing a situation that is contrary to the key idea and that will be refuted in the article, or by asking provocative questions that will be answered in the development of the article.

Read the following first paragraph, or introduction, of a reading selection entitled "Photographing Emotions." What is the function of this introduction? It tells you the topic—photographing emotions—and introduces the key idea that the author will explain in the selection: "Photographs that appeal to basic human emotions have a special kind of impact." What else does the author include in the introduction? The author states that "some of the subjects that appeal to basic human emotions are related to conflict, sex, ambition, and escape." Ways of appealing to each of these four basic human emotions are the subtopics. Now you know what the topic, key idea, and subtopics of this selection are, and you can predict the author's major points and the probable order in which he will discuss them.

Photographs that appeal to basic human emotions have a special kind of impact. The viewer does not simply observe the subject, but reacts emotionally to it. The viewer may laugh, feel sad, or simply empathize with the emotions of the subjects. Some of the subjects that appeal to basic human emotions are related to conflict, sex, ambition, and escape.

The Development of the Topic

After you have read the introduction and have answered the questions, *Who or what is this about?* and *What is the author's most important idea about the topic?* you are ready to move on to the development of the selection. The development elaborates on the ideas that were mentioned in the introduction. It forms the bulk of the selection because it restates the key idea, includes the supporting ideas and the supporting details, and answers the questions for identifying the key idea, supporting ideas, and supporting details: *What is the most important thing the author is saying about the topic?* and *Who? What? Why? How? When? Where? Which? What kind?*

In the development part of the reading, the author may connect the supporting ideas by listing the information, by putting the information in a specific order, by comparing and contrasting two or more ideas, by discussing the causes or effects of the key idea, or by presenting the causes and effects of and the solution to a problem. (These ways of organizing information are discussed in the next chapter, Chapter 8.)

Let's return to the reading selection "Photographing Emotions" to see how the development of this passage builds on its introduction. What did you learn from the introduction to "Photographing Emotions?" You learned that the topic is photographing emotions, that the key idea is the importance of appealing to basic human emotions when taking photographs, and that the subtopics are the ways of appealing to each of four basic human emotions: conflict, sex, ambition, and escape.

Now read the next four paragraphs of "Photographing Emotions," looking for the ways the author connects the subtopics presented in the introduction to the ideas he presents in the development of the selection. Each of the subtopics mentioned in the introduction is expanded on or supported in the development of the passage. The author explains each of the appeals to human emotions and gives examples of pictures that may arouse these emotions. Your predictions from reading the introduction will help you understand and retain the material you encounter in this part of the passage.

Conflict exists when people compete against others or against the forces of nature or society. It may be seen in photographs of firefighters battling a blaze, residents sandbagging to fight a flood, ordinary people struggling against disaster. The human competitive spirit is seen also in sports, in elections, in business, and in a grimmer way, in war. Accidents are another context in which we can observe basic human conflict against the forces of nature and society.

Sex appeal has become a standard phrase in our language and it describes another appeal to basic human emotions. Photographs of attractive men and women, singly, in couples, and in groups, usually appeal to human beings of both sexes: they attract the eye and trigger emotional responses. Sex appeal may be observed in action in newspaper and magazine advertisements and in human interest stories and articles.

The *appeal to ambition* can be seen in pictures of people who have achieved success in any area of business, science, athletics, cultural activities, industry, or in other human pursuits. People are interested in others who have achieved success, who have overcome odds, or who by the workings of chance have attained a measure of fame or a notable position.

Finally, photos of people in recreational activities possess *escape appeal*. Escape is represented when the subjects portrayed are shown attempting to escape the monotony of everyday life by having fun, in the pursuit of pleasure and adventure. The person with an interesting hobby, the surfer, or the mountain climber, appeals to the viewer's desire for escape. For a moment the viewer can empathize with the subject and escape the routine of life.

The Conclusion

The final part of the basic structure of a reading selection is the conclusion, which pulls together the ideas presented in the introduction and the development. You can find the conclusion in the last paragraph or paragraphs of a reading or as a separate section or chapter.

The conclusion may be a summary of or a commentary on the selection. If it is a summary, it will review the most important ideas of the passage, usually in the order presented in the reading, as the introduction frequently does. Like the introduction, the conclusion will answer the questions, *Who or what is this about?* and *What is the author's most important idea about the topic?* It may also repeat the subtopics and the supporting ideas. If it is a commentary, the conclusion will tell you what the author believes to be the implications of the material. The author may derive a generalization from the passage or use the conclusion to recommend an action or thought. Sometimes the conclusion consists of both a summary and a commentary.

Let's return to "Photographing Emotions," remembering the connection of the ideas from the introduction to the development. Now read the final paragraph, or conclusion, of the passage. Is it a summary of or a commentary on the ideas the author presented in the development of the selection? Does it review the key idea, make recommendations based on the key idea, or do both? This conclusion does not restate the ideas in the selection; rather, it offers suggestions to the reader based on those ideas. It tells the reader how to develop the skill of taking pictures that appeal to basic human emotions. How is this idea related to the introduction and the development of the selection? The introduction and the development of the passage tell the reader *why* it is important to appeal to basic human emotions when taking photographs; the conclusion tells the reader *how* to appeal to basic human emotions. Even though it is not a summary of the reading, this conclusion builds on the introduction and the development of the selection and extends the key idea of the selection.

> Seeing picture possibilities that appeal to basic human emotions is a skill that can be developed. Look at your photographic subjects. Ask yourself what feeling or emotion the subject generates in you. Then consider how best to convey that same feeling or emotion to your viewer. Ask yourself not only what the idea of your photograph is to be, but also what the emotion of the photograph is to be. Your own emotional sensitivity to the scenes you perceive can be developed.

Now look at the entire selection to see how the three parts—introduction, development, and conclusion—fit together.

Photographing Emotions

Key Idea

Subtopics

> Photographs that appeal to basic human emotions have a special kind of impact. The viewer does not simply observe the subject, but reacts emotionally to it. The viewer may laugh, feel sad, or simply empathize with the emotions of the subjects. Some of the subjects that appeal to basic human emotions are related to conflict, sex, ambition, and escape.

1

Introduction

Conflict exists when people compete against others or against the forces of nature or society. It may be seen in photographs of firefighters battling a blaze, residents sandbagging to fight a flood, ordinary people struggling against disaster. The human competitive spirit is seen also in sports, in elections, in business, and in a grimmer way, in war. Accidents are another context in which we can observe basic human conflict against the forces of nature and society.

Sex appeal has become a standard phrase in our language and it describes another appeal to basic human emotions. Photographs of attractive men and women, singly, in couples, and in groups, usually appeal to human beings of both sexes: they attract the eye and trigger emotional responses. Sex appeal may be observed in action in newspaper and magazine advertisements and in human interest stories and articles.

The *appeal to ambition* can be seen in pictures of people who have achieved success in any area of business, science, athletics, cultural activities, industry, or in other human pursuits. People are interested in others who have achieved success, who have overcome odds, or who by the workings of chance have attained a measure of fame or a notable position.

Finally, photos of people in recreational activities possess *escape appeal*. Escape is represented when the subjects portrayed are shown attempting to escape the monotony of everyday life by having fun, in the pursuit of pleasure and adventure. The person with an interesting hobby, the surfer, or the mountain climber, appeals to the viewer's desire for escape. For a moment the viewer can empathize with the subject and escape the routine of life.

Seeing picture possibilities that appeal to basic human emotions is a skill that can be developed. Look at your photographic subjects. Ask yourself what feeling or emotion the subject generates in you. Then consider how best to convey that same feeling or emotion to your viewer. Ask yourself not only what the idea of your photograph is to be, but also what the emotion of the

> photograph is to be. Your own emotional sensitivity to the scenes you perceive can be developed.
>
> —Marvin Rosen, *Introduction to Photography*

Signal Words for Basic Structure

Understanding the basic structure of a reading helps you comprehend and retain the author's ideas. You can identify the structure of a reading more easily by recognizing special words called **signal words.** Authors use signal words to connect ideas and to help readers follow the directions of the authors' thoughts.

Signal words can indicate that a key idea, supporting idea, or supporting details are about to appear. You can think about signal words as road signs: Some tell you to continue in the same direction as you were proceeding, whereas others indicate a change in course or the introduction of a new thought.

Words That Indicate a Continuing Thought

also	first
besides	next
furthermore	then
in addition (to)	one reason
likewise	another reason
similarly	for example
moreover	for instance

Words That Indicate a Shift in Direction

although	on the contrary
but	on the other hand
despite	otherwise
however	rather
in spite of	whereas
nevertheless	yet
notwithstanding	

Signal words also indicate the introduction and the conclusion of a reading selection. Many textbook chapters begin with the words "We shall study." You have probably read these words many times, but you may not have thought of them as announcing the introduction and predicting the key idea. Following are some of the phrases that indicate the introduction and that may help you predict the key idea:

> The main point is...
> There are three major ideas shown here...
> This chapter deals with...
> In the following chapter...

For example, the introduction of a book about Great Britain during World War II might state:

> The main point is that Britain's military force was weak in 1941.

Or a chapter in a book used in an English literature class might begin:

> This chapter deals with the elements of drama.

Some words mark the beginning of a summary or the consequence of ideas previously presented. These words indicate that you are about to read a conclusion. For instance:

accordingly	in summary
consequently	therefore
finally	thus
in conclusion	to sum up

A conclusion about test-taking strategies, for example, might end:

> Therefore, he passed the exam.

Or an author of a writing textbook might state the consequence of learning rules of grammar:

> Finally, when you understand and can apply the grammar and usage rules, you have a sense of confidence in your ability.
>
> —Barbara Fine Clouse

You do not need to memorize these signal words, but you should recognize them and think about them when you read and write. They enable ideas to flow smoothly, and they help you follow those ideas. You can anticipate the meaning of what you will read by being aware of signal words as cues to shifts in the author's thoughts.

Exercise 7A

Preview and read the following selection.
Then identify the introduction, development, and conclusion by labeling them in the text.
Describe the function of the introduction (presents a plan of the reading, provides background information, and/or explains the importance of the key idea) and the conclusion (summary or commentary).
Finally, circle the signal words and explain the purpose of each signal word. What type of signal words are used most frequently in this reading selection—signal words that indicate a continuing thought or signal words that indicate a shift in direction?

1. The radical *behaviorists* led first by John B. Watson (1913) and later by B. F. Skinner (1938) argued that science must investigate public, observable events. The behaviorists concluded that since mental events such as thoughts and images and consciousness cannot be observed directly, they have no place in the science of psychology.

2. The behaviorists' arguments had tremendous impact on American psychology and, indeed, on American society. From the early 1920's through the late 1950's almost all experimental psychologists abandoned the investigation of mental events and substituted the study of behavior, the latter being more readily observable and, thus, more amenable to study by scientific methods. As a consequence of this choice of subject matter, these decades led to many statements about the effects of reinforcement on the behavior of people and laboratory animals, but they provided little insight into the mysteries of memory, language, and thought. Since the late 1950's, however, a revolution has occurred. Experimental psychologists have turned their talents increasingly to the investigation of the mind, and there has been a rebirth of interest in what is now called the cognitive approach to psychology.

The Cognitive Approach

3. The essence of the cognitive approach can be summarized by considering three of the major characteristics that distinguish it from behaviorism. First, it emphasizes knowing, rather than responding. Cognitive psychologists are concerned with finding scientific means for studying the mental processes involved in the acquisition and application of

knowledge. This means that their major emphasis is not upon stimulus-response bonds, but on mental events. This stress on mind as opposed to behavior is consistent with intuition; we define ourselves at least as much by our thoughts as by our actions. Descartes said *"Cogito ergo sum"* ("I think; therefore I am"). His words would not have rung so true had he proclaimed, "I behave; therefore I am."

Of course, the cognitive approach does not ignore behavior, but rather than being the object of study, responses are used as indicators that enable inferences regarding mental events. Perhaps the best way to state the distinction is to paraphrase Noam Chomsky, the great linguist, who wrote that calling psychology "behavioral science" is like designating natural science "the science of meter readings" (Chomsky, 1968, p. 58). Chomsky eloquently expresses the cognitive viewpoint: to call psychology the *science of behavior* is to confuse the evidence studied (behavior) with the goal of the study (an understanding of the mind). Indeed, in attempting to banish unobservables from the realm of psychology, the behaviorists were striving to impose a restriction on psychological theorizing that is not imposed in any of the other sciences. No one has ever observed directly either gravity or a quark, yet physicists are not deemed unscientific for including these concepts in their theories.

A second characteristic of the cognitive approach is that it emphasizes *mental structure* or *organization.* It is argued that an individual's knowledge is organized and that new stimuli are interpreted in light of this knowledge. This stress on organization is particularly apparent in the theory of Jean Piaget, the Swiss scholar who has contributed so much to our understanding of human development. Piaget has argued that all living creatures are born with an invariant tendency—to organize experience—and that this tendency provides an important impetus for cognitive development.

The third characteristic of the cognitive approach is that the individual is viewed as being active, constructive, and planful, rather than as being the passive recipient of environmental stimulation. The analogies frequently used by the behaviorist reveal a passive view of the organism. Humans are described as blank slates upon which the environment writes, wax upon which the environment impresses itself, and mirrors that reflect the environment. On the other hand, the cognitive theorist views the individual as an active participant in the process of acquiring and using knowledge. The individual is thought of as actively constructing a view of reality, selectively choosing some aspects of experience for further attention, and attempting to commit some information to memory. The cognitive theorist assumes that any complete theory of human cognition must include an analysis of the plans or strategies people use for thinking, remembering, and understanding and producing language.

A good way to highlight the distinctions between the behaviorist and the cognitive views of human nature is to examine how proponents of each approach have attempted to study morality, a topic outside the realm of this book. Behaviorists have focused on certain moral (or immoral) behaviors, such as cheating, helping others, and disobeying authority (reflecting characteristic 1). They have assumed that moral development involves nothing more than the learning of additional moral behaviors (characteristic 2), and have viewed such moral development as the result of reinforcement and punishment to which the individual has been subjected (characteristic 3). Cognitive theorists, on the other hand, have focused on the thought processes by which people decide between right and wrong (characteristic 1). They have argued that moral development brings with it increasingly complex and organized rules for making moral decisions (characteristic 2), and that such development is dependent upon the active construction of the individual (characteristic 3). It is hard to imagine two more radically different approaches to the same topic!

—Darlene Howard, *Cognitive Psychology*

Function of introduction _____

Function of conclusion _____

Exercise 7B

Preview and read "The Feminization of Academe." Identify the introduction, development, and conclusion by labeling them in the text.

Describe the function of the introduction and the conclusion.

Next, identify the key ideas and subtopics by marking them in the text.

Finally, circle the signal words and explain the purpose of each signal word (for instance, to indicate a continuation of the same thought, to introduce a new thought, or to introduce the introduction or the conclusion).

The Feminization of Academe

American colleges once devoted themselves almost exclusively to the preparation of young men for the ministry and teaching. By the middle of the nineteenth century this practice appeared to be placing colleges in ever greater financial trouble. As commercial growth agitated a country in the midst of rapid industrial expansion, the country's young men sought business success and shunned both the ministry and teaching. With declining enrollments, colleges faced three alternatives: They could go bankrupt, they could open their doors to women, or they could revise their curricula to cater to the needs of youth determined to exploit the possibilities of an industrial society.

Turning to women seemed natural enough to many, though there was little precedent for it. As men focused their attention on commercial success, women came increasingly to be seen as the guardians of culture. Because colleges had long been the repositories of culture in America, women and colleges seemed ideally suited to one another. When schools opened their doors, women flocked to them, some seeking training for careers as teachers, a very few hoping to break the barrier of such traditionally male domains as the ministry or medicine, and many more searching for literary and artistic fulfillment. It seemed a happy marriage.

But at the same time that the colleges were encouraging the enrollment of young women, they were revamping their curricula in the hope of recapturing their male audience. Through courses in political science, economics, sociology, engineering, medicine, law, and business administration, college administrators sought to convince the public of the colleges' utilitarian character. Many colleges, emulating the example of European institutions, transformed themselves into universities with graduate departments and professional schools and began to argue that science could speed economic and social development. At the turn of the century these schools were often available to women; because of overexpansion, some had little choice. But it was assumed from the beginning that they would appeal primarily to men.

These curricular and institutional innovations proved tremendously successful, but the success was tinged with irony. By welcoming young women at the same time that they were altering their curricula to appeal to young men, universities found themselves with a growing female student body dedicated to an educational ideal that the university was trying to abandon. The danger, as many saw it, was that women would overrun the university and jeopardize the reform effort.

In 1902 fear gripped many at the University of Chicago, who foresaw the imminent feminization of their school. One professor, economist J. Lawrence Laughlin, sought to reassure his colleagues. He was aware that in the ten years since the university's opening the female enrollment had increased from 25 percent to 50 percent of the student body, but he predicted that once the university's scientific programs and professional schools became firmly established the trend would be reversed.

> The congestion of numbers [of women students] is now due largely to the fact that the undergraduate courses are practically used by women as an advanced normal school to prepare for teaching, the one profession easiest to enter by them. At present, this part of the university is the main part. The best men are going less and less into teaching. Just so soon as proper support and endowments are given to the work which offers training for careers in engineering, railways, banking, trade and industry, law, medicine, etc. The disproportion of men will doubtless remedy itself.

On one level the concern over female enrollment at Chicago, as well as Laughlin's reassurances, reflected the new university's parochial desire for status; but on another level it reflected the pervasive fear of feminization that plagued American society in the early twentieth century. As the economic change of a rapidly industrializing society brought social dislocation, Americans clung ever more tenaciously to their most basic assumptions about sexual identity and fought any changes in accepted sex-role divisions.

Education played a singularly important role in this drama, because the special circumstances of the development of the university placed American higher education at the fulcrum of social change. No sooner had higher education been opened to women as a relatively unnecessary pursuit in a commercial, industrializing society, than it became clear to many that education could make a significant contribution to that industrialization. But by the time education's potential value was perceived, women had flooded the schools, filling 50 percent of the student body at many schools by 1900. Society was faced with two alternatives. It could acquiesce in the surrender of education to women and thereby protect the separation of sexual spheres, but suffer the loss of a valuable institution for male training, or it could continue trying to make higher education more attractive to men and risk the danger to sex-role divisions posed by sexual integration. Apprehensively, society chose the latter alternative and accepted coeducation.

—Carol Ruth Berkin and Mary Beth Norton,
Women of America: A History

Function of introduction _____

Function of conclusion _____

Summary Exercise

Write a summary of this chapter. Make sure your summary includes an introduction, development, and conclusion. Use signal words to indicate how the ideas are related.

Chapter 8

Analyzing Patterns of Organization

In this chapter you will find answers to these questions:

What are patterns of organization and how do they differ from basic structure?
How do you use patterns of organization when you think about something?
What are the most common patterns of organization?
Why is it important to recognize signal words?
Why is it helpful to predict patterns of organization?

Recognizing how authors structure reading selections helps the reader understand and remember the information. This chapter examines the more specific methods, or **patterns of organization,** authors use to present their ideas and considers how these patterns of organization clarify the topics and subtopics, help the reader understand the key idea, and show the relationship between the supporting ideas and supporting details.

Authors typically use standard patterns of organization to present their material. The most common patterns of organization are the **list pattern,** the **order pattern,** the **compare/contrast** pattern, the **cause-and-effect pattern,** and the **problem-solution pattern.** Although authors frequently use more than one pattern of organization in their writing, most reading selections have a dominant pattern. Recognizing that dominant pattern will help you predict what the author is going to say.

Exercise 8A

The following exercise will help you see different patterns of organization and the relationships they signify. The names of eleven people and events are listed below. Organize these names in as many groups or categories as you can, designating a topic for each category. A category does not need to include all the listed items but must include at least two of them.

George Washington
Indira Gandhi
Civil War
John F. Kennedy
United Nations
Revolutionary War
Martin Luther King, Jr.
Margaret Thatcher
desegregation
World War II
Abraham Lincoln

For example, one group might be as follows:

American Presidents
    George Washington
    John F. Kennedy
    Abraham Lincoln

After you have grouped the items, think about the different ways in which the items might be connected. Relating these items will show you different patterns of organization. For instance, you could connect the group of American presidents simply by a list. The topic is American presidents; the subtopics are Washington, Kennedy, and Lincoln. You would thus be organizing your information in a list pattern. Another possibility is order—you could read or write about these American presidents in chronological order, the order in which they lived. A third option would be to compare and contrast different characteristics of these American presidents: their leadership styles, their beliefs, and so on. Another relationship among these American presidents might be cause and effect: The American presidents from further back in time might have had an effect on the presidents who lived more recently. The final type of connection among these American presidents might be problem-solution; this arrangement would be an extension of the cause-and-effect pattern and could include defining a problem caused by Washington's presidency, describing its effects on Lincoln's term, and discussing its solution during Kennedy's tenure.

In each of these examples the same topic and subtopics appear; however, each example has a different key idea, and so the connection among the supporting ideas will be unique for each method of organization. The following statements demonstrate how the key idea varies as each of these patterns of organization is used.

> List: *Washington, Lincoln, and Kennedy are three American presidents who are interesting to study.*
> Order: *It is interesting to follow the development of the American presidency by studying presidents from the eighteenth, nineteenth, and twentieth centuries.*
> Compare/contrast: *Several similarities and differences exist among three American presidents.*
> Cause and effect: *George Washington's policies during his presidency affected Abraham Lincoln's and John F. Kennedy's ideas.*
> Problem-solution: *Problems during Washington's administration affected Lincoln's presidency and were solved during Kennedy's tenure.*

List Pattern

The list pattern is simply a series (or list) of ideas, facts, or details about the key idea. The order in which the ideas or details are listed is not important and can be switched without changing the meaning. This arrangement is the least structured of the patterns of organization, and it shows the simplest relationship of ideas. Authors typically use this pattern when they want to present straightforward information with a list of examples, clarifications, or attributes. Statistical information is also often presented in the list pattern.

Signal Words for List Pattern

The following words may signal that the author is using the list pattern:

many
much
a few
a number of
several
most
another
besides
also
furthermore
too
in addition
one, two, three, and so on

The paragraph below is an example of information organized in the list pattern. The topic of the paragraph is legitimate authority. You learn from the first sentence of the paragraph that the key idea is that there are three types of legitimate authority: traditional, legal, and charismatic. In addition to telling you the key idea and the subtopics, the author indicates that the paragraph is organized in the list pattern by using the signal words *three types*. With this knowledge, you can predict that the author will tell you about the three types of authority without showing another relationship among them and that the author could explain these subtopics in any order without changing the meaning of the paragraph.

> Max Weber distinguishes three types of legitimate authority: traditional, legal, and charismatic. Traditional authority gets its legitimacy from its history. Such authority is right and legitimate because that is the way it has "always" been, because "God made it that way when He created the world," whether the monarch was called king, pharaoh, Inca, sultan, shah, khan, patriarch, or Papa (pope). Legal authority, however, is based on "rational" claims. Those who hold office do so because of rules and procedures arrived at by reasoning and approved by general agreement such as the vote, the electorate, the plebiscite. Charismatic authority rests on a very special quality of leadership to which Weber gave the name charisma. Its original meaning was "grace," but he added to that a heroic, sacred, or magical quality in the individual that makes the leader close to superhuman. He becomes the symbolic embodiment of a cause, a nation, or an idea, and attracts loyalty from his followers.
>
> —Jane Dabaghian, *Mirror of Man*

Order Pattern

The order pattern also presents readers with a list, but the list must be in a certain order. There are many variations of the order pattern. The ideas, facts, or details that support the key idea can be ordered chronologically, or according to a time sequence; according to a process, or sequence of steps; according to size or place; or according to importance. In each variation of the order pattern, the author arranges the material in a logical order, with each step related to the steps preceding or following it.

Chronological Order

When authors organize material in **chronological order,** they list the steps or events in the order in which they occur (or occurred). Each step or event relates to the steps or events that precede or follow it. Chronological order is often used to tell stories and is found in history texts.

Here is an example of a paragraph using chronological order to discuss events:

> Archimedes was said to have used solar reflecting mirrors more than 2000 years ago to set fire to ships in a Roman fleet. In the mid-1800s a French scientist developed the first known solar device able to convert water into steam and power an engine. There were some rather surprising solar technological developments in the early parts of the twentieth century. Tens of thousands of solar water heaters were sold and used in California and Florida in the early 1900s, and some of these reportedly are still in operation.
>
> —Charles E. Kupchella and Margaret C. Hyland,
> *Environmental Science*

Process

When authors are explaining a **process**—the steps necessary to do or make something—they are also using a version of the order pattern. When describing a process, authors must be careful to show that each step closely follows the preceding one and must ensure that no step is left out. Examples of a process are often found in chemistry textbooks; you must follow laboratory procedures carefully to get the desired results.

The following example of the process pattern of organization presents a step-by-step test to determine whether flies taste with their feet.

> The first step is to provide a fly with a handle since Nature failed to do so. Procure a stick about the size of a lead pencil. (A lead pencil will do nicely. So will an applicator stick, the kind that a physician employs when swabbing a throat.) Dip one end repeatedly into candle wax or paraffin until a fly-sized gob accumulates. Next anaesthetize a fly. The least messy method is to deposit him in the freezing compartment of a refrigerator for several minutes. Then, working very rapidly, place him backside down on the wax and seal his wings onto it with a hot needle.... Lower the fly gently over a saucer of water until his feet just touch. Chances are he is thirsty. If so, he will lower his proboscis (eating and sucking part of some insects) as soon as his feet touch and will suck avidly. When thirst has been allayed, the proboscis will be retracted compactly into the head.
>
> —Vincent C. Dethier, *To Know a Fly*

Size or Place

Arranging material according to **size or place** is also a variation of the order pattern. A group of items can be presented from the largest to the smallest, or vice versa. Sometimes a paragraph shows how the details of a particular place (for example, a room, a field, or a city street) are arranged. The paragraph might describe the details from right to left (or left to right), from top to bottom (or bottom to top), from near to far (or far to near), and so forth. The important thing to remember is that the details are logically arranged according to where they are located. This type of order pattern is usually found in descriptions, which occur in all academic disciplines and especially in literature.

The following paragraph is an example of an order pattern that arranges material according to size or place—in this case, place. The author traces the American offensive in the Pacific during World War II.

> General Douglas MacArthur's strategy was to "island-hop" toward Japan itself, skipping the most strongly fortified points whenever possible and taking weaker ones.... The first American offensive was at Guadalcanal in the Solomons

(1942). Over the next few years U.S. troops attacked the Gilberts (1942), the Marianas (1944), and the Philippines (1944).

—Mary Beth Norton et al., *A People and a Nation*

Importance

Authors use a version of the order pattern when they arrange ideas or details by importance—that is, from most to least important or from least to most important. This kind of order pattern can be useful; once you have determined how the author has arranged the ideas or details, you can quickly zero in on what he or she considers the most important. Try doing so with the following example:

> The federal court system is organized on both a geographic and a hierarchical basis. The lowest level of the system is the district court. There are more than ninety districts, at least one in every state and territory of the United States, and there may be as many as thirty judges in a single district. The district court is the general trial court, where most federal, civil, and criminal actions begin. The large number and geographic distribution of the district courts are necessary to ensure convenient and timely adjudication of disputes involving parties subject to federal jurisdiction. The next level of federal courts is the court of appeals. There are eleven such courts, one for the District of Columbia and ten others for numbered "circuits," which each include up to ten states and territories. The court of appeals primarily hears appeals taken from decisions at the district court level. The purpose is to ensure that the district courts do not make serious errors of judgment and that laws are interpreted and applied uniformly in all the district courts in the circuit. The ultimate level in the federal court system is the Supreme Court. The Supreme Court reviews those relatively few cases appealed from the courts of appeal which raise substantial and important questions of federal law. With its national focus, the Supreme Court is designed to resolve conflicts in interpretation that might exist among different circuits.

In the preceding paragraph the author moves from the lowest level of the court system, the district court, to the next level, the court of appeals, and finally to the highest level, the Supreme Court.

When you recognize the order pattern in a reading selection, you can look for the specific variation of the pattern and predict the order in which the author has arranged the ideas.

Signal Words for Order Pattern

The following words may signal that the author is using the order pattern.

first, second, and so on	at last
next	ultimately
then	begins
soon	ends
later	more, most
after	less, least
finally	better, best
subsequently	worse, worst

Compare/Contrast Pattern

To **compare** is to explain the similarities between two or more ideas, people, places, events, things, and so forth. To **contrast** is to explain the differences. People compare and contrast all the time. In fact, comparing and contrasting can be seen as the foundation for understanding, for learning, and for making decisions. Whenever you encounter something new, you can ask how it is similar to or how it is different from something you already know.

Whenever you make a choice, you compare and contrast two or more things to reach your decision. For example, if you are trying to decide what to have for lunch you may think about whether a hamburger or a tuna fish sandwich appeals more to you. They are both lunch foods, and so they have that in common—they have a *basis for comparison.* In evaluating the nutritional value of lunch foods, you could not compare or contrast, for example, a hamburger and a toy; they do not have a basis for comparison. You make your choice by thinking about how a hamburger and a tuna fish sandwich are alike and how they are different. Of course, this example is a simple one, but more complicated ideas or items can be compared and contrasted as well.

An author may use the compare/contrast pattern to inform the reader, to emphasize or evaluate particular qualities, or to persuade the reader that one thing is better than another. One of the most frequent uses of the compare/contrast pattern is to explain the unfamiliar in terms of the familiar. By comparing and/or contrasting new information with familiar material, the author is building on prior knowledge. The preview question, *What do I already know about this topic?* helps you to understand new material by comparing and contrasting it with what you already know.

Once you identify the pattern of organization, you can see how the ideas are related. In the case of the compare/contrast pattern, the key idea usually states that there are similarities and differences between the items that make up the topic. As you are looking for what is being compared, you can ask yourself, *What is the basis for comparison?* For example, if an author is comparing the United States and Canada, the basis for comparison is that they are both countries in North America. Countries in North America is the topic; that there are similarities and differences between countries in North America is the key idea. After you have determined the key idea, you can find the subtopics by asking, *What North American countries is the author comparing and contrasting?* The United States and Canada are the subtopics. You can then move on to determine the supporting ideas by identifying the similar and dissimilar aspects of the subtopics the author compares and contrasts. The supporting ideas answer the question, *What aspects of the subtopics are being compared and contrasted?* For example, the author might include the following aspects of the United States and Canada: area, population, official language, and health care systems. As you recognize the specific characteristics of each of the supporting ideas, you see the supporting details. The author might compare and contrast the areas of the two countries: The area of the United States is 3,679,245 square miles; that of Canada, 3,831,033 square miles.

Figure 8.1 depicts a useful chart for recognizing and understanding the relationships among these components.

	Area	Population	Official language	Health care system
United States	3,679,245 square miles	264,149,210	English	Private
Canada	3,831,033 square miles	28,434,545	English and French	National

Figure 8.1   Comparing the United States and Canada

Authors may organize the information they are comparing and contrasting in two ways: (1) by presenting all the supporting ideas and supporting details about one subtopic and then comparing and contrasting those elements with all the supporting ideas and supporting details about another subtopic or (2) by presenting one supporting idea and its supporting details as compared and contrasted for both (or all) the subtopics, followed by another supporting idea and its supporting details as compared and contrasted among the various subtopics, and so forth. Sometimes authors may combine the two methods—they may begin with one way of comparing and contrasting and then move on to the other.

Applying the first method to the example of North American countries, the author would begin by providing all the supporting ideas and details about the United States. Then the author would compare and contrast those elements with all the supporting ideas and details about Canada. Using the second method, the writer would begin by comparing and contrasting the area of the United States with the area of Canada. Next the author would compare and contrast the population of the United States with the population of Canada. The author would then continue comparing and contrasting for all the other supporting ideas and supporting details, taking them up one by one.

Signal Words for Compare/Contrast Pattern

Some signal words tell you that two or more ideas are being compared or contrasted. Words indicating comparison signal that the author is telling you how this thought is the same as another; words indicating contrast signal that the idea following the signal word is different from the previous concept.

Words That Indicate Similarities
like
as
again
still
same
similarly
in comparison

Words That Indicate Differences
but
on the other hand

on the contrary
however
rather
different
in contrast
instead

The following reading selection, entitled "Dispute Resolution," is an example of material arranged in the compare/contrast pattern of organization. The key idea of the passage and the basis for comparison are that there are similarities and differences between types of dispute resolution. The author compares and contrasts two types of dispute resolution: mediation and arbitration. These are the subtopics. Specifically, the author compares and contrasts three aspects of these two types of dispute resolution: the characteristics of mediators and arbitrators, the power of mediators and arbitrators, and the result of arbitration and mediation. These are the supporting ideas.

Dispute Resolution

Often newspaper reporters writing about labor or international disputes use the terms *mediation* and *arbitration* interchangeably. Many people therefore believe that the terms are synonymous. Although mediators and arbitrators share some attributes, they in fact have fundamental distinctions. Both mediators and arbitrators are disinterested, or neutral, persons who intercede between or among two or more parties for the purpose of resolving the parties' dispute. They may be private citizens or members of some governmental agency. There the similarities end. A mediator is armed only with the power of persuasion. He or she first listens to the respective positions and demands of the various parties and then tries to bring the divergent positions together to some mutually beneficial settlement point. This process is done by helping parties see the strengths and weaknesses of their own and their adversary's positions; prioritize their demands; and explore different avenues for meeting the essential needs of all disputants. If the parties cannot be made to see that settlement is in their mutual interest, that the costs of confrontation are greater than the costs of compromise, then the mediator's job is done. A mediator has no power to impose a settlement on recalcitrant parties. In contrast, an arbitrator is more like a judge, chosen by the parties to make a binding decision. After listening to the parties' presentations and considering relevant agreements or laws, an arbitrator issues an award, or ruling. With rare exception, the parties have no choice but to comply with the award. If one or more parties feel the arbitrator's award was deficient in some way, their only real remedy is not to use that arbitrator in the future.

—Mark Irvings

Exercise 8B

The subtopics and supporting ideas of Dispute Resolution *are shown in the following chart. Fill in the supporting details.*

	Characteristics of Persons	Power	Result
Arbitration	1. _____	2. _____	3. _____
	_____	_____	_____
	_____	_____	_____
Mediation	4. _____	5. _____	6. _____
	_____	_____	_____
	_____	_____	_____

Cause-and-Effect Pattern

When one event happens as a direct result of a previous occurrence, the two events are linked by a causal relationship. Our lives are made up of cause and effect. For example, in the sentence "I was late for class because I overslept," the cause is oversleeping; the effect is being late for class. Several effects may sometimes be cited for one cause, or several causes may explain one effect. For instance, the writer of the preceding sentence may have been late for class because he or she overslept, the bus was late, and the writer stopped to speak with friends.

When you recognize the cause-and-effect pattern, you can more easily find the key idea and can state it in terms of causes or effects. The question, *What is the author saying about the topic?* might become more specific by asking, *What does the topic affect or cause?* or *How is the topic affected or caused?* If an author states that the failure of the government to enforce pollution controls has resulted in many problems, you can find the key idea by asking, *What does the lack of enforcement cause?* After determining that the key idea is that unenforced pollution controls cause many problems, you can find the supporting ideas by specifically identifying the subtopics, the problems or effects. These might include health problems, dead fish, and a decrease in tourism. A diagram of the key idea and supporting ideas is presented in Figure 8.2.

Looking for the supporting ideas in terms of causes and effects will make a reading selection easier to understand. Supporting ideas may also be introduced by such statements as these:

The list of [causes or effects of the key idea] is . . .
The reasons for [the key idea] are . . .
The results of [the key idea] are . . .
[The effect] happened because of [the cause].

Signal Words for Cause-and-Effect Pattern

The simple "because" statement is not difficult to understand ("I was late for school because I overslept"). But more obscure cause-and-effect situations may not be so easily recognized. Signal words help the reader to connect ideas and to find the causal relationship between two or more ideas. Here are some possible signal words:

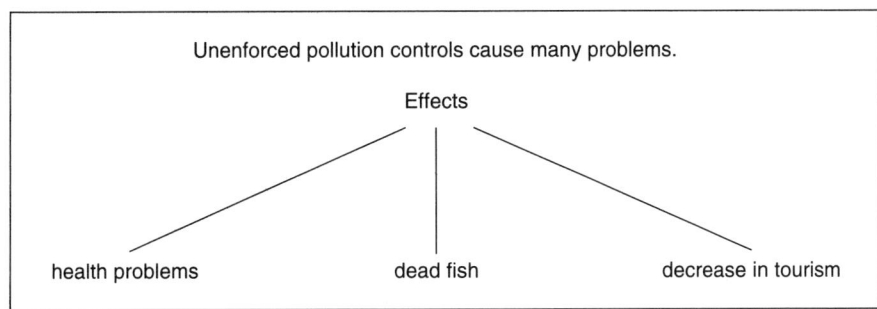

Figure 8.2 Key idea, subtopic, and supporting ideas

because	results
since	resulted in
therefore	as a result (of)
consequently	for this reason
so	leads to
brought about	becomes
is the outcome of	thus
determine	effects
if, then	affects
causes	

The following selection about stretching is an example of information presented in the cause-and-effect pattern. The key idea of the passage is that stretching too far causes your muscles to contract (the stretch reflex).

The italicized signal words indicate the primary cause-and-effect relationship, as well as secondary relationships that introduce supporting details.

> Your muscles are protected by a mechanism called the stretch reflex. Any time you stretch the muscle fibers too far (either by bouncing or overstretching), a nerve reflex responds by sending a signal to the muscles to contract: this keeps the muscles from being injured. *Therefore,* when you stretch too far, you tighten the very muscles you are trying to stretch!
>
> Holding a stretch as far as you can go or bouncing up and down strains the muscles and activates the stretch reflex. These harmful methods *cause* pain, as well as physical damage *due to* the microscopic tearing of the muscle fibers. This tearing *leads to* the formation of scar tissue in the muscles with a gradual loss of elasticity. The muscles *become* tight and sore.
>
> —Bob Anderson, *Stretching*

Problem-Solution Pattern

The final pattern of organization, the problem-solution pattern, is an extension of the cause-and-effect pattern. The problem-solution pattern may be familiar to you because many authors use it in writing magazine articles about everyday problems or concerns. For example, the author of such an article may offer the reader solutions to shyness, or ways to make more money, or methods of becoming healthier. When using the problem-solution pattern, an author may begin with a statement of a problem, then cite the causes and effects of that problem, and end with a possible solution to the problem. Or the author may begin with one or more solutions and then state the problem and its causes and effects.

The signal words for the problem-solution pattern are the same as those for the cause-and-effect pattern. The following selection about stress is an example of material presented in the problem-solution pattern. The problem, causes, effects, and solution have been labeled to aid your understanding.

Stress: Its Nature, Causes, and Management

Problem

1 Stress involves a complex pattern of negative emotions and physiological reactions occurring in situations where individuals perceive threats to their major goals which they may be unable to meet. To understand stress fully we must take account of reactions to it, stimuli that produce it *(stressors),* and *cognitive appraisal* (individuals' perceptions that events pose a threat to their important goals or beliefs).

Causes

2 Many factors contribute to stress. Major life changes (e.g., divorce, death of a close relative) are often highly stressful and can exert adverse effects upon physical and psychological health. Recent evidence, though, suggests that minor *daily hassles* of everyday life may be even more important in this regard. Many aspects of jobs (e.g., work overload, responsibility for others, role conflict) contribute to stress. Finally, certain features of the physical environment (e.g., noise, extreme temperatures) can be highly stressful.

Effects

3 Prolonged exposure to high levels of stress exerts adverse effects upon individuals' physical and psychological well-being. Stress also interferes with the performance of many tasks and with effective decision-making. Job-related stress can sometimes lead to burnout, a psychological state characterized by physical, mental, and emotional exhaustion, as well as feelings of low personal accomplishment....

Solution

4 The harmful effects of stress can be reduced by physical fitness, relaxation techniques, learning to leave job-related stress at the office, and developing networks of social support (persons in

whom one can confide, and to whom one can turn for help and guidance).

—Robert A. Baron, *Psychology*

Exercise 8C

Read each of the sentences that follow and predict which pattern of organization would be used if each sentence were the key idea of a paragraph.

Example:
There are five buildings on campus.
Pattern: *List*

1. The right and left hemispheres of the brain differ in their ability to recognize and communicate emotion.

    Pattern: _____

2. You will need to bring several items on the camping trip.

    Pattern: _____

3. Hormones exert profound effects on a wide range of processes related to the basic functioning of our bodies.

    Pattern: _____

4. Babies acquire language in a series of steps.

    Pattern: _____

5. Different cultures hold sharply contrasting views about how many marriage partners an individual should have at a given time.

    Pattern: _____

6. If we run short of energy sources, we run the risk of creating food shortages among many of the world's people.

    Pattern: _____

7. Having fewer students in the classroom would improve teaching and learning.

   Pattern: _____

8. Although many people believe that the women's movement began in the 1960s, its history goes back to the previous century.

   Pattern: _____

9. He hung the pictures around the room, beginning at the wall near the doorway and moving toward the far wall.

   Pattern: _____

10. We examined the parts of the respiratory system.

    Pattern: _____

Exercise 8D

Using each of the patterns of organization, make up a key idea for each of the following topics. For an example, see the various key ideas for the listing of American presidents on page 181.

1. college courses

   List: _____

   Order: _____

   Compare/contrast: _____

   Cause and effect: _____

   Problem-solution: _____

2. drugs

   List: _____

Order: _____

Compare/contrast: _____

Cause and effect: _____

Problem-solution: _____

3. the environment

List: _____

Order: _____

Compare/contrast: _____

Cause and effect: _____

Problem-solution: _____

Exercise 8E

Read the following selections and identify the pattern of organization of each of them.

Example:
Shortly after World War II, decades of investigation into internal workings of the solids yielded a new piece of electronic hardware called a transistor. Transistors, a family of devices, alter and control the flow of electricity in circuits.... They are solid. They have no cogs and wheels, no separate pieces to be soldered together, it is as if they are stones performing some useful work. They are durable, take almost no time to start working, and don't consume much power. Moreover, as physicists and engineers discovered, they could be produced cheaply in large quantities.

—Tracy Kidder, *Soul of a New Machine*

Pattern: *List*

1. Every new administration at Washington began in an atmosphere of expectant good will, but in this case the airs which lapped the capital were particularly bland. The smile of the new President was as warming as a spring thaw after a winter

of discontent. For four long years the gates of the White House had been locked and guarded with sentries. Harding's first official act was to throw them open, to permit a horde of sightseers to roam the grounds and flatten their noses against the executive window-panes and photograph one another under the great north portico; to permit flivvers [old, cheap automobiles] and trucks to detour from Pennsylvania Avenue up the driveway and chortle right past the presidential front door. The act seemed to symbolize the return of the government to the people. Wilson had been denounced as an autocrat, had proudly kept his own counsel; Harding modestly said he would rely on the "best minds" to advise him.... Wilson had seemed to be everlastingly prying into the affairs of business and had distrusted most business men; Harding meant to give them as free a hand as possible "to resume their normal onward way." And finally, whereas Wilson had been an austere academic theorist, Harding was "just folk": he radiated an unaffected good nature, met reporters and White House visitors with a warm handclasp and a genial word, and touched the sentimental heart of America by establishing in the White House a dog named Laddie Boy.

—Frederick Lewis Allen, *Only Yesterday*

Pattern: _____

2. A number of factors led to the eventual transition to the centralized federal government which we know today, but several are outstanding. First,... the transformation of the United States from a nation of farmers to an industrial power, as well as the growth in population, demanded a greater coordination of activities. This became increasingly evident as the country entered the international market and it became necessary to regulate imports and exports. In addition, as international trade expanded, the federal government extended its contacts with other nations in the form of embassies and consulates. Second,... as industrialization took place, the government took a more active role in the economy, attempting to protect the interests of the people. The Sherman Anti-Trust Act of 1890 is a good example. Third, the conflict between the federal government and the individual state governments escalated, culminating in the secession of the Southern states and the Civil War. The victory of the Northern states established the power of the national government over that of the individual states. Finally, the history of almost constant U.S. mili-

tary activities required the formation of a strong national hierarchy to guide such actions.

—Daniel J. Curran and Claire M. Renzetti, *Social Problems*

Pattern: _____

Exercise 8F

Read "Gender and Substance Abuse"; then make a chart showing the subtopics, supporting ideas, and supporting details the author is comparing and contrasting. Refer to the charts on the United States and Canada (p. 187) and arbitration and mediation (p. 190).

Gender and Substance Abuse

With the widespread use of drugs in American culture beginning in the 1960s, it was generally believed that "the drug revolution" would eventually eliminate differences in patterns of substance abuse between women and men. People assumed that as women took on more "male" roles, such as working in the paid labor force, women's use of alcohol and drugs would more nearly approximate men's. This has not generally occurred (Robbin, 1989), although there is some convergence in drinking rates among young people, particularly college students (Temple, 1987). 1

With regard to alcohol, men drink more frequently than women and drink more on any given occasion. Men are more likely to be classified as problem drinkers. In drug use, men use marijuana, inhalants, cocaine, hallucinogens, PCP, and heroin more than do women. Women do exceed men in the use of mood-modifying drugs that are medicinal and legal, such as prescribed medications, tranquilizers, barbiturates, antidepressants, and over-the-counter drugs (Robbins and Clayton, 1989). In fact, two-thirds of the prescriptions for psychotropic drugs are written for women. The only illicit substances used equally by young women and young men are amphetamines (Johnston, Bachman, and O'Malley, 1982).... 2

Most women receiving drug treatment are being treated for barbiturate, sedative, and tranquilizer use, although women make up a small (25 percent) proportion of those treated for drug abuse. Women are approximately 20 percent of the heroin addict population, but, although they are a 3 minority of heroin addicts, they tend to be in more difficult situations. Women heroin addicts, compared with men, are more likely to be unemployed, unmarried, and with dependent children. They also have lower self-esteem than male heroin addicts and have more symptoms of depression and anxiety, and they are more likely to have other health problems (Colten and Marsh, 1984). Women's careers as addicts also narrow their life options more than male addicts' careers (Rosenbaum, 1981).

One explanation of the differential patterns of substance abuse among men and women is that gender roles encourage different social responses to drug and alcohol use by men and by women. There is no evidence that confusion about one's gender identity is a cause of substance abuse; in fact, for both men and women, it would appear that patterns of substance abuse are consistent with images of masculinity and femininity in the culture. But, according to traditional gender roles, women are not expected to drink and use drugs to the same extent as men. Indeed, women who become alcoholics tend to be perceived as more masculine and "hard" than other women, indicating that this violates expected roles for women. Women heroin addicts are also seen as more deviant, more reprehensible, and less treatable than male addicts. So, while traditional gender roles may protect women from substance abuse, they also pose constraints on the treatment and societal reaction to women with substance abuse problems.

—Margaret L. Anderson, *Thinking About Women*

Exercise 8G

Read the excerpt from Life in a Mexican Village: Tepoztlán Restudied, *and identify the dominant pattern of organization. Then determine the key idea and the subtopics of the passage.*

Life in a Mexican Village: Tepoztlán Restudied

Collective Labor

Collective labor, known as the *cuatequitl*, is in all probability an ancient tradition in Tepoztlán. At present it takes a number of forms, the village *cuatequitl*, the barrio *cuatequitl*, the *cuatequitl* of neighbors, and, on rare occasions, an inter-village *cuatequitl*. The village *cuatequitl* is a compulsory form of collective labor organized by the village authorities for public works such as improving the roads, constructing public buildings, or doing other work which, in theory, will benefit the village as a whole. Each able-bodied man between ages twenty-one and fifty can be called upon for service to the community. Failure to respond to such a call is punishable by a fine or jail sentence. However, a man can pay the daily wage of a substitute if desired. When the task is a relatively small one and more men are called up than are needed for the actual work, some are asked to contribute food or drink instead of labor.

The better-to-do families generally do not participate in the village *cuatequitl,* since they consider such work beneath their dignity and prefer to pay for substitutes. The main source of labor for the village *cuatequitl* are the poor who cannot afford substitutes or fines. The men from the smaller and poorer barrios have the reputation of being the most industrious and reliable workers for the *cuatequitl.* This is related to the fact that they have little political influence and have greater fear of the authorities.

The village *cuatequitl* is organized in terms of the eight *demarcaciones* or wards into which the village is divided. The *ayudante* or representative of each *demarcación* is ordered to announce a *cuatequitl* in his ward, and specific men are designated to appear at a given time and place. The attendance of the men is checked by the *ayudante* from his list.[1] Sometimes, when men are needed at short notice, more direct means are used to assure successful recruitment.

In a recent boundary dispute with the municipio of Tejalpa, the authorities posted aides at all the roads and paths leading out of the village to intercept the men as they went to their fields early in the morning. In this way 600 men were recruited in one day, and they were set to work to cut through the forest overgrowth which covered the disputed boundary line. In this case, since it was a municipio boundary, men from the other villages were also recruited. Other instances of inter-village *cuatequitl* have occurred in the repair of bridges which are used in common.

In recent years there have been very few village *cuatequitls* of major importance. In 1934 some work was done to improve the market place. The last important village *cuatequitl* was organized in 1926–27 while Redfield was in the vil-

---

[1]Some men will work until the check-off and then slip away.

lage.² At this time, under the initiative of the local political faction known as the Bolsheviki, communal washbasins were constructed. During the twenties, political feelings ran so high and cleavages were so marked that members of the opposition group refused to work in *cuatequitls* organized by those in power. Fines were out of the question at the time because authority could not be enforced.

During the early thirties, when political schisms were still strong, there occurred an unusual type of voluntary village *cuatequitl* for the construction of the road to Cuernavaca. Led by two enterprising non-Tepoztecan schoolteachers and with the backing of the colony of Tepoztecans in Mexico City, the villagers decided to build a road to Cuernavaca. The two political factions, the Bolsheviki and the Fraternales, refused to work side by side, and each organized separate shifts, one beginning at Tepoztlán and working toward Cuernavaca, the other working from Cuernavaca toward Tepoztlán.

Although the village *cuatequitl* is intended as a means of aiding the village as a whole, there are many obstacles to its successful operation, and it is gradually declining. Perhaps the fundamental difficulty is the inherent individualism of Tepoztecans, the suspiciousness and critical attitude toward the local government, and the paucity of local funds. The village *cuatequitl* has been traditionally associated in the minds of the villagers as a coercive rather than a voluntary institution. This may be the result of having lived under an authoritarian system in which the local government had been imposed for years. Since the local government, generally the *síndico* or the presidents has the power to designate the citizens who are to work in the *cuatequitl*, there is ample opportunity for favoritism and vengeance against political opponents or personal enemies.

It may be significant in this connection that children in their games will often say, "Unless you do this I will give you your *cuatequitl*," suggesting that the *cuatequitl* is viewed as a punishment. It should also be noted that historically the existence of a native institution for collective labor was a distinct aid to the Spanish conquerors in their organization and control of the labor supply.

The second type of *cuatequitl* is the barrio *cuatequitl*. This is the collective working of the lands of the barrio

---

²Before the Revolution, when there was more money in the local treasury and when the local government was in the hands of *caciques* whose tenure was quite stable, there were many more *cuatequitls* than now.

saints. Barrio members are expected to cooperate in the preparation of the land, planting, cultivating, and harvesting of the crops from the saints' field. The sale of the produce goes for the upkeep of the local chapel. In contrast to the village *cuatequitl*, participation in the barrio *cuatequitl* is entirely voluntary. The barrio *mayordomo* goes through the barrio announcing at each house the time of the *cuatequitl*. While there are no fines or penalties for nonparticipation, there is strong social pressure as well as fear that the saint may be offended by failure to work for his upkeep. Still, in recent years there has been increasing difficulty in obtaining barrio cooperation. Now three of the seven barrios rent out the land and use the rental for the expenses of the chapel.

The barrio *cuatequitl* cleans the churchyard and repairs the chapel. Barrio differences in this connection are interesting. Although the smaller barrios of San Pedro, San Sebastián, and Los Reyes are the most reliable workers on the village *cuatequitl*, they appear to be the most neglectful in the upkeep of their respective chapels, indicating perhaps that Catholicism has less of a hold in these barrios. Indeed, it was in the barrio of San Sebastián that a Protestant sect won over about fifteen families. The barrio of Santa Cruz, also very poor, is known for its superior care and great devotion to its chapel. The larger barrios, too, keep their chapels in repair.

The third occasion for the *cuatequitl* is that of a group of neighbors within the barrio who may agree among themselves to repair the street or to build a water tank or some other local improvement. This *cuatequitl* generally involves fewer people and still occurs quite frequently. During our visit to the village four new water founts were built in this way. The *cuatequitl* of the barrio and of neighbors would seem to be a natural mechanism for a great deal of cooperative endeavor on a purely voluntary basis. But the poor quality of human relations in the village, and the fear to take the initiative in any venture, keep cooperative undertakings at a minimum. Yet the fact that there exists a tradition of cooperative forms of labor has occasionally led to truly heroic and dramatic undertakings. The most recent example of this was the construction of the road to Cuernavaca.

—Oscar Lewis, *Life in a Mexican Village: Tepoztlán Restudied*

1. Pattern: _____

2. Key idea: _____

3. Subtopics: _____

_____

_____

Exercise 8H

Preview and read "Daydreams and Fantasies: What Function Do They Serve?" and determine the principal pattern of organization. Then identify the introduction, development, and conclusion by marking them on the text, and circle the signal words.

Daydreams and Fantasies: What Function Do They Serve?

1   If people spend a considerable amount of time engaging in daydreams and fantasies—changing their own consciousness, if you will—then these activities must serve some useful functions. But what, precisely, do they accomplish? No clear-cut answer to this question has as yet emerged, but existing evidence points to several interesting possibilities.

2   First, daydreams and fantasies may serve as a kind of safety valve, permitting persons to escape, however briefly, from the stress and boredom of everyday life. Perhaps this is one reason why many students tend to daydream in class or while reading their textbooks. (Not this one, I hope!)

3   Second, daydreams and fantasies often provide us with a ready means of altering our own moods, primarily in a positive direction. If you've ever felt happier after a daydream filled with desirable activities and events, you are already familiar with such benefits (Forgas & Bower, 1988).

4   Third, it is possible that daydreams and fantasies help people find solutions to actual problems in their lives. By imagining various behaviors and the outcomes they may produce, we can examine potential courses of action carefully and from the safe perspective of our own minds. This can help us formulate useful plans of action.

5   Finally, fantasies may play an important role in the self-regulation of behavior. By imagining negative outcomes, people may strengthen their inhibitions against dangerous or prohibited behaviors (Bandura, 1986). Similarly, by dreaming about potential rewards, people may enhance their own

motivation and performance. In sum, fantasies and daydreams may be much more than a pleasant diversion; they may actually yield substantial benefits to those who choose to induce them.

—Robert A. Baron, *Essentials of Psychology*

Pattern of organization: _____

Exercise 8I

Preview and read "Threats to the Natural Environment," an example of the problem-solution pattern of organization. Label each part of the reading—problem, cause, effect, and solution. Then fill in the blanks on page 205.

Threats to the Natural Environment

1   Of future concern is the fact that in contrast to many of the more industrial nations which have implemented policies to restore harvested woodlands, the Third World tends to perceive the forests as a perpetual rather than a renewable resource. We need only examine two factors to recognize the impending crisis: the rate of recovery for damaged forests and the ratio of acres deforested versus acres replanted in developing regions. One indicator of recovery is the *total biomass*—the point where there is no total restoration of living plant matter on a forested area. Research on tropical forests has found that after slash-and-burn farming, total recovery of the biomass accumulation would take at least 150 years. When the forested land experienced prolonged degradation, such as use as a pasture, the rate of recovery is slowed. When the land was subjected to extreme abuse, like clearing by a bulldozer, "close to 1000 years may pass before biomass levels reach those of mature forest" (Uhl, 1983).

2   The second factor is the ration of deforested areas to replanted ones: in Asia, one acre is planted for every five harvested; in Latin America, one acre in ten is replaced; and in Africa, one acre is replanted for every twenty-nine acres deforested. The United Nations Food and Agriculture Organization projects that by the year 2000, over half the world's developing population either will be lacking adequate fuelwood or will be depleting the existing supply to meet their needs....

Just as the need to compensate for the loss of soil leads to the need to extend farmlands into wooded areas, deforestation also has its impact on the ecosystem. First, when trees and ground cover are removed, the interaction between vegetation and the soil is disrupted. Moreover, in areas where trees serve to shield crops from severe wind, both wind and water erosion increase significantly. In semiarid regions, the removal of trees results in expanding deserts, a process known as *desertification.* Second, the ecological system is further altered because deforested areas fail to return rainfall to the atmosphere. In comparison to the normal rainforest where 74 percent of rainfall is returned to the atmosphere, only 25 percent of rainfall in deforested areas finds its way back into ecological cycle. This means that the earth must adapt itself to three times the normal amount of run-off rainfall, which causes more soil erosion. The natural cycle is further disrupted, because when the amount of moisture returned to the atmosphere is reduced, the level of rainfall in the adjacent area is reduced accordingly, a situation which could lead to droughts and other problematic conditions.

Hopefully, the preceding discussion has given you some understanding of the ecological process and the interrelationships among its various elements. What should be apparent is the fact that even natural resources that are generally considered inexhaustible can be depleted significantly because of misuse. Moreover, the misuse of one resource can lead to problems in related elements of the ecosystem. Fortunately, the ecological problems related to rainfall, soil, and forests can be remedied if proper measures are taken to conserve and renew the existing reserves. Often, the solution to the problem is quite simple. For example, the introduction of vetiver grass, a deep rooted and thickly tufted grass commonly referred to as *klus,* in the Deccan Plateau region in southern India has ended years of flooding and soil erosion. The farmers in the Deccan Plateau, who like most of their counterparts in developing nations had cleared the forests, enjoyed a 300 percent increase in their crops only three years after the klus was planted.

—Daniel J. Curran and Claire M. Renzetti, *Social Problems*

1. Key idea: _____

2. Subtopics: _____

_____

Summary Exercise

Briefly explain the patterns of organization, giving examples of signal words used in each pattern. Which pattern(s) of organization did you use to write your summary?

Chapter 9

Becoming a Critical Reader: Determining the Author's Purpose

In this chapter you will find answers to these questions:

Which preview question helps you determine an author's purpose?

What qualities distinguish a critical reader?

What is the major difference between informational writing and persuasive writing?

What techniques do authors use to convey their points of view?

Why do authors use connotative and figurative language?

Most nonfiction is written to inform the reader about something or to persuade the reader to believe or do something. What does the author want the reader to know or to believe or do? Is the author writing to tell you about something, to transfer information from his or her head to yours? Does the author want to convince you of something or persuade you to take certain actions or think along certain lines? Is the author recounting an experience or telling a story? Knowing the author's purpose helps you determine your task as a reader and how to accomplish it.

It is important to realize that authors frequently do not state explicitly why they are writing a particular selection. **Critical reading** begins with being able to recognize whether an author is writing to inform or to persuade. You, the reader, must infer the author's purpose by reading "between the lines." A critical reader is as interested in why or how something is written as in what is written. You can learn to distinguish between **informational writing** and **persuasive writing** by becoming aware of the clues that indicate the author's purpose.

Distinguishing between Informational Writing and Persuasive Writing

You can assume that in informational writing, the data are presented in a straightforward, objective manner. The author presents facts and explains the material. A direct transmission of knowledge takes place, with no argument involved. The author does not try to convince you of anything but simply gives you the facts as he or she knows them. News articles, for example, are written to inform. When, however, the author's purpose is to persuade, he or she wants you to accept an argument, to take action, or to change your behavior or attitude. The author states a position, an opinion, and tries to support it by citing facts and authorities and by reasoning from evidence. Newspaper editorials are good examples of persuasive writing. Persuasive writing needs to be read with close attention to the supporting evidence it presents.

The first step in determining an author's purpose is to ask the preview question, *Why did the author write this?* Sometimes you can learn the author's purpose simply by asking this question as you read the title or by knowing something about the author's background. The title *Problem Solving and Structured Programming in Pascal,* for example, tells you that the author's purpose is to explain programming in the computer language Pascal; the author is writing to inform you. In contrast, the title "What the Human Mind Can Do That the Computer Can't" tells you that the author wants to persuade you that computers cannot do everything the mind can do. And an article written by a member of the National Rifle Association will probably try to convince you that gun control limits constitutional freedoms.

Exercise 9A

From reading the following descriptions, do you think the author is trying to inform or to persuade? Write your answer on the line that follows each description.

1. "The Special Theory of Relativity," by James Q. Coleman, a distinguished physicist who has done theoretical research on guided missiles at Johns Hopkins University

   _____

2. *The Civil War: A Northern Perspective*, by Ulysses S. Grant, general of the Union Armies

   _____

3. *Eat to Win*, by Dr. Robert Haas

   _____

4. *Desert: The American Southwest*, by Ruth Kirk, a nature writer and photographer

   _____

5. "Why You Should Become a Nurse," by Jane Sherman, director of a graduate nursing program

   _____

If the author's purpose is not clear from the title, you need to look further. As you learned in the chapter about previewing, it is helpful to pay special attention to the introduction of a reading, because frequently this section is where you will find the author's intent. If you still cannot find or infer the author's purpose, then continue to read the selection and continue to ask, *Why did the author write this?*

In the following introductory paragraph, the author is writing to inform you about a specific aspect of Japanese painting.

> The floating silk thread line of Japanese painting was introduced by the Tosa school of artists eight hundred years ago and has been in favor ever since. It is the purest or standard line and is reserved for the robes of elevated personages. The brush is held firmly and the lines, made to resemble silk

threads drawn from the cocoon, are executed with a free and uninterrupted movement of the arm.

—Henry P. Bowie, *On the Laws of Japanese Painting*

In contrast, the author of the following selection is writing to persuade you. He wants to convince you of the constitutional right of self-determination, particularly as it pertains to terminating life-sustaining treatment.

Every competent adult is considered to be the master of his own body. He may treat it wisely or foolishly. He may even refuse life-saving treatment, and it's nobody else's business. Certainly not the state's. That is the law of the land.

Cold comfort for Peter Cinque of Lynbrook, L.I., who, locked in like an uncharged prisoner, was kept joined to a life-sustaining device—from which he had begged to be released—until reduced to a comatose, vegetative state. His last few days were shorn of dignity, his family was humiliated and his death became a media event.

—Willard Gaylin, "Still, a Prisoner Owns Himself"

The discussion of the characteristics and examples of informational writing and persuasive writing in this and the next chapter will also help you to differentiate between them and to define your task as reader.

Informational Writing

Articles in which authors want to tell you about something, such as the taking of a picture or the performing of an experiment; a journal article outlining a research program in the social, natural, or physical sciences; a geology textbook; a newspaper report—all of these are examples of informational writing. If you determine that the author's purpose is to inform, you know that she or he will try to present the material as clearly as possible so that you can easily understand and that she or he will use facts to support the key idea. The author will present ideas by using the patterns of organization you learned in Chapter 8. The pattern might list various detailed applications to illustrate a new concept; it might order information according to some scheme like time, importance, or place; it might compare or contrast to make an explanation more vivid; it might present the causes of an event. In each case, the author develops the basic topic and key idea by providing generalizations or informational statements supported by factual details and illustrations that explain, clarify, emphasize, and develop.

The following passage is an example of informational writing. The author's key idea is the healing process of a broken bone. The supporting ideas include the sequence of events that occur during that process. The author does not try to convince you, the reader, of anything, but rather, presents the facts that explain the way a broken bone mends.

Sticks and Stones—The Repair of Broken Bones

1 With a thud accompanied by a sickening crack, a boy falls from high in a tree amidst a cracking of small branches and a shower of leaves. The rapidly swelling, awkwardly bent forearm confirms his parents' worst fears: a bone is broken. Let's examine the sequence of events that occur during the next 6 weeks or so, as the bone heals.

2 First, blood from ruptured vessels forms a large clot surrounding the break. Phagocytic cells and osteoclasts in the blood ingest and dissolve the cellular debris and bone fragments.

3 Second, bones are normally covered with a thin layer of connective tissue (the **periosteum**), rich in capillaries, osteoblasts, and osteoblast-forming cells. A fracture ruptures the periosteum and stimulates the production and release of numerous osteoblasts. These, in conjunction with cartilage-forming cells, secrete a porous mass of bone and cartilage called a **callus** surrounding the break. The callus replaces the original blood clot, and holds the ends of the bones together while remodeling processes re-form the original shape of the bone.

4 Third, osteoclasts, osteoblasts, and capillaries invade the callus. Nourished by the capillaries, osteoclasts break down the cartilage, while osteoblasts replace it with bone.

5 Finally, osteoclasts remove excess bone, restoring the original shape.

—Gerald Audesirk and Teresa Audesirk, *Biology*

You, too, write informationally. When you write an account of a trip, you are giving information, when you tell someone how to do an experiment, you are transmitting knowledge, when you describe the actions of the opposing sides in the French and Indian Wars, you are imparting the relevant facts to the extent you know them. In none of these cases are you trying to convince the reader to think in a certain way or take a specific action.

Exercise 9B

Preview and read the following two examples of informational writing. Then answer the question, What is the author's most important idea about the topic? Write the key idea, the subtopics, and the supporting ideas of each selection on the lines provided.

1. Attitudinal Analysis

1   It is important for a speaker to distinguish among *attitudes, beliefs, and values*. The attitudes, beliefs, and values of an audience may greatly influence a speaker's selection of a topic and specific purpose, as well as various other aspects of speech preparation and delivery.

2   An attitude reflects likes or dislikes. Do you like health food? Are you for or against capital punishment? Do you think that it is important to learn cardiopulmonary resusitation (CPR)? Should movies be censored? What are your views of nuclear energy? Your answer to these widely varied questions will express your attitudes.

3   A belief is what you hold to be true or false. Beliefs underlie attitudes. Why do you like health food? You may believe that natural products are better for your health. That belief explains your positive attitude. Why are you against capital punishment? You may believe that it is wrong to kill people for any reason. Again, your belief explains your attitude. It is useful for a speaker to probe audience beliefs. If the speaker can understand why audience members feel the way they do about a topic, he or she may be able to address that underlying belief, whether trying to change an attitude or reinforce one.

4   Values are enduring concepts of good and bad, right and wrong. More deeply ingrained than either attitudes or beliefs, they are therefore more resistant to change. Values support both attitudes and beliefs. For example, you like healthy food because you believe that natural products are more healthful. And you value good health. You are against capital punishment because you believe that it is wrong to kill people. You value human life. As with beliefs, a speaker who has some

understanding of an audience's values will be better able to adapt a speech to them.

—Steven A. Beebee and Susan J. Beebee, *Public Speaking*

a. Key idea: _____

b. Subtopic: _____

c. Supporting idea: _____

d. Subtopic: _____

e. Supporting idea: _____

f. Subtopic: _____

g. Supporting idea: _____

2. Personal Saving

Economists define saving as "that part of after-tax income which is not consumed"; hence, households, have just two choices with their incomes after taxes—to consume or to save.

Saving is defined as that portion of current (this year's) income not paid out in taxes or in the purchase of consumer goods, but which flows into bank accounts, insurance policies, bonds and stocks, and other financial assets.

Reasons for saving are many and diverse, but they center around security and speculation. Households save to provide a nest egg for unforeseen contingencies—sickness, accident, unemployment—for retirement from the work force, to finance the education of children, or simply for the overall financial security of one's family. On the other hand, saving might well occur for speculation. One might channel part of one's income to the purchase of securities, speculating as to increases in their monetary values.

The desire or willingness to save, however, is not enough. This willingness must be accompanied by the ability to save, which depends basically on the size of one's income. If income is very low, households may dissave; that is, they may consume in excess of their after-tax incomes. They do this by borrowing and by digging into savings they may have accumulated in years when their incomes were higher. However, both saving and consumption vary directly with income; as households get more income they divide it between saving and consumption. In fact, the top 10 percent of income receivers account for most of the personal saving in our society.

—Campbell R. McConnell and Stanley L. Brue,
Economics: Principles, Problems, and Policies

a. Key idea: _____

b. Subtopics: _____

_____

_____

c. Supporting ideas: _____

_____

_____

_____

Persuasive Writing

Authors writing to persuade the reader build on writing to inform the reader; however, the interaction between the reader and the author becomes more direct when the author's purpose is to persuade than when it is just to inform. When writing to persuade, the author is trying to engage the reader in order to obtain the desired response. Whereas with informational writing the reader has the task of gathering and digesting information, with persuasive writing the reader must also identify the author's point of view and understand what the author wants the reader to do with this knowledge. As reader, you need to read critically to **evaluate** the author's ideas and to judge whether and how the author has supported his or her convictions.

You can also ask more specific questions to find the key idea of persuasive writing than you can when you are looking for the key idea of informational writing. Rather than asking the question, *What is the author's most important idea about the topic?* you can find the key idea of persuasive writing by asking, *What is the author trying to persuade me of?* or *What is the author trying to prove?* The answer to these latter questions may be called an assertion, a proposition, an opinion, a claim, a thesis, a generalization, or a conclusion. If the key idea of a reading selection is that frustrated children tend to become aggressive, this thought is the author's assertion and answers the question, *What is the author trying to prove?* The author wants to convince you that frustrated children behave this way. What does the author want to persuade you of if the assertion is that decent housing for all people is possible? The author wants you to believe that all people could have adequate housing.

Although the author of the following example of persuasive writing does not explicitly state why he wrote it, you can infer that he is trying to prove something; he presents his assertion that "Despite its [Brazil's] receptive splendors, this development is a banquet to which few are invited" and supports it with specific examples of this situation. He wants to convince you that Brazil's economy benefits only some people.

Surplus People, Surplus Regions

"Grow with Brazil." Display ads in New York newspapers exhort U.S. businessmen to join the precipitous growth of the giant of the tropics. The city of São Paulo sleeps with its eyes open. The din of development shatters its eardrums; factories and skyscrapers, bridges and highways, sprout with the suddenness of tropical plants. But if accuracy had a place in publicity, the slogan would be: "Grow *at the expense of* Brazil." Despite its deceptive splendors, this development is a banquet to which few are invited and whose main dishes are reserved for foreign stomachs. Brazil already had ninety million inhabitants and will double that number by the end of the century, but its modern factories economize on labor and, in the hinterland, the intact latifundio [area of large estates] is no more promising a source of jobs. A small boy in rags gazes with shining eyes at the world's longest tunnel, recently opened in Rio de Janeiro. The ragged boy is rightly proud of his country, but he is illiterate and steals in order to eat.

—Eduardo Galeano, *Open Veins of Latin America*

Exercise 9C

Preview and read the following examples of persuasive writing. On the line after each reading, write the answer to the question, What is the author trying to persuade me of or to prove?—*that is, the key idea*.

1. Teacher Expectations and Student Achievement

Researchers have studied teacher expectations for the last twenty-five years. Early studies of teacher expectations and student achievement have led educators to emphasize the importance of having high expectations for all students.

A recent study of teacher expectations by Goldenberg (1992) revealed that teacher expectations can be a mitigating factor. Goldenberg studied two first-grade Hispanic girls in the same classroom. The teacher held low expectations for one girl and high expectations for the other. Contrary to the theme of the earlier expectations studies, the student that had lower teacher expectations did well in reading achievement, while the student with high teacher expectations did not do well! Goldenberg observed the students and the teacher carefully for long periods of time and was able to explain why these unexpected findings occurred, as well as point out a very important lesson about the way more effective teachers teach.

Goldenberg observed that although the teacher held different expectations for the two students, the teacher's behaviors were not influenced in the same way. The teacher worked very hard to help the low-expectation student engage with and complete assignments. The teacher understood that this student would need extra attention. At the same time, although the high-expectation student was not completing assignments, the teacher "assumed" that she would succeed and so did not monitor and push the student. The result was that the low-expectation student succeeded and the high-expectation student did not.

Goldenberg concluded: "My principal contention is that the teacher's behavior is what matters—what a teacher expects matters less than what a teacher does."

—James A. Johnson, et al., *Introduction to the Foundations of American Education*

Key idea: _____

2. Hypnosis: Contrasting Views about Its Nature

What does hypnosis involve? In other words, what changes—if any—does it produce in consciousness and other psychological processes? Systematic research has led to the formulation of two major theories of the nature of hypnosis.

The Social-Cognitive or Role-Playing View

The first of these views suggests that the seemingly strange and mysterious effects of hypnosis can best be understood by reference to the relationship between hypnotized persons and the hypnotist. Specifically, this theory argues that hypnotized persons are actually playing a *special social role*—that of *hypnotic subject*. Having seen movies and read stories about hypnosis, most people have a clear idea of what it supposedly involves. They believe that when hypnotized they will lose control over their own behavior and will be unable to resist strong suggestions from the hypnotist. When exposed to hypnotic inductions (instructions to behave in a certain way or to experience specific feelings), therefore, many people tend to obey, since this is what the social role they are enacting suggests *should* happen. Further, they often report experiencing the changes in perceptions and feelings that they *expect* to experience (e.g., Lynn, Rhue, & Weekes, 1990; Spanos, 1991).

It's important to note that this does not mean that persons undergoing hypnosis engage in conscious efforts to fool others. On the contrary, they sincerely believe that they are experiencing an altered state of consciousness and that they have no choice but to act and feel as the hypnotist suggests. Thus, in an important sense, their behavior and their reports of their experiences while hypnotized are genuine (Kinnunen, Zamansky, & Block, 1994). These behaviors and experiences, however, reflect beliefs about hypnosis and the role of hypnotic subject as much as—or perhaps even more than—the special skills of the hypnotist or the effects of hypnosis on consciousness.

The Neodissociation Theory

The second major theory of hypnosis is very different. The **neodissociation theory** suggests that hypnosis operates by inducing two kinds of splits or *dissociations* in consciousness (Bowers, 1990; Hilgard, 1977). The first of these, *dissociated experience*, involves the erection by hypnosis of an amnesia-like barrier that prevents experiences during hypnosis from entering normal consciousness. The second split, known as *dissociated control*, implies a split in normal control over behavior. Persons who have been hypnotized, the theory argues, obey suggestions from the hypnotist in a direct, uncritical fashion; the higher centers of control or *will* are essentially cut out of the picture. According to Hilgard (1977), then, persons who have been hypnotized are in an altered state of consciousness in which one part of their mind accepts suggestions from the hypnotist, while the other part (which Hilgard terms "the hidden observer") observes the procedures without participating in them. So, for example, if hypnotized persons are told to put their arms into icy water but told that they will experience no pain, they will obey and will report no discomfort. However, if asked to describe their feelings in writing, they may indicate that they did experience feelings of intense cold (Hilgard, 1979). So it seems as if one part of consciousness obeys hypnotic suggestions while another does not.

Which of these theories is correct? While support for both views exists (e.g., Miller & Bowers, 1993), most psychologists believe that the social-cognitive view is more accurate. It appears that most of the unusual or bizarre effects observed under hypnosis can readily be explained in terms of hypnotized persons' belief in the effects of hypnotism and their efforts—not necessarily conscious—to behave in accordance with their expectations and the hypnotist's suggestions. Several forms of evidence lend support to this conclusion.

Evidence for the Social-Cognitive View of Hypnosis

First, consider the potential effects of hypnosis on memory. Can hypnotism help people remember events they have forgotten? This is an important question, for as we'll see in Chapter 6, hypnotism is sometimes used to help eyewitnesses to crimes "remember" events they have observed (Loftus, 1993). Critics of such procedures suggest that, in fact, hypnotism does not improve memory: All it does is induce hypnotized persons to remember what the hypnotist suggests they *should* remember. However, research on this issue indicates that when offered rewards for being accurate, hypnotized persons can do so, despite suggestions from the hypnotist (Murrey, Cross, & Whipple, 1992). These findings suggest that hypnotism does not produce actual changes in memory; rather, it simply suggests to hypnotized persons what they should remember—a conclusion consistent with the social-cognitive view.

Additional evidence for the social-cognitive view is provided by studies focused on the question of whether hypnotism produces actual changes in perception—for example, whether hypnotism can induce people to perceive stimuli that aren't there or render them incapable of perceiving stimuli that are present (Miller & Bowers, 1993; Spanos et al., 1990). Again, the weight of existing evidence suggests that when such effects occur, they do not stem from real changes in perception; rather, they arise out of efforts by hypnotized persons to behave as they think the hypnotist wants them to behave.

In sum, existing evidence offers considerable support for the conclusion that the effects of hypnosis stem mainly from efforts (perhaps unconscious ones) by hypnotized persons to meet the expectations of the hypnotist, plus their beliefs concerning the powerful impact of hypnotism. This does not imply that hypnotism is a fraud or involves actual faking. On the contrary, in describing their experiences when hypnotized, most persons appear to be quite truthful (Kinnumen, Zamansky, & Block, 1994). What existing evidence *does* suggest, in brief, is that hypnotism is better understood in terms of such processes as influence and demand characteristics than in terms of mystical powers of hypnotists.

—Robert A. Baron, *Essentials of Psychology*

Key idea: _____

3. Early one morning I received a telephone call from a friend—the mother of a five-year-old boy. "I'm calling from upstairs," she said in a low voice: "so Greg won't hear this." There was a pause. "Ernest died this morning! What shall I tell Greg?" "How terrible!" I said. "But who is Ernest?" "Ernest is Greg's hamster!" she said. "This will break his heart. I don't know how to tell him. Bill is going to stop off at the pet shop on his way home from work tonight and pick up a new hamster, but I just dread breaking the news to Greg. Please tell me what to say to him." "Why don't you tell him that his hamster died?" I said. "Died!" said my friend, shrinking at my crudity. "What I want to know is how I can break the news gently to him and spare him the pain of this whole experience! I thought I would tell him that Ernest went to heaven. Would it be all right to tell him that?" "Only if you're sure that Ernest went to heaven," I said in my best consulting-room voice. "Oh, stop!" my friend begged. "This is very serious. I don't mean the hamster. I mean this is Greg's first experience with death. I don't want him to be hurt."

"All right," I said. "Then what right do we have to deprive Greg of his feelings? Why isn't he entitled to his grief over the death of his pet? Why can't he cry and why can't he feel the full measure of pain that comes with the discovery that death is an end and that Ernest is no more?" "But he's only a child!" said my friend. "How can he possibly know what death means?" "But isn't this how he will know what death means? Do we ever know more about death than this- the reaction to the loss of someone loved?"

And so we argued, my friend wanting to prevent her son from feeling a loss and I defending Greg's human rights in feeling a loss. I think I finally convinced Greg's mother when I told her that Greg would be better able to endure the loss of his pet if we allowed him to realize the experience fully, to feel all he needed to feel.

In our efforts to protect children from painful emotions we may deprive them of their own best means of mastering painful experiences. Mourning, even if it is mourning for a dead hamster, is a necessary measure for overcoming the effects of loss. A child who is not allowed feelings of grief over a pet or a more significant loss is obliged to fall back on more primitive measures of defense, to deny the pain of loss, for example, and to feel nothing. If a child were consistently reared on this basis, deprived of the possibility of experiencing grief, he would become an impoverished person, without quality or depth in his emotional life. We need to respect a child's right to experience a loss fully and deeply. This means, too, that we do not bury the dead pet and rush to the pet store for a replacement. This is a devaluation of a child's love. It is like saying to him, "Don't feel badly; your love is not important; all hamsters, all dogs, all cats are replaceable, and you can love one as well as another." But if all loved things are readily replaceable what does a child learn about love or loss? The time for replacing the lost pet is when mourning has done its work and the child himself is ready to attach himself to a new animal.

Other stories come to mind which illustrate the problems of parents in dealing with the painful emotions of children. I once knew a little boy who was unable to cry and reacted to loss and to separations from loved persons with an inscrutable indifference, although he regularly produced allergic symptoms at such times. Often he spoke to me about his grandfather whom he had loved dearly and who died when my patient was five. He had many memories of his grandfather and spoke of him with much affection, but he had no memory of the grandfather's death or the year that followed his death. Neither was there any emotion attached to the idea of grandfather's death. But the death of the grandfather had been a great calamity in this child's family and the circumstances of the death were tragic in the extreme. Why was nothing of this remembered? And why was there no emotion attached to the loss of the grandfather or to death or separation from loved persons? All of this was exceedingly complex, but one very significant factor was the reaction of the child's mother at the time of the grandfather's death. Her own grief had been nearly unsupportable, but she was determined not to break down in the presence of the children: "It would make things harder for them." With heroic self-discipline she contained her feelings and presented a facade of her accustomed self to the children. With this I could understand my patient's strange reaction to death and loss. It was not "indifference" as it appeared on the surface, but an identification with his mother's outward behavior at the time of his grandfather's death. Since mother had not permitted her own grief to be revealed, the child behaved as if grief were an impermissible emotion. His suppressed longing to cry could only be satisfied by the symptomatic weeping that accompanied his allergy. It would have been much better for this child if his mother had not concealed her grief from him, for if he could have shared her grief in some way he would have received permission, as it were, to have his own feelings, and mourning for the loved grandfather would have helped him to overcome the shock of his death.

—Selma Fraiberg, *Magic Years*

Key idea: _____

The Author's Techniques

After you have determined what the author wants to prove, you look for how the author tries to persuade you—the ways in which authors employ basic structure, patterns of organization, and connotative and figurative language as techniques to try to get you to believe their points of view.

Basic Structure and Patterns of Organization

Persuasive writing may be introduced with the author's stating the assertion and providing background information about the situation. The development of such a reading includes the reasons and evidence that support the author's belief. And the conclusion appeals to the reader to agree with the writer's opinion. It is important to note, however, that to engage the reader, the supporting material is sometimes placed first and the proposition at the end.

Recognizing the patterns of organization authors use in persuasive writing also helps you evaluate how an author tries to convince you. Although all patterns of organization are evident in persuasive writing, three you will encounter often are compare/contrast, cause-and-effect, and problem-solution. If an author wants to persuade you that you will be more successful if you study business rather than liberal arts, he or she may compare and contrast the income of people in these two fields, making sure the data show that people who have studied business earn more money than liberal arts graduates do. If an author wants you to believe that vitamins are good for you, he or she may present the beneficial effects of taking vitamins. And if an author wants you to take action against the use of alcohol on campus, he or she may first explain the problem of too much drinking on campus, next present the causes and effects of this situation, and then try to convince you that you should work toward alleviating the problem.

Connotative and Figurative Language

Authors also use language to try to convince you of their points of view. They influence your perception of reality by deliberately choosing words that may cause you to react in a certain way because the words create a visual image and appeal to your emotions or biases. Connotative language and figurative language are two types of emotive language that an author may use to express and arouse emotion.

In contrast to a word's **denotation**—its literal meaning—is a word's **connotation.** The connotation of a word is its *implied* meaning, one suggested by or reflecting people's attitudes or what they associate with that word. Although the words *thrifty* and *cheap* have similar denotations, if an author wanted to elicit a negative response about someone's character, he or she would choose *cheap* rather than *thrifty,* because a *cheap* person is seen as being stingy or miserly, and a *thrifty* person as being industrious and good at managing money. As a critical reader, you need to be alert to the negative or positive connotations of words an author may use in persuasive writing.

Exercise 9D

For the items below, put a plus sign (+) next to the words or phrases that evoke a positive response and a minus sign (–) next to the words or phrases that evoke a negative response.

Example: _+_ thrifty _–_ cheap

a. _____ gullible   _____ trusting

b. _____ proud   _____ conceited

c. _____ childlike   _____ childish

d. _____ militant   _____ politically active

e. _____ aroma   _____ smell

f. _____ odor   _____ fragrance

g. _____ noise   _____ racket

h. _____ story   _____ tall tale

i. _____ chatter   _____ speak

j. _____ slender   _____ skinny

You probably hear and use figurative language every day. The sports pages' headlines may say "Sox Pound A's" or "Cubs Rip Pirates." Neither team is violently demolishing another, of course, but these words create a vivid image, and you, the reader, understand who the winners and losers of these decisively won games were. Or if you say, "John eats like a pig," you are speaking figuratively. You do not mean that John actually rolls around in the mud and eats food as pigs do. Instead, you are conveying a message about the way John puts food into his mouth, and your audience "sees" how he does so. Figurative language shows comparison by representing one concept in terms of another.

Exercise 9E

Refer to the readings in Exercise 9C (see pp. 215-221) and answer the following questions,

1. From *Teacher Expectations and Student Achievement*

   a. How does the author want you to react to the title, *Teacher Expectations and Student Achievement?* _____

   _____

   _____

   b. What is the principal pattern of organization of this selection? _____

   c. What are the subtopics? _____

   _____

   _____

2. From *Magic Years*

   a. In which paragraph does the introduction end? _____

   b. What is the purpose of the introduction in this selection?

   _____

   c. In which paragraph does the development end? _____

   d. Is the conclusion a summary, or is it a commentary? ____

   _____

   e. What are the subtopics? _____

   _____

   _____

f. What is the principal pattern of organization? _____

g. Does the author use connotative or figurative language? If so, cite examples and indicate type(s). _____

Summary Exercise

How do you distinguish between informational writing and persuasive writing?

Chapter 10

Becoming a Critical Reader: Evaluating Evidence and Reasoning

In this chapter you will find answers to the following questions:

Why is it important to consider the author's credibility and possible bias?

How do you distinguish between fact and opinion?

What questions can you ask to evaluate facts?

How do you determine if the author's reasoning is valid?

In what ways do authors use emotional appeal?

In the previous chapter you took steps toward becoming a critical reader by learning to recognize an author's purpose. That process continues in this chapter as the focus moves to evaluating the evidence and reasoning that authors of persuasive writing use to support their points of view.

You encounter persuasion daily in conversations, advertisements, and newspaper editorials and letters to the editor. In fact, there are even times you try to persuade yourself to do something, as when you say to yourself, *It's time to study. I really must begin to study. I must turn off the television set. I won't pass the course unless I study.* Here you are trying to get yourself to take action and, by appealing to reason and emotion, are attempting to convince yourself to take that step. When authors try to persuade you to take action or believe something, they too provide evidence that appeals to reason and/or emotion. It is the assertion, or key idea, that an author will try to support with evidence and conclusions drawn from reasoned arguments. Your job as a critical reader is to evaluate that evidence and reasoning and then determine the author's persuasive effectiveness. You can read critically by asking the following questions:

- What are the author's credentials?
- Is the evidence sound?
- Is the reasoning logical?
- How is the author trying to persuade me?
- What supporting information does the author provide?

The Author's Credibility and Bias

The first thing to consider when evaluating persuasive writing is the author's credibility. Although you may not have sufficient knowledge of a discipline to conduct a thorough evaluation, you can learn something about the author by undertaking a simple investigation. Is the author an expert in the field? What are the author's credentials? A chemist analyzing the latest sociological trends is probably less well qualified than a sociologist writing about the same information. Usually, you can learn the author's credentials from the title page and preface of a book and from the information beneath the author's name or at the bottom of a page of an article. If a book or article does not offer such information before you begin reading the material, you may discover something about the author as you read the selection, or you can ask your instructor.

Assessing the author's bias is also important. Does the author have a special interest in persuading you of something? Was the author paid to advocate a position? Does the author gain anything if he or she succeeds in convincing you, or lose anything if he or she fails to convince you? If, for example, you read that drinking three beers a day is good for you, the fact that a spokesperson for the beer industry is making that statement will influence your perception of the legitimacy of the statement; the author's bias is clear.

You will find that informational writing is often contained in material written mainly to persuade, appearing there as part of the argument, although not an argument in itself. Unfortunately, the reverse is also true: Some writing that purports to be informational is also subtly persuasive, based on the bias of the author. For example, historical accounts of events may vary from author to author because the author's opinion influences the presentation of the material. The reporting of events during the Civil War may differ depending on whether the author is from the North or the South.

The following excerpt, from a sociology textbook, is not as free of opinion as you might expect. Rather than merely citing the social problems that exist, the authors also state and support their opinion that social change is the solution to these problems.

Social Problems

We have come to the end of this textbook on social problems. In it we have documented that although the United States is a wealthy nation, many Americans do not share the advantages of this abundance. Much of the suffering of the "have-nots," we have learned, is the result of inequalities that are built-in features of our social arrangements. That is, we live in a social system that itself breeds inequality—one in which a powerful few reap tremendous rewards, while the powerless majority get by as best they can. And we have seen here that the problems of American society frequently spill over into the world community and are tied to crises in other societies, many far less fortunate than our own.

Certainly, there are no easy solutions to any of these serious social problems, but the conflict perspective we've utilized throughout the text does suggest ways to bring about greater social justice.... [C]onflict theorists argue that what makes humans different from other animals is our ability to make rational choices and to transform our environment to better meet our needs. Although we are born into a social world with established social arrangements, our rationality allows us to evaluate this structure and to change it. Put another way, our "highest freedom is not simply [our] ability to take [a] place on the social ladder, but the opportunity to assume control over and constantly reshape the basic institutions of society" (Buell and De Luca, 1977:26). To conflict theorists, then, the solution to social problems starts with people purposely acting to change their social system.

Of course, not everyone will support social change. Those who benefit from existing social arrangements have a vested interest in preserving them. As one observer explains:

> I do not here suppose that the rich and/or powerful are incapable of or unwilling to re-examine and change the society. But I do assume that their understandable interests in remaining rich and/or powerful prevent them from making as critical an examination of the fundamentals of their society as would

be made by those whom the society is not serving so well (Harding, 1979:218).

Change, therefore, must be initiated by those who perceive that their needs and the needs of others like them are going unmet by existing institutions and policies. When this happens, a *social movement* is likely to form. A social movement is a group that has organized to promote a particular cause. Social movements are *issue-oriented*; their members take a stand for or against a specific social issue and work to get their position written into official public policy (Manis, 1984).

As we've already noted, two conditions must exist for a social movement to develop: first, individuals must recognize that the problems they are experiencing are shared by others like themselves and second, individuals must see the social system as the source of these problems. Both factors are critical catalysts for political action, because the dominant ideology of American society leads us to believe that social problems are the result of personal failures and that they could be solved if some people would just work a little harder. Consequently:

> Having a hard life and being a member of an exploited group does not in itself lead to political unrest.... Only when [people] see that their problems are shared by other people like them, the group, can they attribute the source of their concerns to social conditions, such as discrimination, and look to political solutions (Klein, 1984:2).

We have identified a number of social movements in the preceding chapters; the civil rights movement and the women's rights movement are two examples. These groups have mobilized their resources—e.g., money, political connections, or just their sheer numbers—to convince policy makers and the general public that they have legitimate claims and that their interests should be represented more fully and more fairly. Most of the movements we've discussed have broad-based support, but it's important to keep in mind that many of these started with small memberships, and that many small-scale movements are quite successful in achieving their goals. In any event, despite the variation in the sizes and strategies of social movements, what they share in common is their ardent intention to influence the course of social events.

Social movements are important precisely because they deliberately intervene in history. Their members are not content to be passive playthings of social forces; instead they try to affect the social order through direct action. Many of these movements, of course, have little or no impact, but others have brought about lasting and profound social and cultural changes. Our lives today would be utterly different had it not been for the efforts of the diverse social movements that were responsible for, say, the American Revolution, the abolition of slavery, the introduction of compulsory schooling, the extension of the vote to women, or the legalization of birth control devices (Robertson, 1983:582).

Indeed, anyone who doubts the power of a social movement to affect far-reaching change need only look to the Philippines where, in 1986, the Liberal Party, headed by Corazon Aquino, toppled the dictatorial government of Ferdinand Marcos, remarkably with relatively little bloodshed. The Liberal Party began as an opposition movement against the Marcos regime.

Short of a revolution, though, can anything be done to solve the social problems we've examined? As we stated earlier, the conflict theorist would respond that the key to solving social problems is political pressure for social change. Throughout the text, we've discussed a variety of programs and policy changes that we see as steps toward remedying specific problems. To some extent you probably view these kinds of solutions as beyond your control, since we tend to think of the creation of public policy and programs as the job of politicians, not average citizens. But what we must remember is that politicians "are not immune from internal and external pressures. When large numbers of citizens... take sides on major issues, policy makers in Washington and elsewhere are apt to take notice" (Manis, 1984:517).

Importantly, students have a long history of activism in such political pressure groups. During the 1950s and early 1960s, for example, college students played a vital role in the civil rights movement. "Their efforts in the south, particularly in organizing sit-ins at segregated facilities and in encouraging blacks to register as voters, lent great impetus to the movement" (Robertson, 1983:583). Throughout the 1960s and into the 1970s, students staged numerous rallies and demonstrations to protest U.S. involvement in what they judged to be an unjust war in Southeast Asia (Zaroulis and Sullivan, 1984). Today, student groups continue to organize and collectively make known their views on pressing social issues, such as the arms race, U.S. policy in Latin America, and apartheid. In fact, students are at the forefront of the U.S. anti-apartheid movement. They have marched in protest in front of South African diplomatic offices and the corporate headquarters of companies doing business in South Africa. And it was students who were among the first to organize against apartheid by pressuring university boards of directors for divestiture in South Africa (Cowell, 1984b). Despite widespread reports of apathy and growing conservatism on college campuses, it appears that students who feel strongly about particular social problems will continue to join together to act on those concerns.

Perhaps we are being too optimistic here. After all, change is not always for the better; history unfortunately provides us with innumerable examples of groups who, in trying to take their society one step forward, instead moved it two steps backward. We've also read in many chapters of this text how real change can be a frustratingly slow process, and that tremendous effort can result in only piecemeal improvements. Still, we must consider our other options. It seems that we are faced with the choice of allowing our freedoms to be controlled by the demands of existing social arrangements or working together to develop a more satisfying social system (Buell and De Luca, 1977).

Obviously, building an alternative social structure is a difficult task at best, but it's not totally out of reach. Ours is a society of relative affluence, so the means are available. What remains is for those resources to be distributed more equitably both here and abroad. In the final analysis, whether or not this is accomplished largely depends on our willingness as world citizens to become actively involved in the collective process of solving social problems.

—Curran and Renzetti, *Social Problems*

Exercise 10A

From reading the following selection, what do you think is the author's opinion about North and South America?

These two opposite systems of internal colonization reveal one of the most important differences between United States and Latin American development models. Why is the north rich and the south poor? The Rio Grande is much more than a geographical frontier. Is today's profound disequilibrium, which seems to confirm Hegel's prophecy of inevitable war between the two Americas, to be traced to U.S. imperialist expansion, or does it have more ancient roots? In fact, back in the colonial beginnings, north and south had already generated very different societies with different aims.* The *Mayflower* pilgrims did not cross the sea to obtain legendary treasures; they came mainly to establish themselves with their families and to reproduce in the New World the system of life and work they had practiced in Europe. They were not soldiers of fortune but pioneers; they came not to conquer but to colonize, and their colonies were settlements. It is true that a slave-plantation economy like Latin America's developed later south of the Delaware, but there was a difference: the center of gravity in the United States was from the outset the farms and workshops of New England, from which came the victorious armies of the Civil War. New England colonists, the original nucleus of U.S. civilization, never acted as colonial agents for European capitalist accumulation; their own development, and the development of their new land, were always their motivation. The thirteen colonies served as an outlet for the army of European peasants and artisans who were being thrown off the labor market by metropolitan development. *Free* workers formed the base of that new society across the ocean.

Spain and Portugal, on the other hand, had an abundance of *subjugated* labor in Latin America. Enslavement of the Indians was followed by the wholesale transplantation of Africans. Through the centuries, a legion of unemployed peasants was always available to be moved to production centers: as precious metal or sugar exports rose and fell, flourishing centers coexisted with centers of decay, and the latter provided labor for the former. This structure persists to our time; today, as yesterday, it means low wage scales because of the pressure of the unemployed on the labor market, and frustrates the growth of an internal consumer market. But also in contrast to the northern Puritans, internal economic development was never the goal of the ruling classes of Latin American colonial society. Their profits came from outside; they were tied more to the foreign market than to their own domain. Landlords, miners, and merchants had been born to fulfill the mission of supplying

---

*Lewis Hanke and the other authors of *Do the Americas Have a Common History?* stretch their imaginations in vain trying to find parallels between northern and southern historical processes.

Europe with gold, silver, and food. Goods moved along the roads in only one direction: to the port and overseas markets. This also provides the key to the United States' expansion as a national unit and to the fragmentation of Latin America. Our production centers are not interconnected but take the form of a fan with a far-away vortex.

—Eduardo Galeano, *Open Veins of Latin America*

Evidence

Once you have identified an author's purpose, ascertained his or her credibility, and determined what the author is trying to prove (the key idea), you can continue to read critically by evaluating the supporting ideas and supporting details. Here you will ask more questions:

> *How is the author trying to persuade me?*
>   *What kind of evidence does the author offer—*
>   *personal experience?*
>   *statistics?*
>   *experts' and authorities' opinions?*
>   *examples and illustrations?*
>   *results of observations and experiments?*
>   *Is the evidence fact or opinion?*

Distinguishing between Fact and Opinion

Facts are objective and can be proved. Factual evidence can be tested by experimentation, research, and/or observation and are used in both informational writing and persuasive writing. **Opinions** are subjective and cannot be proved. Opinions are beliefs, feelings, or judgments. Although opinions may be based on facts or may be interpretations of facts, opinions by themselves cannot be objectively verified by referring to sources. And though facts are objective, authors often use them to support a subjective point of view when trying to persuade readers to do or believe something.

Examples of assertions supported by facts are commonly found in scholarly, scientific, and legal writing. Here the facts may be in the form of examples, statistics, or observations. (Observations can be objective/fact, as in "There are three women here," or they can be subjective/opinion, as in "He looked sad.") Examples of assertions supported by opinions are often found in literary criticism, newspaper editorials, book and movie reviews, and advertisements. The difference between facts and opinions is the difference between "I know" and "I think"—"I know something is true and I can prove it," versus "I think something is true because..."

Exercise 10B

The following ten statements will give you practice in distinguishing between fact and opinion. Determine whether each statement is fact or opinion, and write F (fact) or O (opinion) on the line preceding each statement. Be prepared to explain your choice.

____ 1. Mary is taller than John.

____ 2. History is the most difficult class in college.

____ 3. *A Streetcar Named Desire* was Tennessee Williams's last great play.

____ 4. Some parents assume an active role in the education of their children.

____ 5. Studies have shown that the effective reader reads widely and frequently.

____ 6. John F. Kennedy was a good president.

____ 7. The results of the survey showed that 75 percent of the students were satisfied with the course.

____ 8. *Gone with the Wind* by Margaret Mitchell is the best book ever written.

____ 9. In his research, Van Gilder found that the differences in the skills required in various fields lie not so much in the materials themselves as in the type of thinking required.

____ 10. College students enjoy reading more than high school students do.

Exercise 10C

Read this selection about democracy. Underline the facts and bracket the opinions.

1   Many people in the United States accept the notion promoted in high school civics books that the country is a "government of the people, by the people, for the people." **Democracy** is the form of government in which the people have the ultimate power. The will of the majority prevails, there is equality before the law, and decisions are made to maximize the common good. In a complex society of more than 257 million persons, the people cannot make all decisions; they must elect representatives to make most decisions. So, decision making is concentrated at the top, but it is to be controlled by the people who elect the decision makers....

2   The most important component of a democratic model is that the representatives, because they are elected by the people, are responsive to the wishes of the people. This model, however, does **not** conform to reality. The United States is undemocratic in many ways. The people, although they do vote for their representatives every few years, are quite powerless. For example, who makes the really important decisions about war and peace, economic policies, and foreign policy? The people certainly do not. The record shows that many times, the people have been deceived when the object was to conceal clandestine illegal operations, mistakes, undemocratic practices, and the like. These illicit activities have been carried out by Democratic and Republican presidents alike.

3   Not only have the people in the United States been misinformed sometimes, but the basic democratic tenet that the public be informed has also been defied on occasion. On the one hand, Congress has shown its contempt for the electorate by the use of secret meetings. The executive branch, too, has acted in secret. Recent presidents have gone months without holding a press conference, have used executive privilege to keep presidential advisors from testifying before congressional committees, and have refused to debate opponents in election campaigns.

—D. Stanley Eitzen and Maxine Baca Zinn,
In Conflict and Order: Understanding Society

Evaluating Facts

Although all facts are verifiable, not all facts can support all assertions. You can evaluate facts by determining whether they are *current* (if that aspect is significant), *sufficient*, *relevant*, and/or *reliable*. Following are examples of the kinds of questions you might ask to evaluate facts.

Current?

Are ten-year-old data on the effects of acid rain valid?

Sufficient?

Is it sufficient for an author to say that 90 percent of the seniors from Getaway High School went on to college solely because they had a terrific English teacher? Or were there other factors that might have contributed to this outcome?

Relevant?

If an author is trying to convince you that imported Swiss cheese tastes better than domestic Swiss cheese does, is it relevant that the imported kind costs more?

Reliable?

Are statistics about airplane safety reliable when their source is the airline industry?

It is also important to note whether the author cites specific sources or makes only general statements. Referring to specific data or to a specific authority in a field to support an assertion is certainly more credible than stating, "Scientists say..." or "Studies prove..." If the author has included footnotes to cite the sources of assertions made, you can verify the assertions, rather than merely relying on the author's statements.

Exercise 10D

Refer to the earlier reading about democracy (p. 235) and evaluate the facts. Write each fact on one of the lines below and note whether it is current (if that aspect is significant), sufficient, relevant, and/or reliable.

_____

_____

_____
_____
_____

_____

Reasoning

In addition to being aware of the credibility of the author and the reliability of the evidence, you must also understand the **reasoning** of the author, or how the author moves from an assertion to a conclusion. To determine whether the reasoning is valid, a critical reader evaluates the way an author uses the supporting material to reach the conclusion. Asking the following questions will help you understand the author's reasoning:

How does the author interpret the evidence?

Are other interpretations possible?

How does the author arrive at the conclusion?

What is the connection between the assertion and the evidence?

Is the reasoning sound? Does one point follow from another?

Exercise 10E

Preview and read the excerpt from "The Poverty of Criminals and the Crime of Poverty," Then answer the questions that follow.

1. Any criminal justice system like ours conveys a subtle, yet powerful message in support of established institutions. It does this for two interconnected reasons: first, because it concentrates on *individual* wrongdoers. This means that *it diverts our attention away from our institutions, away from consideration of whether our institutions themselves are wrong or unjust or indeed "criminal."*

2. Second, the criminal law is put forth as the *minimum neutral ground rules* for any social living. We are taught that

no society can exist without rules against theft and violence, and thus the criminal law is put forth as politically neutral, as the minimum requirements for *any* society, as the minimum obligations that any individual owes his fellows to make social life of any decent sort possible. Thus, it not only diverts our attention away from the possible injustice of our social institutions, but *the criminal law bestows upon those institutions the mantle of its own neutrality.* Since the criminal law protects the established institutions (e.g., the prevailing economic arrangements are protected by laws against theft, etc.), attacks on those established institutions become equivalent to violations of the minimum requirements for any social life at all. In effect, the criminal law enshrines the established institutions as equivalent to the minimum requirements for *any* decent social existence—and it brands the individual who attacks those institutions as one who has declared war on *all* organized society and who must therefore be met with the weapons of war.

This is the powerful magic of criminal justice. By virtue of its focus on *individual* criminals, it diverts us from the evils of the *social* order. By virtue of its presumed neutrality, it transforms the established social (and economic) order from being merely *one* form of society open to critical comparison with others into *the* conditions of *any* social order and thus immune from criticism. Let us look more closely at this process.

What is the effect of focusing on individual guilt? Not only does this divert our attention from the possible evils in our institutions, but it puts forth half the problem of justice as if it were the *whole* problem. To focus on individual guilt is to ask whether or not the individual citizen has fulfilled his obligations to his fellow citizens. *It is to look away from the issue of whether his fellow citizens have fulfilled their obligations to him.* To look only at individual responsibility is to look away from social responsibility. To look only at individual criminality is to close one's eyes to social injustice and to close one's ears to the question of whether our social institutions have exploited or violated the individual. *Justice is a two-way street—but criminal justice is a one-way street.* Individuals owe obligations to their fellow citizens because their fellow citizens owe obligations to them. Criminal justice focuses on the first and looks away from the second. *Thus, by focusing on individual responsibility for crime, the criminal justice system literally acquits the existing social order of any charge of injustice!*

This is an extremely important bit of ideological alchemy. It stems from the fact that the same act can be criminal or not, unjust or just, depending on the conditions in which it takes place. Killing someone is ordinarily a crime. But if it is in self-defense or to stop a deadly crime, it is not. Taking property by force is usually a crime. But if the taking is just retrieving what has been stolen, then no crime has been committed. Acts of violence are ordinarily crimes. But if the violence is provoked by the threat of violence or by oppressive conditions, then, like the Boston Tea Party, what might ordinarily be called criminal is celebrated as just. This means that when we call an act a crime *we are also making an implicit judgment about the conditions in response to which it takes place.* When we call an act a crime, we are saying that the conditions in which it occurs are not themselves criminal or deadly or oppressive or so unjust as to make an extreme response reasonable or justified, that is, to make such a response noncriminal. This means that when the system holds an individual responsible for a crime, *it implicitly conveys the message that the social conditions in which the crime occurred are not responsible for the crime,* that they are not so unjust as to make a violent response to them excusable.

Judges are prone to hold that an individual's responsibility for a violent crime is diminished if it was provoked by something that might lead a "reasonable man" to respond violently and that criminal responsibility is eliminated if the act was in response to conditions so intolerable that any "reasonable man" would have been likely to respond in the same way. In this vein, the law acquits those who kill or injure in self-defense and treats lightly those who commit a crime when confronted with extreme provocation. The law treats leniently the man who kills his wife's lover and the woman who kills her brutal husband, even when neither has acted directly in self-defense. By this logic, when we hold an individual completely responsible for a crime, we are saying that the conditions in which it occurred are such that a "reasonable man" should find them tolerable. In other words, by focusing on individual responsibility for crimes, *the criminal justice system broadcasts the message that the social order itself is reasonable and not intolerably unjust.*

Thus the criminal justice system focuses moral condemnation on individuals and deflects it away from the social order that may have either violated the individual's rights or dignity or literally pushed him or her to the brink of crime. This not only serves to carry the message that our social institutions are not in need of fundamental questioning, but it further suggests that the justice of our institutions is obvious, not to be doubted. Indeed, since it is deviations from these institutions that are crimes, the established institutions become the implicit standard of justice from which criminal deviations are measured.

—Jeffrey Reiman, "The Poverty of Criminals and the Crime of Poverty"

1. What does the author want you to believe? (What is the author's assertion?)

   _____

   _____

2. List the reasons given to support the assertion.

   _____

   _____

   _____

You also need to be aware of what you, the reader, bring to your reading. Your thoughts and the way you reach them are shaped by your experiences, your biases, and your expectations. Examining your prior assumptions about a topic and an assertion is particularly important when you have previous knowledge about the topic of an article you are reading. Your response to Reiman's article, above, depends on such factors as your socioeconomic status, whether you have committed a crime or been a victim of one, and your knowledge of criminology. Without this awareness of your own preconceptions and reasoning strategies, you may find it difficult to understand what the author is saying, or you may easily misunderstand the author's message.

Emotional Appeal

To try to convince the reader, authors of persuasive writing frequently include emotional appeal as well as reasoned argument. The degree to which authors employ these two strategies is determined by their purpose in writing a selection and the audience to which they are writing. Advertising is at the emotional end of the persuasion continuum. Most ads are designed to evoke an emotional response by trying to make you feel, for example, that if you buy the product you will have a good life and become rich and beautiful or handsome.

Often people find it difficult to separate reason from emotion. The effective use of emotive language, such as figurative and connotative language (see Chapter 9), makes the reader more likely to accept a proposition. It is therefore important to be able to (1) recognize when and to what extent authors are writing to arouse an emotional response and (2) evaluate the tools of language they may use for that purpose.

Propaganda

Propaganda techniques are used by nearly everyone and every group. Although they may be used for what some people consider good purposes, too frequently they are not; they cloud thinking and get people to react emotionally rather than rationally. A critical reader knows how to distinguish between propaganda and reasoned argument and can detect such propaganda techniques as the following:

Appeal to tradition. The author claims you should believe or do something because people have thought or done something this way for a long time.

> There has always been a Democratic mayor, and so you should vote for the Democratic mayoral candidate.

Appeal to authority. The author asserts that you should believe or do something because an expert or authority believes or does it.

> My friend the doctor gives his dog ice cream once a week because, he says, it is good for the dog's bones; therefore, you should feed your dog ice cream.

Appeal to pity. The author describes the misfortunes of someone and encourages you to be compassionate and take action to help that person.

> Solicitations from charities use this propaganda technique.

Appeal to get on the bandwagon. The author encourages the audience to support a cause or buy a product because everyone is doing so.

> Try this. Everyone else is doing it.

Exercise 10F

Preview and read this article on criminal behavior. Then compare it with the article in Exercise 10E by answering the questions that follow.

The needs and motivations of people who engage in crime may be biological in origin, psychological in nature, or socially induced. Thus, a murder may be committed by one person because a brain tumor led to violence, by another person because of delusions about persecution by others, or by a member of a juvenile gang who is trying to impress peers by being tough.

Having certain needs, desires, or motivations is a necessary but not sufficient reason to commit a crime. Because all people to some extent learn that they should abide by the law, potential offenders must reduce their commitment to the law before they violate it. The critical question becomes, "Why, in a society in which such actions are widely known to be criminal and severely punishable, are they committed?" (Walker, 1974: 61–62). People who violate the law are often only weakly attached to it and to people and institutions that support the law, including parents, teachers, and peers. Being unconcerned about the opinion of others who are committed to a conventional way of life makes it easier to neutralize the constraints of the law. People also neutralize the influence of the law by using rationalizations to justify their violations; for instance, they may claim that their circumstances make it acceptable for them to commit a crime.

Another factor critical to the perpetration of many crimes is the learning of skills needed to commit a crime. This learning may be from the general culture, from the mass media, from other criminals, or from noncriminals who convey values conducive to crime. Safecrackers must learn how to "blow" a safe or pick a lock. Armed robbers have less to learn, because holding a pistol and demanding money requires few specific skills. Some offenders use specialized skills that they have employed for legitimate purposes to commit crime; one example is an accountant who uses bookkeeping skills to embezzle funds from a company by manipulating the books.

Given the need or desire to commit a crime, the reduction in commitment to the law, and the learning of the requisite skills, yet another factor is needed before a crime can be committed: the opportunity to violate the law. Crime is sometimes situational in nature; that is, people who might not otherwise think of breaking the law may commit a crime if they are confronted with a tempting opportunity to make an illicit gain with little risk. Others systematically seek opportunities to commit profitable crimes, planning their offenses in advance and organizing a group of criminals to carry out illegal acts. Social changes can increase opportunities for crime. For example, bank robberies have increased with the development of suburban branches that lack good security, and auto thefts have increased as the number of cars available to be stolen has grown.

Our conceptual scheme can help us to understand the reasons that people commit criminal acts. When individual acts of crime by an offender accumulate over time, we speak of a criminal career, a sequence of criminal acts that may lead an offender to a life of crime. An understanding of criminal behavior requires knowledge of the factors that give rise to individual acts that violate the law, but it also requires detailed information about the way that those acts add up to a criminal career.

—John E. Conklin, *Criminology: The Study of Criminal Behavior*

1. What does each author want you to believe?

   Jeffrey Reiman: _____

   John Conklin: _____

2. Does the author use facts or opinions to support the assertions? Write an F next to each fact and an O next to each opinion.

3. Evaluate each fact by identifying it as current, sufficient, relevant, and/or reliable.

4. Which author included more emotional appeal? Provide examples. _____

   _____

   _____

5. Which article did you find more persuasive? Why?

   _____

6. How did your previous assumptions and experiences affect your responses to these two articles?

_____
_____
_____
_____

Summary Exercise

What techniques do authors use to persuade readers?

_____

Chapter 11

Putting It Together: Flexible Reading and Active Learning

In this chapter you will find answers to these questions:

How does efficient reading depend on flexible reading?
What are the three basic approaches to reading?
When and how do you skim?
What is sectioning?
How does mapping relate to note taking?

In the previous chapters you have built a strong foundation in the basic reading skills and have learned how to move beyond the basic skills to become an analytical and critical reader and thinker. In this chapter, "Putting It Together: Flexible Reading and Active Learning," you will learn how to become an efficient and powerful reader and learner by evaluating your reading tasks and applying learning techniques that will help you to organize material for study.

The link connecting flexible reading and active learning is time. Often the amount of reading you are required to do in college seems to take every spare minute of every day. How do students who are carrying several courses, perhaps devoting many hours a week to a job, and taking care of their everyday lives make time for studying? The answer is that efficient students allow for learning time by adjusting their reading time to suit their purposes. In this way, knowing how to be a flexible reader leads directly to efficient learning.

Reading flexibly means being aware of what you want to get from your reading and knowing what strategies will help you adapt your reading time and effort to your purpose and the task. Not everything you pick up to read is written with the same density. Some texts, such as those in science or philosophy, compress much information into a relatively small space. Other texts, such as those in some of the social sciences, depend on example and illustration to explain the concepts they cover. How you deal with the different kinds of reading you have to do should be determined by your purpose and by the way the material is presented.

The Three Approaches to Reading

The reading questions you have learned in this book enable you to read critically and to determine how authors organize ideas. Once you have defined your purpose in reading, have given thought to what you already know about the topic, and have asked the other preview questions to identify the topic, key idea, and subtopics you can use three different approaches to reading—*skimming, reading,* and *studying*—to adapt how you read to what you need to get from the material. You will find as you complete this chapter that these three approaches, described below, echo the three levels you examined in Chapter 6: Level 1, the key idea; Level 2, the supporting ideas; and Level 3, the supporting details.

- *Skim* to acquire an overview of your reading. In skimming, you get a sense of what the whole reading and its parts are about. Skimming, like Level 1, involves reading for the *topic, key idea,* and subtopics.
- *Read* to have a better grasp of the author's ideas, the kind of support the author uses, and the organization of the material. Reading, like Level 2, centers on reading for the topic, key idea, subtopics, and *supporting ideas.*
- *Study* to understand the material fully. Studying, like Level 3, entails reading for the topic, key idea, subtopics, supporting ideas, and *supporting details.* Studying is necessary when your previewing indicates that you will need every bit of information provided if you are to understand thoroughly what the author is saying.

These three approaches put you in control of your reading and give you the tools to adapt your reading style to the task. Sometimes previewing and/or skimming will be sufficient for your purposes; at other times you may need to follow those activities with reading or studying. You are the one who decides what needs time and what does not; by setting your purpose, you know what you are after and when you have accomplished it. The time you save in skimming easy material to find the topic, key idea, and subtopics is the time you will have for reading that requires more time—material that is closely packed with ideas, that is sequential and demands attention to all the steps, or that is by its nature hard to understand.

Reading Strategies

In his book *Skimming and Scanning,* Edward Fry, a noted reading expert, assigns the following reading rates to the three approaches:

- Skimming at 800+ words per minute with 50 percent comprehension
- Reading at 250–500 words per minute with 70 percent comprehension
- Studying at 200–300 words per minute with as close to total comprehension as possible

Fry's figures demonstrate the relative time and attention given to each approach. Also associated with each approach are strategies, or ways to carry out each approach, that will enhance your ability to be a flexible but thorough reader:

- *Strategies for skimming* include skimming to preview (described in Chapter 2), skimming to gain an overview, skimming to scan, and skimming to review.
- *Strategies for reading* include **sectioning,** a technique that breaks down new information into comprehensible sections by finding and labeling the subtopics.
- *Strategies for studying* include marking up, note taking, mapping, and diagraming—organizational strategies to use when you are studying and reviewing.

Skimming

Skimming is one of the most useful techniques available to an efficient and flexible reader. Although the definition of skimming depends in part on what each reader needs to get out of the process and how much time he or she has to give to it, the following sections offer general guidelines.

Skimming to Gain an Overview

Skimming a reading, like skimming cream from milk, is moving lightly over the surface and separating the richest or most important aspects from the many facts, opinions, and details the material contains. Skimming takes courage, because many people think that one must read for every word, that not to do so is wrong—is somehow cheating oneself or the author. But the efficient reader reads for ideas, not words, and skimming is a skill that develops from questioning and reading for ideas. As Fry's reading rates indicate, skimming is fast reading, or fast processing, of written material, and this skill is developed through steady and persistent practice. Skimming gives you a general, rather than specific, understanding of a reading and establishes the context in which the details take their subordinate place. You will find that once you have mastered the art of skimming, you can substantially reduce the time it takes to read an assignment without losing much comprehension.

Good skimming takes place when you understand the points the author is making from the topic, key idea, and subtopics without reading the supporting ideas and details that make up the explanations, examples, or definitions. It helps you learn the author's point of view, see what kinds of evidence are being used to support the arguments, and discern how the material is organized—what is being contrasted with what and how, or what was the cause of what effect. And when you are short of time, skimming your assignment will at least provide you with some understanding of the material when you go to class and will give you some context on which to base questions.

How to skim to gain an overview.

1. After you have found the topic and key idea of the entire reading and established your purpose in reading it, look for the topic, key idea, subtopics, and possibly some supporting ideas of each *part* of the reading. This step entails reading the headings, first paragraph, and last paragraph in each section. If there are no headings, start looking for the subtopics by reading the first and last sentences of each paragraph.

2. Look for key phrases and signal words that are clues to key and supporting ideas—"The problem is," "The answer to," "We discovered that," "First, second, third," "To conclude," and so on.

3. Try to recognize patterns of organization. This is an essential part of skimming. If you know the author's organization, you will know what questions to ask as you skim the material. One question follows another almost automatically when you ask such questions as *What caused this problem? What happened next? What effect did Y have on X?* and *In what ways is A like B?*

4. Skip what you can identify as background or similar information that merely sets the stage; such information is usually found at the beginning of a reading.

5. Skip supporting details, such as examples, definitions, and other explanatory material, if you already know this information or can understand the author's point without the supporting details.

6. Don't panic when you see dates and numbers. Instead, realize that they are being used to illustrate relationships and to indicate movement and comparison. By observing the dates cited in a reading, you can roughly place an event as being in the first third, middle third, or last third of a century or as being in a certain decade—the exact date is rarely important. Similarly, numbers and percentages in a reading show whether there is movement up or down and how big or small one thing is compared with another. Understanding the relationship between two events or two quantities is usually more significant than remembering a specific date or number.

If you were skimming the following paragraph, what would you identify as the topic and key idea? What does the rest of the writing consist of?

> The word *reading* can take a variety of meanings depending on the context in which it appears. Sometimes, for example, the verb *to read* clearly implies comprehension; it would usually be redundant if not rude to say to a friend, "Here's a book you might like to read and comprehend." But at other times the verb does not entail comprehension; our friend might reply, "I've read that book already and didn't understand it." Obviously, there is little to be gained by asking such abstract questions as "Does reading involve comprehension, or thinking, or inferential reasoning or does it not?" Everything depends on the context in which the words are used. In its specific detail the act of reading itself depends on the situation in which it is accomplished and the intention of the reader. Consider, for example, the differences between reading a novel, a poem, a social studies text, a mathematical formula, a telephone book, a recipe, an advertisement, and a street sign.
>
> —Frank Smith, *Understanding Reading*

Your skimming tells you that this selection is about reading and that the key idea is that the meaning of the word *reading* depends on how it's used. The rest of the paragraph consists simply of illustrations—supporting ideas and supporting details—answering the questions, *How? When?* and *What?* Do you need to read these illustrations word by word to understand what Frank Smith is saying?

The article below, on muscle activity, is underscored to show you what to look for as you practice the skimming technique. Notice that the underlining tends to occur at the beginning and end of the article and of each paragraph.

Types of Muscle Activity

1. When your skeletal muscles receive a stimulus from your nervous system to act, they respond by developing tension and producing a measurable force. Your skeletal muscles act in three different modes—isometric, concentric, and eccentric—to produce this force. An **isometric muscle action** is one in which force is produced by the muscle without a change in the length of the whole muscle. Isometric muscle actions do not create any joint motion. Muscles act isometrically to stabilize a particular body part while another body part is moving, or when a maximal resistance is met and the force produced by your muscles cannot overcome the resistance. Isometric exercise routines were popular in the 1960s and can develop strength, but they are not commonly used today.

2. One example of an isometric muscle action is the unsuccessful attempt to push a car out of snow or mud. Although you push with all your might, the car (as well as your joints) does not move. The muscles involved all are producing forces, but in an isometric way. Another example, and one more related to resistance training, is attempting to lift a barbell too heavy for you. The more you try, the more tired your muscles become, but the barbell never leaves the floor.

3. A **concentric muscle action** is one in which force is produced while the muscle shortens. Joint movement is always produced during concentric muscle actions. Raising a 20-pound dumbbell in an elbow flexion movement (curl) is an example of a concentric action of the elbow flexor muscle (biceps). In general, concentric muscle actions occur in a direction opposite of the downward pull of gravity.

4. **Eccentric muscle action** describes a muscle's ability to produce force while lengthening. Typically, eccentric muscle

actions occur when movement is in the <u>same direction as the pull of gravity</u>. If you want to be sure that a given resistance exercise has an eccentric phase, you must use the type of resistance training equipment that requires you to perform an eccentric action in order to achieve the starting position prior to your next repetition. For example, with a 20-pound dumbbell biceps curl, you lower the weight slowly to the starting point of the exercise in an eccentric action of the elbow flexors. Even though the motion produced during this phase of the curl is elbow extension, it is the force exerted by the controlled lengthening of the elbow flexors (biceps) that is responsible for the motion, not the elbow extensor muscles (triceps).

All factors being equal, <u>the greatest amount of force is produced during eccentric muscle actions, followed by isometric and then concentric muscle actions</u>. Changes in muscle size and strength are affected both by the type of resistance exercise you employ and by the type of muscle action(s) you use during your workout. When using free weights (barbells, dumbbells), <u>the typical sequential pattern of concentric-eccentric muscle actions during resistance training contributes to improved muscle strength and muscle fiber size</u>. According to current research, if your resistance exercise program uses only concentric muscle actions, you'll need to perform at least twice as many concentric-only repetitions to achieve the same results as you would attain by using concentric-eccentric combinations.

—Rebecca J. Donatelle and Lorraine G. Davis, *Health: The Basics*

Exercise 11A

Referring to the selection above and to the six points, listed earlier, on how to skim to gain an overview, use a highlighter to shade the following excerpts from textbooks as you skim them, looking for the topic, key idea, subtopics, and patterns of organization. The underscoring of the first few paragraphs of item 1 serves as an example.

1. In the history of human social interaction, <u>few concepts</u> have been <u>so widely misunderstood as race</u>. Although the word *race* has a specific scientific meaning, that meaning has seldom served as the basis for human race relations. <u>Social conceptions of race, rather than scientific definitions, have been</u>

crucial in shaping interracial patterns (Pitchford, 1992). In practice, the word has been widely misapplied, with a host of significant results. In different times and places, people have believed that race is the single most important determinant of individual mental, physical, emotional, and moral capacities, and they developed drastic and tragic policies toward millions of fellow human beings purely on that basis. The subjugation of blacks by whites in the South African system of racial segregation known as **apartheid,** and the "final solution" to the Jewish "problem" in Nazi Germany are two blatant examples that come readily to mind, but they hardly exhaust the supply of historical cases. Ironically, as with Hitler's answer to the Jewish "racial" issue, these social policies were often constructed on a fundamental distortion of what race and membership in a particular racial group really mean.

2 From a strictly scientific standpoint, the term **race** refers to a classification of human beings that is based on biological attributes. Specifically, Webster's Dictionary defines it as "a population that differs from others in the relative frequency of some gene or genes" (1983, p. 1484). These gene differences are hereditary and may manifest themselves as observable differences in skin color, body shape, hair texture, and other physical characteristics (Schaefer, 1990).

3 Although this definition seems straightforward, attempts to translate the concept into empirical terms have not been successful. The question of which specific biological characteristics are of most importance in defining the various human races has not yet been answered. Nor has the related question of how many different races there really are.

4 Ethnologists (scholars who study races and their origins) often speak of three major racial groups: **Caucasoid,** or "white"; **Negroid,** or "black"; and **Mongoloid** or "yellow." This classification scheme is imprecise and inaccurate, however. Variations in physical characteristics, including skin color, are often greater among individuals within a given racial group than they are between individuals of different racial groups (Gould, 1981). Further adding to the confusion is the fact that, throughout the long course of human history, there has been a tremendous amount of **amalgamation;** that is, biological reproduction across various racial group lines. The notion that any sort of pure races may still exist in the contemporary world is extremely naive.

5 Objective truths have seldom been the only determinants of human social beliefs and actions, however, and nowhere is this more evident than in the case of race. It is inherently difficult, if not impossible, to establish definitive boundaries to distinguish human races clearly. It is equally

difficult to chart the psychological and other consequences of membership in a particular racial group. Nonetheless, <u>people in many societies have acted toward one another as though it were possible to do so and as though race per se were of fundamental importance in shaping individual abilities and disabilities.</u>

Ethnicity Defined

Race represents a way of classifying people on the basis of biological differences. In contrast, ethnicity represents a way of classifying or grouping people on the basis of cultural differences. **Ethnic groups** consist of people who share a common orientation toward the world, who thus have developed a sense of "peoplehood" or identification with one another, and who are perceived by others as possessing and sharing a distinctive culture (Bahr et al., 1979).

In this sense, there is no such thing as a "Jewish race"; that is, a population sharing a set of specific genes. Rather, Jews represent an ethnic group based on a set of religious and cultural traditions. To the extent that they lack effective power and are the targets of prejudice and discrimination, Jewish Americans represent a minority ethnic group in the United States. Similarly, the Irish are an ethnic group, not a race. Irish Americans represent a recognizable ethnic group to the extent that their common ancestry and cultural traditions make them identifiably different from the majority or dominant Anglo-Saxon Protestant group. Since Irish Americans generally are no longer the objects of prejudice and discrimination, they no longer constitute a minority in this society.

As is true with race, the concept of ethnicity has been subjected to misunderstanding and misapplication in social relations in many societies. Although ethnicity itself has nothing to do with biological differences among people, many ethnic groups in fact possess specific physical characteristics that differentiate them from others. For example, many Mexican Americans display a number of features including hair color and skin tone that distinguish them from their Anglo neighbors. These physical features sometimes lead them to embarrassing and volatile interactions with U.S. Border Patrol agents, who mistake them for undocumented Mexican nationals attempting to enter into the United States illegally.

By the same token, people who appear indistinguishable on the basis of physical characteristics may be members of vastly different ethnic groups. For example, in regions of the

United States having large Southeast Asian immigrant populations, many Anglos simply lump the newcomers together under the generic title "Indochinese." In the process, they ignore important cultural distinctions that Vietnamese, Laotians, Cambodians, and Thais make among themselves.

In similar fashion, although ethnic groups are often defined at least partially on the basis of common ancestry or nationality, ethnicity is not equivalent to common political or geographical background. Throughout the last part of the nineteenth and early part of the twentieth centuries, immigrants to the United States from any part of what was then Russia were listed officially as being of "Russian" origin. It was only later that specific ethnic groups from within that country's geographic boundaries (e.g., Lithuanians, Latvians, Georgians, Ukrainians) were recognized as distinct entities. In the aftermath of the dismantling of the Soviet Union, former "Soviet" peoples throughout the newly created republics are reasserting their ethnic identities, often with frightening results (Sneider, 1992). Switzerland is a recognized political entity whose citizens claim Swiss nationality, yet there is no "Swiss" ethnic group per se. Rather, that country is made up of three recognizable and different ethnic populations, German, Italian, and French, each of which maintains its own identity and sense of peoplehood. On the other hand, many of the formerly hyphenated-American ethnic groups (e.g., Irish American, Polish American) can trace their ancestors to a common geographic or political area (e.g., Ireland, Poland). Given these complexities, perhaps it is no wonder that we have such a difficult time making sense out of the distinctions among racial, ethnic, political, and other groups.

In the United States, at least, it appears that "ethnic group" has become something of a blanket or umbrella term. It includes groups that are recognizably different on the basis of cultural or physical characteristics or some combination of the two. This might not reflect a great deal of scientific or objective validity, but it does seem to reflect common social practices, as well as people's apparent need for some way of classifying themselves and others in their social relations (Bahr et al., 1979).

—George J. Bryjak and Michael P. Soroka,
Sociology: Cultural Diversity in a Changing World

2. Opportunity cost is a concept you did not see in the definition of economics. But not seeing it doesn't mean that it isn't there. There is yet more to say about the definition, but this is the logical place to introduce a related concept.

Opportunity costs are everywhere, due to scarcity and the necessity of choosing. Opportunity cost is not what you choose when you make a choice—it is what you did *not* choose in making a choice. **Opportunity cost** is the value of the forgone alternative—what you gave up when you got something.

Your brain is wrestling with the idea of opportunity cost now. You have temporarily given up the opportunity to think of food. But what about your stomach? If it is full, it has temporarily given up the opportunity to be empty. Or vice versa. You open your mouth to protest the existence of opportunity cost. You could have laughed or yawned or sung the *Star Spangled Banner* at full volume instead. All are opportunity costs. You buy the blue shirt rather than the green, or 1,700 pieces of bubble gum, or leave the dollars in your checking account. Opportunity cost. Your state uses its limited budget to build more roads rather than schools. Opportunity cost. Your government chooses more defense spending and sacrifices human services. You guessed it.

Look back at the scarcity discussion. It was concluded there that the concept of free goods is not a realistic concept. Economists are fond of saying that there is no such thing as a free lunch. Even if your friend buys your lunch, you give up something—namely, time. That time could have been used for some other purpose, so there is an opportunity cost associated with lunch, no matter who buys. From the point of view of society, resources are used up to provide the lunch. These resources are limited. Resources applied to this production cannot be applied to that production. Consequently, the production of a good to satisfy a want imposes an opportunity cost. So opportunity cost is why goods are not free, but scarce. . . .

Choice also imposes opportunity cost over time. The use of resources now means that those resources will not be available for future use. A decision must be made, an opportunity cost encountered, as to whether to allocate for present needs or future needs. Today versus tomorrow.

Some goods will be consumed today and some in the future. By reducing consumption today, future consumption may be increased. Isn't that one reason you are in school? If you are not working full time, you are not consuming all you could. You are postponing consumption. Why? Because you believe you could get a better job (and one with more pay) if you have more training and education. So you can consume even more later. Thus you postpone current consumption while building up your skills so as to increase consumption later. Again, a barrel of oil pumped from the ground now is a barrel of oil that will not be available for consumption any day in the future. So to use the oil today imposes forgone opportunities in the future.

—Arleen J. Hoag and John H. Hoag, *Introductory Economics*

Exercise 11B

Skim the following paragraph, noting the significance of the numbers, and answer the questions that follow.

The developed countries, with less than a quarter of the people in the world and an average per capita income of more than $9,000, control some 80 percent of the global economy. In stark contrast, the less developed countries with an average per capita income of less than $1,000, control only about 17.6 percent of that economy. Further, the developed countries consume about 80 percent of the total world supply of energy, the less developed countries about 12 percent. As a final index to the disproportionate distribution of wealth, the consumption of iron, copper and aluminum by developed countries ranges from 86 to 92 percent, by the less developed countries, even including China, from 8 to 14 percent.

—Peter H. Raven, in "Third World in the Global Future"

1. What pattern of organization is the author using?

   _____

2. What do the numbers tell you about per capita income in the developed and the less-developed countries?

   _____

   _____

3. What do the numbers tell you about control of the global economy?

   _____

   _____

4. What do the numbers tell you about energy consumption?

_____

_____

5. What do the numbers tell you about consumption of metals?

_____

_____

6. What do all the statistics together tell you about distribution of wealth?

_____

_____

Skimming to Scan

The skimming you do when you need to search through a document to find a particular piece of information—like a date, a number, or a name, or whether or not the author treats a certain topic—is often called scanning.

How to skim to scan. Follow these suggestions:

1. Define precisely what information you are looking for.

2. Refer first to the table of contents and to the index to see what may be listed under your topic or a topic somewhat similar to your topic.

3. Skim only that portion of the book which seems likely to contain relevant information.

Say that for a sociology course, you have decided to write a research paper on "The Division of Labor between the Sexes in Rural India." Your first task is to visit the library to see how much information you can collect on this subject. Although the library's card catalog lists nothing on this exact topic, it does list two books on life in rural India. So you find those books and skim them to see whether their contents are useful to you. The quickest method is to look at the index, but what should you look under? You try "Work," "Labor," and "Men and women." You also look at the tables of contents; there you find a chapter on family life. You then turn to the appropriate pages and skim until you come to something that is relevant. At that point, you read carefully, taking notes (see p. 287) on material you want to include in your paper.

Exercise 11C

1. For your course in psychology you have chosen to write a paper on twins. Which of the following chapters would you skim to see whether they contain information you could use?

    a. Stress and Adjustment

    b. Learning

    c. Infancy and Childhood

    d. Therapies

    e. Family Structure

2. You have located a biography of Thomas Jefferson and want to determine his views on slavery. Which index headings would you look under?

    a. Agriculture

    b. Labor

    c. Race relations

    d. Federalism

3. You skim to scan

    a. when you are in a hurry.

    b. to find a particular piece of information.

    c. when you want an overview of your reading.

    d. as a way of previewing.

Exercise 11D

Skim to scan the article on dowsing. Then answer the specific questions that follow.

1. What is dowsing?

   _____

2. What are the main explanations for the phenomenon?

   _____

   _____

   _____

3. In which paragraphs do you find examples of dowsing?

   _____

   _____

   _____

Dowsing and Dowsers

When a person walks across a field with just a stick in his hand, and by the movements of that stick detects minerals buried far below, he is dowsing. There are few virtuosos at this ancient art, but many people can achieve occasional success. Usually a forked stick is used, one fork held in either hand, but sometimes a single straight twig is preferred. If the stick turns in the hand, this indicates the presence of minerals below. Hazel and peach twigs are the traditional favorites, though other fruit or nut woods have their advocates. In today's society, however, 2 L-shaped lengths of coat hanger or copper wire are often easier to come by than a peach tree, and these seem to do the job just as well.

In England and America dowsers have searched mainly for water (hence the expression "water witching") but early European miners dowsed to detect metals. A few people were even able to track down criminals with the rod, but this led to widespread abuses, so the Inquisition condemned this form of dowsing, while approving it for finding water. The subject has always been controversial: Some sects believed the rod was moved by the devil, and Martin Luther stated that dowsing violated the 1st commandment. Not many agree with this today, but we still have no certain explanation of the dowser's successes.

For instance, what can we make of John Mullins, a famous English dowser? Wealthy Sir Henry Harben had spent over £1,000 (in the last century, and pre-inflation) on professional geological advice and on well-drilling based on that advice. His estate remained short of water. Finally, Sir Henry sent for Mullins, who promptly indicated locations for 5 wells, giving the depths at which water would be found. In all cases he was correct. Many similar tales are told of him and of his contemporary, William S. Lawrence, both of whom "outguessed" experienced geologists on a number of occasions.

The same thing happened in Saratoga Springs, where fortunes were made and lost by men trying to find mineral water. The large companies involved in the search often used several dowsers independently to confirm one another's findings before expensive well-digging was begun.

The popular image of a dowser has him striding across the countryside, rod in hand, but this is not always the case. Two of the best-known dowsers have worked successfully while sitting comfortably at a table, dowsing with a pendulum suspended over a map of the area concerned. Henry Gross of Maine, probably America's best-publicized dowser, frequently used this method, as did Britain's Evelyn Penrose. Miss Penrose perhaps brought dowsing full circle in that she dowsed as much for metals as for water. She found metals, oil, and water for the Government of British Columbia, and worked for tough-minded businessmen located in the U.S., England, and Australia. An interesting point about her dowsing was that she described different physical sensations according to which metal she was seeking. Silver, she said, itched, while tin gave her a feeling of exhilaration.

While dowsing has brought fertility to previously arid farmland and financial success to miners, it is also credited with saving lives. In Vietnam, American forces made good use of the L-shaped coat-hanger dowsing rod to detect mines and other booby traps. Most of the men did not profess to know how or why the rods turned to give them warning—they were just glad that they did!

Perhaps prompted by the news reports from Vietnam, the U.S. Dept. of Interior and Utah State University conducted a dowsing research project in which over 150 people were asked to place wooden blocks wherever they got a dowsing reaction along a certain course. Each subject walked separately, not knowing where his predecessors had placed their blocks, yet there was a strong tendency for the blocks to be grouped in specific locations. These locations also tended to be where the earth's magnetic field changed abruptly. Such changes may be caused by water below the ground, so in this sense the experiment's results may help explain dowsing. However, magnetic-field changes are not necessarily due to water, and Professor Duane Chadwick, who conducted the experiment, emphasizes that since no wells were dug, there is no proof that any of the places chosen by several subjects would actually yield water.

8   One explanation put forward is that the dowsing rod may serve as a sort of "amplifier" of ESP impulses. This is supported by the fact that Dutch psychic M. B. Dykshoorn often uses a divining rod to supplement his clairvoyance. Perhaps the dowser receives information by ESP, and, though he is unaware of it, his muscles react just enough to move the rod. Some believe the dowser perceives the water itself; others say he senses the change in the magnetic field. Since the 5 senses do not perceive magnetism, the latter would still be a form of ESP, but with a rather more physical tie-in.

9   Another theory is that different substances give off specific vibrations to which a dowser is physically sensitive, making his muscles twitch so that, unconsciously, he turns the rod. The study of the effects of different substances and their vibration is termed radiesthesia, and its proponents consider it a science that can be used in medical diagnosis.

10   Yet another theory maintains that the rod itself is affected by the substances being dowsed. Most dowsers sincerely try to hold the rod still, yet it moves anyway. Unwilling to accept the unconscious muscle-movement theory, some are convinced that the rod moves of its own volition. In 1530 Georgius Agricola commented that if this were the case the rod would move for everyone, which it does not with any degree of accuracy. Nearly everyone can get *some* dowsing reaction, whether right or wrong (of Chadwick's more than 150 subjects, only one got no reaction at all), but few can approach Evelyn Penrose's purported 80% success rate. An even higher rate of 93% "hits" was reported for American John Shelley, former president of the American Society of Dowsers, based in Schenectady, N.Y.

11   Skeptics dismiss the whole subject as a sham. They say that a dowser's successes are due to an understanding of geology, a surveying of the lie of the land, vegetation, and so on. The record of the many dowsers who have repeatedly suc-

ceeded where geologists have failed suggests that this is not the whole story.

—David Wallechinsky and Irving Wallace, *The People's Almanac*

Skimming to Review

Skimming is an important part of reviewing. When you want to remember the content of a reading, you should skim it immediately after you have read it. This technique is the same as previewing but comes after, rather than before, you read. You may recall from the piece on memory (p. 000), the best way to remember something is to review, consolidate, and organize new information as soon as possible after learning it. But you do not need to reread every word; you can fix it in your mind by remembering the main points and the organization. You can also use the same technique when you are reviewing for tests and exams.

How to skim to review.

1. Consolidate information by going back over the chapter titles, the headings and subheadings (or section titles), the introduction, and the summary or concluding paragraphs to review the topic, key idea, subtopics, and some supporting ideas.

2. Test yourself by turning the headings into questions and reciting what you know about the title and each section. If, for example, the heading is "The Laws of Gravity," your question would be, *What are the laws of gravity and how do they work?* If you can answer the question to your satisfaction, then move on to test yourself on the next heading. You thus need to reread only that portion you feel you have not adequately mastered.

Exercise 11E

1. Skim to preview the article on poetry, below, by answering the following preview questions:

    a. What is the article about?

b. What is the key idea?

c. Why are you reading the material?

d. What do you already know about the topic?

e. Why did the author write the article?

Poetry—Personal and Public

The most influential poets and critics of the early twentieth century advocated a poetry that, in its ideal form, was impersonal and without ambition to make changes in the world. Archibald MacLeish provided the best-known formula for this "New Poetry" in "Ars Poetica," concluding: "A poem should not mean/But be." At its best, poetry that was written in accord with the new principles was aesthetically rewarding and classically compelling. But at its worst, it was dry, hard, allusive, intellectual poetry that neither involved nor moved the reader. By the time of World War II, in the 1940s, the New Poetry had lost its revolutionary momentum and had become an academically approved movement, producing a poetry that was predictable in form and subject.

But during the 1950s and 1960s, poets rediscovered the possibilities of making poems out of their personal lives. The personal was revived in part, no doubt, because poetry was threatened with annihilation in a mass culture in which individual identity was becoming a mere annoyance to the ever larger and more impersonal institutions of government, industry, education. And the meaning of poetry was renewed in part because of the growing realization that injustices not only existed but were often embedded in the very institutions created to protect and extend human rights.

Thus it was that poets rediscovered the personal voice with all its human inflections; and thus it was that this personal voice was raised at times in a cry of anguish and protest, grief and outrage.

The Beat poet Allen Ginsberg is credited by some critics with dragging poetry, screaming, out of the classrooms into the streets. Representing a general disillusionment with the Establishment in all its forms, the Beat movement reached its peak during the late 1950s. Poets like Ginsberg became the wandering minstrels of an urban culture, appearing in offbeat bookstores and bohemian clubs to read their poetry to enthusiastic crowds.

As the civil rights movement of the period grew stronger, oppressed groups of all kinds began to demand more and more from a too often complacent society. And the Vietnam War turned the 1960s into America's "long, dark night of the soul." Then it was that poets—especially young ones, but also many of an older generation—proclaimed a renewed public role for poetry, a poetry that not only meant, but also declaimed, and sometimes howled.

The new-found freedom of poetry to say what it wanted or needed to say was accompanied by new freedoms of language and form. The language of poetry became more relaxed, more conversational, more clearly the language of the streets than of the universities. At the same time poets tended to throw over the old forms and create their own. Robert Creeley said: "Form is never more than an extension of content." Denise Levertov refined this formula: "Form is never more than a *revelation* of content." Content—the meaning of a poem—was thus proclaimed a poem's main excuse for being.

Some poets used the new freedoms to write a kind of free-flowing poetry that is sometimes called "process poetry," in which the poem remains open to whatever thoughts or feelings the poet experiences in the process of creating the poem. The poem becomes a kind of ramble through a segment of life with the poet. "This Is the Land," by Carlos Cortez, has elements of this kind of poetry.

The new freedoms breathed new life into poetry. As the restrictive, academic formulas were overthrown, new poets appeared, writing a simple, clear poetry, sometimes understandable on a first reading or hearing. Audiences that had been baffled and bored by poems of the past discovered that poetry could delight and instruct, move and amuse, depress and inspire.

—James E. Miller, Jr. et al., *United States in Literature*

2. Now skim the same article to gain an overview of it. Then answer the following questions.

   a. What are three subtopics found in this reading?

   _____

   _____

   _____

   b. What are the two principal patterns of organization found in this reading?

   _____

   _____

   c. What do the authors conclude?

   _____

   _____

3. Now skim to scan the article, to answer the question, What did Allen Ginsberg do?

   _____

4. List three questions you would ask yourself in reviewing the article.

   a. _____

   b. _____

   c. _____

Reading and Sectioning

A strategy closely associated with the second approach, reading—wherein you read for the topic, key idea, subtopics, and supporting ideas—is that of dividing the material into its component sections to see how the authors develop and support their ideas. You were introduced to this strategy in Chapters 4, 5, and 6, when you looked for the subtopics of your readings; in Chapter 2, when you grouped chapter titles; and in Chapter 8, when you organized lists of names and events according to certain categories.

Sectioning

A section is a unit of one or more paragraphs that are grouped together because they have the same subtopics As a reading strategy, such grouping, or sectioning, is done as you read, by giving each section a different and appropriate title derived from your answer to the question, *Who or what is this about?* A good analogy is a department store. What subtopics or sections would you use to develop the key idea that a department store carries a variety of goods? One section might be shoes, another might be linens, and a third might be toys. These categories can be further divided into different kinds of shoes, linens, and toys. What the department store doesn't do is to mix children's shoes with bed linens or men's shoes with toys. Such an arrangement would be poor marketing—so disorganized that people would be unable to find their way around.

Similarly, as you saw in Chapter 8, most authors aim to organize information in a way that you, the reader, will easily comprehend. Their ideas are not thrown at you randomly but are arranged coherently. For instance, if you tell someone about a book you've read, you set out the details in some kind of order. Bill may start at the beginning and go right through, chapter by chapter, until the end; Diane may prefer a different arrangement, first addressing why she chose the book, then giving a brief summary of the most interesting parts, and finally stating her opinion of it. These are quite different structures. But in each case the information is sectioned into subtopics under the general topic of "A Book I Have Read." In the first case, the pattern of organization is chronological; in the second, the pattern moves from subtopic to subtopics as in a list. In both cases, the material is connected and presented in meaningful units that you can follow. You discover the system existing in a particular reading by asking, as you read, *What is this part about?* You then section it according to subtopics.

The effort you put into finding the threads that join topic with subtopics and key idea with supporting ideas helps you understand and become familiar with the ideas contained in the material. It also provides you with an easily remembered package in which each unit is labeled, rather than with an unrelated scattering of thoughts. The titles you give to each section become your clues, or memory joggers, to what is contained in the reading.

How to section.

1. Note where one subtopic ends and another begins, either by marking the text or by making notes.

2. Write a title for the section, based on its subtopics in the margin or in your notes.

3. Write out the key idea of the section, remembering that this concept is also a supporting idea for the key idea of the entire reading.

As you gain experience in sectioning, you will probably use larger and larger units of subdivision as you see the connections between subtopics. The fewer subtopics you have, the easier they will be to remember as you try to reconstruct the reading.

The following two articles have been marked up to illustrate sectioning. The first example is sectioned by subtopic.

Piano Manufacturing

Topic—piano manufacturing

Changes — *Subtopic— changes in piano industry*

The piano manufacturing business has seen dramatic changes in the twentieth century, particularly over the last twenty years. In 1900, there were 7000 piano manufacturers in America, including families who made pianos in their homes. One out of every six people in America was involved in some aspect of the piano business, including the production of raw or manmade materials used in constructing a piano. Today, however, there are only about ten independent piano manufacturers and just six major piano companies. A far cry from the mom-and-pop piano makers of the past, these are Steinway, Baldwin, Sohmer, Kimball, Wurlitzer, and Aeolian. Despite the transition from family to corporate ownership, the hand craftsmanship and pride in the product seem to have prevailed. Combined with the most modern business and manufacturing techniques, the piano industry in the 1980s is unique—and healthy, if somewhat pared down.

According to the National Piano Manufacturers Association and industry estimates, piano manufacturing is a half-billion-dollar-a-year industry. In 1982, 203,000 American-made pianos were sold in the United States, a slight decrease over the past two to three years, but an overall increase over a ten-year period.

The sales figures of new American instruments tell only part of the story. Piano manufacturers say that the secondhand piano business is doing remarkably well, and they estimate that nearly 1 million used pianos are sold in America yearly.

In the past decade the American piano industry has been faced with intense competition from the Koreans and the Japanese, the latter having already cornered twenty percent of the American market with Yamaha and Kawai pianos. In fact, in Hamamatsu, Japan, where the Yamaha is manufactured, more pianos are made per year than in any other part of the world. But United States piano manufacturers have risen quickly to the challenge. Piano companies are rapidly increasing their know-how in engineering as well as in marketing and manufacturing. These firms are developing more efficient, profitable methods, and new products that the public can more easily afford, such as the practical spinet, a much smaller and cheaper piano than a grand.

The two basic types of pianos are grands and uprights. Grand pianos are constructed on a horizontal plane, which means that the strings are stretched horizontally across the plate and framework, and come in three sizes; a baby grand is four and a half feet to six feet long; a medium grand, six to eight feet long; and a concert grand, eight to nine feet long and sometimes longer. While only five percent of the pianos manufactured today are grand pianos, they are played and featured most often because they tend to be far more responsive and powerful than uprights.

Upright pianos, also called vertical pianos, have strings that are stretched vertically across the plate and framework. Uprights vary in height: a full-size is forty-eight inches or more; the studio model is forty-four inches; the console is thirty-nine to forty-two inches; and a spinet, popular because of its small size, is thirty-six to thirty-eight inches. Upright pianos have two major types of actions: direct blow action and drop action. Direct blow action makes for a better piano because the action is mounted above the ends of the keys, allowing direct movement of the parts, a strong hammer blow, and maximum tonal response. Drop action, mounted behind and below the keys, sacrifices sound and is harder to fix because the space is so cramped.

rebuilding pianos

Today, there is a slowly developing renaissance in piano making. With the high cost of new pianos, many people are buying used pianos and having them rebuilt or refinished. At least a dozen companies in New York City alone are now starting to rebuild old pianos, which are being sent from all over the country. Trained piano makers are also in considerable demand.

—Judith Oringer, *Passion for the Piano*

In this article we were able to connect the subtopics of each paragraph into larger units. Now we have an article with three sections, each with a title, and have followed the author as she has moved from subtopic to subtopic under the topic of piano manufacturing. You may find it difficult initially to make the move from a subtopic for each paragraph to subtopics for the larger sections. In time, however, you will find that the process becomes easier. Test your memory by reconstructing the article, using only the three section titles as clues.

The second article, taken from a chemistry textbook, has the general title "The Origins of Chemistry." The object here is to break down the article into sections, which may consist of more than one paragraph, following the change in subtopics by asking, *Who or what is this about?* The exercise was completed by discovering the supporting idea contained in each section, that is, by asking, *What is the most important idea the author has about the subtopic?*

Topic—origins of chemistry	The earliest attempts to explain natural phenomena led to fanciful inventions—to myths and fantasies—but not to understanding. Around 600 B.C., a group of Greek philosophers became dissatisfied with these myths, which explained little. Stimulated by social and cultural change as well as curiosity, they began to ask questions about the world around them. They answered these questions by constructing lists of logical possibilities. Thus Greek philosophy was an attempt to discover the basic truths of nature by thinking things through, rather than by running laboratory experiments. The Greek philosophers did this so thoroughly and so brilliantly that the years between 600 and 400 B.C. are called the "golden age of philosophy."
Key idea— three steps lead to modern chemistry	
Subtopic A— Greek philosophers	Some of the Greek philosophers (scientists, really) believed they could find a single substance that everything else was made of. A philosopher named Thales believed that this substance was water, but another named Anaximenes thought it was air. A third, Empedocles, said that the world was composed of four elements: earth, air, fire, and water.
Supporting idea—Greek philosophers attempted to discover the basic truths of nature by thinking things through.	During this period, the Greek philosophers laid the foundation for one of our main ideas about the universe. Leucippus (about 440 B.C.) and Democritus (about 420 B.C.) were trying to determine whether there was such a thing as a smallest particle of matter. In doing so, they established the idea of the atom, a particle so tiny that it could not be seen. At that time there was no way to test whether atoms really existed, and more than 2,000 years passed before scientists proved that they do exist.
Subtopic B— the alchemists	While the Greeks were studying philosophy and mathematics, the Egyptians were practicing the art of chemistry. They were mining and purifying the metals gold, silver, and copper. They were making embalming fluids and dyes. They called this art *khemia*, and it flourished until the seventh century A.D., when it was taken over by the Arabs. The Egyptian word *khemia* became the Arabic word *alkhemia* and then the English word *alchemy*. Today our version of the word is used to mean everything that happened in chemistry between A.D. 300 and A.D. 1600.
Supporting idea—The alchemists practiced the art of chemistry instead of thinking about it.	

| | A major goal of the alchemists was to transmute (convert) "base metals" into gold. That is, they wanted to transform less desirable elements such as lead and iron into the element gold. The ancient Arabic emperors employed many alchemists for this purpose, which, of course, was never accomplished. | 5 |

The alchemists also tried to find the "philosopher's stone" (a supposed cure for all diseases) and the "elixir of life" (which would prolong life indefinitely). Unfortunately they failed in both attempts, but they did have some lucky accidents. In the course of their work, they discovered acetic acid, nitric acid, and ethyl alcohol, as well as many other substances used by chemists today. 6

Subtopic C—Boyle

Supporting idea—Boyle realized that every theory had to be proved by experiment.

The modern age of chemistry dawned in 1661 with the publication of the book *The Sceptical Chymist*, written by Robert Boyle, an English chemist, physicist, and theologian. Boyle was "skeptical" because he was not willing to take the word of the ancient Greeks and alchemists as truth, especially about the elements that make up the world. Instead Boyle believed that scientists must start from basic principles, and he realized that every theory had to be proved by experiment. His new and innovative scientific approach was to change the whole course of chemistry. 7

—Alan Sherman, et al. *Basic Concepts of Chemistry*

The preview and initial skimming provided the topic and key idea. We found the subtopics fairly easily, and the supporting ideas of sections A and C were directly stated in the text. We did, however, have to infer the supporting idea found in section B: What distinguished the alchemists from the Greek philosophers was that they practiced the art of chemistry instead of just thinking about it.

Exercise 11F

Turn to the article on dowsing (p. 259) that you skimmed to scan.

1. Reread the article and note the subtopic found in each paragraph.

Paragraph	Subtopic
1	Introduction—definition
2	Controversy about dowsing
3	Success of Mullins
4	Success in Saratoga Springs
5	a. _____
6	b. _____
7	c. _____
8	d. _____
9	e. _____
10	f. _____
11	g. _____

2. Put together those paragraphs which have the same subtopics, to form seven sections, as follows:

Section	Subtopic
Paragraph 1	Introduction—definition
Paragraph 2	Controversy about dowsing
Paragraphs 3–4	Examples of success
Paragraph 5	a. _____
Paragraph 6	b. _____
Paragraphs 7–10	c. _____
Paragraph 11	d. _____

Exercise 11G

This exercise applies the techniques of skimming and sectioning to an article on smoking.

1. Preview the following article to establish what the topic is. Think about what your purpose in reading it is and what you already know about the topic.

   Topic:_____

2. Now skim the article to find the key idea and the main patterns of organization.

The Battle for Minds and Lungs

Tobacco companies in the United States are under siege. Clinical evidence mounts that cigarettes can be devastating to health. The government wants to slap an additional 75-cents-a-pack tax on cigarettes. Anti-smoking zealots are targeting smokers and shaming them about their habit. Physician groups and the health lobby have mounted mighty campaigns against tobacco products.

For the tobacco industry, a tremendous amount is at stake. Although fewer Americans smoke today than in the past, cigarettes remain a tremendously profitable business. One British conglomerate bought American Tobacco Company for $1 billion in 1994. At the time, analysts were expecting huge profit growth in the industry, led by RJR Nabisco at 35.5 percent. The earnings of Philip Morris, RJR Nabisco and American Brands, which represent more than 80 percent of the domestic market, were expected to create excess cash flow of $3 billion.

Naturally, the tobacco industry is not taking these attacks lying down. Much of the battleground is the mass media, which traditionally are viewed as well suited as a forum for opposing views. On the cigarette issue, however, there is some thinking that there need to be restraints on the tobacco interests because, among other things, their advertising is so effective.

Some of the catchiest ads around are for tobacco products. Take Joe Camel. Studies say he's more recognized among kids than Mickey Mouse.

Some advertising is subtle in its appeal. Marlboro became a successful brand with ads featuring macho cowboys doing their work. The product was in a noble context of rugged masculinity, hard work and honest values. Over the years, Marlboro ads have shifted to dramatic Western vistas, placing the product in a natural, outdoor healthy context. The new implied message: Smoking is healthful.

Benson and Hedges is making a badge of honor out of the ostracism that smokers feel. Ads show smokers on the wings of airliners in flight and at desks hanging outside office skyscrapers.

All told, the U.S. cigarette industry spends about $400 million a year on advertising.

Meanwhile, the government runs media announcements about the dangers of smoking. In 1994, the American Medical Association launched a major television campaign for a quit-smoking kit.

The government also has narrowed the forums in which cigarette makers can advertise. Since 1971, cigarette ads have been banned from television and radio. In response, tobacco manufacturers beefed up print media and billboard advertising and shifted to sponsoring events that would promote their products through association. Marlboro, Camel and other brands have moved into the mail order business, offering brand-related products in exchange for proof-of-purchase bar codes. Marlboro, for example, offers Western boots, cowboy hats, belt buckles, denim shirts and leather jackets.

Both sides in the tobacco war vie for news media attention. RJR Nabisco was delighted, for example, to go public rebutting criticism that Joe Camel glamorizes smoking among kids. The study, by the respected Roper Organization, confirmed that Joe Camel was widely recognized among young people, but that only 3 percent of 16- and 17-year-olds who recognized Joe had a positive attitude about smoking.

Meanwhile, with news conferences and briefings and news releases, the health lobby, often led by the U.S. surgeon general, feeds the negative message about smoking to the media. Articles on the horrors of smoking abound in newspapers and magazines and on television and radio.

The battle for the public's mind is perhaps its most direct on talk shows, where articulate representatives of the tobacco industry make their freedom of choice defense. With patriotic fervor in their voices, they say government is going too far, being un-American even, to consider taking away the "right" of people to enjoy pleasures like a cigarette. This is an appeal that goes to the heart of what it is to be an American.

The tobacco spokespersons are always well equipped with data that challenge many of the health studies. And, correctly, they point to flaws in the sometimes-overstated and hysterical points made by anti-smoking zealots. On talk shows, this makes good drama.

The greatest fear of tobacco companies is that someone, somewhere will prevail in a product liability suit. Many people have sued, blaming health problems on cigarettes, but no one has succeeded. The tobacco companies put major resources into defending against these actions, knowing that a loss could result in a cascade of suits that could wreck their industry, just as 20 years earlier product liability suits wrecked the U.S. asbestos industry.

The forum for product liability trials is the courtroom, and the tobacco companies know that the cases are widely reported. Their defense is part of the battle to win popular support for their cause. Admittedly, it's an uphill battle in the courtroom—rich tobacco companies with attorneys in three-piece suits versus terminally ill victims of lung cancer and heart disease. But, from the tobacco companies' perspective, it is better to make their case in the public courtroom than to lose one of these cases or let the sad stories of the ailing plaintiffs go unaddressed.

A theme in these cases is that the plaintiffs say the cigarette companies used advertising to entice them into a fatal addiction. The courtroom then becomes a forum for tobacco lawyers to point out that tobacco is not addictive. Their evidence? Forty million Americans have quit.

Traditionally, tobacco companies sparred with their opponents in the media. Now Philip Morris has changed its rules of engagement. In 1994 the company filed a $10 billion libel suit against ABC for a television report that the company had spiked cigarettes with extra nicotine to make them more addictive. ABC stood by its report.

Philip Morris may or may not prevail in the suit, but more important long term is that the mass media are now on notice not to take sources who criticize the tobacco industry at face value—or they may be faced with an expensive libel suit. Under American law, the media are responsible for the truth of what sources tell them. That means that one upshot of the Philip Morris vs. ABC is that news reporters may be more cautious in the future in reporting criticism of the tobacco industry.

In its new aggressiveness, Philip Morris is suing governments that adopt antismoking policies. The company has sued San Francisco to drop a strict smoking ban in the workplace. In another action, Philip Morris has sued the U.S. Environmental Protection Agency for a claim that secondary smoke can cause cancer.

20 The battle for people's minds includes events that attract media attention. Philip Morris, for example, helped organize a tobacco farmers' protest at the nation's capitol against a proposed cigarette tax. The protest underscores how important tobacco is to the economy of many states from Wisconsin into the Deep South.

21 The tobacco companies also curry public favor by associating themselves with good causes. They share their profits with dance companies, theaters, art museums and educational institutions. They contribute to causes like promoting racial equality. In this sense, the companies are good citizens.

22 Anti-smoking lobbyists accuse cigarette companies of targeting minors and teenagers, women and minorities in their advertising. The companies are quick to deny they are encouraging young people to smoke. The companies point to thousands of signs they provide retailers about customers needing to provide proof of age. With a straight face, RJR Nabisco says Joe Camel, and also his friend Josephine, are just lovable characters that kids like, noting too, that the adults the company seeks to reach also like the characters.

23 U.S. tobacco companies have learned that their brands have appeal abroad, where governments and health lobbies generally are less vigorous. The companies have been especially successful in Asia, and they have moved into the former communist bloc with major marketing and advertising programs in Czechoslovakia, Hungary, Kazakhstan, Lithuania and Russia.

24 The media battle for minds and for lungs continues—on a broader and more intense scale than ever.

—John Vivian, *Media*

a. Key idea: _____

b. Principal patterns of organization:

_____

_____

3. Now read the article, divide it into sections, and title the subtopic of each section according to the following pattern:

Section	Title of Subtopic of Section
Paragraph 1	Introduction
Paragraph 2	Profitability
Paragraph 3	The Fight
Paragraphs 4–9	Advertising
a. _____	_____
b. _____	_____
c. _____	_____
d. _____	_____
e. _____	_____
f. _____	_____
Paragraph 24	Conclusion

Studying and Organizing

The third approach to reading—studying—involves understanding and remembering new concepts and information. It is achieved by reading deeply and thinking hard. Your aim is to be able to put your new learning to use as you move further into a field of study. For instance, understanding the background and problems of postrevolutionary America makes the outbreak of the Civil War more comprehensible; knowing how the heart works provides insights into the circulatory system.

Understanding and remembering result from the following:

- Reading the supporting material—the details that explain and illustrate
- Thinking about and analyzing the new ideas and concepts
- Integrating the new information with what you already know

- Organizing the new information so that you can store it as part of what you know

The best ways to organize new material are (1) to mark up your reading and (2) to condense the material and impose some order on it. You can organize information either by **note taking** and outlining, that is, using your own words to describe your understanding of the author's ideas and information, or by **mapping** and **diagraming,** which are ways of illustrating what you want to learn by developing your own graphics.

When you are reading new material, material that may be hard to grasp, you need to actively engage all your senses in the effort. It is not enough just to say you will remember, unless you're one of the .00001 percent of people who have a photographic memory.

You will find that involving your pencil in the task, through marking up your text, through note taking and outlining, and through mapping and diagraming, will greatly enhance your comprehension and your ability to remember.

Marking Up

In this book we have stressed marking up your text because this practice is an excellent way of analyzing your readings and participating actively in the reading process. Some students mark up their texts only by using brief check marks in the margin to indicate an important point. Most, though, go to the other extreme, underlining or highlighting virtually every sentence so that each page becomes blue or yellow or whatever the color of the highlighter is. Neither of these methods is very efficient. The first does not give enough information, and the second does not discriminate the truly important from the less important. Further, both these methods are mentally passive and provide a false sense of security. It is as if the information went directly from the page, through the hand, and back to the page, leaving no trace on the mind. Underlining by itself is not enough; you have to process the words through your mind to extract the author's ideas. Thoughtful marking, based on your reading questions, is the best approach.

In the following example, the key idea, subtopics, supporting ideas (single line), and some supporting details (double lines) have been noted, as have the patterns of organization. In doing your own text marking, you may find it easier to use a code of underlining and bracketing, as was done in Chapter 6; or you may want to write marginal notes; or you may want to use a combination of techniques. You may also choose to mark passages you find particularly difficult, ones to which you'll want to return later. It is important only that your marking be consistent and not too complicated; otherwise, you won't use it.

Topic: The corporation
Key idea: Corporations need to be watched because ownership is disperse, and it is hard to fix accountability.

The Corporation

History

Corporations <u>began</u> in the <u>sixteenth century</u>, <u>when</u> the great <u>explorers</u> <u>needed larger sums of money</u> than any single person or partnership could provide to equip and finance their expeditions. <u>Shares of stock</u>, representing a share in the future profits of the enterprise, were <u>sold</u> to <u>groups</u> of backers. The practice of buying shares extended to the <u>general public</u> and financed <u>colonization and trade</u> in the <u>seventeenth</u> and <u>eighteenth centuries</u> and the <u>big business</u> of the <u>nineteenth and twentieth centuries</u> that resulted from the industrial revolution. [1]

Definition

As more people and funds became involved, it became necessary to refine and <u>legally define</u> the corporation. Who owns a corporation? Who is legally responsible? In a partnership, individuals pool resources and become owners, but <u>corporation ownership</u> is <u>widely dispersed</u> <u>through the sale of shares</u>, each indicating a degree of proprietorship. <u>The stockholders own the corporation</u>. And whereas in a partnership each partner involved is personally liable for all the activities of the enterprise, in a corporation individual stockholders are protected by <u>limited liability</u>. The <u>business exists independently</u> of them and <u>only its asset can be seized</u>. [2]

Ownership

Legal responsibility

<u>Corporations are legal entities</u>, acting through their <u>boards of directors and managers</u>. They can <u>buy and sell, hire and fire, take legal action, and commit crimes</u>. But these activities do not go on in a vacuum. <u>Federal and state governments</u> have set up <u>agencies and</u> enacted <u>legislation to protect</u> the <u>public</u>, such as the <u>Securities and Exchange Commission</u>, which monitors the buying and selling of stocks and bonds, and the various <u>antitrust laws</u>, which inhibit unfair business practices. [3]

Accountability growth

Corporations have come a long way from the small groups that banded together to finance a voyage to the Indies. There are <u>giant corporations within</u> certain <u>industries</u> that control billions of dollars, <u>like IBM</u>, and holding <u>companies that extend ownership</u> and control <u>over a large variety of businesses</u>, <u>like ITT</u> (formerly International Telephone and [4]

Need for supervision Telegraph), which owns the Hartford Insurance Company, the Sheraton hotel chain, and businesses involved in the automotive, defense, and pulp and timber industries. In this era of mergers, acquisitions, interlocking directorates, and other complicated managerial and financial maneuverings, it is <u>hard to know who is making the decisions and difficult to fix accountability</u>. For these reasons, it is increasingly <u>important that we require our state and federal watchdog agencies to continue to be alert in protecting the public against unfair and possibly criminal activity</u>.

The marking up of "The Corporation" is based on the fundamental reading questions. You may choose to add more detail. You may also want to add your critical evaluation as you go along or at the end of the reading. In marking up, your mind is hard at work thinking about your reading—analyzing and organizing. Marking up is the first step in organizing to understand, remember, and review.

Exercise 11H

Mark up the following text by making marginal notes, by underlining and bracketing, or by using a combination of methods. In any case, your marking should clearly indicate the topic, key idea, subtopics, and supporting ideas, and possibly the patterns of organization as well.

Black Macho and the Myth of the Superwoman

1. As the function of the Southern white woman changed, the life of the black woman continued just as if the country were in its first stages of growth. She labored in the fields beside her husband, developed muscles in her arms, bore the lash and the wrath of her master. Her labor and trials became inextricably associated with her skin color, even though not so long before, the colonial woman had not been much better off.

2. Whether slavery would continue seemed in doubt during the Revolutionary War and immediately afterward. The truth is that the Revolutionary forces had enlistment problems. When the British offered blacks freedom if they fought with them, the Revolutionaries had no choice but to enlist blacks too. Five thousand blacks, in integrated and all-black regiments, fought in the Revolutionary War. They did so because they believed it would win them their freedom. The

Rights of Man, they had reason to assume, would be extended to them. After the war, when many masters did not make good their promises, many blacks escaped to Canada and to other territories. Others sued for their freedom in the American courts and won. The new government seriously considered the abolition of slavery, but because of cotton and tobacco it was not to be.

Gradually a network of lies developed to justify the continuance of the master/slave relationship, the selling of children away from their mothers, the separation of wives and husbands, the breeding of slaves like animals. After the constitutional ban on slave importation, which took effect in 1808, the market required that a brutal emphasis be placed upon the stud capabilities of the black man and upon the black woman's fertility. The theory of the inferiority of blacks began to be elaborated upon and to take hold. It was at this point that the black woman gained her reputation for invulnerability. She was the key to the labor supply. No one wished to admit that she felt as any woman would about the loss of her children, or that she had any particularly deep attachment to her husband, since he might also have to be sold. Her first duty had to be to the master of the house.

She was believed to be not only emotionally callous but physically invulnerable—stronger than white women and the physical equal of any man of her race. She was stronger than white women in order to justify her performing a kind of labor most white women were now presumed to be incapable of. She had to be considered at least the physical equal of the black man so that he would not feel justified in attempting to protect her.

She was labeled sexually promiscuous because it was imperative that her womb supply the labor force. The father might be her master, a neighboring white man, the overseer, a slave assigned to her by her master; her marriage was not recognized by law.

Every tenet of the mythology about her was used to reinforce the notion of the spinelessness and unreliability of the black man, as well as the notion of the frivolity and vulnerability of white women. The business of sexual and racial definition, hideously intertwined, had become a matter of balancing extremes. That white was powerful meant that black had to be powerless. That white men were omnipotent meant that white women had to be impotent. But slavery produced further complications: black women had to be strong in ways that white women were not allowed to be, black men had to be weak in ways that white men were not allowed to be.

It has become a national belief that because the black woman's master was the slaveowner, and not her husband, she became abusive to her husband, overly aggressive, bossy, domineering. But those who trace such characteristics in the contemporary black woman back to her slave ancestry will have to find some other basis for their arguments. So far as circumstances would permit, she was a loyal, faithful and dutiful wife and mother. In partnership with her slave husband, the black woman slave fought to preserve her family, and everything that she did can be seen in that light. Her family structure was simply different from that of whites; it had no fewer rules and allowed women no greater measure of equality.

If circumstances permitted, a slave woman often lived with a single man most of her life. If her husband was to be sold, he might assign a friend to look after his wife and children. Or after a time, the woman might take another husband. She would act just as if her previous husband were dead.

In choosing a husband, a woman might live with a succession of men, but once she had settled upon a mate, she would be faithful to him. Adultery was vigorously frowned upon by the slave community. Often she was pregnant before she settled down. Her behavior did not indicate what the slaveowners claimed was a unique immorality or moral devastation; it was a carryover from her African home, where it was fairly common behavior, just as it was in many agrarian societies. If the black woman could not get along with her husband, she was allowed to separate from him. These practices were all acceptable under the code the slaves devised for themselves and necessary to their survival. It is easy to see how slaveowners used them to support their contentions that slaves were amoral and socially chaotic.

The work of historian Herbert Gutman has revealed that the threat slavery posed to the black family did not prompt the slave to give up all hopes of family life but rather to value it above all else. For the black man and woman family life was their only daily refuge. It offered them companionship, some modicum of comfort, a positive and reinforcing view of themselves and a future. Gutman describes the slaves as having been considerably preoccupied not only with their husbands and wives and children but with their cousins, nieces and nephews, aunts and uncles and grandparents. Whenever it was possible, they maintained family ties across generations.

Eugene Genovese suggests that the reputation the slave woman had for beating her children might have resulted from her attempts to teach them to obey quickly that they might later avoid death at a white man's hand. Plantation owners had a habit of spoiling black children, allowing them to play and roam freely with white children until the age of twelve or thirteen. Then abruptly everything would change. The white children would go off to school and the black children would be sent to the fields. The black children would become subject to the whippings and plantation discipline administered to adults. Slave mothers evidently tried to minimize that transition. No precedent for harsh parental discipline existed in African society, where mothers traditionally indulge their younger offspring. It is also known that some black women slaves in America traveled much of the night in order to see their children on another plantation and arrive back home before dawn.

12 In many ways the black woman's plight in slavery was worse than the black man's, not because she fought against a traditional woman's role but because she willingly assumed it. In addition to her labors in the fields or in the big house, she also did the same work expected of early colonial women, and all poor women, in her own house. Certain rituals in which she participated, like the annual corn-shucking parties which Genovese cites in *Roll, Jordan, Roll*, indicated that she believed in the notion of the male slave as provider: The men shucked the corn, competed for prizes, while the women looked on and prepared the food.

13 In this and various ways, the slaves showed that they had not forgotten what constitutes a desirable relationship between male and female. And no matter what the white master might whisper in the black woman's ear, she usually showed herself to have a mind of her own in matters that concerned her own people. For instance, although their mistresses encouraged them to shun the attentions of the field hands, black female house servants quite commonly married field hands. Whites had little success in effecting a division between house and field slaves like the one that developed in the West Indies.

14 Assimilation was simply not a possibility, much less a problem for the slave woman. Although she often lived in close proximity to whites, the emotional reality of her world remained distant from direct white influence. She was never able to relate freely to whites—the consciousness of the barrier was always there, even in bed with the master—and thus she was unable to absorb the intricate rationalizations for their racism and to adapt them to her image of herself. She had to depend upon her own people for her self-image.

—Michele Wallace, *Black Macho and the Myth of the Superwoman*

Note Taking and Outlining

Although marking up a text is a useful technique for analyzing your reading, if you want to have a record of what you have read or a basis for recalling what you have read, then you need to take notes. Translating the author's thoughts into your own words makes for better understanding and longer retention than simply copying an author's words does. Engaging in note taking increases your attention; however, in note taking as in marking up, there is a fine balance between taking so many notes that in effect you duplicate the text and taking notes that are informative enough to ensure your understanding of the concepts when you review them. Some students use a formal outline, others use the Cornell Method, and all students, at one time or another, have to take notes for writing research papers. These techniques are discussed below.

The formal outline. Note taking, particularly outlining, is a written representation of an order-of-importance chart, proceeding from most important to least important under each heading. One could also view an outline as moving from the general to the specific. Outlining helps you see the structure and connections. As you can see from the following example, an outline of the corporation article on page 279, the supporting ideas are followed by supporting details. Reflected in the example is the common practice of using a standard format to indicate the levels in an outline—I, II, III for subtopics; A, B, C for supporting ideas; 1, 2, 3 for supporting details; and a, b, c if another level is needed.

The Corporation
  I. History
     A. Need for funds
        1. Exploration
        2. Colonization
        3. Big business
     B. Increased funds by selling shares
        1. Groups
        2. General public
  II. Definition
     A. Ownership
        1. Stockholders—dispersed (comparison with partnership)

  2. Position of management and directors
 B. Legal responsibility
  1. Stockholders—limited liability (comparison with partnership)
  2. Corporation a legal entity
  3. Establishment of agencies and laws

III. Accountability
 A. Size and complexity of modern corporations
  1. Large corporations within industries—IBM
  2. Large corporations owning diverse companies—ITT
 B. Need for greater supervision
  1. To identify decision makers
  2. To protect the public

Outlining is also an essential organizing tool when you are preparing to write a research paper, for it allows you to structure your own ideas as key ideas, supporting ideas, and supporting details.

The Cornell Method. The Cornell Method of taking notes was developed by Walter Pauk at Cornell University and has been used successfully by thousands of students for taking both reading notes and class notes. The method, described below, is particularly appropriate for readers of *Active Reading* because it is based on the questions you have been using and gives you space for noting patterns of organization, your summary of the material, and your own comments.

1. Draw a line down a sheet of paper about a third of the way in from the left margin. (Some college bookstores carry paper ruled this way.)
2. Write the topics and subtopics to the left of the line, and write the key idea and supporting material—the supporting ideas and details—to the right of the line.
3. Include notes on patterns of organization—as a reminder of how the author developed the material—also on the right.
4. Use the bottom of the page for adding a summary (discussed in Chapter 5) and a few notes containing your evaluation or critical comments.

Using the Cornell Method, notes on the corporation article would look like this:

Topic and Subtopics	Key Idea, Supporting Ideas, Supporting Details
T: The Corporation	KI: Corporations need to be watched because ownership is disperse, and it is hard to fix accountability.

ST: History	SI: Need for money
	  SD: 16c explorers
	      17c & 18c colonization and trade
	      19c & 20c big business
	SI: Sold shares of stock
	  SD: Groups then general public

ST: Definition
—Ownership
	SI: Dispersed among stock holders
	  SD: Own shares of company
	      Not like partnership
	SI: Business run by managers and directors

—Legal responsibility	SI: Stockholders have limited liability SI: Corporation a legal entity SI: Establishment of supervising agencies and laws

ST: Accountability	SI: Modern corporations large and complex
	  SD: One industry—IBM
	      Diverse industries—ITT
	SI: Need for greater supervision
	  SD: Identify decision makers
	      Protect public
	Patterns of organization: principally list

Summary: Corporations started in the sixteenth century as a means of raising money and have grown ever since. They are legal entities owned by the stockholders, who own shares of the profits but have limited liability. Because of the complexity of corporations, the government needs to be particularly watchful to fix accountability and protect the public.

In addition to helping you distinguish an author's ideas and clarify connections, the Cornell Method provides an ideal arrangement for reviewing reading notes and class notes. Remember, reviewing your notes is as important as taking them. Most students quiz themselves by covering up the right-hand side of the page to see whether they can recite the key and supporting ideas from the clues provided by the topics and subtopics. Others reverse the process, testing to see whether they can abstract the subtopics from the key and supporting ideas.

Note taking for research papers. Taking notes on articles and books you plan to use in writing a research paper represents a special case, one whose procedure is different from that of note taking for review. Here it is easiest to organize your notes if you use note cards that you can rearrange according to subtopics as your thoughts develop. Following is the information to include on these cards and the recommended steps for preparing them.

1. Write the author's full name (list all names if there is more than one author).
2. Cite the complete title of the work you are referring to.
3. Include the facts of publication: the name of the publisher and the date and place of publication.
4. Put the subtopic to which the card refers in the upper-right-hand corner so that you can easily identify it.
5. Distinguish your words from the author's by placing the author's words in quotation marks. Plagiarism, or using someone else's ideas and words as if they were your own, is not allowed in academic circles. Your instructors can recommend one or more books that provide guidelines for the proper way of using and quoting secondary sources.

Exercise 11I

Listed below, at random, are the key words and phrases produced from a review of Active Reading. *Look them over, think carefully about how these ideas are connected, and arrange them in an outline that makes sense to you.*

supporting details   key idea
author's purpose   studying
to inform   conclusion
to persuade   order

cause and effect
patterns of organization
supporting idea
list
previewing
compare/contrast
reader's purpose
subtopic

development
topic
introduction
basic structure
skimming
reading
reviewing
organization

Exercise 11J

Return to the article on poetry (p. 263) that you earlier previewed and skimmed. Now read the article, and then complete the following partial set of notes, keeping to the established arrangement of the Cornell Method.

Topic and Subtopics	Key Idea, Supporting Ideas, Supporting Details
T: 20th century	KI: a. _____
ST: Early 20s (impersonal)	SI: Archibald MacLeish SD: "Not mean but be" SI: Some good points SD: Beautiful, traditional SI: Some bad points SD: Dry, not moving, predictable
ST: 50s and 60s (personal)	SI: b. _____ SD: c. _____ SD: d. _____ SD: e. _____ SI: f. _____ SD: g. _____ SI: h. _____ SD: i. _____ SD: j. _____

Topic and Subtopics	Key Idea, Supporting Ideas, Supporting Details
	SI k. _____
	SD: l. _____
	SD: m. _____
	Pattern(s) of organization
	n. _____
Summary: _____	
_____	

Mapping and Diagraming

Note taking by outlining is one way to organize notes and clarify connections. Another way to assist understanding is to organize material pictorially or visually, rather than verbally—that is, to draw maps, diagrams, or graphs, and to make tables.

For many students, seeing things in a different way, or adding the pictorial to the verbal, is of great value in understanding relationships, making comparisons, and recognizing cause and effect. For many people, dealing with material visually helps memory and recall, because a picture is easier to remember than a string of words. You can help yourself be a better organizer of material and a better reader of graphics by making them yourself. You have, in fact, been using various kinds of graphic aids in progressing through *Active Reading*—the diagrammatic arrangement of supporting material in Chapter 6 and the charts analyzing comparisons in Chapter 8 are examples.

A general word for illustrating relationship is mapping. Thinking of a map can tell you why. A map of the world, for example, shows where countries are, how big countries are in relation to one another and to the great bodies of water, and what different countries' important geographical features, such as mountains and deserts, are. Now think of trying to convey in words the information you see on a map—doing it would take pages, maybe even a book. Like maps, diagrams consolidate and condense information to make the relationships easy to understand.

Following are the most useful kinds of maps and diagrams for you to draw yourself:

1. A *map* that follows the list pattern by organizing material around a central concept without dealing with a specific order, as in Figure 11.1, concerning the article on corporations.

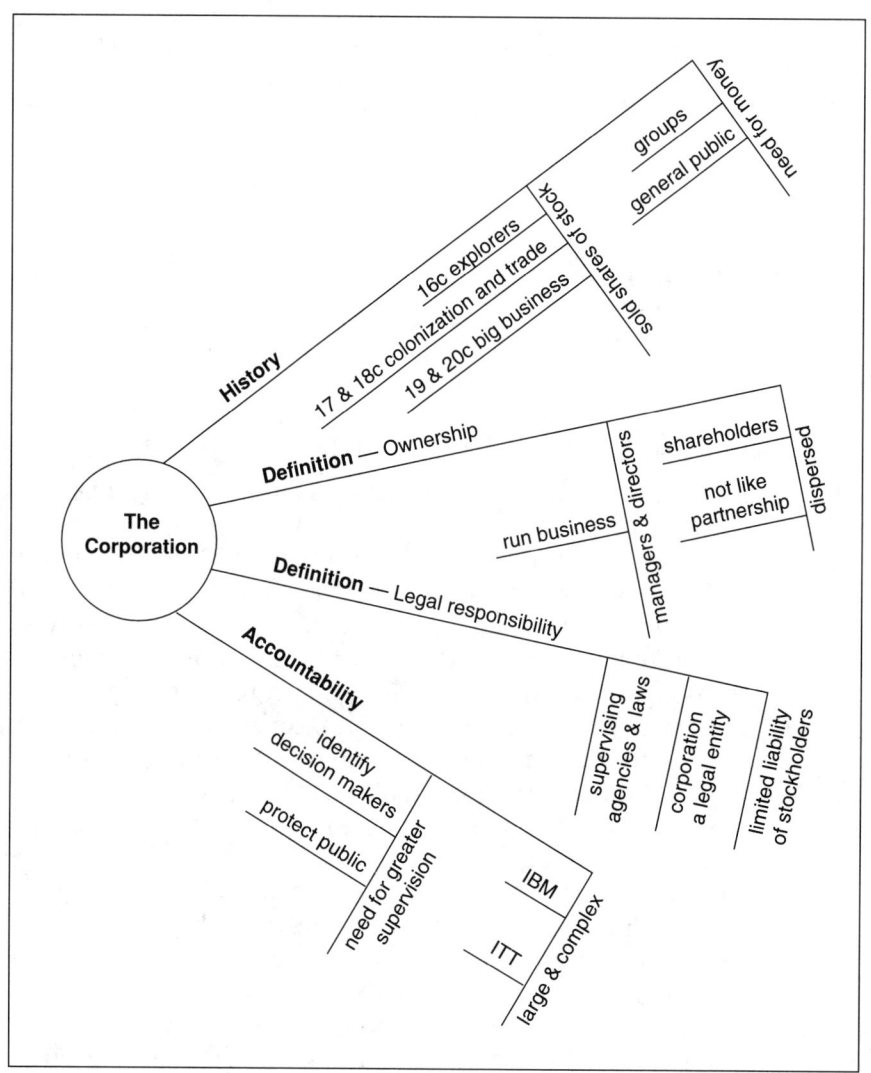

Figure 11.1 Organizing material around a central concept

2. *Flowcharts,* which show how something works by indicating the process in which each step depends on the one before it, as in Figure 11.2. Flowcharts are useful in studying scientific topics, such as the influence of magnetic fields in physics or the digestive system in biology.
3. *Time lines,* which indicate chronological order, as in Figure 11.3. Time lines are particularly useful in studying the historical chronology of any field and can also be used to track the events in a novel.

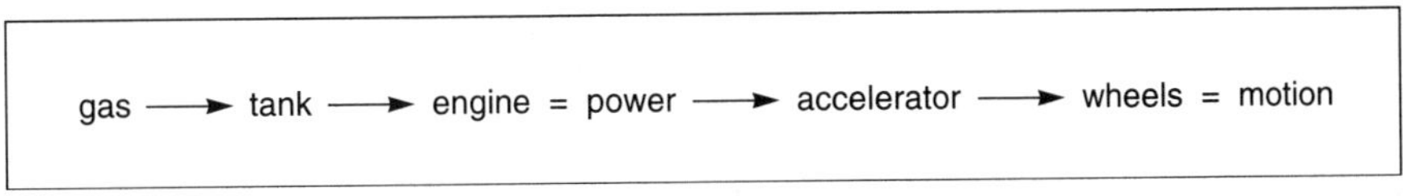

gas ⟶ tank ⟶ engine = power ⟶ accelerator ⟶ wheels = motion

Figure 11.2 Flow charts show how something works by indicating the process in which each step depends on the one before it.

4. Vertical diagrams, or *pyramids*, that break down material according to topic, key idea, subtopics, supporting ideas, and supporting details, indicating order of importance, such as the ones you completed in Chapter 6. These diagrams can be used in any field; a good example is a company's table of organization, which helps you to see clearly the hierarchy, how the various departments relate, and the lines of communication between them.
5. *Graphs,* which show how two or more variables relate by indicating cause and effect, such as those described in Chapter 8. You may occasionally want to use a simple line graph or a pie chart to illustrate relationships. You will learn much about graphing in math, physics, and economics.
6. *Tables* comparing and contrasting information, such as those in Chapter 8.

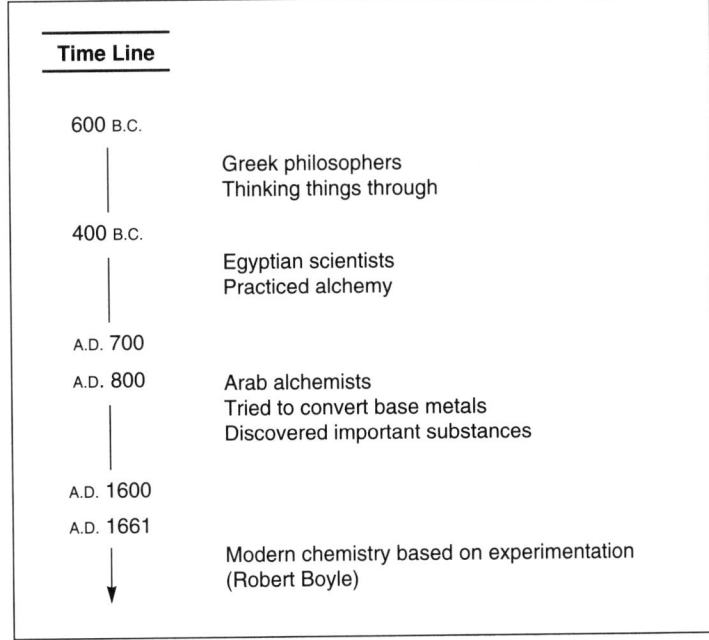

Figure 11.3 Time lines indicating chronological order

11 / Putting It Together: Flexible Reading and Active Learning

Exercise 11K

1. Set the material contained in the following short article into a time line.

   The British-Irish playwright, Richard Sheridan, was born in Dublin in 1751. His father was an actor and his mother a successful writer. Young Richard was educated at Harrow and eloped at the age of 22 with Elizabeth Linley. In 1776 he became part owner of the Drury Lane Theatre, a year after the the publication of one of his most popular plays—*The Rivals*. *The School for Scandal* appeared the next year followed by *The Critic*, in 1779, and *A Trip to Scarborough* in 1777. Sheridan's plays are known for their wit and sensibility as he satirized the life of fashionable England of his time. In 1780 he entered Parliament, where he became known for his brilliant speeches and subsequently became secretary of the treasury (1783), treasurer of the navy, and member of the Privy Council (1806), as well as a leader of London society. But in 1809 he was financially ruined by the burning of the Drury Lane Theater, and he was imprisoned for debt in 1813. He died in 1816.

2. Using Figure 11.4, make a rough graph of the information on p. 293. Use the months as the horizontal axis and one line

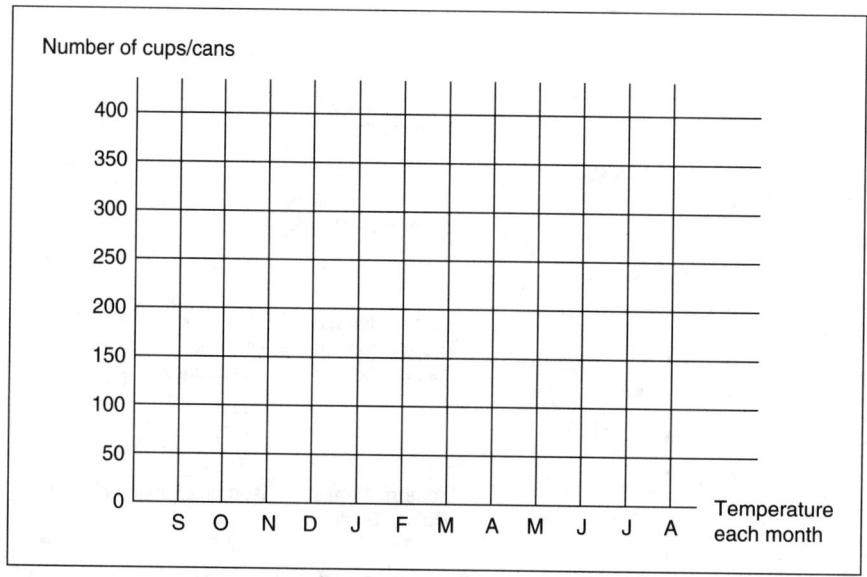

Figure 11.4 A graph for predicting coffee and soda sales

3 / *Analytical and Critical Reading Skills*

each for coffee and soda on the vertical axis. (You may want to refer to the material on graphs, p. 406.)

Al runs a small neighborhood convenience store. He wants to be able to predict the sales of coffee and soda, particularly in the winter, because he doesn't have a lot of room to store cases of soda. With his wife, Anna, he decides to estimate how many drinks of each, coffee and soda, they sell each month. They come up with the following figures:

Month	*Cups of Coffee*	*Cans of Soda*
September	250	300
October	275	200
November	300	100
December	300	60
January	300	50
February	310	75
March	300	100
April	275	125
May	275	175
June	250	300
July	200	400
August	200	400

a. Does the month make much difference in coffee sales?

_____

b. Does the month make much difference in soda sales?

_____

c. When does the demand for coffee equal the demand for soda?

_____

d. When can Al cut back on the storage of soda?

_____

3. Prepare a comparison chart that compares the formal outline and the Cornell Method of outlining. Remember to think about the different points of comparison (see p. 188).

Summary Exercise

Using the information this chapter presents on studying, complete the map depicted in Figure 11.5.

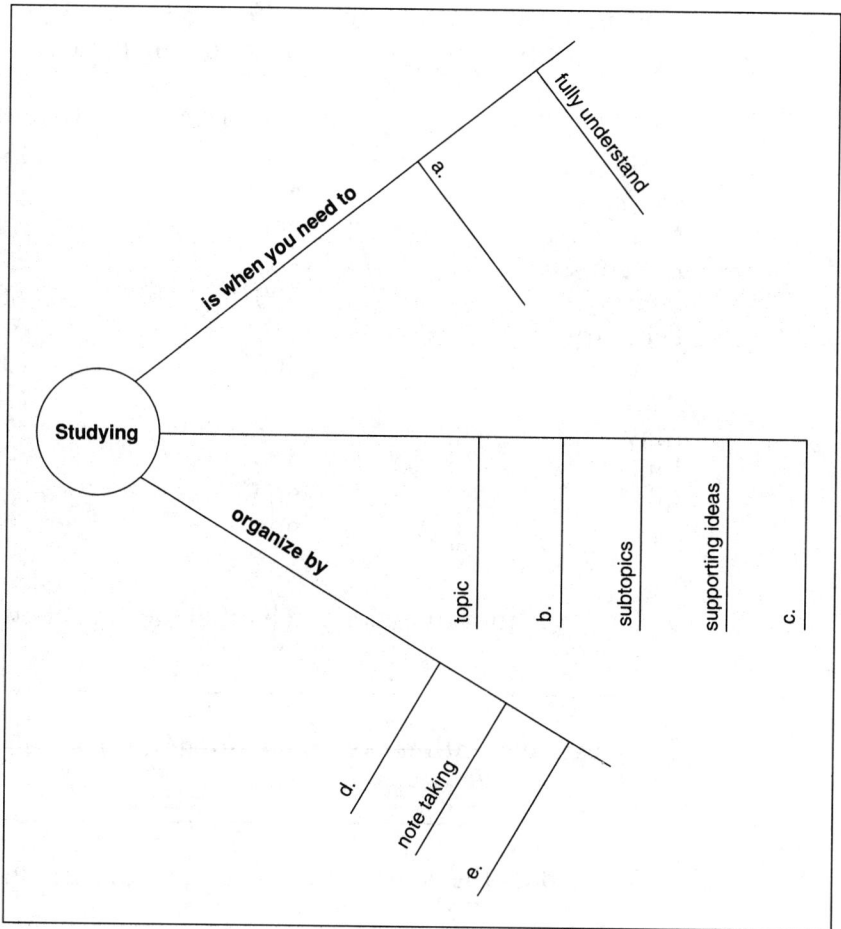

Figure 11.5

Mastery Exercise

Mastery Exercise II, like Mastery Exercise I, provides an opportunity for you to review the basic reading skills presented in Chapters 1 through 6; in addition, this mastery exercise includes analytical and critical reading skills discussed in Chapters 7 through 11. You will apply the techniques of questioning; setting purpose, associating, and predicting; finding topics and subtopics; reading for the key idea, supporting ideas, and supporting details; previewing; determining the author's purpose; recognizing basic structure; analyzing patterns of organization; and evaluating evidence.

A. Preview the article and answer questions 1 through 8.

1   There were 5½ million immigrants in the 1880s, 4 million in the 1890s, creating a labor surplus that kept wages down. The immigrants were more controllable, more helpless than native workers; they were culturally displaced, at odds with one another, therefore useful as strikebreakers. Often their children worked, intensifying the problem of an oversized labor force and joblessness; in 1880 there were 1,118,000 children under sixteen (one out of six) at work in the United States. With everyone working long hours, families often became strangers to one another. A pants presser named Morris Rosenfeld wrote a poem, "My Boy," which became widely reprinted and recited:

> I have a little boy at home,
> A pretty little son;
> I think sometimes the world is mine
> In him, my only one....
>
> 'Ere dawn my labor drives me forth;
> Tis night when I am free;
> A stranger am I to my child;
> And stranger my child to me....

2   Women immigrants became servants, prostitutes, housewives, factory workers, and sometimes rebels. Leonora Barry was born in Ireland and brought to the United States. She got married, and when her husband died she went to work in a hosiery mill in upstate New York to support three young children, earning 65 cents her first week. She joined the Knights of Labor, which had fifty thousand women mem-

bers in 192 women's assemblies by 1886. She became "master workman" of her assembly of 927 women, and was appointed to work for the Knights as a general investigator, to "go forth and educate her sister workingwomen and the public generally as to their needs and necessities." She described the biggest problem of women workers: "Through long years of endurance they have acquired, as a sort of second nature, the habit of submission and acceptance without question of any terms offered them, with the pessimistic view of life in which they see no hope." Her report for the year 1888 showed: 537 requests to help women organize, 100 cities and towns visited, 1,900 leaflets distributed.

In 1884, women's assemblies of textile workers and hatmakers went on strike. The following year in New York, cloak and shirt makers, men and women (holding separate meetings but acting together), went on strike. The New York *World* called it "a revolt for bread and butter." They won higher wages and shorter hours.

That winter in Yonkers, a few women carpet weavers were fired for joining the Knights, and in the cold of February, 2,500 women walked out and picketed the mill. Only seven hundred of them were members of the Knights, but all the strikers soon joined. The police attacked the picket line and arrested them, but a jury found them not guilty. A great dinner was held by working people in New York to honor them, with two thousand delegates from unions all over the city. The strike lasted six months, and the women won some of their demands, getting back their jobs, but without recognition of their union.

What was astonishing in so many of these struggles was not that the strikers did not win all that they wanted, but that, against such great odds, they dared to resist, and were not destroyed.

Perhaps it was the recognition that day-to-day combat was not enough, that fundamental change was needed, which stimulated the growth of revolutionary movements at this time....

In Chicago, the new International Working People's Association had five thousand members, published newspapers in five languages, organized mass demonstrations and parades, and through its leadership in strikes was a powerful influence in the twenty-two unions that made up the Central Labor Union of Chicago. There were differences in theory among all these revolutionary groups, but the theorists were often brought together by the practical needs of labor struggles, and there were many in the mid-1880s.

In early 1886, the Texas & Pacific Railroad fired a leader of the district assembly of the Knights of Labor, and this led to a strike which spread throughout the Southwest, tying up traffic as far as St. Louis and Kansas City. Nine young men recruited in New Orleans as marshals, brought to Texas to protect company property, learned about the strike and quit their jobs, saying, "as man to man we could not justifiably go to work and take the bread out of our fellow-workmen's mouths, no matter how much we needed it ourselves." They were then arrested for defrauding the company by refusing to work, and sentenced to three months in the Galveston county jail.

The strikers engaged in sabotage. A news dispatch from Atchison, Kansas:

> At 12:45 this morning the men on guard at the Missouri Pacific roundhouse were surprised by the appearance of 35 or 40 masked men. The guards were corralled in the oil room by a detachment of the visitors who stood guard with pistols...while the rest of them thoroughly disabled 12 locomotives which stood in the stalls.

In April, in East St. Louis, there was a battle between strikers and police. Seven workingmen were killed, whereupon workers burned the freight depot of the Louisville & Nashville. The governor declared martial law and sent in seven hundred National Guardsmen. With mass arrests, violent attacks by sheriffs and deputies, no support from the skilled, better-paid workers of the Railway Brotherhoods, the strikers could not hold out. After several months they surrendered, and many of them were blacklisted.

By the spring of 1886, the movement for an eight-hour day had grown. On May 1, the American Federation of Labor, now five years old, called for nationwide strikes wherever the eight-hour day was refused. Terence Powderly, head of the Knights of Labor, opposed the strike, saying that employers and employees must first be educated on the eight-hour day, but assemblies of the Knights made plans to strike. The grand chief of the Brotherhood of Locomotive Engineers opposed the eight-hour day, saying "two hours less work means two hours more loafing about the corners and two hours more for drink," but railroad workers did not agree and supported the eight-hour movement.

So, 350,000 workers in 11,562 establishments all over the country went out on strike. In Detroit, 11,000 workers marched in an eight-hour parade. In New York, 25,000 formed a torchlight procession along Broadway, headed by 3,400 members of the Bakers' Union. In Chicago, 40,000 struck, and 45,000 were granted a shorter working day to prevent them from striking. Every railroad in Chicago stopped running, and most of the industries in Chicago were paralyzed. The stockyards were closed down.

A "Citizens' Committee" of businessmen met daily to map strategy in Chicago. The state militia had been called out, the police were ready, and the Chicago *Mail* on May 1 asked that Albert Parsons and August Spies, the anarchist leaders of the International Working People's Association, be watched. "Keep them in view. Hold them personally responsible for any trouble that occurs. Make an example of them if trouble occurs."

Under the leadership of Parsons and Spies, the Central Labor Union, with twenty-two unions, had adopted a fiery resolution in the fall of 1885:

> Be it Resolved, That we urgently call upon the wage-earning class to arm itself in order to be able to put forth against their exploiters such an argument which alone can be effective: Violence, and further be it Resolved, that notwithstanding that we expect very little from the introduction of the eight-hour day, we firmly promise to assist our more backward brethren in this class struggle with all means and power at our disposal, so long as they will continue to show an open and resolute front to our common oppressors, the aristocratic vagabonds and exploiters. Our war-cry is "Death to the foes of the human race."

On May 3, a series of events took place which were to put Parsons and Spies in exactly the position that the Chicago *Mail* had suggested ("Make an example of them if trouble occurs"). That day, in front of the McCormick Harvester Works, where strikers and sympathizers fought scabs, the police fired into a crowd of strikers running from the scene, wounded many of them, and killed four. Spies, enraged, went to the printing shop of the *Arbeiter-Zeitung* and printed a circular in both English and German:

> Revenge!
> Workingmen, to Arms!!!
> ...You have for years endured the most abject humiliations;...you have worked yourself to death...your Children you have sacrificed to the factory lord—in short: you have been miserable and

obedient slaves all these years: Why? To satisfy the insatiable greed, to fill the coffers of your lazy thieving master? When you ask them now to lessen your burdens, he sends his bloodhounds out to shoot you, kill you!

...To arms we call you, to arms!

A meeting was called for Haymarket Square on the evening of May 4, and about three thousand persons assembled. It was a quiet meeting, and as storm clouds gathered and the hour grew late, the crowd dwindled to a few hundred. A detachment of 180 policemen showed up, advanced on the speakers' platform, ordered the crowd to disperse. The speaker said the meeting was almost over. A bomb then exploded in the midst of the police, wounding sixty-six policemen, of whom seven later died. The police fired into the crowd, killing several people, wounding two hundred.

With no evidence on who threw the bomb, the police arrested eight anarchist leaders in Chicago. The Chicago *Journal* said: "Justice should be prompt in dealing with the arrested anarchists. The law regarding accessories to crime in this State is so plain that their trials will be short." Illinois law said that anyone inciting a murder was guilty of that murder. The evidence against the eight anarchists was their ideas, their literature; none had been at Haymarket that day except Fielden, who was speaking when the bomb exploded. A jury found them guilty, and they were sentenced to death. Their appeals were denied; the Supreme Court said it had no jurisdiction.

The event aroused international excitement. Meetings took place in France, Holland, Russia, Italy, Spain. In London a meeting of protest was sponsored by George Bernard Shaw, William Morris, and Peter Kropotkin, among others. Shaw had responded in his characteristic way to the turning down of an appeal by the eight members of the Illinois Supreme Court: "If the world must lose eight of its people, it can better afford to lose the eight members of the Illinois Supreme Court."

A year after the trial, four of the convicted anarchists—Albert Parsons, a printer, August Spies, an upholsterer, Adolph Fischer, and George Engel—were hanged. Louis Lingg, a twenty-one-year-old carpenter, blew himself up in his cell by exploding a dynamite tube in his mouth. Three remained in prison.

The executions aroused people all over the country. There was a funeral march of 25,000 in Chicago. Some evidence came out that a man named Rudolph Schnaubelt, supposedly an anarchist, was actually an agent of the police, an *agent provocateur*, hired to throw the bomb and thus enable the arrest of hundreds, the destruction of the revolutionary leadership in Chicago. But to this day it has not been discovered who threw the bomb.

While the immediate result was a suppression of the radical movement, the long-term effect was to keep alive the class anger of many, to inspire others—especially young people of that generation—to action in revolutionary causes. Sixty thousand signed petitions to the new governor of Illinois, John Peter Altgeld, who investigated the facts, denounced what had happened, and pardoned the three remaining prisoners. Year after year, all over the country, memorial meetings for the Haymarket martyrs were held; it is impossible to know the number of individuals whose political awakening...came from the Haymarket Affair.

—Howard Zinn, *A People's History of the United States*

1. What is the reading about?

2. Why might you want to read about this topic?

3. What do you think is the author's most important idea about the topic?

4. Why did the author write this article?

5. What are four subtopics you expect to learn about in the reading?

6. What do you already know about the topic? What three statements come to mind when you think about the topic of this reading?

7. What are three points you predict the author will make?

8. What three questions do you have on this topic?

B. Now go back and read the article. Then complete the tasks outlined below.
   1. Diagram the information in the article, indicating topic, subtopics, supporting ideas, and supporting details. (You may want to refer to the diagrams in Chapter 6, pp. 00 and 00).
   2. Mark up the article by labeling the introduction, development, and conclusion.
   3. Write the answers you found to the questions you asked in part A, item 8.

_____

_____

4. Following are a few terms whose meanings you may have had to guess at. Infer the meaning of each word or phrase by using context clues, and write the explanation on the lines provided.

   a. "revolt for bread and butter" (paragraph 3, line 5):

   _____

   b. scabs (paragraph 14, line 6):

   _____

   c. "agent provocateur" (paragraph 19, line 5):

   _____

   d. recognition (paragraph 4, line 11 and paragraph 6, line 1)—explain the differences in the ways *recognition* is used in paragraph 4, line 9 and paragraph 6, line 1:

   _____

   _____

   _____

   _____

5. Complete the following questions by filling in the blanks.

   a. The principal pattern of organization of this article is

   _____.

   b. The workers used _____ and _____ to try to attain equal rights for all.

   c. The workers wanted an _____-hour day.

   d. The Knights of Labor was a _____.

e. Three results of the Haymarket Square demonstration were _____ , _____ , and _____ .

f. The author uses _____ to support his key idea.

Write a summary of the article.
_____

Critical Reading Skills Applied to Academic Fields

PART 4

Chapter 12

Reading the Humanities

In this chapter you will find answers to the following questions:

What are the humanities?
What kinds of reading can you expect in the humanities?
What role does critical reading play in the humanities?
How do you analyze fiction?
In what ways does studying the humanities prepare you for a career?

The Nature of the Humanities

The **humanities** are the branches of learning concerned with human thought and culture as represented in literature, philosophy, and the fine arts—art, music, dance, cinema, and photography. You are probably most familiar with literature, having read and studied fiction in high school.

Like reading in the natural sciences and the social sciences, reading in the humanities involves recognizing the author's purpose and evaluating the author's evidence and reasoning. In the humanities, however, the author's purpose and reasoning may be obscure. Thus, what may initially seem to be an easier reading task may in fact be harder. Reading critically is particularly important because much of the writing in the humanities is interpretive and subjective in an effort to convince or persuade. It is therefore necessary to evaluate constantly the authors' ideas and to make informed judgments about how they support these ideas and the reasoning behind them.

Writing in the humanities can take three forms: **informational** or expository writing, which is found in every field of the humanities; **imaginative** writing, or literature; and **persuasive** or critical writing, which is found in the literary essay, in philosophical writing, and in literary and fine arts criticism.

Informational Writing

In the humanities, authors write to inform you in many ways. These methods can be classified into three types of informational writing: factual, descriptive, and process.

Factual Writing

Factual writing provides background information on an author, composer, or artist or on a type or piece of music, literature, or art. Examples of factual writing include (1) notes on a book jacket or album cover and (2) longer pieces, such as a biography of an author (which you might read in a literature course) or an article describing a style of music (which you might read in a music appreciation course). This kind of writing provides a context for your study of the humanities.

The following example of factual writing provides background information about rock and roll by explaining its origins.

> But who's to say precisely where rock and roll began, anyway—does it date back to the "hillbilly" and "race" records issued by the nascent music industry in the 1920s? Was it born from the blues movement of the post–World War II era, in songs like Wynonie Harris's "Good Rockin' Tonight"? Perhaps it was a hard-rocking ode to a then-current car ("Rocket '88'") by an Ike Turner sideman, Jackie Brenston, that turned the corner from blues into rock and roll. Or did Elvis Presley, Scotty Moore, and Bill Black stumble onto it in Sun Studios while goofing around between takes with an Arthur "Big Boy" Crudup number, "That's All Right (Mama)"?
>
> If this were a test question, then the answer "all of the above" would have to be deemed acceptable. And that is by no means the whole picture. Into the melting pot you can add other seminal influences—jazz, folk, country, western swing, ragtime, gospel, ethnic balladry, and Broadway pop. Simmer for four decades and through two world wars. At

some time in the early fifties, rock and roll emerged as an entity quite distinct from its antecedents. Nurtured during an era of affluence by a generation that would find its voice and vocabulary through music, rock and roll set off on its headlong, reckless course.

—Jann S. Wenner, in Rock of Ages: The Rolling Stone History of Rock and Roll

Descriptive Writing

As its name implies, descriptive writing simply describes, or provides an image of, a piece of music, art, or literature. For example, descriptive writing might list the colors an artist used in a painting or the instruments a composer included in a musical composition, so as to make pictures or sounds in the reader's mind by calling up specific details of the work. Descriptive writing in the humanities, particularly in literature, is often mixed with critical writing.

The following paragraph vividly describes a scene painted by William Hogarth, an eighteenth-century English artist.

> In an episode [from Hogarth's painting] of the "Rake's Progress" the poor rake [dissipated man] has become a raving maniac and has to be put in irons in Bedlam. It is a crude scene of horror with all types of madmen represented: the religious fanatic in the first cell writhing on his bed of straw like the parody of a Baroque picture of a saint, the megalomaniac with his royal crown seen in the next cell, the idiot who scrawls the picture of the world on to the wall of Bedlam, the blind man with his paper telescope, the grotesque trio grouped round the staircase, the grinning fiddler, the foolish singer, and the touching figure of the apathetic man, with two men and a woman putting him in irons, the cruel equivalent of the strait-jacket. It is a tragic scene, made even more tragic by the grotesque dwarf who mocks it, and by the contrast with the two elegant visitors who had known the rake in the days of his prosperity.

—E. H. Gombrich, The Story of Art

Process Writing

Process writing explains a series of actions that bring about a result. It tells the reader how to do something or how something was done—for example, explaining the technique used to shoot film. This kind of writing is often found in art and music appreciation courses, where understanding how an artist or musician created a certain effect is important.

The following example explains how to use a feather duster to paint scenery.

> The household feather duster made of turkey feathers provides an extremely fast method of applying either a uniform or a varied texture on large areas of scenery that are laid flat on the floor. The feather duster should have an extended handle so that it can be easily manipulated while you are standing. It is used by dipping the feathers into a large pail of thin paint or dye, letting the excess drain off slightly in the container, then applying the color on the surface by holding the feather duster vertically and working it in an up-and-down motion while twirling it gently between strokes. The feather duster can be used for texturing on almost any kind of material or fabric that is a flat surface. It may be used for applying texture with dyes on a velour cut drop, vinyl or latex on a Masonite deck, or casein on canvas-covered flats.
>
> —Lynn Pecktal, *Designing and Painting for the Theatre*

Authors may also use more than one type of informational writing in a given selection, as in the following example from an art history textbook. The writing in this paragraph combines the first two types: factual and descriptive writing.

> Scenes from the world of entertainment—dance halls, cafés, concerts, the theater—were favorite subjects for Impressionist painters. Auguste Renoir (1841–1919), another important member of the group, filled his with the joie de vivre of a singularly happy temperament. The flirting couples in "Le Moulin de Galette," under the dappled pattern of sunlight and shadow, radiate a human warmth that is utterly entrancing, even though the artist permits us no more than a fleeting glance at any of them.
>
> —H. W. Janson, *History of Art*

The first part of the above passage is an example of factual writing. In the first two sentences the author tells you specific information about the impressionist painters and places Renoir in that period. After giving you this background material, the author moves on to descriptive writing by verbally explaining Renoir's painting *Le Moulin de Galette*.

Exercise 12A

Read the following selections and label in the margins the different types of informational writing the author uses in each article: factual, descriptive, or process. Then answer the questions that follow each article.

1. A movie audience sits in relative darkness watching a dominant, framed area on the screen. There is movement there, and it powerfully draws the eye. There are two other attractions as well. There are patterns of light: shifting textures and contrasts. And there are shifting arrangements of figures inside the apparent depth of the picture. In the movie house, then, space is no longer a given factor of ordinary life but something special—a *design* of movement, light, and spatial relationships.

   This design space is a movie's *mise en scène*. Derived from a French term for a stage setting ("that which is placed on stage"), *mise en scène* refers to the whole movement of performers, costuming, and set design, as well as the use of light. It excludes dialogue or any effects that result from joining shots together in the editing process. Some writers employ the term as a general synonym for a film's overall visual style. *Mise en scène* is specifically a matter of composition.

   —George Wead and George Lellis, *Film: Form and Function*

   a. What are the three attractions on the movie screen? _____

   _____

   b. What is *mise en scène*? _____

   _____

   c. From which language is *mise en scène* derived? _____

2. As far as Jamaican record-buyers are concerned, the word *reggae* was coined on a 1968 Pyramid dance single, "Do the Reggay [sic]," by Toots and the Maytals. Some believe the term is derived from Regga, the name of a Bantu-speaking tribe on Lake Tanganyika. Others say it is a corruption of "steggae," Kingston street slang for prostitute. Bob Marley claimed the word was Spanish in origin, meaning "the king music." Veteran Jamaican studio musicians offer the simplest, and prob-

ably the most plausible, explanation. "It's a description of the beat itself," says Hux Brown, lead guitarist on Paul Simon's 1972 reggae-flavored hit, "Mother and Child Reunion," and the man widely credited with inventing the one-string quiver/trill that kicked off Simon's single as well as many of the top island hits of the preceding years. "It's just a fun, joke kinda word that means the ragged rhythm and the body feelin'. If it's got a greater meanin', it doesn't matter."

—Timothy White, *Catch a Fire: The Life of Bob Marley*

a. What is this selection about? _____

b. What is the author's most important idea about the topic?

_____

c. What are three supporting ideas? _____

_____

_____

d. What did Hux Brown mean when he said, "If it's got a greater meanin', it doesn't matter"? _____

_____

Patterns of Organization

You will find all the patterns of organization used in the humanities. Authors may describe or list the characteristics of a style of painting, provide chronological information about a composer, compare and contrast two types of literature, cite the influence or effect of one sculptor on another, or propose one or more solutions to problems in recording music.

Most informational writing in the humanities includes a variety of patterns of organization; however, one pattern is usually dominant. The following example of the order pattern provides background information about Kate Chopin, the author of "The Story of an Hour," a work analyzed later in this chapter.

Of French and Irish ancestry, Kate O'Flaherty was born in 1851 in St. Louis, Missouri. A wide reader from early youth, she received her educational training at the Sacred Heart Convent, from which she graduated in 1868. Two years later she married Oscar Chopin, a native of Louisiana, who took her to live in New Orleans, where he was a cotton broker. She and her husband participated in the social life of that exotic city, despite the responsibilities of a steadily growing family, which ultimately numbered six children—five boys and one girl. When her husband gave up his cotton brokerage business to manage a large plantation he owned on the Red River in central Louisiana, the family relocated there, and the writer was thus brought to the section of the country which was to provide her with the distinctive settings and characters of her stories. Her husband died in 1882, and feeling herself unable to assume the responsibilities of operating the plantation, she sold it and returned to St. Louis with her six children.

Encouraged to write by friends who had admired her letters, she first produced an amateurish novel, *At Fault* (1890). Then she began publishing skillfully written stories in *Century* and *Harper's* magazines. Two collections soon appeared: *Bayou Folk* (1894) and *A Night in Acadie* (1897). Her final work, *The Awakening* (1899), a novel, received unfavorable critical notices because of its treatment of mixed marriages and adultery. She died suddenly in 1904.

—Eugene Current-Garcia and Walton R. Patrick,
American Short Stories

The following chart shows the patterns of organization for particular situations in informational writing.

	Pattern of Organization	Application	Example
Factual and descriptive	List	Style of painting	"Renoir" reading
	Order	Background information	"Kate Chopin" reading
	Compare/contrast	Different definitions of musical term	"Reggae" reading
	Cause and effect	Influence on another	Tuchman reading (See Exercise 12B)

	Pattern of Organization	Application	Example
Process	Order Problem-solution	How to use something How to fix something	"Feather duster" reading

Example 12B

Read the following examples of informational writing and determine the topic, key idea, and dominant pattern of organization of each one.

1. **East Texas Furniture** The presence of German craftsmen accounts for most of the furniture built in Texas from the late 1830s to the turn of the century. And the workmanship has a special character. Generally solid and simple, the furniture conforms little to the fashions of England and France that dominated most other styles. It combines a kind of German precision and practicality with a western American feeling for size and strength; the furniture utilizes decorative details that speak both of origins and of adopted symbols.

   —Robert Morton, *Southern Antiques and Folk Art*

   a. Topic: _____

   b. Key idea: _____

   c. Pattern of organization: _____

2. As to the mechanics of research, I take notes on four-by-six index cards, reminding myself about once an hour of a rule I read long ago in a research manual, "Never write on the back of anything." Since copying is a chore and a bore, use of the cards, the smaller the better, forces one to extract the strictly relevant, to distill from the very beginning, to pass the material through the grinder of one's own mind, so to speak. Eventually, as the cards fall into groups according to subject or person or chronological sequence, the pattern of my story will emerge. Besides, they are convenient, as they can be filed in a shoebox and carried around in a pocketbook. When ready to write I need only take along a packet of them,

representing a chapter, and I am equipped to work anywhere; whereas if one writes surrounded by a pile of books, one is tied to a single place, and furthermore likely to be too much influenced by other authors.

2   The most important thing about research is to know when to stop. How does one recognize the moment? When I was eighteen or thereabouts, my mother told me that when out with a young man I should always leave a half-hour before I wanted to. Although I was not sure how this might be accomplished, I recognized the advice as sound, and exactly the same rule applies to research. One must stop *before* one has finished; otherwise, one will never stop and never finish....

3   Research is endlessly seductive; writing is hard work. One has to sit down on that chair and think and transform thought into readable, conservative, interesting sentences that both make sense and make the reader turn the page. It is laborious, slow, often painful, sometimes agony. It means rearrangement, revision, adding, cutting, rewriting. But it brings a sense of excitement, almost of rapture; a moment on Olympus. In short, it is an act of creation.

—Barbara Tuchman, *In Search of History*

a. Topic: _____

b. Key idea: _____

c. Pattern of organization: _____

3. According to the Realists and the Naturalists, the function of art, like that of science, was the betterment of humankind, and so the method of the artist should be that of the scientist. Because truth resided in material objects, art had to depict the material, tangible world. Because problems could be solved only through application of the scientific method, dramatists should emulate scientists and strive to become objective observers of the social milieu. Plays should be set in contemporary times and places, for only they could be observed firsthand by the playwright. As the highest purpose of art was the betterment of humanity, the subject of plays should be contemporary life and its problems.

—Kenneth M. Cameron and Patti P. Gillespie,
The Enjoyment of Theatre

a. Topic: _____

b. Key idea: _____

c. Pattern of Organization: _____

Imaginative Writing: Fiction

Imagination and creativity are essential parts of the humanistic tradition. The artist—whether author, painter, dancer, filmmaker, sculptor, or composer—provides a different, exciting, and meaningful interpretation that is meant to give not only pleasure but also a deeper understanding of and new insights into the human experience. Although an artistic interpretation of experience takes place in art and music, we shall confine our discussion in this chapter to a brief look at the imaginative writing found in fiction—novels, short stories, and plays—using the short story as our primary example.

The specific difference between fiction, or imaginative writing, and nonfiction is that in reading fiction you deal not only with what the authors say, but also with how they say it. And so in fiction, the medium is at least as important as the message. Imaginative writing appeals primarily to the reader's imagination or emotions and is evaluated for its style and artistic effect as well as for its logic.

Most colleges offer a variety of courses in reading and interpreting literature; whole books are devoted to just one aspect of literary interpretation. Although this book cannot go into the same amount of detail, you will find that applying the skills you have learned in *Active Reading* will help you arrive at a better understanding of a piece of fiction.

Previewing Fiction

Previewing imaginative writing is different from previewing other material. Literary works are not textbooks, set up with headings and helpful study aids; nor do they fall into the realm of objective argument, supported by proofs or evidence. Instead, fiction is subjective and usually subtle. It does not yield easily to quick surveys. Nevertheless, there is something to be gained by applying the following three preview questions to your reading:

1. *What is this book (or story, or play) about?*
   The title and chapter headings may provide clues about the author's plot or theme. And a quick glance at the text may give you an idea of the setting and a sense of who the main characters are.

2. *Why are you reading it?*
   This question calls for an examination of your motives so that you can adapt your reading to your purpose. Are you reading simply for enjoyment, as one does when reading a detective story? If so, you will read quickly, to find out how the story ends. Or are you reading to discover meaning and thus to understand the author's ideas, as when you read a classic like *Moby Dick?* In this case, you will study the work closely, probably reading it several times: first very quickly, to get a sense of the story or plot, and later, more deeply, to discover the author's **theme,** or key idea, by analyzing the development of events and the characters' reactions to them.

3. *What do you already know about the topic?*
   Literary works are based on experience. Authors expect a reader to react to their writings on the basis of the reader's own experiences and feelings. Therefore, it is important to start associating with the contents of books or stories as soon as you can. Sometimes you'll do so through identifying with place—if, for instance, you live on a farm, you'll be more likely to understand the plight of the migrant farmers in John Steinbeck's *Grapes of Wrath* than will a city dweller, reading the same novel from a more objective and broader historical **perspective.** At other times you'll identify with the characters—if you know someone who has struggled with emotional illness, your reading of and reaction to Ken Kesey's *One Flew over the Cuckoo's Nest* will be much more direct than it would be if you did not connect with the characters that way. And finally, if from your knowledge and experience you recognized the title of Lorraine Hansberry's *Raisin in the Sun* as a quotation from a Langston Hughes poem in which the poet compares a dream postponed to a raisin that withers in the sun, you would immediately have an insight into Hansberry's play. Awareness of this subjective dimension forms an important part of the active reading of literature.

If you find that you get very little information from asking these preview questions, you might try to make connections to the individual authors and to the background of their works by consulting biographical and other relevant material in the library.

Analytical and Critical Reading of Fiction

Fiction consists of stories about characters whose thoughts and actions portray an image of life—the author's theme. The questions, *Who? What? Where? When?* and *Why?* will have different emphases in different works but will always serve to move the story forward. Sometimes it is the characters that are most important, as in *Hamlet*, and sometimes it is the action, as in a story by Edgar Allan Poe. An analysis of a literary work requires an examination of action, characters, setting, plot, and language in an effort to discern the theme.

Action

The **action** in fiction is a series of connected events that may or may not be presented chronologically—some fiction begins at the middle or end and includes flashbacks. The dominant pattern of organization in fiction is problem-solution, generally referred to as *conflict-resolution.* Authors usually begin their stories by setting the scene and introducing the characters. A problem, in the shape of a conflict, soon appears, complicating the situation with various causes and effects as the story moves toward its climax. At the end is a resolution—that is, a solution of the problem that leaves the characters changed and the reader with a situation different from the one at the beginning of the story. For example, Holden Caulfield's experiences mature and shape him so that at the end of the story he faces life as a different person from the confused boy we met at the beginning of *A Catcher in the Rye.* Questions based on action might include *What are the principal actions? Why is this particular action happening at this particular time? What is its effect? What is the conflict? How is it resolved?* and *What changes have taken place?*

Characters

Characters are usually introduced by description; the more vivid the description, the better you see them. Yet, the reader comes to know the characters through their actions: what they think, say, and do. Noting these actions helps you understand why the characters behave as they do, why they are important to the plot, and whether a given action is consistent with a given character. It would not be in character, for example, for the mean-spirited, hard-driving Fagin in *Oliver Twist* to turn into a "nice guy." Much of the relevance of particular characters derives from their relationships with the other characters in a story. The reader's task is to try to understand these relationships through asking such questions as *Why was a particular character included? How does this character influence the plot?* and *What is the author conveying through this character's actions?*

Setting

Setting—time and place—may also play a role in the story, depending on the author's purpose. The author may use setting as a part of the story, as in Thornton Wilder's *Our Town;* as a microcosm in which the actors play out a story with universal significance, as in Herman Melville's *Moby Dick;* or as a realm in which the characters are influenced by historical events, as in Charles Dickens's *A Tale of Two Cities.* Occasionally the setting has no particular significance in itself. The following questions are useful in discovering the role of setting: *Is the setting significant? What purpose does it serve?* and *Could the story have occurred somewhere else or at some other time?*

Plot and Theme

Plot, defined as the outline, or skeleton, of the narrative, is usually the element in fiction that initially interests the reader. The plot is introduced by the answer to the question, *What is this about?* But authors have a deeper purpose than just to tell stories; stories are the vehicles for the ideas and insights that make up the authors' **themes.** It is this message—often not set out in words but made explicit through the actions of the characters—that is the object of the reader's search. A beginning to the search for theme is to ask, *What is the author's most important idea about the topic?* Let's return to the example of *Moby Dick.* The novel is about the pursuit of the white whale by Captain Ahab; that is the subject matter of the plot. The theme is Herman Melville's idea that Captain Ahab brings ruin on himself and others by pursuing an impossible dream. Or, a more universal statement is that it is fatal, but heroic, to attempt to achieve the impossible. An author's theme is always closely related to the central conflict. The author presents his or her view of life by showing how the characters react in certain circumstances and how they are affected by the conflict. The reader may not agree with this view of life—in fact, the author is usually asking only for a reaction—but the reader should make every effort to recognize why the author wrote the story and how the plot supports the theme.

Language

In imaginative writing, unlike what is found in most nonfiction, use of language is the writer's art. The choice of words and the style of writing are carefully worked out to express feelings or ideas in new images. Words are authors' only tools for conveying meanings and for suggesting, implying, and so arousing feelings, as you will see in "The Story of an Hour," analyzed on page 323. Through their interpretations and insights authors aim to help you understand yourself and others.

Evaluating Fiction

At the risk of making perhaps too simple a generalization, it can be said that the topic introduces the plot and the key idea leads to the theme, whereas the action, characters, setting, and language provide the supporting ideas and supporting details. An analytical reading helps us see how an author uses the supporting ideas and details to tell the story on which the key idea or theme is based.

As a critical reader, you will use these analytical tools in examining imaginative writing and will then go on to decide (1) how successful authors are in accomplishing their aims and (2) your reactions to their writings.

As noted earlier, much of the pleasure in reading fiction is that each reader filters an interpretation of it through his or her own experience and outlook. There are thus many different ways of looking at an individual text, none of them necessarily "right." Nevertheless, the more you read and learn, the more knowledge and insights you can bring to your reading and the more skillful you can become in working out what the author's theme is and how well it is conveyed. Even so, from the beginning you can have opinions based on your reactions to the text. You can start with such questions as *Do the characters seem real? Do they behave consistently? Does everything—characters, setting, action—work together to move the story forward?* And you can ask yourself: *Can I work out how the plot provides evidence for the author's theme? Do I agree with the author's ideas, and if not, why not?* and *Do I like what I read, and why or why not?*

Now we will apply some of the questions introduced in this section to the reading of a short story entitled "The Story of an Hour," by Kate Chopin, whose biography you read on page 313.

First, a preview to see what can be discovered about the story: What is it about? Where is it set? Who are the principal characters?

The Story of an Hour

Knowing that Mrs. Mallard was afflicted with a heart trouble, great care was taken to break to her as gently as possible the news of her husband's death.

It was her sister Josephine who told her, in broken sentences, veiled hints that revealed in half concealing. Her husband's friend Richards was there, too, near her. It was he who had been in the newspaper office when intelligence of the railroad disaster was received, with Brently Mallard's name leading the list of "killed." He had only taken the time to assure himself of its truth by a second telegram, and had hastened to forestall any less careful, less tender friend in bearing the sad message.

She did not hear the story as many women have heard the same, with a paralyzed inability to accept its significance. She wept at once, with sudden, wild abandonment, in her sister's arms. When the storm of grief had spent itself she went away to her room alone. She would have no one follow her.

There stood, facing the open window, a comfortable, roomy armchair. Into this she sank, pressed down by a physical exhaustion that haunted her body and seemed to reach into her soul.

She could see in the open square before her house the tops of trees that were all aquiver with the new spring of life. The delicious breath of rain was in the air. In the street below a peddler was crying his wares. The notes of a distant song which some one was singing reached her faintly, and countless sparrows were twittering in the eaves.

There were patches of blue sky showing here and there through the clouds that had met and piled above the other in the west facing her window.

She sat with her head thrown back upon the cushion of the chair quite motionless, except when a sob came up into her throat and shook her, as a child who has cried itself to sleep continues to sob in its dreams.

She was young, with a fair, calm face, whose lines bespoke repression and even a certain strength. But now there was a dull stare in her eyes, whose gaze was fixed away off yonder on one of those patches of blue sky. It was not a glance of reflection, but rather indicated a suspension of intelligent thought.

There was something coming to her and she was waiting for it, fearfully. What was it? She did not know; it was too subtle and elusive to name. But she felt it, creeping out of the sky, reaching toward her through the sounds, the scents, the color that filled the air.

Now her bosom rose and fell tumultuously. She was beginning to recognize this thing that was approaching to possess her, and she was striving to beat it back with her will—as powerless as her two white slender hands would have been.

When she abandoned herself a little whispered word escaped her slightly parted lips. She said it over and over under her breath: "Free, free, free!" The vacant stare and the look of terror that had followed it went from her eyes. They stayed keen and bright. Her pulses beat fast, and the coursing blood warmed and relaxed every inch of her body.

She did not stop to ask if it were not a monstrous joy that held her. A clear and exalted perception enabled her to dismiss the suggestion as trivial.

She knew that she would weep again when she saw the kind, tender hands folded in death; the face that had never looked save with love upon her, fixed and gray and dead. But she saw beyond that bitter moment a long procession of years to come that would belong to her absolutely. And she opened and spread her arms out to them in welcome.

There would be no one to live for during those coming years; she would live for herself. There would be no powerful will bending her in that blind persistence with which men and women believe they have a right to impose a private will upon a fellow-creature. A kind intention or a cruel intention made the act seem no less a crime as she looked upon it in that brief moment of illumination.

And yet she had loved him—sometimes. Often she had not. What did it matter! What could love, the unsolved mystery, count for in face of this possession of self-assertion which she suddenly recognized as the strongest impulse of her being!

"Free! Body and soul free!" she kept whispering.

Josephine was kneeling before the closed door with her lips to the keyhole, imploring for admission, "Louise, open the door! I beg; open the door—you will make yourself ill. What are you doing, Louise? For heaven's sake open the door."

"Go away. I am not making myself ill." No; she was drinking in a very elixir of life through that open window.

Her fancy was running riot along those days ahead of her. Spring days, and summer days, and all sorts of days that would be her own. She breathed a quick prayer that life might be long. It was only yesterday she had thought with a shudder that life might be long.

She arose at length and opened the door to her sister's importunities. There was a feverish triumph in her eyes, and she carried herself unwittingly like a goddess of Victory. She clasped her sister's waist, and together they descended the stairs. Richards stood waiting for them at the bottom.

Some one was opening the front door with a latchkey. It was Brently Mallard who entered, a little travel-stained, composedly carrying his grip-sack and umbrella. He had been far from the scene of accident, and did not even know there had been one. He stood amazed at Josephine's piercing cry; at Richard's quick motion to screen him from the view of his wife.

But Richards was too late.

When the doctors came they said she had died of heart disease—of joy that kills.

—Kate Chopin

Your preview starts with the title, "The Story of an Hour," which tells you that the tale is set in a particular time frame: one hour. A glance at the rest of the material shows that it is about a woman—there are many references to "she" and "her"; perhaps "she" is Mrs. Mallard—and that the action seems to take place in a house or a room.

Now go back and study the story to see whether you agree with the answers to the questions below.

What is the story about?

You can expand on your preview by saying that the story is about a Mrs. Mallard, whose husband died suddenly.

Who are the main characters? How do they relate to one another?

There is really only one main character, Mrs. Mallard, although one could say Mr. Mallard plays a role.

What is the conflict?

The conflict is within Mrs. Mallard; it consists of her sense of loss as opposed to her new feelings of freedom.

What is Mrs. Mallard's motivation?

She wants to be free.

How is the conflict resolved?

By Mrs. Mallard's death.

What is Kate Chopin's theme, or underlying message?

That a woman's need for independence is more important than her need for love.

Does Mrs. Mallard behave realistically?

Yes. She seems to be a woman of some passion who responds in dramatic ways, as when she cried on hearing the news of her husband's death and while she was alone.

Are the setting and timing of the story significant?

That the events took place in an hour is significant. What happens in such a short time is the climax to what were probably years of conflict between repression and expression.

What does Kate Chopin want the reader to feel or think as a result of having read the story?

The author seems to want the reader to understand and have sympathy for Mrs. Mallard's intense desire to be her own person.

Has Kate Chopin accomplished that purpose? If so, how?

Our subjective answer is yes, because of the way Chopin shows us the change that came over Mrs. Mallard. Compare the description and language in paragraph 8—"She was young, with a fair, calm face, whose lines bespoke repression...dull stare...suspension of intelligent thought"— with those in paragraphs 10 and 11—"Now her bosom rose and fell tumultuously...she abandoned herself...the vacant stare and the look of terror...went from her eyes. They stayed keen and bright. Her pulses beat fast...."

This analysis is one reading of the story. You may not agree with it, but if you do not, you need to be able to justify your differing opinions by referring directly to the story. You will learn more about judgment and evaluation as they are used in the humanities when you read the section on criticism that appears later in this chapter.

Although we have used a short story to illustrate previewing and reading imaginative literature, the points made here can be applied equally well to novels and plays. Novels differ principally because of their length. In a short story, the author has to jump right in and give the reader as much information as is necessary to the story, as quickly as possible (look back to see how much information is contained in the opening paragraph of "The Story of an Hour"). In a novel, there can be a much more leisurely presentation of background, characters, and setting. In a short story, there is usually only one conflict, and once it is resolved the story comes to a rapid close; in a novel, there may be a main conflict and several minor ones, all contributing to the forward movement of the plot, and their resolution may be delayed. A play is more like a short story than a novel, except that everything the reader knows about the plot and characters comes from the dialogue and the setting. In all these types of literature, the characters, setting, action, and language combine to provide the author's vision or insight into people and the ways they live their lives.

When you are studying literary texts, the following steps will help your understanding:

1. Read through once quickly, to see what the story is about. Then reread carefully, noting action, characters, setting, plot and theme, and language.
2. Mark words and passages that seem important to you. This technique is particularly useful as a way of having material on hand to refer to or quote from when you are writing a paper on the text.
3. Make a chronological outline of the events.
4. Diagram the relationships among the various characters. Write brief character sketches.
5. Write a summary of how the plot is used to work out the author's theme.
6. Make notes of your reactions to the text.

Exercise 12C

Preview, read, and reread the following story, entitled "The Portrait." It was written by Tomás Rivera, an author, scholar, and educator from Texas. Answer the questions that come after it.

The Portrait

As soon as the people returned from up north the portrait salesmen began arriving from San Antonio. They would come to rake in. They knew that the workers had money and that was why, as Dad used to say, they would flock in. They carried suitcases packed with samples and always wore white shirts and ties; that way they looked more important and the people believed everything they would tell them and invite them into their homes without giving it much thought. I think that down deep they even longed for their children to one day be like them. In any event, they would arrive and make their way down the dusty streets, going house to house carrying suitcases full of samples.

I remember once I was at the house of one of my father's friends when one of these salesmen arrived. I also remember that that particular one seemed a little frightened and timid. Don Mateo asked him to come in because he wanted to do business.

"Good afternoon, traveler. I would like to tell you about something new that we're offering this year."

"Well, let's see, let's see..."

"Well, sir, see, you give us a picture, any picture you may have, and we will not only enlarge it for you but we'll also set it in a wooden frame like this one and we'll shape the image a little, like this—three dimensional, as they say."

"And what for?"

"So that it will look real. That way...look, let me show you...see? Doesn't he look real, like he's alive?"

"Man, he sure does. Look, vieja. This looks great. Well, you know, we wanted to send some pictures to be enlarged ...but now, this must cost a lot, right?"

"No, I'll tell you, it costs about the same. Of course, it takes more time."

"Well, tell me, how much?"

"For as little as thirty dollars we'll deliver it to you done with inlays just like this, one this size."

"Boy, that's expensive! Didn't you say it didn't cost a lot more? Do you take installments?"

"Well, I'll tell you, we have a new manager and he wants everything in cash. It's very fine work. We'll make it look like real. Shaped like that, with inlays...take a look. What do you think? Some fine work, wouldn't you say? We can have it all finished for you in a month. You just tell us what color you want the clothes to be and we'll come by with it all finished one day when you least expect, framed and all. Yes, sir, a month at the longest. But like I say, this man, who's the new manager, he wants the full payment in cash. He's very demanding, even with us."

"Yes, but it's much too expensive."

"Well, yes. But the thing is, this is very fine work. You can't say you've ever seen portraits done like this, with wood inlays."

"No, well, that's true. What do you think, vieja?"

"Well, I like it a lot. Why don't we order one? And if it turns out good...my Chuy...may he rest in peace. It's the only picture we have of him. We took it right before he left for Korea. Poor m'ijo, we never saw him again. See... this is his picture. Do you think you can make it like that, make it look like he's alive?"

"Sure, we can. You know, we've done a lot of them in soldier's uniforms and shaped it, like you see in this sample, with inlays. Why, it's more than just a portrait. Sure. You just tell me what size you want and whether you want a round or square frame. What do you say? How should I write it down?"

"What do you say, vieja, should we have it done like this one?"

"Well, I've already told you what I think. I would like to have m'ijo's picture fixed up like that and in color."

"All right, go ahead and write it down. But you take good care of that picture for us because it's the only one we have of our son grown up. He was going to send us one all dressed up in uniform with the American and Mexican flags crossed over his head, but he no sooner got there when a letter arrived telling us that he was lost in action. So you take good care of it."

"Don't you worry. We're responsible people. And we understand the sacrifices that you people make. Don't worry. And you just wait and see, when we bring it, you'll see how pretty it's gonna look. What do you say, should we make the uniform navy blue?"

"But he's not wearing a uniform in that picture."

"No, but that's just a matter of fixing it up with some wood fiber overlay. Look at these. This one, he didn't have a uniform on but we put one on him. So what do you say? Should we make it navy blue?"

"All right."

"Don't you worry about the picture."

And that was how they spent the entire day, going house to house, street by street, their suitcases stuffed with pictures. As it turned out, a whole lot of people had ordered enlargements of that kind.

"They should be delivering those portraits soon, don't you think?"

"I think so, it's delicate work and takes more time. That's some fine work those people do. Did you see how real those pictures looked?"

"Yeah, sure. They do some fine work. You can't deny that. But it's already been over a month since they passed by here."

"Yes, but from here they went on through all the towns picking up pictures...all the way to San Antonio for sure. So it'll probably take a little longer."

"That's true, that's true."

And two more weeks had passed by the time they made the discovery. Some very heavy rains had come and some children, who were playing in one of the tunnels leading to the dump, found a sack full of pictures, all worm-eaten and soaking wet. The only reason that they could tell that these were pictures was because there were a lot of them and most of them the same size and with faces that could just barely be made out. Everybody caught on right away. Don Mateo was so angry that he took off to San Antonio to find the so and so who had swindled them.

"Well, you know, I stayed at Esteban's house. And every day I went with him to the market to sell produce. I helped him with everything. I had faith that I would run into that son of a gun some day soon. Then, after I'd been there for a few days, I started going out to the different barrios and I found out a lot that way. It wasn't so much the money that upset me. It was my poor vieja, crying and all because we'd lost the only picture we had of Chuy. We found it in the sack with all the other pictures but it was already ruined, you know."

"I see, but tell me, how did you find him?"

"Well, you see, to make a long story short, he came by the stand at the market one day. He stood right in front of us and bought some vegetables. It was like he was trying to remember who I was. Of course, I recognized him right off. Because when you're angry enough, you don't forget a face. I just grabbed him right then and there. Poor guy couldn't even talk. He was all scared. And I told him that I wanted that portrait of my son and that I wanted it three dimensional and that he'd best get it for me or I'd let him have it. And I went with him to where he lived. And I put him to work right then and there. The poor guy didn't know where to begin. He had to do it all from memory."

"And how did he do it?"

"I don't know. I suppose if you're scared enough, you're capable of doing anything. Three days later he brought me the portrait all finished, just like you see it there on that table by the Virgin. Now tell me, how do you like the way my boy looks?"

"Well, to be honest, I don't remember too well how Chuy looked. But he was beginning to look more and more like you, isn't that so?"

"Yes, I would say so. That's what everybody tells me now. That Chuy's a chip off the old block and that he was already looking like me. There's the portrait. Like they say, one and the same."

—Tomás Rivera, *And the Earth Did Not Devour Him*

1. What is the story about?

2. Who are the main characters?

3. How do they relate to each other?

4. What motivates the principal characters?

5. What is the conflict?

6. How is the conflict resolved?

7. What do you think is Rivera's theme?

8. Do the characters behave realistically?

   _____
   _____

9. Are the setting and timing of the story significant?

   _____
   _____

10. What does the author want the reader to feel or to think as a result of having read the story?

    _____
    _____
    _____

11. Has the author accomplished his purpose? If so, how?

    _____
    _____
    _____

12. Do you agree or disagree with Rivera's theme. Why?

    _____
    _____
    _____

Persuasive Writing and Critical Reading

In the humanities, frequently the purpose of persuasive writing is to persuade or convince the reader that the author is right. Therefore, authors' writing in the humanities may be more overtly subjective than in the natural and social sciences. Authors in the humanities offer their own opinions with reasons to support their ideas; they offer evidence from a text, a piece of art or music, or a film, or from the writer's own thinking, as in philosophy. As you learned in Chapters 9 and 10, reading critically to evaluate an author's ideas is important when reading persuasive writing. Persuasive writing can be further distinguished as being **criticism** or **argument.**

Criticism

When an author is examining the work of someone else, subjecting it to analysis and critical evaluation, the result is critical writing. You read criticism to get a deeper understanding or a different interpretation of an author's or artist's work. Criticism can provide a greater appreciation of a work because the critic or reviewer looks carefully at what the author or the artist set out to do, analyzes how the author or artist went about it, and evaluates how well the artist or author succeeded. The most obvious example of critical writing is found in reviews of books, movies, concerts, and art shows, in which the reviewer presents an account of the product and then gives an opinion of how good it is. Comparing and contrasting one work with another one produced by the same artist or by another person are also frequently done.

Critics present examples and details from a work that illustrate its strengths and weaknesses, the reviewer's reactions to these aspects, and analyses of their responses. As a type of persuasive writing, criticism is based on opinion and uses the questions introduced in Chapters 9 and 10:

- What is the author or artist trying to prove?
- What techniques did the author or artist use to persuade the reader?
- How well did the author or artist succeed?

Book reviews. Both in nonfiction and in fiction, book reviewers discuss the author's purpose in writing the book and how the author tries to accomplish this purpose. Usually a book review also treats the value and usefulness of the book on its own merits, as well as in comparison with other, related books.

Movie and play reviews. In addition to the criteria mentioned above, reviewers of plays provide evaluations of the actors' performances, the action, the dialogue, the director's work, the costumes, and the set.

Music and dance reviews. Critics of music and dance review concerts and dance presentations by evaluating the composition, the performers' interpretation of the composition, and the performers' techniques.

Art reviews. Reviewers of artwork usually present a descriptive analysis of their observations and reactions by discussing the artist's use of space, shape, color, and proportion. A reviewer may discuss these characteristics by presenting the material in an order pattern of organization, perhaps from most dramatic to least dramatic use of color (order of importance) or from one side of the painting to the other (size or place).

Following is a book review of *The Mandarins*, a novel by the French writer Simone de Beauvoir. Knowing that a mandarin is a person having influence or high status, especially in intellectual or political circles, enables you to predict the topic of the reviewed book. This will help you understand how the reviewer supports her belief that Simone de Beauvoir deals successfully with the topic of her book.

Purpose and value of book

By writing [in *The Mandarins*] about men corroded by their inner life, perpetually busy reconciling irreconcilables—their ideals, their private lives, and political reality—[Beauvoir] has written the most humane novel that has appeared in France in recent years.   1

How author accomplishes purpose

Humane, for there can be no more representative description of man than one that presents intellectuals forced by their very craft to harmonize the happenings of their lives and the dictates of consciences. It is also a novel that is true in the purest sense of the term, for Simone de Beauvoir, a philosopher, cannot handle fiction otherwise than by describing step by step things she has experienced.   2

—Madeleine Chapsel, *Reporter*

Exercise 12D

Preview and read the following reviews. Answer the questions that follow each one.

1. Encouraged by the attention her work received, Chopin wrote the truly daring "The Story of an Hour" in April 1894. The story described the complex and certainly untraditional response of a woman who received the news that her husband had been killed in a railroad accident; she weeps pro-   1

fusely and then exults that she is now unencumbered: "Free, free, free!" she exclaims. The narrator elaborates Louise Mallard's excitement:

> She did not stop to ask if it were or were not a monstrous joy that held her. A clear and exalted perception enabled her to dismiss the suggestion as trivial.... She saw...a long procession of years to come that would belong to her absolutely. And she opened and spread her arms out to them in welcome.
>
> There would be no one to live for during those coming years; she would live for herself. There would be no powerful will bending her in that blind persistence with which men and women believe that they have a right to impose a private will upon a fellow-creature.

Embedded in this text is an extremely radical, even subversive, view of the institution of patriarchal marriage and family, in which the power is traditionally held by husbands, not by wives and certainly not by children.

—Wendy Martin, *New Essays on The Awakening*

a. What is the reviewer trying to prove? _____

_____

b. How does the reviewer support this opinion? _____

_____

c. Having read "The Story of an Hour," do you agree or disagree with the reviewer's opinion? Why?

_____

_____

_____

2. Even if Gabriel Garcia Marquez had not won the Nobel Prize in 1982, he would still be of the greatest interest to readers in the United States. As one of the world's best known and loved living authors, his novel *One Hundred Years of Solitude* had sold 30 million copies in 36 languages by its twentieth anniversary in 1987.

The term *magic realism* is not as popular today as it once was, but it still aptly describes much of Garcia Marquez's fiction and prepares the reader a bit for what to expect. Although the writer himself says that he doesn't exaggerate or make things up, a reader accustomed to the realism of earlier fiction will do well to begin Garcia Marquez with a willing suspension of disbelief. Things happen on a colossal scale, and Macondo, where much of his fiction takes place, is no ordinary small town. Garcia Marquez is a master at telling us universal truths that amaze us with candor and charm. His matter-of-fact style of narrating the most incredible happenings makes everything seem possible, and indeed inevitable.

To be read for its literary value, of course, the work of Garcia Marquez, especially his novels, also gives us a kind of history lesson of Latin America. This is a particularly valuable lesson today, for he describes the social reality and background of his country [Colombia], and by analogy other similar countries, with vigor and truth.

—Kathleen McNerney, *Understanding Gabriel Garcia Marquez*

a. What is the author's most important idea about Garcia Marquez's writing?

_____

b. What does the author think are Garcia Marquez's strengths as a writer?

_____

_____

c. How does Garcia Marquez provide historical information about Latin America?

_____

_____

3. Book review:

Archimedes' Revenge: The Joys and Perils of Mathematics. Paul Hoffman. 285 pp. Norton, 1988. $17.95.

In recent years, the "intelligent layman" has been blessed with a good handful of readable, well-informed introductions to contemporary mathematics. Among the most recent are *The Mathematical Tourist,* by Ivars Peterson, and *Mathematics and the Unexpected,* by Ivan Ekeland. Now this book can be added to the list.

The usual dilemma of mathematics popularization is that it is done either by a mathematician or a journalist. If by a mathematician, he or she probably has difficulty writing for a lay audience. If by a journalist, he or she probably has difficulty acquiring a very deep or very accurate knowledge of contemporary mathematics. This dilemma can be broken in several ways. One way is for a journalist to make effective use of advice and criticism from mathematicians. This, I surmise, is what Paul Hoffman has done in this book. The reader will learn about some novel, unfamiliar concepts: infinite minimal surfaces, Arrow's voting paradox, and massive parallel computers. He will also encounter some less fascinating material, for instance, "Archimedes cattle problem," a system of seven Diophantine equations with two geometric constraints.

The author's writing style is breezy, jazzy, and hyperreadable. I, for one, would have asked for some self-restraint in the pursuit of grab-the-reader-by-the-shoulders magazine style. For instance, in his presentation of game theory, he introduces "card-carrying conservatives," Attila the Hun and GI Joe, and liberals, "Hal Handout and Freeda Freelove." "Of the two, Freelove's heart bleeds more profusely." One chapter is titled, "Prime Prostitution." (It's about applications of prime number theory to cryptology). Later on, we read of a "chunky, bespectacled physicist in his late twenties with spaghetti hair, long sideburns, and a craving for ice cream at all hours of the day." We are told that this ice cream eater is certified as a genius by a "prestigious award."

Despite lapses in good taste and some technical errors, this book is good light reading. It will not do much to educate or inform the reader, or to uplift or defend the mathematics profession. It may convince some readers that mathematics can be interesting, even exciting.

—Reuben Hersh, in *American Scientist*

a. What is this review about? _____

b. What is the reviewer's most important idea about the topic? _____

_____

c. Does the reviewer think this book is a useful addition to the field? Why? _____

_____

_____

d. What aspects of this book does the reviewer discuss?

_____

_____

_____

4. Broadcast review:

[I]t ["War of the Worlds"] was calculated to utilize properties inherent in the medium, and it does so better than anyone anticipated, catapulting Welles to international fame and linking his name forever to the greatest hoax (however unintentional it may have been) in the history of broadcasting. 1

Presumably it was Welles's idea to have writer Howard Koch update H. G. Wells's science fiction novel by casting the first part of the program in the form of fake news bulletins, with Herrmann imitating everything from "Ramon Raquello and his orchestra" to a solitary piano playing Chopin. At first an announcement breaks into a music program to say that "disturbances" have been sighted on the planet Mars, and then gradually the whole show is taken over with reports of disaster. At the midway point, a reporter (Ray Collins) is heard from atop "Broadcasting Building" on Times Square, describing the destruction of New York and ultimately falling dead at the mike. A ham radio breaks the silence, asking "Isn't there anyone on the air?" and then, after ten seconds of absolute quiet, a CBS announcer gives a station break. 2

Everyone concerned has recalled that they had little respect for the script, which they though was silly, and at the last moment Welles almost withdrew the project in favor of an adaptation of *Lorna Doone*. But when the broadcast finally aired on Halloween eve 1938, it was acted with customary intensity, and at 8:30, halfway through the program, the cast was surprised to learn that some listeners had been taking the whole thing seriously. For several hours after- 3 ward, groups of people from coast to coast were thrown into panic, believing that monsters from Mars, flying invulnerable spaceships and armed with poison gas, were destroying the earth. Luckily nobody committed suicide or died of heart failure, although people of widely different social classes and educational backgrounds behaved irrationally. They prayed, took flight in cars, or ran out to warn their neighbors that the world was ending; church services were interrupted by hysterics, traffic was jammed, and communications systems were clogged. At Princeton, two distinguished geologists rushed out to search for the Martian "meteor" which was reported to have landed nearby, and scores of citizens were medically treated for shock.

Four times during the show listeners were told that they were hearing a dramatization, and at the end Welles jovially announced that it had all been a friendly joke: "That grinning, glowing, globular invader of your living room is an inhabitant of the pumpkin patch, and if your doorbell rings and nobody's there, that was no Martian...it's Hallowe'en." Nevertheless for many of those who tuned in late to the first half of the program, the news seemed quite real.

4

—James Naremore, *The Magic World of Orson Welles*

a. What was "the greatest hoax in the history of broadcasting"? _____

_____

b. Does the reviewer think Welles was successful? _____

_____

c. What examples and details does the reviewer use to support or illustrate the strengths or weaknesses of the broadcast?

_____

_____

d. Did Welles expect the listeners to react as they did? Why?

_____

_____

Argument

One of the best illustrations of writing based on argument is found in philosophy. Philosophers attempt to understand and explain the nature of the universe, sometimes even questioning whether there is a universe. Some philosophers are interested in finding out why things are the way they are; others, in why people believe as they do. For example: What is justice? What is truth? What is the best form of government? Does God exist? These are the kinds of questions philosophers ask as they speculate on and challenge existing notions. Philosophers write about their beliefs, building their arguments on a foundation of rational thinking. Very often they derive their hypotheses from their responses to the thinking of other philosophers. Subsequently, the new **hypothesis** (a prediction based on some fact that is used to point the way to further investigation) becomes the subject to challenge, and thus it goes in a never-ending—because never-provable—spiral of higher and higher levels of thinking.

Reading philosophy requires thinking and questioning. There is nothing concrete or tangible on which to base the information you are reading, because you are dealing with the product of philosophers' thoughts, which come from their minds, not from research, experiments, or secondary sources.

Knowing that philosophy has a specialized vocabulary will help you understand your reading. Philosophical terminology is often taken from common language but used in a special way. In general usage, *practical* means "useful"; however, in philosophical writing, *practical* means "of or pertaining to practice or action," and in *practical reason*, reason is guiding an action. *Idealism* is another example of how the general usage of a word differs from its philosophical meaning: Whereas the common definition of this word is that it pertains to the ideal, in philosophy *idealism* refers to the theory that the nature of what we see around us has to do with ideas, or our minds.

The following paragraph provides an introduction to how philosophers formulate their thoughts. It is about moral philosophy, an important branch of philosophy that concerns how people view standards of right and wrong.

> What we say moral philosophy is will depend on what we think philosophy itself is. Since Socrates, philosophers have tried to shed light on problems of various sorts by becoming clearer about the concepts in terms of which the problems were posed.... Moral philosophy is no exception: the problems on which it tries to shed light are practical

issues about morality. How could you decide what was a fair pay raise, for example, if you had no idea what "fair" meant, and therefore, no idea what would settle such questions?

—Hare, *Men of Ideas*

Philosophers examine many areas of human experience, including forms of government, human knowledge and how it is acquired, and religious and moral belief systems. But regardless of the topic or belief a philosophical work examines, that work always presents the philosopher's opinion, supported by logical reasoning. Once again, by asking the questions you learned in Chapter 10, you can evaluate the author's evidence, reasoning, and persuasive effectiveness:

- *What is the philosopher's opinion?*
- *How does the philosopher support this opinion?*
- *Is the reasoning sound? Does one point follow logically from another?*

A philosophical work often makes for difficult reading. The writing is dense, containing many complex thoughts and few examples. Asking questions, finding the patterns of organization, sectioning the material, and knowing the vocabulary will help you understand this type of writing.

The author of the following reading on philosophic doubt believes that philosophic doubt is a positive characteristic. From the marking up of the selection, you can see that in the first paragraph he explains why he holds this belief. The next paragraph is about the limitations of science and mathematics. The author further supports his assertion by writing about the limitations of human reasoning, claiming that human reasoning is only as valid as our perceptions and offering specific examples of these boundaries as evidence for his opinion.

Introduction

Philosophic doubt is not the pitiable condition of the soul that timid spirits imagine. It is not pessimism or cynicism, but a healthy and cheerful habit. It gives peace of mind. Men who stop pretending can sleep o' nights. There is a certain scepticism which is in no sense the spirit that denies. It is a frank recognition of the things as they come. It is almost a test of a man's honesty, among those who have stopped to think about the nature and limitations of our knowledge. Certainly cultivated people do not exhibit

1

Advantages of philosophic doubt

KI

the same degree of cocksureness as do the ignorant. People think the old saying about "doubting the intelligence that doubts" is funny. Popular audiences will always laugh at it. But why not? It is a platitude that the more a man learns the more he realizes how little he knows. <u>Existence is filled with inscrutable mystery</u>. To none of the profound questions that we ask of it is there any final answer. We must be satisfied ultimately with surmise, with symbol and poetic fancy. Speculations about the soul, God, the ultimate nature of reality and the course of destiny, and as to whether existence has any meaning or purpose beyond our own, or whether our life itself is worthwhile—all these speculations and many others of similar nature lead to no conclusions in fact, and we return always to the point from which we started. The very terms in which we put such questions are often meaningless when closely examined by the intellect, and the answer to them is determined by our own moods.

SI

SD

There is a general belief that science can answer the riddle. But science is only one possible view of things, the one best adapted to the needs of creatures like ourselves. It cannot deal with questions of value. It can tell us how things operate, their relative mass and positions in space and time, but it cannot tell us what they are in themselves, nor why they exist nor anything about their goodness or beauty. The more exact scientific knowledge becomes, the more closely it approaches mathematics. Pure mathematics deals only with abstractions and logical relations and can dismiss the whole world of objects. Science presupposes the data of experience and the validity of its own logical principles. It substitutes its mechanized order of things for things as we experience them.

2
Limitations of science and math

SI

Human reasoning is partial in all its processes. We think successfully about things when we ignore all the aspects or qualities of them except those which are relevant to the purpose at hand. The H_2O-ness of water is no more the ultimate nature of water than is its wetness, or its thirst quenching quality. That it is H_2O is only

3
Limitations of human reasoning

one of the things that may be said about water. Now if we add together bits of onesided and partial scientific knowledge, we do not thereby gain a sum total which is the equivalent of reality as a whole. We have a useful instrument for dealing with our environment, because in thought we have greatly simplified it by ignoring in each instance all that is irrelevant. But what we now have is a universe of discourse, a human construction which is what it is because we are always more interested in some aspects of things than in others.

All our ideas are views—they have been likened to snapshots. The world of which we are part is in flux. It comes to us as process, and our intellect does not grasp the movement any more than we can restore the movement of a man running by adding together a series of photographs. The movement always takes place between the pictures. Intellect is an instrument, not a mirror. Our world is not reducible to a form of thought, and when men speak of truth, reality, cause, substance, they are really only saying what they mean by certain words. The world, as James said, has its meanings for us because we are interested spectators, and so far as we can see none of these meanings are final. Whitehead and others have shown that some of the basic concepts of physical science which have held sway since the seventeenth century are now subject to revision. Santayana says that knowledge is faith—animal faith. It would be strange if it were otherwise, if hairy little creatures such as we are, whose ancestors lived in trees and made queer guttural noises, should so organize human discourse as to be able to say the last word about reality as a whole. It is well that we should marvel at our achievements of knowledge, for they are man's noblest work; but let us remember that human reason, itself a phase and part of the process of nature, can only view the whole process from its own partial standpoint, and that is enough unless we aspire to infallibility.

—Everett Dean Martin,
The Meaning of a Liberal Education

Exercise 12E

Preview and read the following selections about philosophy. Section each reading. Then evaluate the author's reasoning by answering the questions after each reading.

1.   The claim that art is intrinsically valuable and that therefore the school should foster it has often been made, though less often acted on. His [Mr. Read's] theory of art, as I have interpreted it, puts this plea in a slightly different light. For the argument is not that the school should attempt to educate the emotions as well as the intellect, or that the practice of art has a role in the maintenance of mental health, or that, in general, there is something of value in addition to the intellectual with which the school should be concerned. It is rather that art is valuable because intellectual activity is valuable; that because the school has to do with the latter, it should have to do with the former. It is an extension of the scope of the notion of the "intellectual," which is achieved by the definition of art as the discovery of form. For Read this is doubtless the most important reason why the school should be concerned with art, though it may not be the most politic on which to dwell.

    To emphasize that the activity of art is a condition of acquiring an understanding of discursively formulated knowledge, such as the schools have always concentrated on, is to emphasize that in many cases it is equivalent to what we would normally call "insight." For to acquire a new concept involves two logically different steps: learning the word for the new concept and discriminating the kinds of things which are to be counted as cases of the concept. The more important and difficult of these is clearly the latter step of deciding what is to count as a case covered by the concept. This requires the activity which Read calls "art." For example, imagine drawing a triangle on a board and saying to a child: "This is a triangle." (I choose an example from geometry partly to emphasize an earlier point: that "art" is not restricted to the visual arts or to the traditional media.) To understand the word "triangle" the child must discriminate the drawing from whatever other marks and scratches may be on the board; and, contemplating the drawing, he must discriminate its triangularity from its color, its size, and so on. Such a discrimination is done visually, not verbally, that is, using line as the medium, not words. If the discrimination is not made, then learning the word "triangle," Read would say, is useless, and perhaps worse than useless. It is at best an exercise of memory, an external handling of symbols. This is what Read thinks the schools have typically encouraged; they have attempted to hand over the discursive forms of knowledge without the necessary prior engagement in the activity of art. This is done by the method of being told something and then trying to remember it.

—Ralph Smith, *Aesthetics and the Problems of Education*

a. What is Smith's point of view? _____

_____

_____

b. How does Smith support his opinion?

_____

_____

c. How is Read's philosophy of art applied to education?

_____

_____

2. Some people are subject to a certain delicacy of passion, which makes them extremely sensible to all the accidents of life, and gives them a lively joy upon every prosperous event, as well as a piercing grief, when they meet with misfortunes and adversity. Favours and good offices easily engage their friendship; while the smallest injury provokes their resentment. Any honour or mark of distinction elevates them above measure; but they are as sensibly touched with contempt. People of this character have no doubt, more lively enjoyments, as well as more pungent sorrows, than men of cool and sedate tempers: but I believe, when everything is balanced, there is no one, who would not rather be of the latter character, were he entirely master of his own disposition. Good or ill fortune is very little at our disposal: and when a person, that has this sensibility of temper, meets with any misfortune, his sorrow or resentment takes entire possession of him, and deprives him of all relish in the common occurrences of life; the right enjoyment of which forms the chief part of our happiness. Great pleasures are much less frequent than great

pain; so that a sensible temper must meet with fewer trials in the former way than in the latter. Not to mention, that men of such lively passions are apt to be transported beyond all bounds of prudence and discretion, and to take false steps in the conduct of life, which are often irretrievable.

There is a delicacy of taste observable in some men, which very much resembles this delicacy of passion, and produces the same sensibility to beauty and deformity of every kind, as that does to prosperity and adversity, obligations and injuries. When you present a poem or a picture to a man possessed of this talent, the delicacy of his feeling makes him be sensibly touched with every part of it; nor are the masterly strokes perceived with more exquisite relish and satisfaction, than the negligences or absurdities with disgust and uneasiness. A polite and judicious conversation affords him the highest entertainment; rudeness or impertinence is as great a punishment to him. In short, delicacy of taste has the same effect as delicacy of passion: it enlarges the sphere both of our happiness and misery, and makes us sensible to pains as well as pleasures, which escape the rest of mankind.

—David Hume, "Of the Delicacy of Taste and Passion"

a. What is the philosopher's opinion? _____

_____

b. What evidence does he use to support his opinion? _____

_____

c. What is a "delicacy of passion"? _____

_____

d. How does Hume compare a "delicacy of passion" to a "delicacy of taste"?

_____

e. Describe someone you know who has a "delicacy of passion" and a "delicacy of taste."

_____

_____

Applications to Career Fields

Most college programs include courses in the humanities, whether you are majoring in a discipline therein, such as philosophy, art, or music, or an applied course of study, such as business or engineering. Knowledge of language and skillful use of words are great strengths in whatever career field you choose. Studying the humanities provides the best preparation for acquiring these skills. In addition, it gives you considerable experience in evaluating other people's opinions, and this aspect, too, provides an excellent foundation for any field beyond such professions as artist, musician, or writer that are usually associated with the humanities. The training and skills in reading and using language that lawyers, journalists, educators, and businesspeople receive in the humanities help them to recognize not just what is on the surface but the underlying messages—an invaluable asset in their professional careers.

Exercise 12F

Preview and read "Ethics and Journalism." Then answer the questions that follow.

Ethics and Journalism

1   When we enter the area of journalistic ethics, we pass into a swampland of philosophical speculation where eerie mists of judgment hang low over a boggy terrain. In spite of the unsure footing and poor visibility, there is no reason not to make the journey. In fact, it is a journey well worth taking for it brings the matter of morality to the individual person; it forces the journalist, among others, to consider his basic principles, his values, his obligations to himself and to others. It forces him to decide for himself how he will live, how he will conduct his journalistic affairs, how he will think of himself and of others, how he will think, act and react to the people and issues surrounding him.

2   Ethics has to do with duty—duty to self and/or duty to others. It is primarily individual or personal even when it relates to obligations and duties to others. The quality of human life has to do with both solitude and sociability. We do right or wrong by ourselves in that part of our lives lived inwardly or introvertedly and also in that part of our lives

where we are reacting and responding to other persons. This duality of individual and social morality is implicit in the very concept of ethics. The journalist, for example, is not simply writing for the consumption of others; he is writing as self-expression, and he puts himself and his very being into his journalism. What he communicates is in a very real way what he himself is. He pleases or displeases himself—not just those in his audience. What he does to live up to some standard within him not only affects the activities and beliefs of others, but in a very real way, the very essence of his own life.

A concern for ethics is important. The journalist who has this concern obviously cares about good or right actions; such a concern indicates an attitude which embraces both freedom and personal responsibility. It indicates also that the journalist desires to discover norms for action that will serve him as guiding principles or specific directives in achieving the kind of life which he thinks most meaningful and satisfying. Ethical concern is important also for it forces the journalist to commitment, to thoughtful decision among alternatives. It leads him to seek the "summum bonum," the highest good in journalism, thereby heightening his authenticity, as a person and journalist.

—John C. Merrill, *The Imperative of Freedom*

a. What is the key idea of the article? _____

_____

b. How does the author support his assertion? _____

_____

_____

c. What is your reaction to this selection? _____

_____

_____

d. If you were a journalist, how would you react to this passage?

_____

_____

_____

_____

Exercise 12G

Preview and read "Writing." Then answer the questions that follow.

Writing

In the beginning, when you're first starting out, there are a million reasons not to write, to give up. This is why it is of extreme importance to make a commitment to finishing sections and stories, to drive through to the finish. The discouraging voices will hound you—"This is all piffle," they will say, and they may be right. What you are doing may just be practice. But that is how you are going to get better, and there is no point in practicing if you don't finish.

I went through a real crisis of faith about two-thirds of the way through my last novel. The thing is that I had gotten twenty-seven bad reviews in a row on my previous novel, and I was feeling just the merest bit unsure about my skills and the joys of publication. But during that crisis of faith, I made a commitment to the characters in the new novel, instead of to the book itself. So I spent a little time at my desk every day, just writing down memories of my family, my youth. I went for walks and to lots of matinees, and I read. I spent as much time as I could outdoors while I waited for my unconscious to open a door and beckon. It finally did. I did not have some beautiful Hallmark moment when I threw back my shoulders with a big smile, dusted off my hands, and got back to work. Rather, it was like catching amoebic dysentery. I was just sitting there minding my business, and then the next minute I rushed to my desk with an urgency I had not believed possible. . . .

All the good stories are out there waiting to be told in a fresh, wild way. Mark Twain said that Adam was the only man who, when he said a good thing, knew that nobody had said it before. Life is like a recycling center, where all the concerns and dramas of humankind get recycled back and forth across the universe. But what you have to offer is your own sensibility, maybe your own sense of humor or insider pathos or meaning. All of us can sing the same song, and there will still be four billion different renditions. Some people will sing it spontaneously, with a lot of soulful riffs, while others are going to practice until they could sing it at the Met. Either way, everything we need in order to tell our stories in a reasonable and exciting way already exists in each of us. Everything you need is in your head and memories, in all that your senses provide, in all that you've seen and thought and absorbed.

—Anne Lamott, *bird by bird*

a. Why did the author write this? _____

b. What is the author's most important idea about writing?
   _____

c. What pattern of organization does the author use? _____
   _____

d. According to the author, what is the importance of practice? _____
   _____

e. Compare your writing experience with the author's. _____
   _____

Summary Exercise

State the three types of writing found in the humanities and summarize the characteristics of each.

Chapter 13

Reading the Natural Sciences

In this chapter you will find answers to the following questions:

How do you read a scientific textbook?
What is special about scientific vocabulary?
How do you solve problems?
What are scientific reports?
What kinds of evidence are used in scientific writing?

Characteristics of the Natural Sciences

The natural sciences are those disciplines which objectively study the natural and physical world around us and our place in it. A knowledge of mathematics is fundamental to studying these fields, because all natural sciences depend on mathematical computation and measurement. The following are the principal fields of study usually included under the general heading of "natural science."

- *Astronomy:* the scientific study of the universe
- *Biology:* the scientific study of living organisms and life processes
- *Chemistry:* the scientific study of matter, or the study of the composition of substances and changes in their composition
- *Geology:* the scientific study of the origin, history, and structure of the earth
- *Physics:* the scientific study of matter and energy and of the interaction between the two

Scientific study of the natural sciences is the investigation of the physical self and natural phenomena. The key word here is *investigation*. Questions are asked whose answers reveal the physical foundations of our existence: *How does it work? What happens? When did this occur? How do they know? How do I know? What is the evidence? How can I make it work?* These questions are as valid in chemistry and biology as they are in physics, astronomy, and geology.

Scientific knowledge evolves from the continual gathering of data and the testing of hypotheses. Science is a dynamic process based on fact. Scientists experiment and observe to test and prove a hypothesis, which then becomes a theory—an explanation supported by evidence. Building knowledge step by step, experiment by experiment, scientists use the known to discover the unknown. Although they rely on past experiments as the basis for their hypotheses, scientists never accept anything as a final truth, because with increased knowledge, accepted truths change. For instance, humankind's view of the world's relation to the sun was radically changed in the seventeenth century by Galileo's theory that the earth rotates around the sun, rather than vice versa, and by the recent planetary data from *Voyager* that have revolutionized the astronomer's vision of the universe.

Reading Mathematical and Scientific Material

Most courses in science and math rely heavily on a main textbook. Nonetheless, in an effort to have students think like scientists or mathematicians, most instructors use other course materials as well, such as study guides, lab manuals, and reports from scientific journals.

The Textbook

Science textbooks are the products of years of experimenting and searching for answers. They are written to instruct and bring the student up to date on the knowledge in a field. Extra exercises and hints for study are contained in the study guides that often accompany such textbooks. Laboratory manuals (or similar material prepared by the instructor) provide a summary of the topic, information about the experiments to be done, and directions for doing them. These manuals also provide space for lab reports, that is, complete and accurate records of what happened in the testing of a hypothesis.

Math and science textbooks are designed to be as comprehensible as possible. Their headings and subheadings are clearly set out, many study aids are included, and graphic material that illustrates and explains the text is abundant.

Previewing and Reviewing

With scientific materials as with all others, you begin reading actively by asking preview questions. Because textbooks in science and math usually follow a pattern that gives first the key idea and then the detail, previewing is a relatively easy task. You will often find that the chapters are already sectioned and that the key ideas or topics are emphasized within the sections. When previewing textbooks in these fields, do not neglect to check the aids provided by the authors—diagrams, graphs, tables, summaries, study questions, glossaries, math reviews, and so forth. These elements are particularly important in studying material that is unfamiliar and initially difficult to understand. Know what your book contains—that math review found in the back of the book may be just what you need when you are faced with a problem in chemistry or physics.

Determining your purpose will help you ascertain how to read the material. New material builds on previous knowledge. The author assumes you have learned the necessary preparatory information and can make the requisite connections between previous knowledge and new material. For example, in algebra you would have a difficult time understanding polynomials if you did not know the properties of exponents and of combining sign numbers; in physics you could not grasp the formula for energy if you did not know the specialized meaning of the term *work*. You also need to review the material frequently to make sure you have a strong foundation before you move on to new information. When you are reviewing, skim back over the material to find what you may not understand.

To apply these points, let's examine a preview of a passage from *Introduction to Physical Geology,* entitled "Earthquake Prediction."

Topic	**Earthquake Prediction**	
	Statement	
Key Idea	Effective earthquake prediction might help minimize loss of life, yet pinpointing earthquakes, which seemed so close at hand during the 1960s, is proving to be an elusive goal.	1

Discussion

Subtopic: Animals as predictors

Chinese scientists claim to have been successful in predicting about fifteen earthquakes in recent years. They rely heavily on the centuries-old idea that animals sense various underground changes prior to an earthquake and behave abnormally. Most of the bizarre behavior is simply increased restlessness. Cattle, sheep, and horses refuse to enter their corrals. Rats leave their hideouts and march fearlessly through houses. Shrimp crawl on dry land. Ants pick up their eggs and migrate en masse. Fish jump above the surface of the water, and rabbits hop aimlessly about.

Supporting Idea: Animals may be able to predict earthquakes.

Chinese scientists successfully predicted the Haicheng earthquake in February 1975 by means of unusual animal behavior. The most intriguingly bizarre behavior occurred in mid-December, when snakes came out of hibernation and froze to death on icy ground, and groups of rats appeared and scurried about in the cold winter weather. These events were followed by a swarm of small earthquakes at the end of December. During January, Chinese scientists received thousands of reports of unusual animal behavior, especially in large animals, in the area that proved to be the quake epicenter.

One hypothesis offered to explain abnormal animal behavior before an earthquake is that certain animals are sensitive to small variations in Earth's magnetic field or to sounds produced by microfractures prior to the larger event. Animal sensors that detect light, sound, odor, touch, and temperature are well known, and they may have the ability to detect subtle changes in other physical phenomena.

Subtopic: Dilatancy theory

Supporting Idea: Rocks swell before they rupture.

Much of the work on earthquake prediction in the United States has been based on the dilatancy theory. Laboratory and field studies in recent years have indicated that a rock subjected to stress swells just before it ruptures. This dilation is caused by the opening and extension of numerous tiny cracks, and it begins at levels of stress that are about half as great as those needed to break the rock. As a rock dilates, changes occur in certain physical characteristics, such as electrical resistance, seismic wave velocities, and magnetic properties. Geologists therefore attempt to monitor uplift and tilting of the ground, electrical resistivity, the number of seismic events, and ground-water pressure.

Supporting Idea: Dilatancy theory is inadequate.

For a prediction to benefit the populace, it must specify the time, the location, and the magnitude of the coming quake. Such accuracy is proving to be difficult to achieve. The problem is not so much that the dilatancy theory is wrong, but rather that it is inadequate. Different kinds of earthquakes apparently have different kinds of precursors. Instead of attempting to predict the time, place, and magnitude of an expected earthquake, geologists are now concentrating on the more modest goal of forecasting which areas of the world may be most susceptible to significant quakes.

Subtopic: Seismic map

Supporting Idea: Seismic maps indicate where stress may be building up.

A major contribution to forecasting has been the compilation of a map showing the seismic potential of the world's tectonic plate boundaries. This map essentially shows locations along the plate boundaries of the Pacific where major quakes are most likely to occur in the near future. Along the plate margins are several gaps in seismic activity, where stress may be building up to a critical level. The most susceptible areas are those where major tremors have occurred in the past but have not occurred within the last one hundred years. These include such heavily populated areas as southern California, central Japan, central Chile, Taiwan, and the west coast of Sumatra. These areas appear likely to experience a major earthquake (magnitude of 7.0 or greater) in the next few decades. One such seismic activity gap existed along the western coast of Mexico until a major quake struck the area on November 29, 1979.

Subtopics: Questions relating to prediction

Supporting Idea: Some want to withhold prediction until techniques are perfected.

If a reliable earthquake prediction system could give from one to ten years' advance warning of a "killer" quake, what would be the appropriate social response? Would the usual flow of mortgage money be terminated? New earthquake insurance would certainly become unavailable. What about fire insurance, business expansion, unemployment, tax revenues, and demands on local government? The fear that false alarms would lead to an adverse social response has led some to call for the withholding of predictions until prediction techniques are perfected to absolute certainty.

—W. Kenneth Hamblin,
Introduction to Physical Geology

Since this section has the title "Earthquake Prediction," you can be sure that it will deal with the way in which earthquakes are or are not predicted. Your preview also reveals that the first sentence of what the author chooses to call the "Discussion" probably provides the key idea—that it is still hard to predict earthquakes. You can assume that the author is informing, not persuading, you of why this is so. Perhaps you are interested because you, or some relatives, live in an area where there have been earthquakes; perhaps you want to know how much scientists know about predicting earthquakes and why it is a difficult task. You may develop some specific questions from your preview, such as, *What are some of the hypotheses connected with earthquake prediction?* or *How long until we get a reliable prediction system?*

A first reading reveals the key idea, sections, titles, and supporting ideas, as shown in the example on pages 351–354.

Although you may not completely understand the details, you have gained a general comprehension and a sense of the connections between what geologists now know and what they need to know. An awareness of the author's strategies provides you with more useful information. The supporting details are presented through cause and effect: for example, the effect on animals caused by changes in the Earth's magnetic field. And the passage ends with a commentary that includes some important questions for you to consider. In a closer reading you will discover what is currently known about where earthquakes might occur.

Exercise 13A

Working in pairs, preview a chapter of a science text. Find the topic of the chapter and discuss the chapter's organization with your partner by answering the questions below.

1. Is the chapter sectioned? If so, what questions should you ask as you read? If not, what are a few reasonable questions you can ask?

2. How does this chapter relate to the ones that precede and follow it? (You may need to refer to the table of contents.)

3. What are some of the points you can predict will be made in the chapter?
4. Are any words unfamiliar to you? If so, note them.

The Organization of the Textbook

Science textbooks are written to inform and teach the reader. In many of them, particularly for those sciences in which problem solving is important, such as mathematics, physics, and chemistry, the chapters are usually divided into three sections: *explanation*, *example*, and *exercises*.

Textbook explanations. The explanation is the initial presentation of an idea. The author will first state and explain the concept or principle in words. She or he may define terms and discuss strategies and relationships, sometimes using formulas or diagrams to illustrate. Here is a typical textbook explanation:

> *Objective:* To find the mean of a set of numbers. The *average*, or *mean*, is the sum of all the numbers in a group divided by the total number of items in the group.

Textbook examples. The explanation does not stand alone. In fact, if you are unaware of the importance of actively reading the example before you continue, you may find science and math textbooks ambiguous or difficult to understand. The author provides an example to illustrate the explanation and assumes that you will read both sets of information before you move on to the exercises.

Most instruction occurs with the examples. As the strategies for solution are laid out into meaningful ideas, you should ask yourself questions to ensure that you see the connection among the ideas the author presents.

When reading examples, ask yourself questions like these:

- *What would I do?* Then look at the example and think about why the author answered the problem in the way he or she did.
- *Do I understand every step in the author's solution?*
- *What calculations did the author perform to get to the next line?*

Here is a typical example you might find in a mathematics textbook:

A student's test scores for five tests are listed below. Find the mean.

$$\begin{array}{ccccc} \text{Test 1} & \text{Test 2} & \text{Test 3} & \text{Test 4} & \text{Test 5} \\ 86 & 95 & 94 & 87 & 93 \end{array}$$

$$\frac{\text{Sum of Scores}}{\text{Number of tests}} = \frac{86 + 95 + 94 + 87 + 93}{5} = \frac{455}{5} = 91$$

The mean is 91.

Textbook exercises. After you have read the explanation and the examples, you then move on to the exercises. Too frequently, students go right to the exercises and try to do them as quickly as possible without first making certain that they understand the explanation and the examples; then their reactions to the exercises are "This makes no sense" or "Where did they get this?"

Here is a typical exercise that might follow the previous example:

Three students hiked the following distances: Student A hiked 20 miles, Student B hiked 17 miles, and Student C hiked 25 miles. What is the mean distance the three students hiked?

There is one right answer to a problem but not always one right way to get to that answer. Not all problems are done the way the example is done. An author may present too much information in one step, requiring you to further break down the procedure to understand what is being done. Or the author may show steps in the example that are unnecessary for doing the exercise. Seeing the connections among the steps will help you determine which steps of an example are applicable to a particular problem. Problem solving is a complex thinking process, as you will see by looking at the section called Problem Solving on p. 372.

Vocabulary

Each branch of science has its own vocabulary and terms. Much scientific work also depends on using **symbols** that, in contrast to specialized words and phrases, are universal.

Terms. Scientific language is often drawn from Latin and Greek to make the terms more understandable to a wider range of people. And each word has a precise, single meaning. For instance, the scientific invention *television* derives its name from the Greek *tele*, meaning "distance," and the Latin *videre*, meaning "to see"; the term can refer only to a single process—that by which you can see at a distance. Familiarity with the list of Latin and Greek prefixes, roots, and suffixes found in Appendix A is particularly useful when your reading entails scientific terms. You cannot depend on gaining the exact meaning of terms from context. Therefore, you have to learn the definitions provided in the text, in the glossary, or by your instructor.

Symbols. It is important to learn the language of the symbols used in mathematics and the branch of science you are studying so that you can start using it and building fluency. Symbols are a shorthand way of naming elements and quantities. No doubt you are already familiar with many symbols—% for percent, MW for megawatt, C for carbon, and so on. Symbols also indicate operations, such as the familiar + ("add") and $\sqrt{}$ ("take the square root of"). Symbols are combined in formulas, which state a general rule or principle in terms of the relationships of the individual symbols. For example, H_2O, the symbol for water, indicates that two parts of hydrogen are added to one part of oxygen to make water.

These methods have been devised to show complicated ideas in simple form. You need to know the meaning of the letters and symbols to understand how the ideas they represent are related. Unfortunately, there is no easy way to learn symbols and formulas; you must work at learning them, as you do with words that you don't know but whose precise meaning is necessary to your task. This is no place to guess—when you come across a symbol you don't know, look it up in your textbook or ask what it means. In addition, you might also reserve a page in the back of your notebook on which to list symbols and their meanings. And if you are more comfortable with words than with numbers and symbols, you may want to translate mathematical language into a language with which you are more familiar. For instance, you might depict an algebraic sequence or a formula as a sentence, with the terms a, x, and so forth, as the nouns, and the symbols +, –, and so forth, as the verbs.

Numbers and symbols are an important part of scientific reading. If you freeze or cannot think confidently when you see numbers, keep in mind that early difficulties may have been caused by factors other than your innate ability. Moreover, as an adult you are now capable of doing things you could not do when you were younger. By using a systematic, active approach and your developed analytical powers, you can treat numbers as just another source of information.

Graphics

You may have noticed that your math and science instructors' offices always have chalkboards in them, whereas that is not so true of faculty offices in the English department. You may also have noticed that when you are talking with math or science instructors, they tend to get up, go to the board, and diagram their explanation of a concept for you. Diagrams, graphs, and tables are often the means of communicating ideas and showing connections in math and the sciences. Therefore, students must understand these graphic representations and know how to read them. Illustrative material is also central to your understanding of the text. A careful reading of this material pays dividends in comprehending, consolidating, and remembering what at first might seem difficult material.

At this point you may find it useful to refer to the sections on reading graphic aids on p. 404. Although these illustrations deal primarily with material from the social sciences, they are equally applicable to the natural sciences.

Exercise 13B

Pages 378–383 contain a section of an early chapter in Introduction to Chemical Principles. *Answer the following questions by first previewing the excerpt. Then skim it, noting (1) how the author has organized the material, and (2) terms and symbols you do not know.*

1. What is this section about?

   _____

2. What is the author's most important idea about the topic?

   _____

3. What two things do you associate with or already know about the topic?

   _____

   _____

4. What three points do you predict the author will take up?

   _____

   _____

   _____

5. What four points do you notice about the organization of this section?

   _____

   _____

   _____

6. What are three terms or symbols that are unfamiliar to you?

   _____   _____   _____

Scientific Reports

Like textbooks in the sciences, scientific reports and articles based on reports are very precisely laid out. Once you know the pattern of presentation of a scientific report or article, you will know exactly where to look for what. This factor, too, facilitates the task of previewing.

Scientific articles report the results of investigation and research, provide the evidence on which the conclusion is based, and interpret the meaning of the observations. They connect current research with past research and form the basis for future research. You may remember news reports about the publication of the findings of two scientists on a safe method of producing nuclear energy through cold fusion; other scientists would not comment until they had seen the written evidence produced in a form they could replicate and test in their own labs. Scientists do not accept new discoveries without extensive testing of the basic hypothesis. Therefore, scientific reports follow specific rules that give scientific writing a more formal structure than is normally found in other fields.

The *scientific method* is a systematic and exact way of analyzing scientific data. Briefly, the scientific method entails the following:

- Stating a problem
- Forming a hypothesis
- Gathering evidence
- Testing the hypothesis
- Drawing a conclusion or general principle

Scientific writing that reports on the results of research and investigation follows this basic structure. It is plain, unadorned, objective writing. Yet one could also say that reports on research are written to persuade, because the authors want to convince the reader that their points of view or conclusions are correct. They support their positions by marshaling the strongest evidence possible from their personal observations or experiments. As always in dealing with persuasive material, the reader asks, *What is the author trying to convince me of? What evidence supports the arguments?*

Sectioning a scientific report reveals the form followed by all authors in presenting the results of research:

- The title, telling us what the report is about
- An abstract, a very brief summary of the report
- An introduction, giving the purpose of the experiment or investigation, the way in which it fits into other research in the field, and, occasionally, the findings
- A section on methodology and materials
- The results of the research, which may include a graphic presentation of the observations and data
- A conclusion or a discussion of the findings

Perhaps it is simpler to think of the form of a research report in terms of the answers to these questions:

What is it about?
Why was it done?
How was it done?
What was found?
What does the researcher conclude?

Reports on scientific research that appear in journals are written for those who work in the field. For persons unfamiliar with a particular discipline, these reports may be hard to read because of the terms used and the procedures described. As a science student, however, you may be asked to read journal articles to see how professionals in the field report on their work. To provide an example, we shall apply the model of a research report to sectioning the following article from a biology textbook.

Mutualism: Acacia and Ant—Partners for Life

What is it about?

1   Daniel Janzen of the University of Pennsylvania, then a doctoral student, was walking down a road in Veracruz, Mexico, when he saw a flying beetle alight on a thorny tree, only to be driven off by an ant. Further observation revealed that the tree, a bull's-horn acacia, was covered with ants. A large ant colony of the genus *Pseudomyrmex* made its home inside the enlarged thorns of the plant, whose soft pulpy interiors are easily excavated to provide secure shelter.

Why was it done?

How was it done?

What was found?

2   To determine how important the ants are to the tree, Janzen began stripping the thorns by hand until he found and removed the thorn housing the ant queen, thus destroying the colony. He later turned to more efficient but dangerous methods, eliminating all the ants on a large stand of acacias with the insecticide parthion. The acacias were unharmed by the poison, Janzen became ill from it, and the ants were all killed. Within a year of the spraying, the recovered Janzen found nearly all the acacia trees dead, consumed by insects and other herbivores, and shaded out by competing plants. The ground surrounding the trees, which the ants normally kept pruned, was overgrown. The trees were apparently dependent on their resident ants for survival.

Why was it done?

How was it done?

What was found?

3   Wondering if the ants could survive off the tree, Janzen painstaking peeled the ant-inhabited thorns off 100 acacia trees, suffering multiple stings in the process. He housed each ant colony in a jar provided with local nonacacia vegetation and insects for food. The colonies all starved. Close inspection of the acacia revealed swollen structures filled with sweet syrup at the base of the leaves and protein-rich capsules on the leaf tips. Together these provided a balanced diet for the ants.

What does the researcher conclude?

Janzen's experiments strongly suggest that this species of ant and acacia have an obligatory mutualistic relationship—that is, that neither can survive without the other. Of course, further observations were required to confirm this. The fact that the ants starved in Janzen's jars did not rule out that they may survive successfully elsewhere, but, in fact, this species of ant is never found living independently. Similarly, the bull's-horn acacia is never found without its resident ant colony. Thus, a chance observation followed by careful research led to the discovery of an important mutualistic association.

—Gerald Audesirk and Teresa Audesirk, *Biology*

Exercise 13C

How would you answer the research report questions as they are applied to "Mutualism"?

1. What is it about?

2. Why was it done?

3. How was it done?

4. What was found?

5. What does the researcher conclude?

Analytical and Critical Reading

How does an active reader approach scientific texts and reports? The key to understanding science lies in making connections and seeing relationships. Close reading is usually necessary, because the material is packed with information that you must unpack by dealing with terms and symbols that have precise meanings. You may have to check backward and forward from text to formula or diagram, but the overall process for understanding what you read is to read for ideas. Asking questions to determine your purpose and the author's purpose, to connect what you already know with what you want to know, to identify what the author is writing about, and to pinpoint what he or she is saying about it helps you see the reasons behind the mathematical and scientific processes. You must thoroughly understand the concepts before you can apply them.

There are several points to bear in mind when you are analyzing and reading math and science textbooks:

1. *The importance of skimming.* Skimming to gain an overview provides a clear picture of the major ideas in a reading. This understanding helps you to make the larger connections and to know which details you need to learn. Does it make sense to know how the heart works without knowing the function of the heart and how it relates to the rest of the body?

2. *The importance of details.* Details define, explain, describe, and support the author's ideas—ideas that may be complex and initially difficult to understand. The details contain the answers to your questions, *What does this mean?* and *How does this work?* Reading for details calls for careful and necessarily slower reading. Although at first it is important to have an overview of the function of the heart and a rough idea of how it works, you need to move on and learn the details well enough to know the vocabulary and to be able to diagram exactly how the heart works.

3. *The importance of precision.* You must be able to understand exactly what the author is talking about at all times. You have to make sure that you have answers to your questions. If you find an explanation in your textbook hard to understand, ask your instructor or the lab assistant to explain the concept, or go to the library to locate another textbook on the same topic. You can't afford to let anything slide. Not understanding step one means that you will never be able to understand steps two and three.

4. *The importance of application.* Scientists test and understand their own and other scientists' thinking by applying the concepts, or hypotheses, to experiments. Aspiring scientists do the same. You will do many experiments in association with your courses. You will also benefit, however, from thinking through a concept like friction and applying it to a situation you know, such as braking a car.

With these considerations in mind, you will find the following analytical questions useful in thinking about reading science texts:

- *Is the reading an explanation of a concept, the steps of a process, or a series of examples from which you need to draw conclusions?*
- *Is the material a report on research or an experiment?*
- *Do you understand the terms that are used?*
- *Are the results the same as those found in other reports, or are they different?*
- *What is the evidence?*
- *Is the methodology logical and complete? Can you follow it step by step?*
- *Is the author trying to persuade, inform, or both?*
- *What are the author's conclusions?*

Exercise 13D

Skim, read, and analyze the following text, using some of the questions listed above.

The Ohio River

In 1936 a Kentucky congressman called the Ohio River a "cesspool." Everything was dumped into the river; pollution control was decades in the future. The Ohio River is a good example of what water pollution has done and can do to a river.

The Ohio River Basin includes nearly 200,000 square miles of Indiana, Kentucky, Ohio, West Virginia, Illinois, Virginia, North Carolina, Tennessee, Maryland, Pennsylvania, and New York. About 20 million people live and work in this basin, and it has over 2,000 major industrial operations. The valley produces about 75%, of the nation's coal and more than one-third of its steel. The Ohio River Basin has over 94 million acres of cropland. Obviously, a proportional share of the water pollution related to these activities ends up in the Ohio River. The river is already polluted at its source, where it is formed by the confluence of the far-from-pure Allegheny and Monongahela rivers at the Golden Triangle in Pittsburgh, Pennsylvania. Things get worse as the Ohio flows some 981 miles to the southwest, where it joins the Mississippi at Cairo, Illinois. The urban centers along the Ohio include Paducah, Covington, Newport, Owensboro. Louisville, and Ashland, Kentucky; Evansville, Indiana; Cincinnati, Portsmouth, Ironton, Marietta, and Steubenville, Ohio; Huntington, Parkersburg, Weirton, and Wheeling, West Virginia; and Pittsburgh, Pennsylvania.

3   According to some sources, many industries along the Ohio still do not meet current emission standards. Numerous reports have identified hundreds of errant chemical compounds in Ohio River water; many of these chemicals are known to produce cancer in humans and other animals.

4   Some of the Ohio River pollution problem stems from the fact that the Ohio has been converted over the years into a series of long lakes created by dams built by the Army Corps of Engineers to ensure navigation depths along the entire length of the river. A related problem is that the percentage of oxygen saturation during the summer drops considerably from Pittsburgh to Cairo.

5   According to the Environmental Protection Agency's Office of Water Planning and Standards, pollution problems of the Ohio River include (1) low alkalinity (high acidity)—a result of the fact that the Ohio drains many coal-mining areas in Pennsylvania, West Virginia, and other states; (2) a high total fecal **coliform** count*—indicating that sewage treatment in a number of cities along the Ohio is inadequate; (3) a high iron and manganese concentration—reflecting the character of the industry along the Ohio; and (4) some toxic substances—DDT and chlordane, for example.

6   A 1987 report released by ORSANCO, an organization of the states bordering the Ohio River, summarized the results of testing for toxics in the Ohio River from 1976 to 1985. Toxic substances were found throughout the length of

---

*Coliforms are bacteria that inhabit the digestive tract of *Homo sapiens* and other animals. Though not usually pathogenic in themselves, their presence indicates contamination by fecal waste and warns of potential infection by less common but more virulent inhabitants of the gastrointestinal tract, such as the causative agents of cholera and hepatitis.

the river, varying in types and amounts depending on the use of the watershed and the types of industrial discharges. The most frequently found toxics were zinc and copper. Others commonly detected were chloroform, lead, phenols, nickel, and chromium. The toxic that most often exceeded the EPA's cancer risk criteria was chloroform. Arsenic also exceeded the cancer risk criteria, but not as frequently. Lead was the toxic that most frequently exceeded the EPA's aquatic life criteria and, at times, the EPA's human health criteria. Only on rare occasions were the safe drinking water standards exceeded for arsenic, cadmium, chromium, copper, lead, or mercury. Although pesticide and PCB residues were not found often in water samples, they were routinely detected in fish. Health officials cautioned against eating, more than once a week, fish caught in the Ohio River. The commission concluded that the river overall, however, is cleaner than is generally perceived.

Some of the things that get into the Ohio River cancel some other things out. For instance, the Ohio has high levels of suspended solids, apparently the result of sediment being washed into the stream during high flows along its length. Although the Ohio also has a great potential for algae growth, the cloudiness of water, caused by suspended solids, blocks out sunlight, inhibiting algal growth.

As late as 1948, still 99% of the raw sewage from toilets, slaughterhouses, and similar sources went directly into the Ohio—untreated. Although there was some very slow progress in the 1950s, significant improvement did not begin until the environmental movement in the late 1960s. Because of the Clean Water Act and other legislation, much of the raw sewage and odor of the Ohio are gone now. Many of the cities along the river are fast approaching the EPA standard of reduction of sewage by 85%. Many of the coal mines have been closed and sealed; operational mines are better controlled. Also on the comeback trail are sauger, crappie, white bass, and freshwater drum and paddlefish. According to ORSANCO, Ohio River fish now carry less heavy metal.

Largely as a result of clean water legislation of the early 1970s, the 700 industrial plants along the Ohio have sharply reduced the amount of waste they dump into the river. But plants are relatively easy to monitor and to regulate. The greatest unresolved problems now come from farms, construction sites, septic tank leakage, and the like—nonpoint sources and sources otherwise difficult to regulate.

A report issued in May 1990 by ORSANCO made an assessment of nonpoint source pollution on the Ohio. It found that agricultural runoff was the most widespread nonpoint source, but mining was the most severe. Impacts from mine runoff were most severe in the northern third of the river. Acid mine drainage carries sulfates and heavy metals into the river. Agriculture is the predominant source of nonpoint pollutants in the bottom third of the river. Sediment, pesticide, and fertilizer residues are all carried into the river. PCBs were found to be a problem along the entire length of the river.

Even the point sources have considerable room for improvement. Because of combinations of technical problems, design problems related to the connection of storm drains to sewage systems, and other problems, some Ohio River towns are removing less than half the contaminants from their sewage.

There has been dramatic though incomplete success with other of the world's great rivers. The Potomac River, which runs through Washington, D.C., used to smell of human excrement; today, the cities that affect the Potomac remove more than 85% of pollutants from the sewage they generate before the Potomac gets it. It was 0% not very long ago, but Congress has apparently acted to get its own house in order. Other notable success stories include the Willamette River in Oregon and the Thames in England—both of which, like the Ohio and the Potomac, were once virtual cesspools and are now relatively clean.

—Charles E. Kupchella and Margaret C. Hyland,
Environmental Science

1. Is the reading an explanation, the steps of a process, or a series of examples?

2. Is the reading a report on research or an experiment?

3. Do you understand the terms that are used?

4. What is the evidence?

5. Are the authors trying to persuade, inform, or both?

_____

6. What are the authors' conclusions?

_____

_____

Patterns of Organization

Most of the patterns of organization described in Chapter 8 appear in scientific writing. The following table illustrates when and how the principal patterns are used.

Pattern	Application	Example
List	Presentation of unordered material	Lists of different types of diseases (biology)
Order	Steps of a process	Directions for conducting an experiment (chemistry)
Cause and effect	Judgment of relationships	Changes in variables in an equation (math)
Problem-solution	Solution of problems	Word problems (physics)

Exercise 13E

From each of the following opening paragraphs, predict the principal pattern or patterns of organization of the entire reading.

1. Fog comes about when (1) moisture is added to a warm air mass or when (2) a moist air mass is cooled to its dew point. In the second case, a mass of air cools either because it comes into contact with cooler ground or water, or because it expands rapidly, or because it receives an invasion

of cooled air. The moisture condenses out of the air mass and a thick cloud forms on the ground....There are several types of fog, classified according to formation and point of origin. These classifications are rather descriptive. For our purposes here, we shall discuss three types of fogs, each formed by a slightly different set of circumstances: radiation fog, advection fog, and frontal fog.

—Joseph S. Weisberg, *Meteorology*

a. Compare/contrast

b. Problem-solution

c. List

d. Cause and effect

e. Order

    2. We have not only seen Earth from space, we have also seen the ocean floor, mapped its topography and structure, and gained insight into its origin and history. Until recently, this part of earth was as inaccessible as the planets in the outer solar system. We now know that the oceanic crust is completely different from the continental crust. It is much younger, composed of different material, and has had a separate history of its own.

    We have also "X-rayed" the interior of Earth and recognized that it is a highly differentiated planet whose materials are segregated into layers according to density. From this new ability to see the internal structure of Earth, we have discovered how it functions as a dynamic system.

    We now know that volcanoes, earthquakes, mountain building, and continental drift are manifestations of Earth's internal heat. In our time the right tools, sophisticated technology, and decisive evidence have come together to allow us to understand how Earth works. In this chapter we will briefly describe the major geologic features of the planet Earth—features that make it unique in the solar system.

—W. Kenneth Hamblin, *Introduction to Physical Geology*

a. Compare/contrast

b. Cause and effect

c. List

d. Problem-solution

e. Order

3. In 1927 the Nobel Laureate H. J. Muller found that high-energy radiation could damage genetic material—the chromosomes of living organisms. Most of what we have found out since then about the specific, direct effects of radiation on the human body comes from studies of survivors of the atomic bomb blasts in Japan and studies of Marshall Islanders who were exposed to radiation during atomic tests in the early 1950s. Data about chronic exposure come from X-ray technicians and radiologists who received large doses in the years before the dangers of radiation were recognized. Still other data come from uranium miners. A considerable amount of additional basic information has come from experiments with laboratory animals.

—Charles E. Kupchella and Margaret C. Hyland, *Environmental Science*

a. Cause and effect

b. Order

c. Compare/contrast

d. List

e. Problem-solution

Organizing for Study

Studying the sciences takes substantial effort and concentration. If you can see the whole picture, you will be able to follow every step, and to tie the details into the whole. Through organizing the material for yourself, you will be thinking about it in a way that leads to greater concentration, understanding, and retention.

Marking Up

Although most math and science textbooks are models of good organization, you can still benefit from the mental exercise of marking up the text in ways that are meaningful to you. Some instructors say students should always read with a pencil in hand to do the following:

- Make marginal notes indicating topics, key ideas, subtopics, and supporting ideas.

- Turn headings into questions, read for the answers, and underline or highlight those answers.
- Note definitions of important terms.

Note Taking

Either the formal outline or the Cornell Method of note taking (see Chapter 11) works well when you are reading math and science texts. You may want to supplement your notes with sketches illustrating conceptual material. When you are reading your textbook before class and come across something that is not clear to you, mark the place in your notes so that you can later ask your instructor, a TA, or a tutor to explain the point. Classroom and lab time is especially significant in the study of math and science. Instructors see their principal role as explaining through lectures and demonstrating through experiments. A wise student integrates reading notes with class and lab notes.

Mapping and Diagraming

Scientists sometimes find visualizing and diagraming relationships more helpful than describing those relationships in words. As a student, you can make relationships more vivid by sketching a map, diagram, or time line, like those described in Chapter 11.

Exercise 13F

First mark up the following selections and then outline or diagram them, using one of these methods: the formal outline, the Cornell Method, mapping, a flowchart, or a time line. Then state why you used the method you did.

1. A basic characteristic of life is a high degree of order. You can see it in the intricate pattern of veins throughout a leaf or in the colorful pattern of a bird's plumage. If you were to scrutinize the vein of a leaf or the feather of a bird under a microscope, you would discover that biological order also exists at levels below what the unaided eye can resolve. 1

   Biological organization is based on a hierarchy of structural levels, with each level building on the levels below it. Atoms, the chemical building blocks of all matter, are ordered into complex biological molecules such as proteins. The molecules of life are arranged into minute structures 2 called organelles, which are in turn the components of cells. Some organisms consist of single cells, but others, including plants and animals, are aggregates of many specialized types of cells. In such multicellular organisms, similar cells are grouped into tissues, and specific arrangements of different tissues form organs....

In the hierarchy of biological organization, there are tiers beyond the individual organism. A population is a group of organisms belonging to the same species; populations of various species living in the same area make up a biological community; and community interactions that include non-living features of the environment, such as soil and water, form an ecosystem. Unfolding biological organization at its many levels, from molecular architecture to ecosystem structure, is fundamental to the study of life.

—Neil A. Campbell, *Biology*

a. Method used: _____

b. Why? _____

2. The earliest traces of life arose 4 billion 600 million years ago, fish and amphibians appeared 345 million years ago, mammals appeared 225 million years ago, primates appeared 65 million years ago, and the spread of humankind began 2 million years ago. Given these statistics, fish have existed for 7 percent of geological time; mammals, for about 5 percent; primates, for 1 percent; and humankind, for little more than .04 percent.

a. Method used: _____

b. Why? _____

Problem Solving

Problem-solving processes are the same whether you are trying to resolve a campus crisis, work through a computer programming procedure, or persuade someone to go out with you. Solving a problem is figuring out how to get from where you are to where you want or need to be. To that end, you need to have strategies.

Problem solving is an aspect of critical reading that involves evaluating an author's thoughts—how they are presented, how they are supported, and what they mean to you. Developing these critical thinking skills requires active learning. In the natural sciences and mathematics, critical thinking means understanding topics conceptually, not only memorizing a set of definitions and rules. For many students, the study of science and mathematics begins and ends with rote memorization; they never move on to question, to understand concepts, or to see the connections among ideas. Instead, they merely passively accept rules and guess at answers because they have never developed effective learning and problem-solving strategies.

The emphasis here is on the *process* by which you as a student discover the answer, rather than on the answer itself. An active problem solver tries different approaches to a problem. First is to see and understand the relationships involved. Next is to solve the problem through reasoning and computation.

Strategies that focus on a representation of a problem through pictures, verbal descriptions, data tables, graphs, and diagrams help get you started. Using such techniques, you are actively representing your understanding of the material by illustrating the connections among its components. The material is thus easier for you to understand, and you are more aware of the ways in which you can work out the problem.

Another method of making things more vivid is to express your thoughts aloud as you are solving problems. When you are doing your homework, try talking through the problems aloud—to yourself or to a problem-solving partner. The benefits of this process include distinguishing between what you know and what you need to learn; recognizing steps you might skip in problem solving and thus avoiding jumping to conclusions; and valuing the importance of working through problems systematically.

As a thinking process, problem solving involves three main steps: *definition, analysis,* and *conclusion.* These steps can be translated into specific questions:

1. *Definition* (defining the problem)
   What is this problem about?
   Do I understand every word or term?
   Can I associate the problem with previous knowledge?

2. *Analysis* (analyzing the parts of the problem)
   What do I need to know?
   What am I asked to find? What are the unknowns?
   What am I told? What facts are given? What are the

knowns?
What symbols are used? What operations do they identify?
What information is needed? What is not needed? What is relevant and what is not?
What is the relationship between the information given and what I am asked to find? What mathematical concepts can I apply to this problem? What process should I use?

3. *Conclusion* (finding the answer)
How can I complete the problem?
What do I estimate or predict the answer will be?
How shall I compute each part of the problem?
Does my result make sense?
Is my result accurate? Is there a way to check the answer?

In doing the following example, you would answer these questions like this:

Joan scored 25 times for 39 points in the last basketball game. Some of her points were for field goals worth 2 points each; the others were for free throws worth 1 point each. How many of each type of basket did she get?

Need to know: How to translate words into numbers and symbols
Asked to find: Number of field goals
Number of free throws
Told: Total points
Total number of times scored
Number of points of each type of basket
Relationship of information given to what you are asked to find:
Concepts: Use information you have to show relationship of known facts to unknown facts
Process: Let a letter represent one thing you do not know:
n = number of field goals Joan scored
Then:
$2n$ = points Joan scored by field goals
25 = number of times Joan scored
$25 - n$ = points Joan scored by free throws
39 = total number of points Joan scored
Specific problem: $2n + (25 - n) = 39$
Completing the problem:
Predict: Fewer than 20 field goals because 2×20 is more than 39

Compute: $2n + (25 - n) = 39$
$2n + 25 - n = 39$
$n + 25 = 39$
$n = 14$ field goals
$25 - 14 = 11$ free throws
Check answer: Put value of n in the equation
$(2 \times 14) + (25 - 14) = 39$ points
$14 + 11 = 25$ times

Evaluation of Evidence

All scientific and mathematical progress depends on what has gone before. The accumulation of knowledge rests completely on objective proofs of hypotheses. Because scientific writing rests on proof, it must be accurate and objective. A scientist at first gets an idea based on his or her familiarity with what has gone before, next tests it, and then publishes the results. Because others must be able to replicate the experiment, there is no room for personal opinion—the experiment works or it doesn't work. Personal conjecture is acceptable in the original hypothesis to be proved, such as "I think I can drink this whole can of soda in thirty seconds." The proof must be irrefutable, such as the evidence of drinking the can of soda before witnesses. Personal opinion can also be found in the conclusions, perhaps in the form of statements about why the experiment didn't work, where future research might be directed, or how the new knowledge might be applied. But it is evidence that plays the primary role in scientific research.

Evidence you are likely to encounter in scientific reading takes three forms:

- The results of an experiment, as in physics or chemistry
- The development of a proof, as in math
- The observation of natural phenomena, as in astronomy or biology

As you learned in Chapter 10, active readers go beyond simply reading a text. They also *evaluate* it, by making decisions about how accurate they think it is, how it relates to what they already know, and how they can make use of it or incorporate it into their own thinking. As a beginner in the field, you can relate what you are learning only to your own experience and observations. Once you have read to see what the author is explaining or proving and have a clear understanding of the methodology employed, you need to assess what you have read by asking the following questions. You will be asked to apply some of these questions to Exercises G and H, the final exercises in this chapter.

1. *Does the author start with a reasonable hypothesis, something that can be proved through experiment or observation?*
2. *What kind of evidence is the author using?*
3. *Is the evidence current; does it need to be?*
4. *Have the proofs been developed systematically, without omitting any steps?*
5. *Does the evidence prove the hypothesis right or wrong?*
6. *Are the author's conclusions consistent with the observations?*
7. *What have I found out?*
8. *Do the results seem right?*
9. *Have I ever observed a similar situation?*
10. *Can I use this knowledge in my current work?*

As you proceed in your study, you will find yourself examining each new concept or principle in relation to what has gone before and what is to come next: *How does it fit in? How can it be used? What is its likely effect?* You will develop many more questions for yourself, always remembering that the more precise your questions, the better the results of your efforts. As you gain knowledge and sophistication, your questions will become sharper and your judgments more accurate, because you will have better criteria on which to base your evaluations.

Applications to Career Fields

Some students have definite careers in mind for which the study of math and science is necessary; others study these subjects as a way of testing their interests. As our society becomes increasingly technical, career fields based on science and math are growing exponentially. One can start with fundamental practical fields, such as those listed below, and go on to new ways of combining fields as demands for new technology increase—such as psychobiology, astrophysics, or biochemistry.

Astronomy: teaching, research, space technology
Biology: teaching, medicine, research
Chemistry: medicine, engineering, pharmaceuticals
Geology: teaching, research, engineering, environmental studies, mineral and petroleum exploration

Mathematics: teaching, research, engineering, medicine, computer science, business

Physics: medicine, teaching, research, engineering, architecture

In most instances, specialization comes later, often at the upperclass or graduate level. At the undergraduate level, the basic mathematics and sciences are taught to provide the necessary foundation for future work. Although in some technical institutions this teaching involves direct application, in a liberal arts program it concentrates on the theoretical background of the field—the questions, *What is it? Why is it?* and *How does it work?* To make the material more meaningful, one can also ask, *How is it used?*

Two skills gained from your study of science that will directly affect how you go about your career training are:

1. *Precision.* Science and math are quantitative and exact. The method used to find the answer is as important as whether or not the answer is right.
2. *Creativity and imagination.* Scientists are constantly playing with ideas, making connections, and testing hunches. These games make for progress.

Exercise 13G

You have already previewed and skimmed the extract from Introduction to Chemical Principles, *on pages 378–383. Now read it, analyze it, and answer the analytical and critical questions that follow.*

1. By marking up, analyze Section 2.1, noting in the margin the supporting ideas and patterns of organization.
2. Using either the formal outline or the Cornell Method, outline Section 2.2.
3. What pattern of organization will be used in Section 2.3?

2.1 THE IMPORTANCE OF MEASUREMENT

1   It would be extremely difficult for a carpenter to build cabinets without being able to use tools such as hammers, saws, and drills. They are a carpenter's "tools of the trade." Chemists also have "tools of the trade." Their most used tool is the one called *measurement*. Understanding measurement is indispensable in the study of chemistry. Questions such as "how much...?," "how long...?," and "how many...?" simply cannot be answered without resorting to measurements.

2   Most of the concepts now considered to be the basic principles of chemistry had their origin in extensive tabulations of experimental data obtained by making measurements. The concepts were "discovered" as these data tabulations (measurements) were subjected to the procedures of the scientific method.

3   It is the purpose of this chapter and the next to help students acquire the necessary background to deal properly with measurement. Almost all the material of these two chapters is mathematical. An understanding of this mathematics is a necessity for students of chemistry who want their encounters with the subject to be successful. The following analogy is appropriate for the situation. Physical exertion in sports can be fun, relaxing, and challenging if you are in good physical shape. If you are not in good physical condition, such exertion is not satisfying and may even be downright painful (especially the day after). Being "in good shape" mathematically has the same effect on the study of chemistry. It can cause that study to be a very satisfying and enjoyable experience. On the other hand, a lack of the necessary mathematical skills can cause "chemical exercise" to be somewhat painful. The message should be clear. The contents of this chapter (and Chapter 3) must be taken very seriously. Skimming over this material is a sure invitation to frustration and struggle with the chemical topics that follow.

2.2 ACCURACY, PRECISION, AND ERROR

4   It is important that measurements made by scientists be precise and accurate. Although the terms *precise* and *accurate* are used somewhat interchangeably in nonscientific discussion, they have distinctly different meanings in science. **Precision** refers to how close multiple measurements of the same quantity come to each other. **Accuracy** refers to how close a measurement (or the average of multiple measurements) comes to the true or accepted value. A simple analogy not directly involving measurement—shooting at a target—illustrates nicely the difference between these two terms (see Fig. 2.1). Accuracy depends on how close the shots are to the center (bull's-eye) of the target. Precision depends on how close the shots are to each other.

Figure 2.1 *The difference between precision and accuracy.*

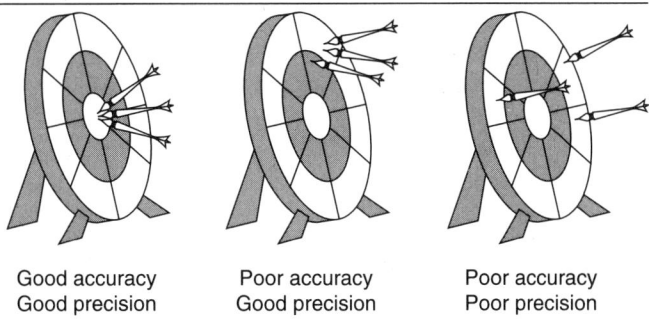

Good accuracy Poor accuracy Poor accuracy
Good precision Good precision Poor precision

5   The preciseness of a measurement is directly related to the actual physical measuring device used; that is, precision is an inherent part of any measuring device. You would expect, and it is the case, that the reproducibility (preciseness) of temperature readings obtained from a thermometer with a scale marked in tenths of a degree would be greater than readings obtained from a thermometer whose scale has only degree marks. A stopwatch whose dial shows tenths of a second is preferred over one that shows only seconds if a precise time measurement is to be made.

6   In contrast to precision, accuracy depends not only on the measuring device used but also on the technical skill of the person making the measurement. How well can that person read the numerical scale of the instrument? How well can that person calibrate the instrument before its use?

7   Normally, high precision results in high accuracy. However, high precision and low accuracy are also possible. Results obtained using a high-precision, poorly calibrated instrument would give precision but not accuracy. All measurements would be off by a constant amount as a result of the improper calibration.

8   Even the most accurate and precise measurements involve some amount of error. It is impossible to have a 100% accurate measurement. Flaws in measuring-device construction, improper calibration of an instrument, and the skills (or lack of skills) possessed by a person using a measuring device all contribute to error.

9   Errors in measurement can be classified as either random errors or systematic errors. **Random errors** are errors originating from uncontrolled variables in an experiment. Such errors result in experimental values that fluctuate about the true value. Variance in the angle from which a measurement scale is viewed will cause random error. Momentary changes in air currents, atmospheric pressure, or temperature near a sensitive balance for weighing would cause random errors. The net result of random errors, which can never be completely eliminated, is a decrease in the precision of measurements.

10 **Systematic errors** are errors originating from controlled variables in an experiment. They are "constant" errors that occur again and again. A flaw in a piece of equipment, such as a chipped weight in a balance, would cause systematic error. All readings would be off by a specific amount because of the improper calibration. Systematic errors affect the accuracy of measurements. Results are consistently either too high or too low compared to the true value.

2.3 SIGNIFICANT FIGURES—A METHOD FOR HANDLING UNCERTAINTY IN MEASUREMENT

11 Two kinds of numbers exist—those that are *counted* or *defined* and those that are *measured*. The difference between them is that we may know the exact values of counted or defined numbers but can never know the exact values of measured numbers.

12 You can count the number of peaches in a bushel of peaches or the number of toes on your left foot with absolute certainty. Counting does not involve reading the scale of a measuring device, and thus counted numbers are not subject to the uncertainties inherent in a measurement.

13 An example of a defined number is the number of objects in a dozen—twelve. By definition, 12 and exactly 12 (not 12.01 or 12.02) objects make a dozen. There are exactly 24 hours in a day, never 24.07 hours. A square has 4 sides, never 3.75 or 3.83 sides. Thus, a defined number always has one exact value.

14 In contrast to counted or defined numbers, every measured number carries with it a degree of uncertainty or error (as previously noted in Sec. 2.2). Even when very elaborate and expensive measuring devices are used some degree of uncertainty will always be present. Let us look at the origin of this uncertainty in more detail.

15 Consider how two different thermometer scales, illustrated in Figure 2.2, are used to measure a given temperature. Determining the temperature involves determining the height of the mercury column in the thermometer. The scale on the left in Figure 2.2 is marked off in one-degree intervals. Using this scale we can say with certainty that the temperature is between 29 and 30 degrees. We can further say that the actual temperature is closer to 29 degrees than to 30 and estimate it to be 29.2 degrees. The scale on the right has more subdivisions, being marked off in tenths of a degree rather than in degrees. Using this scale we can definitely say that the temperature is between 29.2 and 29.3 degrees and can estimate it to be 29.25 degrees. Note how both temperature readings contain some digits (all those except the last one) that are exactly known and one digit (the last one) that is estimated. Note also that the uncertainty in the second temperature reading is less than that in the first reading—an uncertainty in the hundredths place compared to an uncertainty in the tenths place. We say that the scale on the right is *more precise* than the one on the left.

Figure 2.2 Measuring a temperature. A portion of the degree scale on each of the two differently scaled thermometers has been magnified.

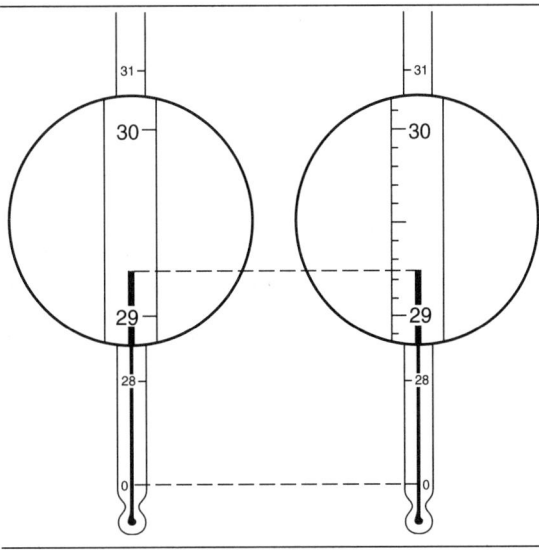

16　　Because measurements are never exact, anytime a scientist writes down a numerical value for a measurement, two kinds of information must be conveyed: (1) the magnitude of the measurement and (2) the precision or reliability of the measurement. The digit values give the magnitude. Precision is indicated by the number of significant figures recorded.

17　　**Significant figures** are the digits in any measurement that are known with certainty plus one digit that is uncertain. Only one estimated digit is ever recorded as part of a measurement. It would be incorrect for a scientist to report that the height of the mercury column in Figure 2.2, as read on the scale on the right, corresponds to a temperature of 29.247 degrees. The value 29.247 contains two estimated digits (the 4 and the 7) and would indicate a measurement of greater precision than is actually obtainable with that particular measuring device.

18　　The magnitude of the uncertainty in the last significant digit in a measurement (the estimated digit) may be indicated using a "plus-minus" notation. The following three time measurements illustrate this notation.

$$15 \pm 1 \text{ seconds}$$
$$15.3 \pm 0.1 \text{ seconds}$$
$$15.34 \pm 0.03 \text{ seconds}$$

Most often the uncertainty in the last significant digit is one unit (as in the first two time measurements), but it may be larger (as in the third time measurement). In this text we will follow the almost universal practice of dropping the "plus-minus" notation if the magnitude of the uncertainty is one unit. Thus, in the absence of "plus-minus" notation you will be expected to assume that there is an uncertainty of one unit in the last significant digit. A measurement reported simply as 27.3 inches means 27.3 ± 0.1 inches. Only in the situation where the uncertainty is greater than one unit in the last significant digit will the amount of the uncertainty be explicitly shown.

19

The precision of a measurement is determined by the number of significant figures in the measurement. A measured length of 2.453 cm (centimeters) for an object is more precise than a measured length of 2.45 cm for the same object. Thus, the term *precision* refers not only to the degree of reproducibility of repeated measurements (Sec. 2.2) but also to the number of significant figures in a measurement. Example 2.1 relates measurement preciseness to actual measuring device scales.

Example 2.1

How many significant figures should be reported in each of the measurements?

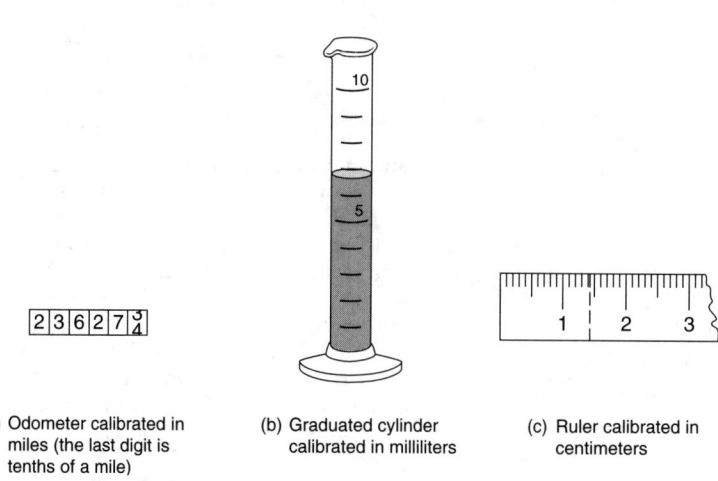

(a) Odometer calibrated in miles (the last digit is tenths of a mile)

(b) Graduated cylinder calibrated in milliliters

(c) Ruler calibrated in centimeters

Solution

(a) We know definitely that the mileage shown on the odometer is between 23,627.3 and 23,627.4 miles. We estimate the final digit (hundredths of a mile) to be a 5, giving a reading of 23,627.35 miles. Thus, *seven* significant figures are reportable.

(b) The level of the liquid is between the 6 and 7 milliliter marks. We estimate the level to be at 6.8 milliliters. *Two* significant figures are to be recorded.

(c) The ruler is calibrated in tenths of a centimeter. The broken line is definitely between 1.4 and 1.5 cm, being closer to 1.4. Estimating the next digit to be 2 we get a measurement of 1.42 cm. Thus, a measurement involving *three* significant figures is obtained.

Practice Exercise 2.1

How many significant figures should be reported in each of the following volume measurements?

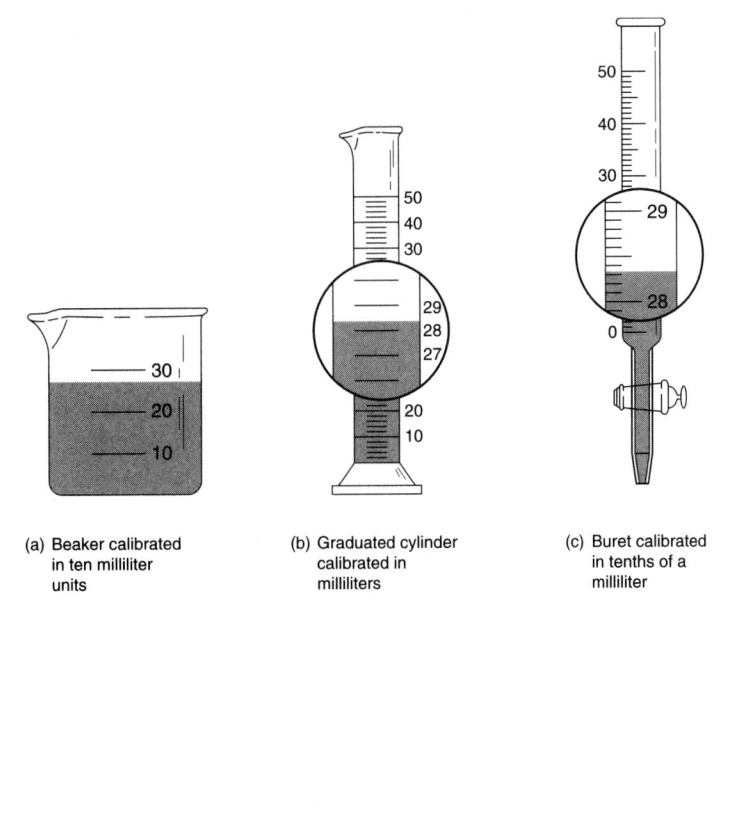

(a) Beaker calibrated in ten milliliter units

(b) Graduated cylinder calibrated in milliliters

(c) Buret calibrated in tenths of a milliliter

—H. Stephen Stoker, *Introduction to Chemical Principles*

Exercise 13G *(Continued)*

4. Did you find the answers to your three prediction questions on page 000? If so, list those answers.

   _____

   _____

   _____

5. Examine Figure 2.1. What does it tell you about accuracy?

   _____

   _____

6. Do the Practice Exercise 2.1. Referring to Example 2.1, what steps did you follow?

   _____

   _____

   _____

7. Does the section consist mainly of fact or mainly of opinion?

   _____

8. What was the source of the author's data? _____

   _____

9. Write a brief summary of what you have learned from this reading. _____

   _____

   _____

   _____

Exercise 13H

Skim the article, "Road Maps of the Mind," excerpted from a biology textbook, and answer questions 1 through 3 that follow it. Then read the article and answer questions 4 through 7.

Road Maps of the Mind: The Role of the Senses in Animal Orientation

Humans have devised elaborate means of orientation: street names, house numbers, odometers to measure distance, and road maps. Without a map, many of us could not drive across town without getting lost. Yet many birds and fish routinely travel hundreds of miles during migrations, often at night, in cloudy weather, or (perhaps most remarkably of all) through or above the seemingly endless sameness of the ocean. How do they find their way?

Orientation by Vision

To a human, the most obvious way to navigate is by sight. Close to home, at least, many animals, including some insects, learn the appearance of their surroundings. For example, the female digger wasp lays eggs in a burrow in the soil. She then flies off to capture insect prey, which she stores in the burrow to feed her offspring when they hatch. The famous ethologist Niko Tinbergen studied the cues used by the female to relocate her burrow. While the female was inside, he surrounded the nest with pine cones. When the wasp emerged, she flew around the nest before departing. While she was gone, Tinbergen moved the cones about a foot away. The returning wasp still sought her nest within the ring of cones. Although the nest was in plain sight nearby, she was unable to locate it because the visual landmarks on which she relied had been shifted.

Birds may also use landmarks, such as rivers and seashores, to find their way, but several species migrate at night or over large expanses of ocean, using the position of the sun or stars to tell direction. Many species seem to have genetically programmed information about the direction of the sun at various times of day, and also possess a biological clock that measures off a roughly 24-hour day. Other birds have the remarkable ability to "read" the night sky. Indigo buntings, for example, seem to have a built-in star map that enables them to find north during spring migration by looking at the stars.

Orientation by Scent

It is difficult to see far under water, and aquatic animals tend to rely on cues other than vision to travel long distances. Pacific salmon, for example, migrate hundreds of miles using scent to locate their final destination. Salmon hatch in freshwater streams, migrate downstream to the ocean to feed and mature, then return to their native stream to spawn. Experiments by Arthur Hasler have conclusively shown that salmon find their home stream by scent. Hasler raised young salmon in a hatchery with a trace of an odorous chemical, morpholine, added to the water. After a month, the salmon were released into the ocean. When they were scheduled to return, Hasler added morpholine to a stream past which the fish would swim on their migration. The salmon stopped at the treated stream, even though they had never encountered that stream before. Other salmon not raised in morpholine ignored the odor.

Orientation by Sound

Animals who hunt in darkness or murky water often rely heavily on their auditory abilities to recognize nearby objects. Some mammals have even evolved a type of sonar, which produces an auditory image of their nearby surroundings. This ability, called **echolocation,** is highly developed in bats and porpoises.

Bats can navigate and hunt insect prey in total darkness using echolocation. An echolocating bat may emit pulses of noise at ultrasonic frequencies (20,000–80,000 cycles per second) that bounce back from nearby objects. The intensity of this sound would make it unpleasantly loud if we could detect it. The patterns of returning sound convey accurate information as to the size, shape, surface texture, proximity, and location of objects in the environment. This system is remarkably sensitive. Little brown bats can detect wires only 1 millimeter thick from a distance of 2 meters. Several specializations of the bat's auditory system contribute to its effectiveness. The enormous, elaborately folded outer ears of the bat collect the returning echos and help the bat locate their source. As the bat emits its cry, muscles attached to the bones of the middle ear briefly contract, temporarily reducing the bones' vibrations and preventing the bat from being deafened by its own calls. The tympanic membrane and bones of the middle ear are exceptionally light and easily vibrated by the faint returning echos.

Porpoises produce ultrasonic clicks within their nasal passages, and emit them through the front of their heads.

Here, a large, flexible, oil-filled sac acts like an acoustic lens, directing the sound forward in a broad beam (for navigation) or a narrow beam (to locate prey). Echolocating porpoises are able to pick up a 5-millimeter object from the floor of their tanks, and distinguish different species of fish. The narrowly focused beam may also be used to stun fish with a blast of sound, making them easier to capture.

Orientation by Magnetic Fields

8   Radar operators have observed flocks of birds migrating at night under heavy cloud cover, when landmarks, sun, and stars were all unavailable, and at altitudes where scent could not possibly be used. Eels of eastern North America and western Europe swim out of streams and rivers into the Atlantic Ocean, and migrate to the Sargasso Sea to spawn. In all that expanse of ocean, it seems unlikely that there could be any consistent chemical cues, and vision certainly cannot be used. How do these birds and eels find their way? The answer seems to lie in responses to the Earth's magnetic field.

9   Homing pigeons are famous for their abilities to fly home after being released some distance away. They can accurately locate their home roost even under cloudy skies in terrain with few landmarks. If a small magnet is strapped to a pigeon's back, it still homes successfully in sunny weather, but loses its way under overcast skies. Apparently, pigeons can navigate either by the sun or by magnetic fields. In sunny weather, the pigeon can orient by the sun, ignoring the magnetic field. In cloudy weather, the magnets throw off the pigeon's magnetic compass, leaving them no way to find home. How do the pigeons detect magnetic fields? No one knows for sure, but in 1979 it was discovered that pigeons have deposits of magnetite (a magnetic iron compound) located just beneath the skull. These deposits may act as a built-in magnet that the pigeons use to tell direction.

10   Eels probably also use magnetic fields for navigation, but in a different way. You may recall from high school physics that when an electrical conductor is moved through a magnetic field, an electric current is induced in the conductor (this is how we generate electricity commercially). Seawater, with its high salt concentration, is a fairly good conductor, and the currents of the Gulf Stream provide movement through the Earth's magnetic field. The Gulf Stream generates extremely weak electric fields, roughly equivalent to a potential created by a one-volt battery with its poles 20 kilometers apart. At first, this was thought to be far too weak to be detected by eels or any other animals.

Remarkable behavioral experiments have shown, however, that eels can do much better. Eels were trained to slow their heart rates in response to electrical fields, and the researchers found that eels can detect electric fields as weak as a one-volt battery with poles *over 3000 miles* (5000 kilometers) apart! For an eel, finding the Gulf Stream must be a piece of cake!

—Gerald Audesirk and Teresa Audesirk, *Biology*

1. What is this article about?

   _____

2. What is the key idea of this article?

   _____

3. What are the principal patterns of organization used in this article?

   _____

4. Read and section the text. How many sections did you discern and what labels did you give them?

   _____

   _____

   _____

5. What is a definition for the term *echo-location*?

   _____

6. What kind of evidence do the authors use to make their points? _____

7. Give three examples of animal orientation.

   _____

   _____

   _____

Summary Exercise

Write a summary that includes the three most important pieces of information or the three most interesting concepts that you learned from the article on animal orientation.

Chapter 14

Reading the Social Sciences/ and History

In this chapter you will find answers to the following questions:

What are the social sciences and history?

How do you preview reading material in the social sciences and history?

What kinds of reading can you expect to find in the social sciences and history?

What is the role of evidence in the social sciences and history?

What career fields are open to students of the social sciences and history?

The Nature of the Social Sciences and History

When you read actively in the social sciences and history, you have to (1) read precisely, as you do when reading mathematics; (2) look for evidence and proof, as you do when reading the natural sciences; and (3) analyze and evaluate, as you do when reading the humanities.

The Social Sciences

Broadly speaking, the social sciences deal with people and how they relate to themselves, to one another, and to their environments. The study of social science is based on studying and analyzing these relationships from various points of view—designated as follows:

- *Anthropology:* the study of the basis for human groupings—for example, by examining why some societies are based on the nuclear family and others on the extended family
- *Archaeology:* the study of the life and culture of ancient peoples—for example, by reconstructing a Mayan village
- *Economics:* the study of the production, distribution, and consumption of wealth—for example, by comparing how wealth is accumulated in pre- and postindustrial societies
- *Political science or government:* the study of the principles and organization of government—for example, by looking at the purpose of county government
- *Psychology:* the study of the mental and emotional processes basic to human behavior—for example, by observing how individuals react to threats of aggression
- *Sociology:* the study of the ways in which people manage living and working together—for example, by analyzing how and why the institutional setup of a corporation differs from that of a hospital

The social sciences are called "sciences" because in these disciplines, as in the natural or physical sciences, practitioners collect data through experimentation, observation, and surveys; analyze the data; and draw conclusions from those analyses. Professionals in the field then present the research and its results in written reports so as to enable a project to be replicated for testing. For a psychological study of whether pigeons can be taught to count, for instance, a researcher might set up an experiment with several pigeons and test the hypothesis (assumption) that pigeons can be taught to count. On the basis of this experiment, the researcher would conclude that these particular pigeons could or could not be taught to count and would then publish the findings in such a way that another experimenter could conduct an identical experiment but perhaps obtain different results. A third experimenter would then take up the challenge. Thus, little by little a hypothesis is tested in different ways and eventually proved valid or invalid.

The social sciences are unlike the natural sciences, though, in an important respect: Often the collection of data in the social sciences cannot be as objective as it can in the natural sciences. Motivation, emotions, and opinions cannot be measured with scientific instruments; whether or not a question is biased depends on the skill of the interviewer. Moreover, outcomes of research cannot always be predicted, because unknown actions or unanticipated events—such as a new oil discovery that makes predictions of energy requirements obsolescent—may affect the results. Thus, the conclusions reached in studies in the social sciences often offer not solutions but more questions to be tested.

Courses in the social sciences entail a substantial amount of reading. Some of this material, such as an economics textbook, is closely packed with information, making the student's task almost like reading a mathematics text, where the student must read very carefully, making sure that each step is thoroughly understood before proceeding to the next. Other material in the social sciences, such as many sociology textbooks, may consist of numerous details and examples that support the opening generalization. Further, some disciplines are more technical than others—for instance, economics and archaeology emphasize mathematical analysis. Nevertheless, all social sciences are alike in that they strive for conclusions based on evidence. When fresh evidence proves some underlying assumptions wrong, old theories are revised and new ones introduced. The fundamental questions to ask in studying the social sciences are *What happens? Why?* and *How?*

History

History can be defined as the record of all human experience. Therefore, the study of history is usually included in every field: the history of science, art history, economic history, and so on. History as a discipline, however, is primarily associated with the social sciences because of its dependence on documentary evidence.

Unlike social scientists, historians rely on primary sources, or original documents like letters and public records, to tell the story of what happened. But how reliable are these documents? Much of the study of history depends on the expert analysis and interpretation of historical evidence by people who have worked in the field for many years and who painstakingly assemble evidence to prove a hypothesis. The value of historical analysis depends not so much on verifiable facts as on the accuracy of the original data and on the interpretive skill of the researcher. History may deal with a sequence of events, such as those which led to World War II, or it may compare historical trends, such as the differences between the growth of the women's movement in Holland and Belgium and the growth of that movement in France. But whichever approach is taken, it is up to the student to seek and understand the significance of the historical data by looking for themes and finding the connections between causes and effects.

In history, too, courses involve considerable reading. Some instructors forgo using a basic textbook in favor of assigning many readings on a particular topic. From the beginning, the student is expected to read and act like a historian, gathering information and challenging assumptions, asking, *What happened?* and *How do I know?*

Previewing

Textbooks

In no other academic area is previewing more important—and often more easily done—than in the social sciences. Modern social science textbooks are written with careful attention to the student's needs. These books are usually well organized, providing clear headings, numerous examples of applications of theoretical material, interesting graphics, and many study aids, such as discussion questions, summaries, and word lists. As you look over textbooks in the social sciences, you will find it useful and easy to follow the methods outlined in Chapter 2 on previewing a textbook. Although most history textbooks are also set up with headings and subheadings, some are not; in these latter cases, you need to be especially conscious of subtopics as you preview so that you can develop your own subheadings.

Nontextbook Material

In contrast to your experience in other courses, particularly those in the natural sciences, you will find that in social science and history courses, your instructors will assign readings beyond the textbook. These may be research reports, case histories or case studies, and sometimes original texts, such as government documents and published or unpublished papers, journals, or diaries. Your reading will probably result in a research paper—for instance, a comparative analysis of the ways in which learning versus cognitive theories evolved (psychology); an examination of the philosophical foundations of constitutional government (political science); a survey on dating habits, based on original data from a questionnaire (sociology); an analysis of statistical evidence on unemployment (economics); or an interpretation of eighteenth-century memoirs (history).

The authors of nontextbook material have not written it with you, the student, in mind. Therefore, you will need to preview more thoroughly, paying particular attention to the following steps:

1. Define your purpose very specifically so that you can focus your search for information.
2. Be aware of who the authors are and why they wrote what they did. What biases might be contained in the material? What points of view can be discerned?
3. Include a preliminary look for the kinds of evidence the authors have used and for the ways they have organized their information and evidence.
4. Distinguish between the author's ideas and the supporting material.
5. On the basis of your preview, predict what you can about the author's arguments and conclusions?

Exercise 14A

Preview the reading, below, from a textbook on health, by answering the following questions.

1. What is the reading about?

2. What do you think is the authors' key idea?

3. What kinds of evidence are used?

4. Is the article written to persuade, to inform, or to do both?

5. What do you think is the authors' point of view?

6. What do you think is the main pattern of organization?

_____

7. What are four subtopics of this article?

_____

_____

_____

_____

Alcoholism

How, Why, Who?

Many people do not limit themselves to one drink per hour. Their express purpose in consuming alcohol is to become intoxicated. Because this type of drinking can become habitual, it is usually labeled irresponsible use, or **binge drinking.** Problem drinking is more likely to occur among people between the ages of 15 and 24 than in any other age group. Alcohol use becomes **alcohol abuse** or **alcoholism** when it interferes with work, school, or social and family relationships or when it entails any violation of the law, including driving under the influence (DUI).

As with other drugs, tolerance, psychological dependence, and withdrawal symptoms must be present to qualify a drinker as an addict. Addiction results from chronic use over a period of time that may vary from person to person. Problem drinkers or irresponsible users are not necessarily alcoholics.

The stereotype of the alcoholic as a skid-row bum applies to only 5 percent of the alcoholic population. The remaining 95 percent of alcoholics live in some type of extended family unit. They can be found at all socioeconomic levels and in all professions, ethnic groups, geographical locations, religions, and races. One in ten Americans is an alcoholic. Moreover, 25 percent of the American population (50 million people) is affected by the alcoholism of a friend or family member. In all, some 18 million American adults are either alcoholics or have alcohol abuse problems.

Women are the fastest-growing component of the population of alcohol abusers. They tend to become alcoholic at a later age and to have fewer years of heavy drinking than male alcoholics. Women at highest risk for alcohol-related problems are those who are unmarried but living with a partner, are in their 20s or early 30s, or have a husband or partner who drinks heavily. Certain ethnic and racial groups also have special alcohol abuse problems.

We know that alcoholism is a disease with biological, psychological, and social/environmental components, but we do not know what role each of these components plays in the disease.

Research into the hereditary and environmental causes of alcoholism has found higher rates of alcoholism among family members of alcoholics. In fact, according to researchers, alcoholism is four to five times more common among the children of alcoholics than in the general population.

Male alcoholics, especially, are more likely than nonalcoholics to have alcoholic parents and siblings. Two distinct subtypes of alcoholism have provided important information about the heritability of alcoholism. *Type 1 alcoholics* are drinkers who had at least one parent of either sex who was a problem drinker and who grew up in an environment that encouraged heavy drinking. Their drinking is reinforced by environmental events during which there is heavy drinking. Type 1 alcohol abusers share certain personality characteristics. They avoid novelty and harmful situations and are concerned about the thoughts and feelings of others. *Type 2 alcoholism* is seen in males only. These alcoholics are typically the biological sons of alcoholic fathers who have a history of both violence and drug use. Type 2 alcoholics display the opposite characteristics of Type 1 alcoholics. They do not seek social approval, they lack inhibition, and they are prone to novelty-seeking behavior.

A 1984 study found a strong relationship between alcoholism and alcoholic patterns within the family. Children with one alcoholic parent had a 52 percent chance of becoming alcoholics themselves. With two alcoholic parents, the chances of becoming alcoholic jumped to 71 percent. The researchers felt that both heredity and environment were significant factors in the development of alcoholism, but were reluctant to specify precisely how these factors worked.

Scientists are on the trail of an "alcohol gene," but so far they have not managed to find one. In 1990, it appeared that a specific gene linked to alcoholism had been discovered. The gene reportedly was a receptor for dopamine, a chemical that plays a crucial role in cell communication and pleasure-seeking behavior. It turned out, however, that not only was the gene not found consistently in every alcoholic studied but that it also existed in some individuals who were not alcoholics.

Because the effects of heredity and environment are so difficult to separate, some scientists have chosen to examine the problem through twin and adoption studies. So far, these studies have produced inconclusive results, although a slightly higher rate of similar drinking behaviors has been demonstrated among identical twins. Moreover, sons living away from their alcoholic parents tend to more nearly resemble them in drinking behavior than they do their adoptive or foster parents.

Although a family history of alcoholism may predispose a person to problems with alcohol, there are numerous other factors that may mitigate or exacerbate that tendency. Furthermore, researchers now believe that social and cultural factors may trigger the affliction for many people who are not genetically predisposed to alcoholism. Some people begin drinking as a way to dull the pain of an acute loss or an emotional or social problem. For example, college students may drink to escape the stress of college life, disappointment over unfulfilled expectations, difficulties in forming relationships, or loss of the security of home, loved ones, and close friends. Involvement in a painful relationship, death of a family member, and other problems may trigger a search for an anesthetic. Unfortunately, the emotional discomfort that causes many people to turn to alcohol also ultimately causes them to become even more uncomfortable as the depressant effect of the drug begins to take its toll. Thus the person who is already depressed may become even more depressed, antagonizing friends and other social supports until they begin to turn away. Eventually, the drinker becomes physically dependent on the drug.

Family attitudes toward alcohol also seem to influence whether or not a person will develop a drinking problem. It has been clearly demonstrated that people who are raised in cultures in which drinking is a part of religious or ceremonial activities or in which alcohol is a traditional part of the family meal are less prone to alcohol dependency. In contrast, in societies in which alcohol purchase is carefully controlled and drinking is regarded as a rite of passage to adulthood, the tendency for abuse appears to be greater.

The entire society suffers the consequences of individuals' alcohol abuse. Half of all traffic fatalities are attributable to alcohol. The annual cost of alcohol-related crimes, medical expenses, accidents, and treatment programs is nearly $117 billion, and it is expected to rise to $150 billion...Direct health-care costs of alcoholics are estimated to exceed $20 billion yearly. Reportedly, alcoholism is directly and indirectly responsible for over 25 percent of the nation's medical expenses and lost earnings. Well over 50 percent of all child abuse cases are the result of alcohol-related problems. Finally, the costs in emotional health are impossible to measure.

14   Alcoholics tend to have a number of behaviors in common.... People who recognize one or more of these behaviors in themselves may wish to seek professional help to determine whether alcohol has become a controlling factor in their lives.

15   Only recently have people begun to recognize that it is not only the alcoholic but the alcoholic's entire family that suffers from the disease of alcoholism. Although most research focuses on family effects during the late stages of alcoholism, the family unit actually begins to react early on as the person starts to show symptoms of the disease.

16   An estimated 30 million Americans (one out of eight) come from an alcoholic household. Twenty-one million members of alcoholic families are 18 or older, and many have carried childhood emotional scars into adulthood. An estimated 7 million children who are under 18 live in an atmosphere of anxiety, tension, confusion, and denial.

17   In dysfunctional families, children learn certain rules from a very early age: Don't talk, don't trust, and don't feel. These unspoken rules allow the family to avoid dealing with real problems and real issues.

18   Dealing with the far-reaching effects of alcoholism strains the alcoholic's entire family. Many families affected by alcoholism have no idea what normal family life is like. Family members unconsciously adapt to the alcoholic's behavior by adjusting their own behavior. To minimize their feelings about the alcoholic or out of love for him or her, family members take on various abnormal roles. Unfortunately, these roles actually help keep the alcoholic drinking.

19   Children in such dysfunctional families generally assume at least one of the following roles:

- *Family hero:* tries to divert attention from the problem by being too good to be true.
- *Scapegoat:* draws attention away from the family's primary problem through delinquency or misbehavior.
- *Lost child:* becomes passive and quietly withdraws from upsetting situations.
- *Mascot:* disrupts tense situations by providing comic relief.

20   For children in alcoholic homes, life is a struggle. They have to deal with constant stress, anxiety, and embarrassment. Because the alcoholic is the center of attention, the children's wants and needs are often ignored. It is not

uncommon for these children to be victims of violence, abuse, neglect, or incest. As we saw, when such children grow up, they are much more prone to alcoholic behaviors themselves than are children from nonalcoholic families.

Fortunately, not all individuals who have grown up in alcoholic families are doomed to have lifelong problems. Many of these people as they mature develop a resiliency in response to their families' problems. Thus they enter adulthood armed with positive strengths and valuable career oriented skills such as the ability to assume responsibility, strong organizational skills, and realistic expectations of their jobs and others.

—Rebecca J. Donatelle and Lorraine G. Davis,
Health: The Basics

Analytical and Critical Reading Skills

Human beings are not nearly as exact or as predictable as things are. Thus, to obtain useful answers to the questions you ask in the social sciences and history, you must be sure to follow your preview questions with *precise* reading questions. Carefully state the answer to your first question: *Who or what is this about?* For instance, "It is about the British government" is not as precise as "It is about the development of the British parliamentary system." Focus succeeding questions the same way: not "What more do I want to know about the British parliamentary system?" but "How did the British parliamentary system develop?" "How does it compare with the U.S. system?" and "What is the role of the House of Lords?" Such specificity will help you understand and retain what you read.

Reading in the social sciences and history requires careful analysis. After previewing and skimming for the topic, key idea, and subtopics, look for the connections between the key idea and the supporting ideas and supporting details. Doing so will help you to locate and distinguish between the author's principal concept, or generalization, and the supporting material, which defines, describes, amplifies, illustrates, or provides factual backup.

In thinking about your reading task, posing analytical questions like these will be useful:

- *Is the author writing to inform or to convince me?*
- *What patterns of organization is the author using?*
- *Is the material an explanation of a concept, the steps of a process, or a series of examples from which I need to draw conclusions?*
- *Is the material a report on research?*

- *Does the material present a different point of view?*
- *What supports the argument or point of view?*
- *What data has the author used?*
- *How were the data collected?*
- *What is the author's conclusion?*
- *Is the methodology complete? Can I follow it step by step?*

Your objective is not only to read with understanding but also, because there is so much reading to do, to read as efficiently and quickly as possible. When reading history and the social sciences, bear in mind the advantages of flexibility. Nontechnical writing in these fields often contains many examples that can be read quickly if you understand the basic concepts. Summarizing sections of chapters and entire chapters will reveal whether you have understood the reading, its development, and its implications or whether there are gaps that you need to go back and fill in.

Vocabulary

In the social sciences you are particularly likely to encounter words that seem familiar but are in fact used in specialized ways. You will usually find, however, that unfamiliar or new terms are printed in boldface in your textbooks and defined in the glossary. Many students benefit from reserving a section of their notebooks to use for listing new terms and their meanings; such lists serve as a ready reference and as a personal word list that can be reviewed for exams.

Patterns of Organization

As you might expect, all the patterns of organization described in Chapter 8 can be found in reading material in the social sciences and history. Authors use lists to explain, define, and illustrate; they order material; they compare one finding with another and contrast two or more phenomena to make their points more vivid and thus more easily comprehensible; they show how one thing caused or was affected by another, and they explore solutions to various problems. Your ability to recognize the signal words and the patterns of organization used will help lead you through the material by indicating what questions you should ask next.

Although most writing in the social sciences and history makes use of a variety of patterns of organization, the following chart shows those patterns which are relevant in particular situations.

Pattern	Application	Example
List	Presentation of material	Types of societies (sociology)
Order	Steps of a process	A lab experiment (psychology)
	Chronology	Steps leading to a peace treaty (history)
Cause and effect	Research analysis	Effects of African colonization (political science) Causes of social differences (anthropology)
Compare/ contrast	Research analysis	U.S. and Japanese production (economics)
Problem-solution	Research report	What to do about the educational system (all fields)

Exercise 14B

Predict the principal pattern or patterns of organization of the entire reading from the opening paragraphs below, by circling the appropriate letter or letters listed. Then answer the question following each reading.

1. The national party convention of the present day is a different animal from that of the past. No longer is it a deliberative forum for choosing the party presidential nominee; rather, the convention now merely ratifies the choices of the preconvention state caucuses and primaries. A look at the Republican and Democratic Party conventions sixty years apart—in 1920 and 1980—illuminates one key contrast between the old-style and new-style conventions: the absence of dark horses—relatively unknown candidates who emerge at the convention and occasionally win a nomination as a compromise choice in order to break a deadlock.

    —Karen O'Connor and Larry J. Sabato, *American Government*

    a. Order _____

    b. Cause and effect _____

c. Compare/contrast _____

d. List _____

e. Problem-solution _____

How would you set up your notes on this article? _____

_____

2.   Much has been written about the changes which have 1
taken place in women's intercollegiate sport during the past
15 years. Most of this writing has focused on the specific
structural and philosophical changes which have transpired,
including discussions related to the pros and cons of both Title
IX and AIAW [Association For Intercollegiate Athletics for
Women] versus NCAA [National College Athletic Association] governance. As an example of such change, growth has
occurred in such areas as budget allocation, athletic scholarship availability, recruitment of athletes, participation rates,
skill level, program offerings, scheduling, travel, post-season
championships, spectatorship, and media coverage....

Little has been written on the central figure in women's 2
sport—the female athlete herself. We know very little about
how the changes in women's sport have affected the sport
experiences of the female athlete or how the female athlete of
today differs from the female athlete of a decade ago.... This
article explores (a) conditions surrounding sport participation, (b) reasons for sport participation, (c) academic performance in college, (d) perceived emphasis of sport program,
(e) reactions to college sport, and (f) post-college sport participation patterns. To address such concerns, this paper summarizes data from several survey and interview studies that have
examined the college sport experience of over 2,000 former
and current female athletes.

—Elaine M. Blinde, "Female Intercollegiate Athletes"

a. List _____

b. Order _____

c. Cause and effect _____

d. Problem-solution _____

e. Compare/contrast _____

Is the author of this article writing to inform or to persuade her audience? How can you tell? _____

_____

_____

3. Many college students today own personal computers that cost anywhere from $1,000 to perhaps $5,000 or more. In addition, it is not uncommon for them to purchase software costing another several hundred dollars. Twenty years ago, computers were available, but they were very large and extremely expensive. Few if any individuals purchased computers for home use. Over the years, the price of the "guts" of a computer—its memory—has declined to less than a thousandth of the price per unit of memory that prevailed twenty years ago. This is the main reason why computers cost so much less today than they used to. Moreover, technological improvements have made it possible to manufacture memory circuitry that is small enough to fit into the transportable personal computers that many of us own and use. In short, as the price of computation has declined the average consumer and business have spent more on purchasing computers.

   By contrast, improved agricultural technology, hybrid seeds, scientific animal breeding, and so on have vastly increased the amount of output a typical farmer can produce. The prices of meat, grains, dairy products, and other commodities have fallen sharply relative to the prices of most other goods and services. As agricultural prices have fallen, many households have decreased their total expenditures on food (after allowing for the effect of inflation on the prices of all goods and services). Even though the quantity of a good purchased generally increases when its price falls, total expenditure on the good may decline. In this chapter, we will examine more closely the response of the quantity of a good or service demanded to a change in its price.

   —Belton M. Fleisher et al., *Principles of Economics*

   a. List _____

   b. Order _____

   c. Cause and effect _____

   d. Problem-solution _____

e. Compare/contrast _____

Do you think the topic of the chapter is computers, agricultural technology, or the relationship between price and goods and services? Why?

_____

Reading Graphic Aids

Graphics are used in textbooks as part of the language of the discipline, as in math or economics, or as study aids. Authors use graphic aids to illustrate and expand on concepts taken up in the text because graphics are yet another way of portraying relationships and clarifying connections.

Graphics are used extensively in the sciences and social sciences to organize, explain, and illustrate concepts and data—they are the means by which material is analyzed and presented. Social scientists work with statistics derived from data, and the best way to present these statistics is in graphic form. Graphics are included not merely as a means of making the information easier for the student to grasp but as an integral part of the way social scientists think. Many textbooks, particularly those in economics, contain appendixes that provide specific information on reading and working with graphic material. It is important that you understand tables, charts, graphs, and diagrams so as to use them and adapt them to your own work in the field.

Make it a practice to preview attentively the titles, captions, headings, and other material connected with graphics. These elements set the stage and usually explain what you are looking at. When you are examining graphics, the principal questions to ask are (1) What is this item about? and (2) What key idea is the author communicating? You can then go on to ask other questions: What is being explained? What relationship or relationships are being illustrated? Can I summarize this information in words?

One warning: Unless you integrate your reading of graphics with the text, you may make a wrong assumption. For instance, from a chart indicating that 33 percent of firstborn children in a research sample did not feel close to their fathers in comparison with 13 percent of middle children, and 15 percent of youngest children in the sample, you might assume that some dreadful influence was at work on the firstborn children. However, a careful reading of the text reveals that most of the firstborn children in the sample were from single-parent homes in which the father was absent.

Explaining graphics to yourself is an important aid in understanding them, and, as you saw in Chapter 11, producing your own graphic depictions—plotting two variables on a graph for economics, diagramming corporate organization for sociology or business, or drawing a time line for history—is a good way to organize, understand, and remember what you are reading.

Most graphics fall under one of three major headings: tables, diagrams, and graphs.

Tables

Tables are used to put information into categories, or groups, and to compare various aspects of two or more concepts or objects; they are also used to summarize and categorize findings. Although tables appear in every field, they are particularly evident in the social sciences, where they condense and clarify data.

Table 14-1, reproduced from a chapter on politics and power, is an example. This table provides a great deal of information in little space. In addition, setting up information this way makes it easy to read the data and to make comparisons. You can see from your preview that the table is about numbers of government employees at various levels and that the key idea is that state and local government offices, combined, employ a larger percent of workers than does the federal government. Later, when you read the table more closely, you will see the precise numbers and can compare employment figures by year. A further message you can infer from the table and wonder about is: Will state and local governments grow rapidly as more and more services that have been

Table 14.1 Government Employment by Level, 1950–1986

Type of Government	Number of Employees (1,000)							
	1950	1960	1965	1970	1975	1980	1985	1990
Total	6,402	8,808	10,589	13,028	14,972	16,213	16,690	18,291
Federal	2,117	2,421	2,588	2,881	2,890	2,898	3,021	3,085
State	1,057	1,057	1,527	2,028	2,755	3,755	3,984	4,284
Local	3,228	4,860	5,973	7,392	8,813	9,562	9,685	10,922
Percent of Total Employment by State and Local Governments								
	66.9	72.5	75.6	77.9	80.7	82.1	81.9	83.1

Source: U.S. Department of Commerce, 1990:229; Bureau of Labor Statistics, 1991:75.

From Daniel J. Curran and Claire M. Renzetti, *Social Problems*

conducted by the federal government are turned over to them? What will be the effect on state taxes?

Diagrams

Diagrams are generally used to illustrate how something works or the process, or **sequence** of steps, that is followed in doing something. Diagrams explain or amplify prose. They can be as simple as the time lines used in history to show the chronology of events, or more complicated, as in the engineering diagram presented in Figure 14.1, showing how a refractory-wall incinerator works.

Here, the topic is a refractory-wall incinerator, and the key idea is that there are many complicated steps in the operation of such an incinerator. You would then go on to examine each step, how it works, and how it fits into the sequence of steps.

Graphs

Graphs are used to show how two or more variables relate. Variables are measurable quantities that can change—for example,

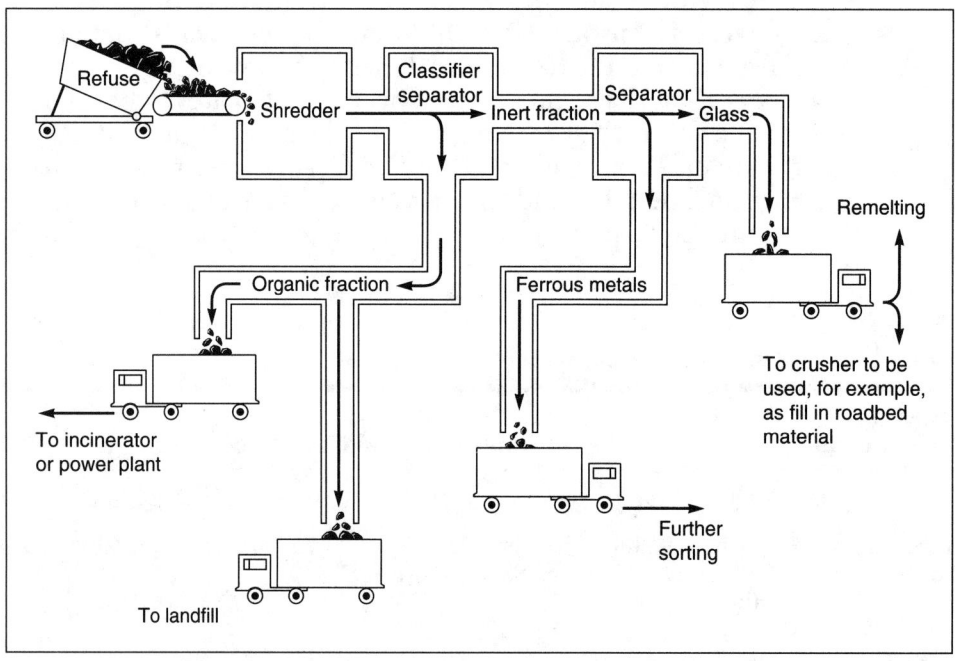

Figure 14.1 Generalized Resource Recovery. In general, all high-technology facilities involve the same basic processes. The refuse is shredded, metals and glass are separated and recovered for sale or use. The organic function may be incinerated, buried, or used in an energy recovery facility.

Source: Charles E. Kupchella and Margaret C. Hyland, Environmental Science

the passage of time and the increase or decrease of amounts. A graph might, for instance, show the annual production of two kinds of cars over a twenty-five year period. Graphs not only compare the variables—for instance, one year with another and one kind of car with another—but may show cause and effect and trends (steady movement up or down). Graphs are used to illustrate data in math and in those disciplines based on mathematics, such as economics, physics, and engineering. They generally fall into three groups: line, bar, and pie. In *Active Reading*, as in most textbooks, diagrams and graphs are referred to as **figures.**

The graphs shown in Figures 14.2 and 14.3 pertain to a reading class in a local college. Both figures have the same title: "A comparison of reading rates of classes A, B, and C, September–February." One is a bar graph and the other a line graph; they each

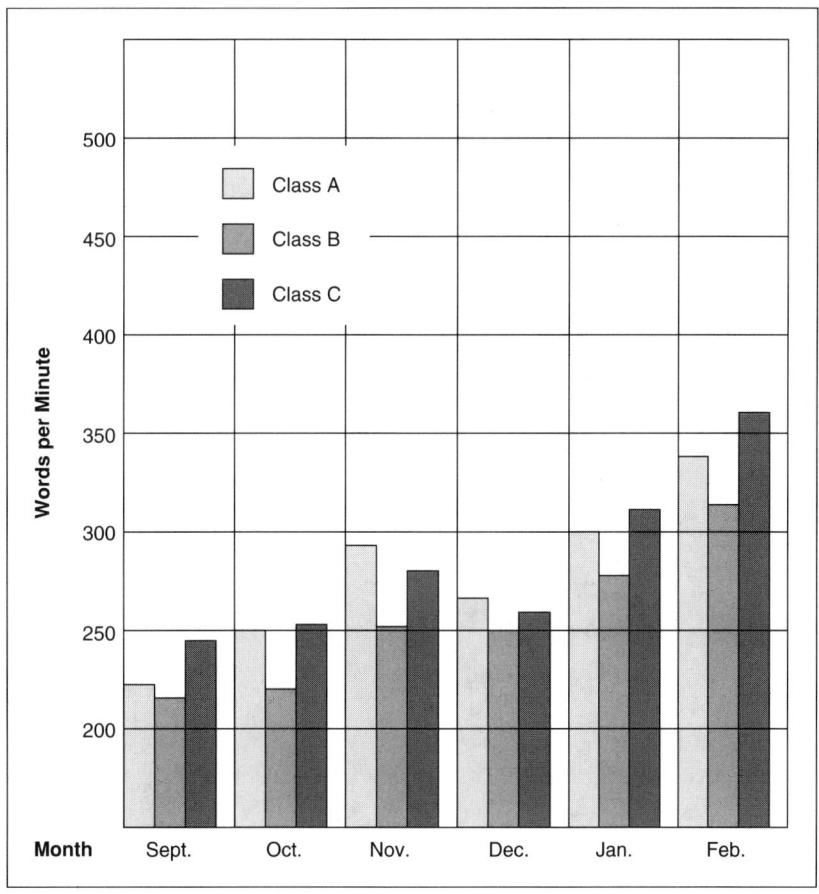

Figure 14.2 A comparison of reading rates of classes A, B, and C, September–February

14 / Reading the Social Sciences and History

show how the rates for the three classes compare. Figure 14.2 makes the comparisons more obvious, but Figure 14.3 gives a better sense of the flow of the rate increase. Both make it easier for the instructor of these classes to see what has taken place than would be the case were the same information written out in prose. From these graphs the instructor can infer that on the whole, Class C is the strongest class; that more time results in higher reading rates, as measured in words per minute; and that this trend will probably continue. Now the instructor needs to ask, What made the rates different? Why was one class slower? Where there the same number of students in each class? Might the age or male-female composition of the class make any difference? These questions point the way to the kind of research that needs to be done.

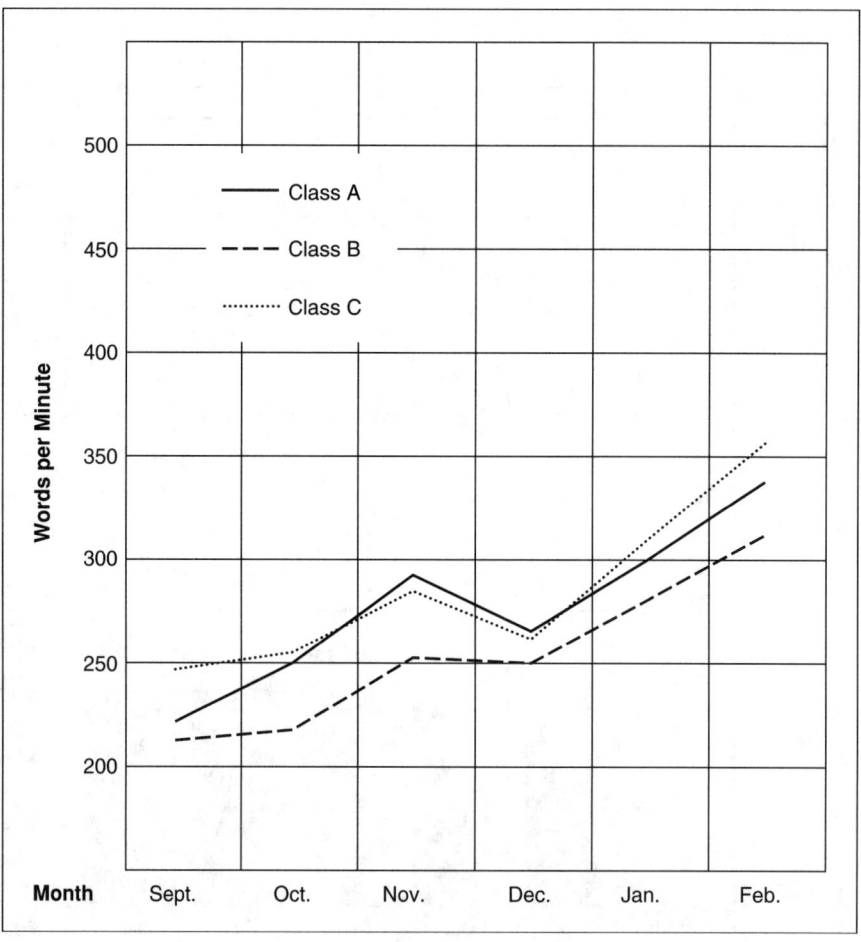

Figure 14.3 A comparison of reading rates of classes A, B, and C, September–February

Exercise 14C

Table 14–2 and Figure 14.4 have been taken from textbooks on sociology and economics. Preview and read them carefully, then answer the relevant questions.

Table 14–2   Who Are The Uninsured?

Characteristic	Percent of the Population without Health Insurance
Total	15.7
Age	
Under 15 years old	15.9
Under 5 years old	17.0
5–14 years old	15.3
15–44 years old	18.1
45–64 years old	10.6
Sex	
Male	16.4
Female	14.9
Race	
White	12.3
Black	21.7
Hispanic	26.5
Mexican American	34.9
Puerto Rican	21.4
Cuban	23.3
Asian	16.3
Native American	n/a
Annual Family Income	
Less than $14,000	37.3
$14,000–$24,999	21.4
$25,000–$34,999	9.3
$35,000–49,999	5.6
$50,000 or more	3.2
Employment Status*	
Employed full-time	62.0
Employed part-time	23.2
Unemployed	14.8

*Percentages are of uninsured population, not general population; excludes elderly.

Source: Lewin, 1991; U.S. Department of Health and Human Services, 1991.

1. a. What is the topic of this table? _____

   b. What is its key idea?

   _____

   c. What percent of the population without health insurance is employed? _____ (full time? _____, part-time? _____)

   _____

   d. Taking the table as a whole, who is the person most likely to be without health insurance? _____

   _____

   _____

2. a. What is the topic of Figure 14.4?

   _____

   b. What is its key idea?

   _____

   _____

   c. Where do most of the receipts come from?

   _____

   d. What is the largest source of receipts for state and local governments?

   _____

   e. What relationship do you see between federal and state income taxes?

   _____

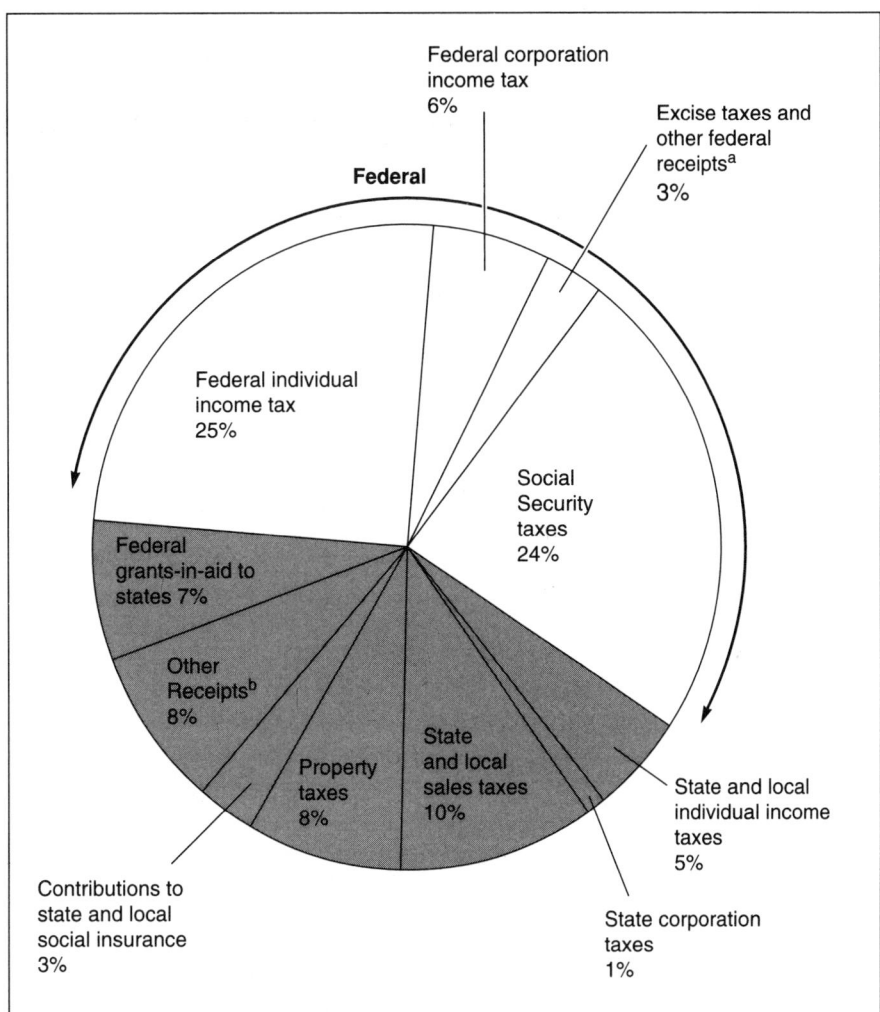

Figure 14.4 Receipts of national, state, and local governments in the United States, first quarter 1990 (percentage of total receipts). [a]Other federal receipts include estate and gift taxes, custom duties, and miscellaneous nontax receipts. [b]Other state and local receipts include fees and charges for services and miscellaneous nontax reciepts.

Source: Survey of Current Business, *May 1990, Tables 3.2 and 3.3. Adapted from* Economics *by Martin Bronfenbrenner et al.*

Exercise 14D

Using one of your own textbooks, find an example of a table, a graph, or a diagram. Then answer the following questions:

1. What is the topic of the table, graph, or diagram?

2. What is its key idea?

3. What relationships (such as comparisons or causes and effects) are being examined?

4. What conclusions can you draw from examining the table, graph, or diagram?

The Research Report

Because most writing in the social sciences and history is in the form of research reports, your textbooks and assignments in these disciplines will often include examples of such reports. You may also be asked to write research reports of your own.

Research reports in the social sciences are based on data from case studies, surveys, observation, and experiments. Let's look at each of these kinds of sources:

- *Case studies*, as the name suggests, are close examinations of specific instances of individual, group, or institutional behavior. Case studies can be valuable in developing hypotheses for future testing. (A sample case on the use of hypnosis in dentistry is presented on p. 414).
- *Surveys* are a means of getting a lot of information from many people; for instance, political surveys are used to predict voting patterns. Surveys are often an example of induc-

tive thinking, wherein the researcher gathers evidence from a small sample to make a general conclusion.
- *Observation* is a way of gathering information about behavior without influencing that behavior—for instance, by watching children through a one-way window in a child care center.
- *Experiments* allow the investigator to study cause and effect by manipulating the components of the experiment. An example would be a study of the effect of an increase in labor costs on the price of a product.

The Report Form

Although the types of data considered valid and the way they are presented may vary somewhat from field to field, in the social sciences a single form is always used for research reports within a *particular* discipline. Familiarity with the form used in a discipline helps readers locate the information they need and anticipate the direction the writing will take. Some professional organizations issue style guides as an aid to writers in the field. These guides can also prove helpful to the reader. You can check on the availability of one in the discipline you are studying by asking your instructor or a librarian. The report form rests on the following commonsense questions, the kinds of questions you would normally bring to your sectioning of the material:

What is the author reporting on?

The answer to this question provides the background and is found in the abstract (brief summary) or in the introduction.

Why did the author undertake the research?

The answer, found toward the beginning of the report, yields the author's hypothesis (the idea he or she is testing) or statement of what he or she wants to find out.

How did the author do the research?

The answer is usually found in the middle of the report, sometimes in a section entitled "Methodology."

What did the author discover?

The answer specifies the author's findings and is usually located about two-thirds of the way through the report. Sometimes it is labeled "Discussion" or "Results."

What are the importance and relevance of the research?

The answer is found in the section entitled "Conclusion" and sometimes in the one labeled "Discussion." The conclusion also summarizes the findings, states what they imply, and links them with the theoretical background and other research in the field.

Let's see how this report form works in the following article on hypnosis, "The Partial Reformulation of a Traumatic Memory of a Dental Phobia during Trance: A Case Study." You will find it easy to summarize this case if you use the questions outlined above.

The Partial Reformulation of a Traumatic Memory of a Dental Phobia during Trance: A Case Study

Abstract: A dental patient undertook hypnosis for the modification of a dental phobia. While she was in trance, the disturbing memory was replaced by a nontraumatic memory. After 2 sessions, the dental phobia was significantly reduced.

In the literature of various clinical disciplines, case studies are often published in journals which serve to illustrate the dynamics of the therapeutic process. Case studies often point to new research directions. The present case study is described with these foregoing points in mind.

Avoidance reactions to dental therapeutics are often found among adults and children who have acquired fearful traumatic associations within their past experience with dental therapy. It is often difficult to treat such patients for their dental problems when their phobic reactions to dentistry elicit thwarting behavior during the course of therapy. Not only is treatment obstructed, but also phobias prevent people from seeking early treatment for dental problems until their problems fulminate into unmanageable physical symptoms. The fear of treatment increases the perceived pain experienced by the patient, which in turn reinforces the phobic behavior....

The present paper is a case-study report which describes how hypnosis was applied in the treatment and subsequent elimination of a long-term dental phobia. It is the intent of this report to support, as other cited researchers have done, the use of psychological techniques to effect patient adaptation to dental therapy....

The case example selected for illustration in the present paper was chosen because the patient presented an intractable dental phobia for 20 years and was unable to come to terms with elements of her phobia.

Case History

The subject is a 30-year-old female Caucasian, married, and wheelchair bound, who had not been to a dentist in almost 20 years. She was in need of extensive dental restoration, but she reported being very fearful of dental treatment.

The initial interview indicated that she could not specify the source of her anxiety, and that she could not go to the dentist until the condition of her mouth became so bad as to make dental restoration imperative. At the point of initial therapy contact, she could not go to a dentist even though she knew it was necessary.

Since the patient proved to be exceedingly responsive after rehypnosis, she was given the suggestion to regress to the time when she became frightened of the dentist. She reported at age 9 that she was taken to the hospital for tooth extraction and that she was frightened when she was wheeled into the operating room. She became terrified when the anesthetic mask was placed over her face. She could not recall anyone giving her comfort; she became terror stricken. She began to abreact to her fear with extremely deep breaths and with the beginnings of tears. The therapist decided to stop the abreaction in its initial stage.

Treatment. In the place of the abreaction, the therapist told the patient that as she was going into the operating room, the doctor would hold her and stroke her forehead and tell her that she should not be afraid because he would take care of her and that he knew that she was frightened. The therapist repeated this script to her and asked her if she now heard the doctor give her reassurance. She asserted that she heard the doctor and she reported after the reassurance that her fear was diminished as she recalled herself being wheeled into the operating room.

One week later she returned for a follow-up session. Trance was rapidly induced and she was again regressed to the age of 9 and to the operation. She recalled that the doctor was telling her not to be afraid, and her degree of abreaction to the event was less. During the regression, she recalled the transplanted memory as an integral part of the scene without altering her reports of the events mentioned during the first regression.

While she was in the trance, the therapist repeated the reassurances of the original therapeutic imagery as well as stroking her forehead and hand as he told her that she was protected. After trance was ended, she reported further reduction of her fear of dentistry. Several weeks later she underwent the extraction of two wisdom teeth and she reported no fear of the dentist or the treatment. Over the last 2 years, she has followed through with cleaning and other forms of tooth restoration.

Discussion

11   The follow-up to this patient indicated that she was able to recall while in trance the implanted event as an integral part of the memory of the original event without awareness of the trauma of the original memory. That is, in recalling the original event at the therapist's request while she was in trance, she reproduced the original event with the implanted memory fully integrated as though it had always belonged there. The mnemonic prosthesis seemed to have been fully assimilated into the original trace pattern, thereby displacing the traumatic event with an event which seemed to elicit a sense of safety which the recall of the original event could not elicit.

12   The change in behavior which occurred after the implantation of the mnemonic prosthesis may in reality have been due to the patient's compliance to the implied therapeutic expectations rather than to the quality of the implanted memory. The improvement might also be a result of our having helped to desensitize the patient to the troublesome aspects of the remembered event by introducing a calm and reassuring tone to the whole situation. It could also be argued that the authors helped to restructure her memory of the past by encouraging the creation of a warm and pleasant confabulation involving an attentive and caring doctor. Whatever the true explanation might be, it is of interest to speculate on the possible usefulness of this technique. It is clearly more dramatic and likely to exert a greater influence on the patient than the unembellished suggestion to relax. It is thus more persuasive and apparently more effective.

13   The procedure just described required only two therapy sessions and two follow-up inquiries. Hypnosis in situations such as this can be successfully applied in the dentist's office for many situations which are related to adaptation to dental therapy. Such a strategy as employed with this study can be applied by a professional dentist with appropriate recognized training in hypnosis or in partnership with a trained psychotherapist.

14   The present authors recognize that patients with phobic configurations such as the one discussed in this case report may present an insurmountable problem to the dentist. The

dentist may, as was done in this patient's interest, call upon the professional skills of a licensed psychologist for assistance with the management of the patient's problem. It may not be an uncommon experience for such professional liaisons to occur. This case study indicates the potential interdisciplinary efforts which may occur when there is an enlightened approach to the wholistic treatment of the patient.

—Sheldon R. Baker and David Boaz,
International Journal of Clinical and Experimental Hypnosis

The title, supplemented by the introduction, gives you the what and the why: This case study is about the use of hypnosis in dental treatment and was undertaken to demonstrate that the use of psychological techniques can help people feel better about having dentistry done. The section labeled "Case History" deals with the methodology, the how: the reassurance of the patient while in a hypnotic trance. In the section headed "Discussion" you find that (1) the research discovered that the patient reacted positively to the experience, and (2) the relevance of the study is the effectiveness of this kind of interdisciplinary treatment. (What about your own reaction—does it bother you that memories were being tampered with?)

Several words in this article are peculiar to the areas of science and psychology. Though you wouldn't need to know them to gain an overview of the article, you probably would need to work out their meanings from the context (or by consulting a dictionary) to completely understand the details. Your personal list of vocabulary words might include *trauma, abreaction,* and *mnemonic prosthesis.*

Exercise 14E

Section and label, in the margin, the article below according to the report form: abstract, introduction, hypothesis, methodology, results, and discussion and/or conclusion. Then answer the questions that come after the article.

Daylight Saving Time and Motor Vehicle Crashes: The Reduction in Pedestrian and Vehicle Occupant Fatalities

Susan A. Ferguson, PhD, David F. Preusser, PhD, Adrian K. Lund, PhD, Paul L. Zador, PhD, and Robert G. Ulmer, MA

Abstract: Fatal crashes were tabulated for 6-hour periods around sunrise and sunset, from 13 weeks before the fall change to standard time until 9 weeks after the spring change to daylight saving time. Fatal-crash occurrence was related to changes in daylight, whether these changes occurred abruptly with the fall and spring time changes or gradually with the changing seasons of the year. During daylight saving time, which shifts an hour of daylight to the busier evening traffic hours, there were fewer fatal crashes. An estimated 901 fewer fatal crashes (727 involving pedestrians, 174 involving vehicle occupants) might have occurred if daylight saving time had been retained year-round from 1987 through 1991. (*Am J Public Health.* 1995;85:92–96)

Introduction

When daylight saving time is implemented in the spring, clock times are advanced 1 hour. In the fall, with the return to standard time, clock times are moved back 1 hour. Daylight saving time has been in effect for most of the United States from the first Sunday in April to the last Saturday in October since 1987.

The transition from standard time to daylight saving time in the spring makes 1 more hour of daylight available in the evening and 1 less hour of daylight available in the morning. Because darkness increases the risk of motor vehicle crashes,[1,2] it has been argued that this shift results in fewer motor vehicle crashes in the evening and more crashes in the morning.[3,4] However, there is typically more traffic during the affected evening hours than during the morning; thus, the net effect of daylight saving time should be an overall reduction in crashes.[5,6]

Susan A. Ferguson and Adrian K. Lund are with the Insurance Institute for Highway Safety, Arlington, Va; at the time of this study Paul L. Zador was also with the Insurance Institute for Highway Safety. David F. Preusser and Robert G. Ulmer are with the Preusser Research Group Inc, Trunbull, Conn.

Requests for reprints should be sent to Susan A. Ferguson, PhD, Insurance Institute for Highway Safety, 1005 N Glebe Rd, Arlington, VA 22201.

This paper was accepted May 17, 1994.

Table 1 Study Design: Light Conditions on Spring and Fall Days of Time Change

	Spring Time Change		Fall Time Change	
Hour	Standard Time	Daylight Saving Time	Daylight Saving Time	Standard Time
Morning				
AM0	Darkness	Darkness	Darkness	Darkness
AM1	Darkness	Darkness	Darkness	Darkness
AM2	*Twilight*	Darkness	Darkness	*Twilight*
AM3	Light	*Twilight*	*Twilight*	Light
AM4	Light	Light	Light	Light
AM5	Light	Light	Light	Light
Afternoon				
PM0	Light	Light	Light	Light
PM1	Light	Light	Light	Light
PM2	*Twilight*	Light	Light	*Twilight*
PM3	Darkness	*Twilight*	*Twilight*	Darkness
PM4	Darkness	Darkness	Darkness	Darkness
PM5	Darkness	Darkness	Darkness	Darkness

In the current study, the effect of daylight saving time on pedestrian and vehicle occupant fatalities was estimated from a model relating light level during morning and evening hours to fatal motor vehicle crashes. The model accounts for both the abrupt changes in morning and evening light levels associated with the April and October time changes and the gradual day-to-day changes in light level in a given hour with the changing seasons of the year.

Methods

In the early morning, there is a period when it is dark, followed by approximately 1 hour of twilight (slightly longer in the northern United States, slightly shorter in the South), followed by the moment of sunrise, and then by daylight. The reverse is true in the afternoon. The left half of Table 1 shows light conditions on the day just before and the day of the spring time change; the right half shows light conditions on the day just before and the day of the fall time change. In Table 1, the 6 morning and 6 evening hours are termed AM 0–AM 5 and PM 0–PM 5. Actual clock times for fall AM and PM hours (that is, from late summer to the end of the year) are defined in relation to the moments of sunrise and sunset on the last day before the change back to standard time. For example, the first minute of AM4 in the fall is sunrise on the last day of daylight saving time. Spring AM and PM hours (from the beginning of the year until early summer) are similarly defined on the last day before the change to daylight saving time. Note that sunrise and sunset times at the fall and spring time changes may differ by up to 1.75 hours because they are at different intervals from the winter solstice.

Sunrise and sunset times are subject to considerable geographic variation as well. This geographic variation was controlled by calculating actual sunrise and sunset times for each year based on the longitude and latitude of the county seat for each county in the contiguous United States, fall and spring. Thus, actual clock hours represented by, for example, AM0 or PM5, vary from county to county and from spring to fall for a given county.

Sunrise and sunset times also vary across the study weeks with the transition from one season to another. For example, fall AM3 is a full hour of daylight in the late summer, shifting gradually to a full hour of twilight before the fall time change, shifting abruptly back to a full hour of daylight immediately after the fall time change, and finally shifting gradually back to twilight as winter approaches.

We estimated variations in light level for the weeks before and after the fall and spring time changes using the midweek sunrise and sunset times applicable to Steelville, MO, the weighted population center of the United States per the 1990 census. The light level was set equal to 0.0 for a full hour of darkness, 1.0 for a full hour of twilight, and 2.0 for a full hour of daylight. Thus, the light level was equal to 0.0, 1.0, or 2.0 for each of the morning and afternoon hours on the days before the fall and spring time changes and was modified accordingly as the light conditions in each hour changed either abruptly or gradually. The value of the light level was computed as a function of the number of minutes of daylight, twilight, or dark in a given hour for each week. For example, if AM3 in a given late summer week had 6 minutes before sunrise (twilight value 1.0) and 54 minutes after sunrise (daylight value 2.0) it was assigned a light level of 1.9.

The data used in this study cover 5 years of fatal crashes, 1987 through 1991, for the contiguous United States.[7] Arizona and most of Indiana were excluded because they do not observe daylight saving time; also excluded were those few counties split between two time zones. Weekly numbers of fatal crashes were tabulated for 13 weeks before the fall time change, 9 weeks after the fall time change, 13 weeks before the spring time change, and 9 weeks after the spring time change (44 weeks centered around the winter solstice; 22 under daylight saving time and 22 under standard time). The data included 14 659 crashes fatal to one or more pedestrians and 60 152 crashes fatal to one or more vehicle occupants (but not fatal to a pedestrian or bicyclist).

Linear regression models were used to relate the natural log of the number of fatal crashes to season (spring and fall), week (22 levels), time (AM and PM), hour (six levels), and light (continuous variable).

Preliminary examination of the data indicated that the most notable changes occurred when the light level was changing from daylight to twilight (or vice versa). Thus, the cube of the light level was selected to more adequately reflect these changes. Light level cubed changed from 0 to 1 for transitions between dark and twilight and from 1 to 8 for transitions between twilight and daylight.

Results

The most notable effects of changing light levels on fatal crashes were seen when light levels changed from light to twilight (crashes increased) and when twilight changed to light (crashes decreased). These effects were greatest for pedestrians.

The increase in pedestrian fatal crashes associated with an abrupt change from daylight to twilight is illustrated in Figure 1 for the fall PM2 hour. During this hour of full daylight for

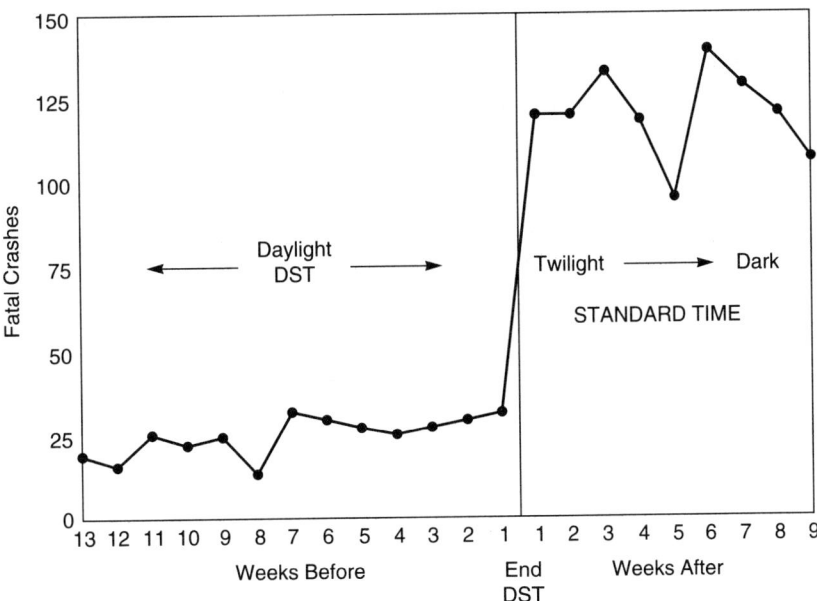

Figure 1 Pedestrian fatal crashes before and after the change to standard time in the fall PM2 hour, 1987 through 1991.

the weeks before the fall time change, crash counts remained relatively stable. With the start of standard time, the fall PM2 hour became a full hour of twilight, and the number of crashes increased substantially. Figure 2 shows the reverse effect for the PM2 hour for the change to daylight saving time in the spring. (Note that clock times for PM2 in the fall and PM2 in the spring are not identical. Thus, the absolute numbers of crashes varied from fall to spring.) Figure 3 shows the fall AM3 hour, in which there were both gradual and abrupt changes in light level from daylight to twilight. Note that the change in fatal crashes was of about the same magnitude whether light conditions changed gradually or abruptly, suggesting that it is light level rather than clock times that affects fatal crashes.

The results of the separate regression models for pedestrian and vehicle occupant fatal crashes had R^2s of 0.87 and 0.91, respectively. Both models had significant main effects for season, week, hour, time, and light level and interactions for time by week and for season by hour. The light level parameters, the standard error of the estimates, and the corresponding percentage change in crashes as a function of light level are given in Table 2.

As expected, there was an inverse relationship between light level and the number of fatal crashes. This effect was

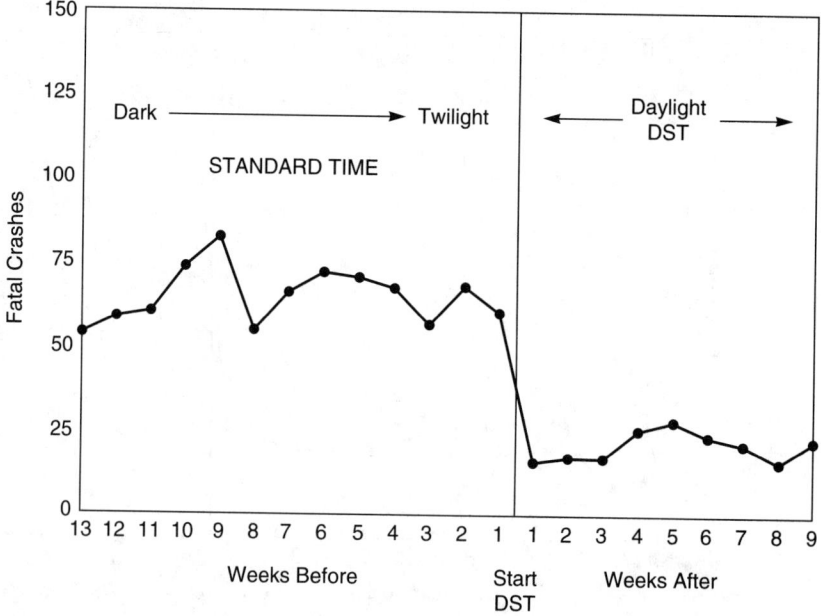

Figure 2 Pedestrian fatal crashes before and after the change to daylight savings time in the spring PM2 hour, 1987 through 1991.

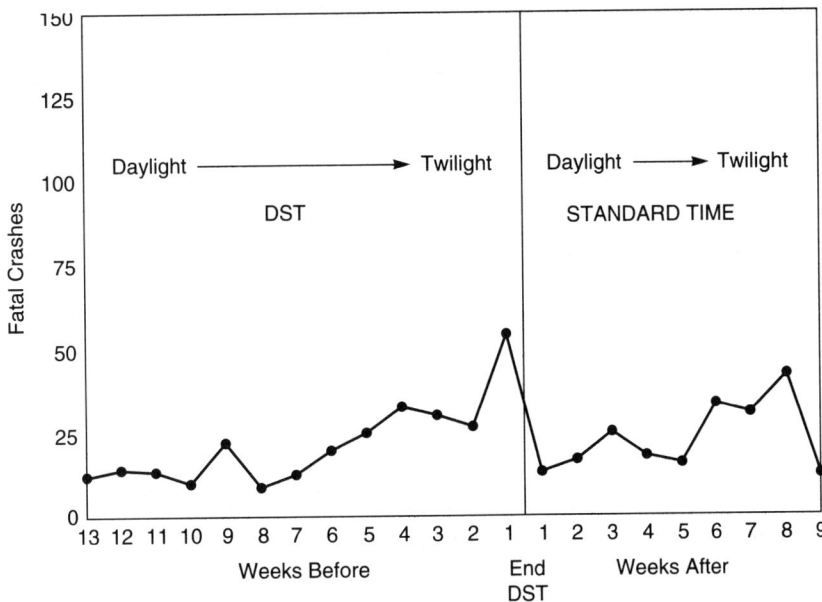

Figure 3 Pedestrian fatal crashes before and after the change to standard time in the fall AM3 hour, 2987 through 1991.

much larger for pedestrians than for vehicle occupants with the change from daylight to twilight. For pedestrians, a change from daylight to twilight was associated with about a 300% increase in fatal crashes.

The pedestrian and vehicle occupant models were used to estimate the number of fatal crashes that would be expected had all weeks been under daylight saving time as opposed to half under daylight saving time and half under standard time. This estimate was done by modifying the light level for each affected hour to reflect a continuation of daylight saving time throughout the year. As shown in Table

Table 2 Light Level Parameters and the Percentage Change in Fatal Crashes with Changes in Light Level

	Parameter Estimates	Standard Error	Percentage Change in Crashes	
			Light to Twilight	Twilight to Dark
Pedestrian	−0.207	.006	+326	+23
Vehicle Occupant	−0.020	.003	+15	+2

Table 3 Estimated Number of Fatal Crashes during the Fall and Spring with Standard Time and Year-Round Daylight Saving Time

	No. of Crashes Predicted		
	Standard[a] Time	Daylight Saving Time	Difference
Crashes fatal to pedestrians			
Fall AM	1 987	2 337	+350
Fall PM	5 725	5 038	−687
Spring AM	1 450	1 882	+432
Spring PM	5 056	4 234	−822
Total	14 218	13 491	−727
Crashes fatal to vehicle occupants			
Fall AM	11 235	11 372	+137
Fall PM	20 751	20 528	−223
Spring AM	9 876	10 044	+168
Spring PM	17 991	17 735	−256
Total	59 853	59 679	−174

Note. Numbers of crashes include the full 44 weeks (22 fall, 22 spring) and the full 6-hour AM and PM periods. Most hour-by-week tabulations would be unaffected by retention of daylight saving time. Differences arise only from those hour-by-week combinations in which there would be a change in light level.

[a]The expected number of fatal crashes under either standard time or daylight saving time were obtained from the models relating light level to the log of fatal crashes. Actual numbers of fatal crashes under standard time were slightly higher than estimated by the model, and their use in calculating the benefits of daylight saving time would have led to an overestimation of the difference in fatal crashes.

3, the predicted net benefit for retaining daylight saving time was a reduction of 727 fatal pedestrian crashes and 174 crashes fatal to vehicle occupants, for an average of about 180 per year.

Figure 4 shows this predicted crash reduction for the 22 weeks of standard time, 1987 through 1991. The greatest benefits from daylight saving time for pedestrians are just before the spring time change and just after the fall time change. Benefits are smallest during the darkest winter months because the PM reduction is increasingly offset by increases during the AM as sunrise gradually occurs later and later, eventually entering the morning rush hours. For vehicle occupants, the reduction in fatal crashes is lower and relatively constant throughout the winter.

Discussion

The effects found in this study are far more pronounced for pedestrians than for vehicle occupants. Vehicles have

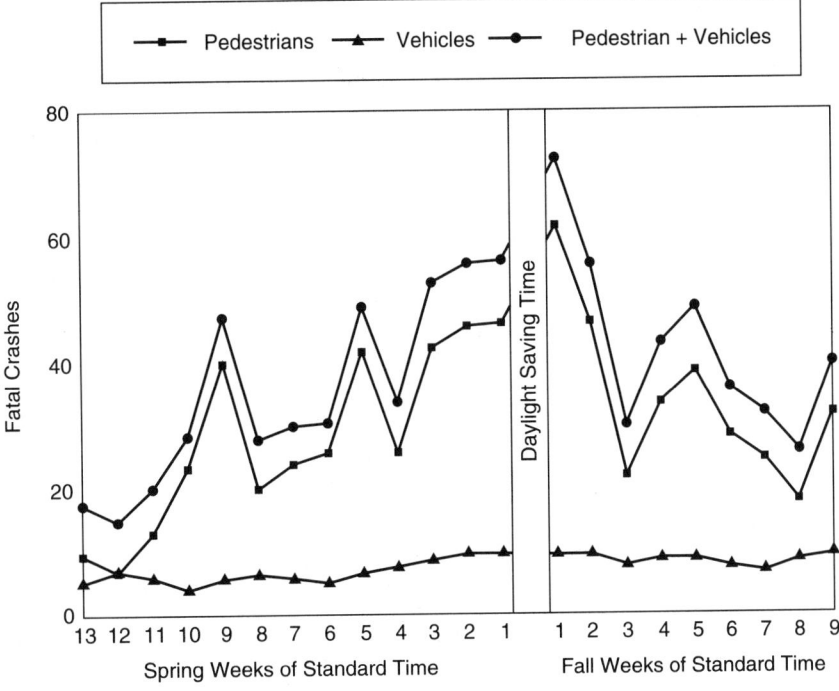

Figure 4 Fatal crashes that would be avoided if daylight saving time were retained.

headlights and taillights that allow them to see and be seen during periods of twilight and darkness. Pedestrians in the United States rarely carry a flashlight during periods of darkness and do not often wear reflective material. Thus, it is not unexpected that the effects of decreased light would be more pronounced for them.

The results of this study provide strong support for the proposition that daylight saving time saves lives; extending it farther into the winter months could save additional lives. This conclusion is consistent with previous research conducted in the United States and Britain.[3-6]

Acknowledgments

The authors wish to thank Dr Scott Fowser, Rocketdyne Division of Rockwell International, for developing the equations needed to calculate sunrise and sunset times for any day at any known latitude and longitude from the sunrise and sunset times on the same day at some other known latitude and longitude.

References

1. Fridstrom L, Ingebrigsten S. An aggregate accident model based on pooled, regional time-series data. *Accid Anal Prev.* 1991;23:363–378.
2. Green H. *Some Effects on Accidents of Changes in Light Conditions at the Beginning and End of British Summer Time.* Crowthorne, Berkshire, UK: Transport and Road Research Laboratory; 1980. Supplementary Report 587.
3. Broughton J, Sedman RJ. *The Potential Effects on Road Casualties of Double British Summer Time.* Crowthorne, Berkshire, UK: Transport and Road Research Laboratory; 1989. Research Report 228.
4. Meyerhoff NJ. The influence of Daylight Saving Time on motor vehicle fatal traffic accidents. *Accid Anal Prev.* 1978; 10:207–221.
5. Joksch HC, Wuerdemann H. The impact of year-round Daylight Saving Time upon traffic deaths and injuries. Hartford, Conn: Center for the Environment and Man Inc; 1974. CEM Report 4166-506.
6. Road Research Laboratory. *British Standard Time and Road Casualties.* Crowthorne, Berkshire, UK: Transport and Road Research Laboratory; 1970. LF213.
7. National Highway Traffic Safety Administration. *Fatal Accident Reporting System.* Washington, DC: US Dept of Transportation; 1992.

—Susan A. Ferguson, PhD, David F. Preusser, PhD, Adrian K. Lund, PhD, Paul L. Zador, PhD, and Robert G. Ulmer, MA in the *American Journal of Public Health.*

1. What kind of evidence did the authors use—personal experience, records, experiment, personal research, testimony of experts, or other reports?

2. What do Figures 1 and 2 tell you about pedestrian fatal crashes?

3. What do the authors consider to be the implications of their study?

The Evaluation of Evidence

The study of social science and history rests on the results of research, and research is based on evidence. The value of a piece of research depends on whether the evidence is relevant, adequate, thorough, precise, based on scholarship, and correct. Why investigators undertook their research and what they make of their findings are also important to the critical reader.

Evidence can be of various kinds. Authors often refer to the results of their previous research, such as experiments, case studies, and their own experience, or to the published work of experts. In each instance, the authors' close observations and accurate reporting are what make a research report useful or valuable. In citing previous research and experts in the relevant field, authors of research reports in particular disciplines may emphasize certain types of evidence:

> *Economics*—statistical data, which come in two forms: (1) descriptive statistics, which summarize and describe data (for example, tables and diagrams), and (2) inferential statistics, which lead to general conclusions based on sample data (for example, graphs)
>
> *History*—original contemporary texts about an event (for example, journals, public records, or newspaper accounts)
>
> *Political science*—government documents, observed behavior, statistical data, and legal precedents
>
> *Psychology*—experiments, systematic observation, and case studies
>
> *Sociology and anthropology*—interviews and systematic observation

As a critical reader in these fields, you can use what you have learned from Chapters 9 and 10 to judge the author, the author's argument, and the author's conclusions by asking:

> *What do I know about the author?*
>
> *Is he or she presenting a particular point of view?*
>
> *What might be influencing the author's point of view?*
>
> *Are there any hidden messages?*
>
> *Does the author start with a reasonable hypothesis, something that might be provable?*
>
> *Does the argument rest mainly on opinions or mainly on facts?*

Are the author's conclusions supported by the evidence?

You can judge the evidence by asking the following:

What kind of evidence is the author using?

Is all the evidence relevant to the author's hypothesis?

Is the evidence current? Does it need to be?

Does the evidence prove what the author set out to prove?

Does the evidence lead to convincing conclusions based on sound arguments?

Is it possible that the sources are biased?

And you can judge the importance of the research to your purposes by asking these questions:

What use can I make of this research?

Will the information support the argument in a paper I am writing?

Does the research contradict the evidence supplied by a different author?

Do I agree with the author's conclusions? Why or why not?

How does the research relate to my previous knowledge in this field?

When I combine the new knowledge with other information I have, can I predict what will happen in a certain situation?

For example, in reading a history text, you may notice that the author usually introduces the key concept and then arranges the material chronologically. But for the concept to be valid, it must result from careful and skilled questioning and analysis of original sources. As a student of history, you must look not only at the content but at the identity and possible bias of the source; the historian must be able to defend a conclusion or interpretation by reference to an accumulation of evidence, not from impressions. Such a defense is known as a *reasoned argument* and involves choosing from a range of possibilities to make a logical case.

The following passage about Bai Bureh, a late-nineteenth-century leader in Sierra Leone, offers a good illustration of the way a historian judges a source:

> One English writer, Elizabeth Hirst, has tried to show, from oral tradition, that at heart Bai Bureh was a man of peace. According to her and her co-author [Kamara]...he had given [1]

up fighting for a long time, taking a vow of peace which he broke only when his sense of Lokko [a tribe] patriotism forced him into action when Samori's *sofa* [leader] menaced the Lokko. While this thesis is apparently supported by some oral Lokko traditions, it conflicts with many Temne [a tribe] traditions which emphasize Bai Bureh's essentially war-like character. Moreover, the archival records reveal that he was almost continuously engaged in war from 1865 until 1898. Indeed many of the events recorded by Hirst and Kamara...do not correspond with what the archives show clearly did happen. Since their book is used in the schools their portrait of Bai Bureh as a man of peace and a model for Christian school children has gained wide currency in Sierra Leone.

It is essential, however, to contradict their thesis... both because it is not true, and because it is clear that the major explanation for [Bai Bureh's] success against the British was his experience as a war leader—unparalleled in those parts not only for its length but also for its continuity.... The significance of his war with the British was that while many other Africans had the will to resist European penetration, he was one of the few who also had the skill.

—LaRay Denzer and Michael Crowder, in
Protest and Power in Black Africa

On what evidence do Denzer and Crowder base their disagreement with the conclusions of Hirst and Kamara? Why did they consider it necessary to point out the disagreement? From this example you can see why it is important to constantly question the basis for statements when you are reading history and the social sciences. Conversely, if you are writing a paper in these fields, you will need to provide complete data to support your conclusions. (Writing a critical evaluation will be your task for one of the exercises at the end of this chapter.)

Applications to Career Fields

Administration, legal studies, psychology, criminal justice, banking and finance, business management, economics, communications, public relations, advertising, marketing, paralegal work, nursing, travel and tourism, public health, social work, environmental science—these are just a few of the career fields that are based in whole or in part on theories and skills developed in the social sciences.

Some courses that deal with the application of theories learned in the social sciences—such as courses in banking and finance—are based on a single discipline (in this case, economics). Others—such as courses in organizational behavior—have an interdisciplinary base, as illustrated in Figure 14.5.

What makes the professional- or career-related courses different from the others? The following description of a course on the principles of marketing gives us a clue.

> Principles of Marketing examines contemporary marketing principles, concepts or managerial practices. Studies marketing environment, consumer behavior, marketing research and information systems. Analyzes marketing in terms or product planning and development, distribution management, pricing strategies, and promotional practices. Focuses attention on the social and legal responsibilities of

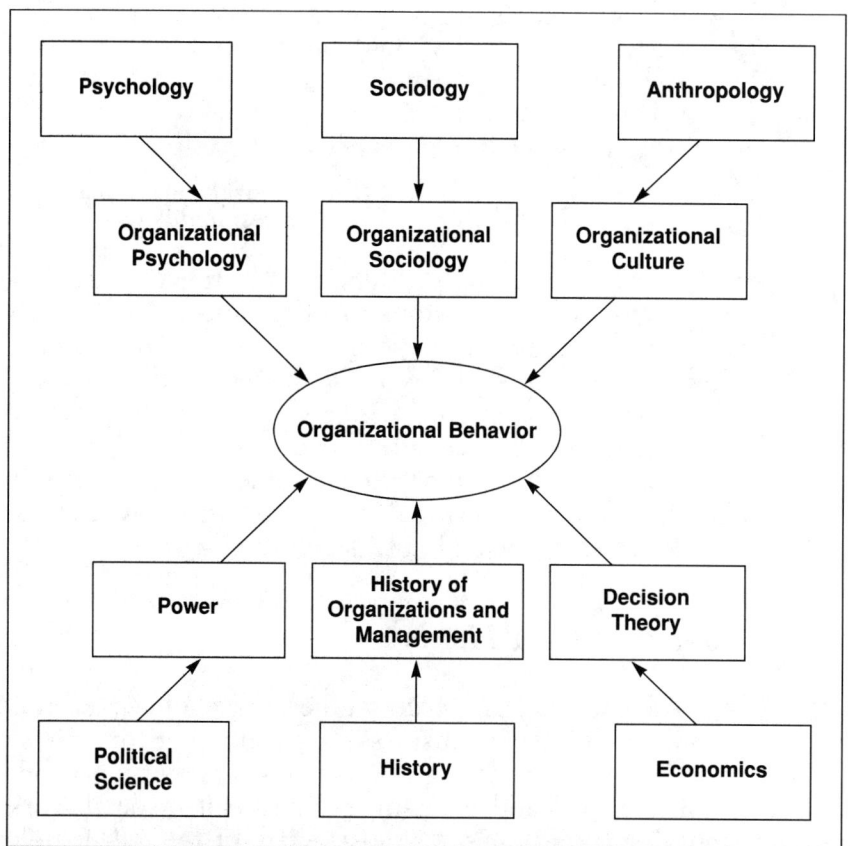

Figure 14.5 The disciplines contributing to the emergence of organizational behavior.

Source: David J. Cherrington, Organizational Behavior.

marketing and consumerism. Case problems and current issues discussed and analyzed.

—Massachusetts Bay Community College

From this description you can see that students taking this course are going to be involved in examining current principles and practices and in analyzing actual marketing situations, with special attention to the social and legal implications. Students will do these things through studying case problems and current issues that take them out of the classroom to observe what actually goes on and through applying the concepts and principles they learn to the solution of actual problems.

When students shift from taking theoretical courses to taking practical or applied courses in these fields, they can generally expect accompanying changes in both the kinds of reading they do and the way they approach evaluation.

Kinds of Reading

Textbooks in the fundamental courses in these fields will share all the attributes of social science textbooks; however, they will probably contain more diagrams illustrating the information and more examples of the ways in which theory is applied. In addition, students will be introduced to the kinds of reading done by professionals in the field—that is, to reports, case studies, and case problems.

- *Reports,* as you have learned, present the results of research. They usually appear in professional journals and are read to ascertain their implications for a particular situation. For instance, a professional employed as a hotel manager would read a report on two new cost-saving plans for food service.
- *Case studies,* as noted earlier, examine one situation closely. They thus enable professionals to see what can be learned from one situation and applied to another—as, for instance, in the development and marketing of a new brand of detergent.
- *Case problems,* or simply "cases," are a teaching and learning device used at every stage of professional development. They describe a problem, its background, and its causes and effects but leave the solution to the reader to work out, either alone or in a seminar. As the following example demonstrates, working out a solution calls for close reading and analysis, tasks that are best accomplished by adhering to the problem-solving steps outlined in Chapter 13.

Case 3: New Truck Assignment

You are the supervisor of a crew of repair technicians. Every so often your department receives a new truck in exchange for an old one, and you have the problem of deciding which technician should receive the new truck. When these decisions have been made in the past, there have been seriously hurt feelings because each technician seems to think he or she is entitled to the new truck. You have a difficult time being fair. In fact, in the past it seems that no matter what you decide, your decision is considered wrong by the majority. Although you consider all six of your technicians highly competent and skilled, you are also convinced that they are a bunch of uncooperative prima donnas. How should you make the decision about who gets the new truck?

—David J. Cherrington, *Organizational Behavior*

Evaluation

When you have to apply what you are learning in these courses to work in the real world, where you will be responsible for how well a job is done, you must read carefully, paying particular attention to why and how something is accomplished. You need to be able mentally to take something apart so as to understand how each part works. It is not enough to know that a good or a bad decision was made about how to handle a particular personnel crisis in Company X; to make use of such knowledge, you need to understand exactly what went into the decision, what factors influenced it, what situation led up to it, and why you believe it was a good or a bad decision.

Here are the key thinking steps:

1. Understand each step of a process.
2. Analyze why it was done that way.
3. Associate and apply what you have learned to a situation you know about or have imagined.
4. Make a critical evaluation. Often there is no "right" answer—there are only judgment calls. Therefore, be able to defend your assessment and recommendations by referring to your careful analysis of the situation.

Exercise 14F

Fill in the blanks in the following statements to test your knowledge of the material contained in this chapter. Refer, if necessary, to the relevant section in the chapter.

1. The social sciences deal with people and how they relate to themselves, to _____, and to their environments.

2. History and the social sciences both depend on _____.

3. Basic questions to ask in studying the social sciences are, *What happens?* _____? and _____?

4. _____, _____, and compare/contrast are the three patterns of organization most often used in writing about history.

5. The two kinds of statistics are descriptive and _____.

6. In reading history, you should watch for bias on the part of the author and of the _____.

7. The form of a research report consists of an abstract, an introduction, and sections labeled _____, "Discussion," and "Conclusion."

8. Observation is a way of gathering information about behavior without _____ the behavior.

9. In management courses, instructors often use _____ as a teaching device.

10. Research reports use evidence gathered from case studies, _____, observation, and _____.

Exercise 14G

This exercise is based on part of a chapter from a textbook on environmental science. The reading is interesting because of the different kinds of graphic material used to illustrate the important points that are made. Preview and read it, using and answering the questions below.

A. Preview questions

1. What is the passage about?

   _____

2. What do you think is the authors' key idea?

   _____

   _____

3. Do you think the authors' main purpose is to inform or to persuade?

   _____

4. What are possible headings for the four principal parts of the reading?

   _____

   _____

5. What are three questions you might ask of the text?

   _____

   _____

   _____

   _____

Historical Perspectives and Trends

Let us look at the historical growth of human population. Two major factors permitted substantial human population increases. One was the increased ability to produce food through agriculture. The second was the substantial lowering of the death rate achieved through improved sanitation and medicine.

World population reached 1 billion in 1850, 2 billion in 1930 (80 years later), 3 billion in 1960 (30 years later), 4 billion in 1975 (15 years later), and 5 billion in 1987 (12 years later). Most projections put world population around 6 billion in the year 2000 or a little before. The momentum of population growth is immense....

At an annual percentage growth rate of 1%, the human population will double in 70 years; at 2%, the doubling time is 35 years; and so on. Average annual growth rate for the world is about 1.8%. This growth rate has a population doubling time of 39 years. However, this rate varies greatly from country to country. Average annual growth rates run around 2.0% in developing nations and 0.6% in developed regions. Figure 8.5 shows annual growth rates by continent from 1960 to 1990. The highest growth rate is in Africa. At the current rate, the population of Africa will double in 28 years. Some subregions of Africa are growing even faster. Kenya and Zambia, with almost a 4% annual growth rate, will double population in only 17 years.

Since 1950, the fertility rates in developed countries have decreased significantly. Many of the developed countries have reached replacement fertility levels, and in Germany, death rates now actually exceed birth rates. For all developed countries the fertility rate is just about at the replacement rate. Should these rates continue, these countries will achieve stable populations or even experience population declines. Although no one knows for certain, it is generally thought likely that once low fertility rates are reached, they will be maintained around replacement levels, with periodic fluctuations. The population problems facing many of the developed countries in the future will stem from increased immigration, urbanization, and wide differences in income.

What about the developing countries? Figure 8.5 shows that annual growth rate has also declined in many of the developing countries since 1960. Although fertility rates in some developing countries are on the decline, there is in the

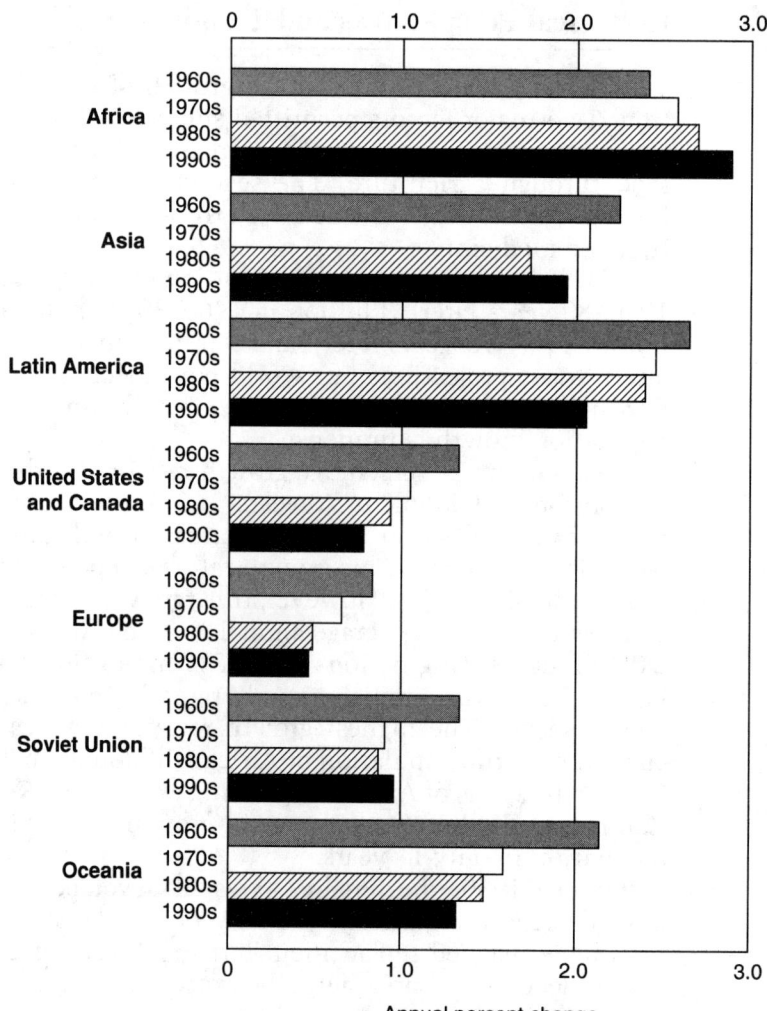

Figure 8.5 World Population: Annual Growth Rate by Continent, 1960 to 1990. This bar graph shows that the annual population growth rate has decreased worldwide since 1960 except for Africa. These figures represent averages for the continents; subregions may reflect growth rates above or below this average.

age structure of the populations of these countries great potential for continued growth.

Almost 90% of current world population growth can be attributed to the developing countries. It has been predicted that of the 6 billion people expected to occupy this planet by the year 2000, fully 5 billion will live in developing countries. According to a U.S. government study, developing countries had 66% of the world's population in 1950, had 72% in 1975, and are likely to have 79% in the year 2000.

Population problems in developing countries include those associated with urbanization and distribution of goods, as in developed countries, but in developing countries these problems will continue to be overshadowed by poverty, hunger, and the need to increase economic output faster than population growth. Historically, population growth in the developing countries has far outstripped resource development and improvement in the quality of life. It has been predicted that simply to maintain present, sometimes very low standards of living in developing countries, economic output must double by the year 2000.

Although total world population will continue to increase for many decades, most population growth *indices* are on the decline and are expected to continue to decline. Crude birth and death rates, gross and net reproductive rates, and general fertility are all expected to drop. The world birth rate appears to be declining at a faster and faster rate. The drop in birth rate in developing countries from 1970 to 1977 was reported to be three times as great as the drop from 1950 to 1970. This dramatic drop in birth rate in developing countries has, since the mid-1960s, exceeded their continuing declining death rate, resulting in an overall decline in the population growth rate (see Figure 8.6). In 1987 the world birth rate did increase slightly due primarily to a jump in birth rate in China. We will discuss this phenomenon later. It is important to keep in mind that even with these promising trends, population growth overall will continue well into the twenty-first century because of the lag effect.

It appears that trends toward urbanization will continue. It is estimated that by the year 2000, 75% of the population in South America, over 40% of Africa's population, and a little less than 40% of the people in Asia will live in cities. Today 20% of the world's people live in a city with a population of 100,000 or greater.

According to the World Commission on Environment and Development, Third World cities alone could grow by 750 million people between 1985 and 2000. This means increased needs for urban infrastructure to provide clean water and sanitation, food and health services, shelter, transportation, and education. Even now problems of inadequate facilities, overcrowding, and disease trouble many urban areas. To achieve the additional infrastructure levels that will be needed would require an enormous development effort and would be extremely costly. There is little likelihood that the means for such an effort are available.

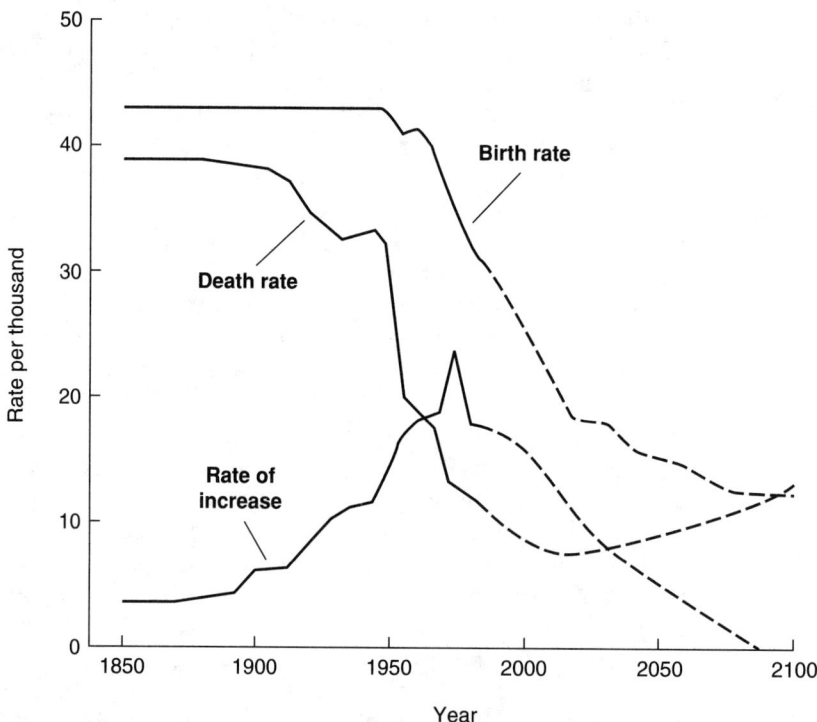

Figure 8.6 Birth Rate, Death Rate, and Rate of Population Increase in Developing Countries, 1850–2100. Since the mid-1960s, the rate of increase in population in developing countries has decreased significantly owing to a dramatic decrease in birth rate. The dashed curves are projections. The increases in death rate shown for the mid to late twenty-first century is due to the large number of older people in the population at that time.

Figure 8.7 shows the historical changes in U.S. population growth. We would like to draw attention to several important points. There was a decrease in the *rate* of population growth in the 1930s, a time of economic depression. A "baby boom" followed World War II and is reflected in the sharp rise in the population growth rate prior to 1950. Population growth since the 1970s appears to be slowing down, but the full effect of the baby boom—as the boom babies have babies—is yet to be seen (Figure 8.7b).

Total births in the United States have risen since 1975 as a result of this large baby boom generation entering their childbearing years, but the *birth rate* has remained low. It is thought that this boom generation is either delaying childbirth or will have a much lower fertility rate, resulting in a continuation of the population growth rate decline. Some

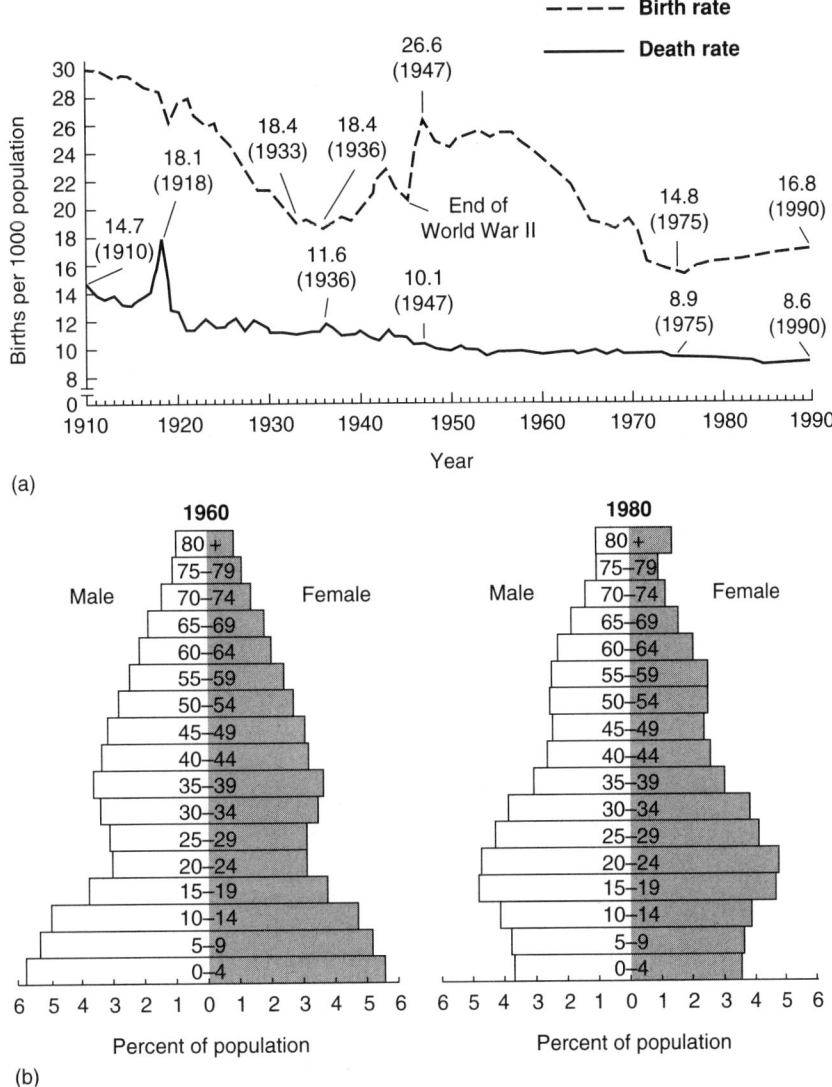

Figure 8.7 U.S. Population Profiles. (a) Birth and death rates per 1,000 from 1910 to 1990. Birth rates slowed in the 1930s, then picked up again after World War II. A leveling-out period began in the late 1970s. Its duration will depend on the reproduction patterns of the baby boom children now in their reproductive years. (b) U.S. population by age and sex, 1960 and 1980. The baby boom bulge has had a significant impact on the economics of American life, from education to job seeking. Even more changes are likely as this predominant portion of the population enters the middle and late years.

think there is little or no reason to expect an increase in fertility rates.

Since the 1950s the birth rate has declined significantly more than the death rate. This decline accounts for a slowdown in the rate of population growth. The fertility rate in the United States is also on the decline. The net population growth rate in the United States has fluctuated around 0.9% in the recent past.

Legal immigrants account for 25% of present U.S. population growth. Illegal aliens add another significant but unknown percentage.

The U.S. Census Bureau has projected U.S. population growth on the basis of high (2.7), medium (2.1), and low (1.7) fertility rates. The Census Bureau estimates that the earliest the population size will stabilize or decline under any of the estimates is around the year 2030.

—Charles E. Kupchella and Margaret C. Hyland,
Environmental Science

B. Reading tasks

1. In the margin, section and title (using the subtopics) one of the principal parts.

2. Analyze one of the parts, noting the supporting ideas and patterns of organization in the margin.

3. Did you find the answers to your three questions? If so, what are those answers?

_____

_____

_____

4. Examine Figure 8.5 carefully, reading the accompanying text, and answer the following questions (Oceania consists of the islands of the South Pacific, Malaysia, Australia, and New Zealand):

a. What is the topic of the figure?

_____

b. What is its key idea?

c. What area of the world is experiencing the slowest population growth?

d. What accounts for the increase in the 1990s in Asia?

e. What does this figure tell you about northern areas of the world compared to southern areas?

C. Critical reading tasks

Write a brief evaluation of what you have read. The following questions will help get you started.

1. Does the passage deal mainly with facts or mainly with the authors' opinion?

2. Where do you think the authors obtained their data?

3. Do you think the authors have come to sound conclusions, based on solid arguments? If so, why? If not, why not?

4. How does this reading affect you? Will you think or behave differently because you read it? If so, in what ways? If not, why not?

Summary Exercise

Summarize the preceding reading emphasizing the conclusions you would draw from it.

Appendixes

Appendix A

List of Prefixes, Roots, and Suffixes

Prefixes

Prefix	Meaning	Examples
ab-	away or from	absent, abduct
ad-	to or toward	advance, admit
ante- pre-	before	antecedent, antedate premise, predict
anti-	against	antisocial, antiwar
auto-	self	autograph, automobile
circum-	around	circumference, circumnavigate
com-, con- sym-, syn-	together	combine, connect sympathy, synonym
contra-	against	contrary, contradict
de-	down from	descent, deduce, depose
dia-	through or around	diameter, diagram
dis-	apart	disconnect, dissect
equi-	equal	equitable, equidistant
ex-	from, out of, former	expel, exit, export, ex-wife
il- in- ir- un-	not	illegal, illegitimate invisible, infrequent irregular, irreducible unhappy, unawake
in-, im-	in or into	invade, insert, immigrant
infra-	below, beneath	infrasonic, infrastructure

Prefix	Meaning	Examples
inter-	between, among	interrupt, interweave
micro-	small	microbe, microscope
ob-	against	obstruct, objection
omni- } pan- }	all	omnipotent, omniscient Pan-American, pantheist
per-	through	pervade, perennial
peri-	around	perimeter, periscope
poly-	much, many	polygon, polygamy
post-	after	postpone, postmortem
pro-	for, forward	progress, proceed
re-	back, again	return, renew
retro-	backward	retrospect, retrograde
semi-, seme-	half	semicircle, semester

Numbers

mono- } uni- }	one	monogamy, monopoly unicorn, unicycle
bi-	two	bicycle, bisect
tri-	three	tricycle, trimester
quar-	four	quarter, quartet
dec-	ten	decimal, decade
centi-	hundred	centimeter, centigrade
milli- } kilo- }	thousand	millimeter, millennial kilogram, kilowatt
mega	{ million { large	megacycle, megaton megabucks, megalomania

Roots

Root	Meaning	Examples
aqua	water	aquamarine, aquarium
audio	hear	audible, auditorium
bene	well	beneficial, benediction
bio	life	biology, autobiography
cor, cord	heart	coronary, cordially
corp	body	corporation, corpse
cred	belief	credible, accredited
dict	say	dictation, diction
ego	self	egoist, egomania
fact	make	factory, manufacture

Root	Meaning	Examples
frater	brother	fraternity, fratricide
gamos	marriage	monogamous, polygamy
geo	earth	geometry, geography
graph	write	biography, graphology
loc	place	locality, dislocate
log	speech, science	monologue, logical
mater	mother	maternal, maternity
mit, mis	send	missive, emit
mort	death	mortal, mortician
navi	ship, sail	navy, circumnavigate
pater	father	paternal, paternity
ped	foot	pedestrian, millipede
philo	love	philosophy, anglophile
phob	fear	hydrophobia, Anglophobia
phon	sound	phonetics, microphone
pos	place	position, depose
pot	strength	potent, impotent
pseudo	false	pseudonym, pseudopod
psych	soul, mind	psyche, psychological
script, scrib	write	inscription, describe
sol	alone	solitary, isolate
struct	build	structure, instruct
tele	far	television, telegram
thesis	to place	antithesis, synthesis
vert	turn	convert, advertisement
vid, vis	see	visible, video
voc	say	vocal, advocate

Suffixes

Suffix	Meaning	Examples
-able, -ible	capable of being	breakable, portable
-age	act, condition	package, postage
-al	of, pertaining to	musical, numerical
-an	person who	electrician, technician
-ant	person who	attendant, participant
-ent	person who	president, incumbent
-ist	person who	novelist, physicist
-or	person who	author, professor
-ance, -ence	action, quality	attendance, instance, prominence

Suffix	Meaning	Examples
-ar	relating to	ocular, jugular
-ive	relating to	active, passive
-ary	place where	library
-ate	to make	fabricate, activate
-fy	to make	pacify, magnify
-ize	to make	sanitize, sensitize
-ee	one who is	enrollee, payee
-er	one who is	preacher, reader
-en	made of	silken, oaken
-fic	causing, producing	scientific, terrific
-hood	state, condition	statehood, brotherhood
-id	state, condition	putrid, liquid
-ic	of, characteristic	fantastic, idiotic
-ice	quality, condition	service, justice
-ile	relating to	docile, infantile
-ion	state of being	attention, motion
-ment	state of being	improvement
-less	without	breathless, heartless
-ology	knowledge of	psychology, theology
-ory	place for	factory, observatory
-ous	abounding in	fabulous, curious
-some	tending to	wholesome, lonesome
-tude	condition of	fortitude, magnitude
-ty	condition of	totality, entity
-ward	direction	northward, forward

Appendix B

An Active Reader's Glossary[1]

The following list of words, with their definitions, has been compiled as an aid to students in understanding the meanings of some of the basic terms that are used in an academic context. Most of these words appear in *Active Reading*, where they are set in boldface.

abstract (*adj*) Thought of apart from any particular instances or material objects; not concrete; expressing a quality of thought separately from any particular or material object. *Example:* Beauty is an abstract word.
(*n*) A brief statement of the essential content of a book, article, speech, etc.; a summary.

analogy (*n*) Similarity in some respects between things otherwise unlike; partial resemblance.

analysis (*n*) A separating or breaking up of any whole into its parts, esp. with an examination of these parts to find out their nature, function, interrelationship, etc.

analyze (*v*) To separate (a thing, idea, etc.) into its parts so as to find out their nature, their relationship to the whole and to each other.

appendix (*n*) Additional or supplementary material at the end of a book or other writing.

application (*n*) The act of putting something to use. *Example:* a job calling for the application of many skills.

argument (*n*) A reason or reasons offered for or against something; proof or evidence.

---

[1] This glossary is derived in part from definitions from *Webster's New World Dictionary*, Third College Edition, Macmillan, USA.

association (*n*) A connection in the mind between ideas, sensations, memories, etc.

classification (*n*) An arrangement according to some systematic division into classes or groups.

compare (*v*) To examine in order to observe or discover similarities or differences.

concept (*n*) An idea or thought, esp. a generalized idea of a thing or class of things; abstract notion.

conclusion (*n*) The final part of a reading selection, the part that pulls together the ideas presented in the introduction and the development. A conclusion can be a summary of, or a commentary on, the selection.

connection (*n*) The logical linking together of words or ideas; the relationship of a word or statement to the context.

connotation (*n*) An idea or notion suggested by or associated with a word, phrase, etc. in addition to its explicit meaning, or denotation. *Example:* "Politician" has different connotations from "statesman."

context (*n*) (1) The parts of a sentence, paragraph, discourse, etc. immediately next to or surrounding a specified word or passage and determining its exact meaning. (2) The whole situation, background, or environment relevant to a particular event, personality, creation, etc.

contrast (*v*) To show differences when compared.

critical reading (*n*) Actively using intelligence, knowledge, and reading skills to analyze and evaluate.

criticism (*n*) The act of making judgments; analysis of qualities and evaluation of comparative worth, esp. the critical consideration and judgment of literary or artistic work.

deduction (*n*) The act or process of reasoning from the general to the specific, or from premises to a logically valid conclusion.

deductive reasoning (*n*) (1) A process of reasoning in which a conclusion necessarily follows from a stated premise. *Example:* All humans are mortal. Socrates is human. Therefore, Socrates is mortal. (2) A process of reasoning from a general statement or idea to a specific instance.

denotation (*n*) The direct, explicit meaning or reference of a word or term.

describe (*v*) (1) To tell or write about; give a detailed account of. (2) To picture in words.

development (*n*) The body of a reading selection; the part that includes the key idea, supporting ideas, and supporting details.

diagram (*n*) (1) A sketch, drawing, or plan that explains a thing by outlining its parts and their relationships. (2) A chart or graph explaining or illustrating ideas, statistics, etc.

discussion (*n*) The examination of a subject in speech or writing.

enumerate (*v*) To name one by one; specify, as in a list.

essay (*n*) A short literary composition of an analytical, interpretive, or reflective kind, dealing with its subject in a nontechnical, limited, often unsystematic way and, usually, expressive of the author's outlook and personality.

evaluate (v) To judge or determine the worth or quality of.

explain (v) (1) To make clear, plain, or understandable. (2) To account for; state reasons for.

explicitly (adv) Clearly stated, leaving nothing implied, definite.

exposition (n) Writing or speaking that sets forth or explains.

fact (n) Something that has been objectively verified.

figurative language (n) An expression in which words are used not in their literal sense but pictorially to create a more forceful or dramatic image. *Example:* the eye of the storm.

figure (n) A diagram.

generalization (n) A general idea, statement, etc. resulting from generalizing; inference applied generally.

generalize (v) To infer or derive (a general law or precept) from (particular instances); to formulate general principles or inferences from particulars.

glossary (n) A list of difficult, technical, or foreign terms with definitions or translations, often included in an alphabetical listing at the end of a textbook.

graph (n) A diagram representing the successive changes in a variable quantity or quantities.

humanities (n) The branches of learning concerned with human thought and relations, as distinguished from the sciences, esp. literature, philosophy, history, etc.

hypothesis (n) pl. **hypotheses** An unproved theory, proposition, or explanation tentatively accepted to explain certain facts or to provide a basis for further investigation, argument, etc.

illustrate (v) To make clear or easily understood with examples, comparisons, etc.

implicit (adj) Suggested or to be understood though not plainly expressed.

imply (v) To indicate indirectly or by allusion; hint; suggest; intimate. *Example:* an attitude implying boredom.

index (n) An alphabetical list of names, subjects, etc., together with the page numbers on which they appear in the text, usually placed at the end of a book or other publication.

induction (n) Reasoning from particular facts or individual cases to a general conclusion.

inductive reasoning (n) The process of using specific facts or individual cases to form a general conclusion. *Example:* Since the number of deaths from automobile accidents has decreased in the states that have seat-belt laws, all states should have seat-belt laws.

infer (v) To conclude or decide from something known or assumed; derive by reasoning; draw as a conclusion.

inference (n) The drawing of a conclusion from fact or premises, the finding of an unstated meaning.

informational writing (n) Writing that presents data in a straightforward and objective way.

interpret (v) To explain the meaning, make understandable.

introduction (n) The beginning of a reading selection, the part that usually includes the key idea of the selection and sometimes contains the subtopics; presents a plan of the material, provides background information, or explains the importance of the key idea.

irony (n) A method of humorous or subtly sarcastic expression in which the intended meaning of the words is the direct opposite of their usual sense. *Example:* to say "that certainly explains it" when in fact the explanation obscures rather than clarifies.

key idea (n) The central thought or principal idea that the author wants to communicate to the reader; the main idea of a reading selection. The answer to the question, *"What is the author's most important idea about the topic?"*

key words (n) The strong words in a sentence, usually nouns and verbs, that convey most of the author's meaning.

learning (n) Getting knowledge of a subject or a skill in an art, trade, etc. by study, experience, or instruction.

logic (n) The science of correct reasoning.

logical (adj) Using or accustomed to using correct or consistent reasoning.

main idea (n) The key idea of a reading selection.

mapping (n) A way of outlining by diagraming the relationships among the various elements.

metaphor (n) A figure of speech containing an implied comparison, in which a word or phrase ordinarily and primarily used for one thing is applied to another. *Example:* The ocean liner plowed the waves.

objective (n) (1) Without bias or prejudice. (2) Being, or regarded as being, independent of the mind; real; actual.

opinion (n) A belief based not on absolute certainty or positive knowledge but on what seems true, valid, or probable to one's own mind; judgment.

outline (n) A summary of a subject, consisting of a systematic listing of its most important points.

paragraph (n) A distinct section or subdivision of a chapter, letter, etc., usually dealing with a particular point; it is begun on a new line, often indented.

pattern of organization (n) A specific method authors use to present their ideas in order to clarify the topics, subtopics, and key ideas and to show the relationship between the key ideas and the supporting ideas and supporting details; patterns of organization include *list, order (chronological, process, size or place, importance), compare/contrast, cause and effect,* and *problem-solution.*

perspective (n) A specific point of view in understanding or judging things or events, esp. one that shows them in their true relationship.

persuasive writing (n) Information presented to convince the reader to do or to believe something.

phrase (n) A sequence of two or more words conveying a single thought or forming a distinct part of a sentence but not containing a subject or a predicate.

predict (v) To state or make an educated guess about the contents of a reading selection in advance, especially to do so by reading actively (previewing, questioning, and so forth).

preface (n) An introductory statement to a book, telling its purpose, plan, scope, etc., usually written by the book's author.

prefix (n) A syllable, group of syllables, or word joined to the beginning of another word or base to alter its meaning or create a new word.

premise (n) A previous statement or assertion that serves as the basis for an argument.

preview (v) To survey a reading selection in advance by asking *What is this about? What is the author's most important idea about the topic? Why am I reading this? What do I already know about the topic? Why did the author write it?*

principal (adj) First in rank, authority, importance, degree, etc.

principle (n) A fundamental truth, law, doctrine, or motivating force.

prove (v) To establish as true; demonstrate to be a fact.

reading (n) Examining and grasping the meaning of written or printed characters, words, or sentences.

reading rate (n) The speed at which one reads, measured in words per minute.

reason (n) An explanation or justification of an act, idea, etc.

reasoning (n) The drawing of inferences or conclusions from known or assumed facts.

refer (v) To send or direct for aid or information.

relation (n) Connection, as in thought, meaning, etc.

root (n) The fundamental element of a word or form.

sectioning (n) A strategy of dividing reading selections into component parts to see how authors develop and support their ideas; a section is a unit of one or several paragraphs that can be grouped under one title because they have the same subtopics.

sentence (n) A word or a group of syntactically related words, usually containing a subject and a predicate, that states, asks, commands, or exclaims something.

sequence (n) The following of one thing after another in chronological, causal, or logical order.

signal words (n) Words that authors use to connect ideas and to help readers follow the direction of the authors' thoughts. *Examples:* also, besides, although, but, finally.

simile (n) A figure of speech in which two unlike things are compared, often by the use of *like* or *as*. *Example:* He was as strong as a bull.

skimming (n) Reading or glancing through quickly without reading word for word.

studying (n) Applying the mind so as to acquire knowledge or understanding.

subjective (adj) Of or resulting from the feeling or temperament of a person; not objective.

subtopic (*n*) Topics or subjects of the various parts that make up an entire reading, such as the units and chapters of a book or the paragraphs of an article.

suffix (*n*) A letter, syllable, or group of syllables added at the end of a word to change its meaning, such as *-ness* in gentleness, or *-ing* in walking.

summarize (*v*) To make a summary of; state briefly.

summary (*n*) A brief statement or account covering the main points.

supporting detail (*n*) Illustrations, examples, verifying statistics, reasons, or descriptions that back up supporting ideas by answering the questions *How? Who? Why? Where? When? What? Which?* and *What kind?*

supporting idea (*n*) The key idea of a section of a reading that elaborates on and develops the key idea of the entire passage and answers the questions *How? Who? Why? Where? When? What? Which?* and *What kind?*

syllabus (*n*) A course outline.

synopsis (*n*) A statement giving a brief, general review or condensation.

synthesis (*n*) (1) The putting together of parts or elements so as to form a whole. (2) A whole made up of parts or elements put together.

table (*n*) A compact arrangement of related facts, figures, or values.

terminology (*n*) The terms or system of terms used in a specific science, art, etc.

theme (*n*) A recurring, unifying subject or idea. *Example:* The theme of this book is that you can become an efficient reader by reading actively.

thesis (*n*) pl. **theses** A proposition maintained or defended in argument.

thinking (*n*) Reasoning about or reflecting on; exercising the power of reason; conceiving of ideas, drawing inferences, and using judgment.

topic (*n*) The subject of a paragraph, essay, or speech.

verify (*v*) To prove to be true by demonstration, evidence, or testimony.

Appendix C

Answer Key

Note: This appendix contains answers to every second item in an exercise, usually starting with item 1 in each. The answers are meant as guides only; your instructor will provide you with more information, such as why a particular answer has been specified or what other answers might also be appropriate. Where an answer may depend on a subjective response—for instance, in those exercises which ask you to refer to your own textbooks, make your own predictions or associations, or draw a diagram or mark up the text—it has not been provided below. Such answers should be discussed with your instructor and with your classmates.

The notation SA indicates that student answers will vary; IM indicates that an answer is too complex to include here but is instead provided in the instructors' manual.

Chapter 1 Reading for Ideas

1:A
1. a
3. b
5., 7., 9., 11. SA

1:B SA

1:C SA

1:D SA

1:E
1., 3., 5., SA

1:F
1.a., b., c. SA
A.
  1. c
  3. a
  5. b

7. d
9. b
11. d
B. SA

Chapter 2 Previewing

2:A

1. Medical Technology and Critical Decisions
3. amniocentesis

2:B

1. names, affiliation, and expertise
3. previewing
5. the glossary

2:C SA

2:D

1. to help the student understand economics
3. The book emphasizes the language of economics and the why of economics.
5. an understanding of basic economic concepts

2:E

1. retail merchandising
3. "Introduction" (Chapter 1); "Pricing" (Chapters 2, 3, 4, 5, 6, 8);

1:G

1. You learn through questioning. Looking for answers provides a purpose and a focus.

"Turning over Stock" (Chapters 7, 9, 10); "Buying" (Chapters 11, 12, 13, 14); "Merchandising and the Computer" (Chapter 15)

2:F

1. the opening paragraphs
3. study questions, summaries, and glossaries
5. the topic, the key idea, and how the chapter fits into the book

2:G SA

2:H

1. maturing and growing old
3. SA

2:I

1. Chicanos in the United States
3. He is probably understanding and sympathetic to Chicanos because he is a Chicano.
5. probably chronologically because it seems to be a history

Chapter 3 Developing Vocabulary: Connecting Words and Ideas

3:A

1. where an animal lives
   definition
   is

3. that one company controls
   example
   an example

5. a hard choice
   logic
   context
7. pertinent
   definition
   commas
9. a fleet
   contrast
   instead of

3:B Possible associations:

1. c society, social
3. d circle
5. d antiseptic, anticlimax
7. b odor
9. a pest

3:C

1. anti-   against
   social   society
   meaning: against society

3. im-   not
   mortal   death
   -al   suitable for
   meaning: can live forever
5. trans-   across
   mitt   send
   -ed   indicates past
              tense
   meaning: was sent
7. mono   one
   gam   marriage
   -ous   characterized by
   meaning: characterized by a
              single marriage
9. kilo-   thousand
   meter   a measure of
              length
   meaning: a thousand meters

3:D SA

3:E SA

Chapter 4   Finding the Topic

4:A

1. b
3. b
5. d

4:B

1. theory or Columbus's theory
3. question
5. he, storeowner

4:C

1. b

4:D

1. Stephen King, he, writer, he, he, Stephen King

3. theory (circle theory seven times)

4:E

1. c

4:F

1. a. Proteins
   b. functions of proteins
   c. composition of proteins

Appendix C / Answer Key   457

d. proteins in food
e. importance of proteins

4:H public broadcasting

4:I malpractice insurance

4:G

1. c

Chapter 5 Discovering the Key Idea

5:A

1. a. vaccination
   b. Vaccination can prevent influenza.
3. a. they
   b. They huddled.
5. a. Joad
   b. He (Joad) licked his lips.

5:B

1. T
3. T
5. KI
7. KI

5:C SA The key idea should be stated in a complete sentence.

5:D

1. c
3. d

5:E

1. What we perceive also depends on our past experience in terms of how "educated" our eyes are.

3. [M]any contemporary black women writers turn to the past.

5. In terms of an invasion route for many bacteria and viruses, our Achilles heel is located at the other end of the anatomy, the respiratory tract.

5F

1. a. Frazier's presentation
   b. Frazier's presentation was faulty.
3. a. brain tumor
   b. Severe consequences occur whether one operates on a brain or not. (The description provides background for later action.)

5:G

1. d; b

5:H

1. a. power
   b. Arthur
   c. Arthur became king by pulling the sword out of the stone.
   d. culture hero
   e. The culture hero derives his power from his knowledge of secrets.
   f. Power is given to the person who can use science or inventions.
3. a. & b. American farmers

c. American farmers in the post–Civil War period protested because they were discontented.

d. causes of discontent

e. The farmers were caught in an economic squeeze.

f. sources of problems

g. The farmers saw the railroads and banks as the sources of their problems.

h. American farmers were discontented during the post–Civil War period because they were poorer than people in the rest of the country.

Chapter 6 Identifying Supporting Ideas and Supporting Details

6:A

1. a. fast-walking
   b. Fast-walking has become the exercise of choice.
   c. throughout many parts of the United States
   d. people of all ages
   e. to improve their health without fuss and bother.

3. a. our fathers
   b. Our fathers brought forth a new nation.
   c. nation
   d. What kind?

5. a. professionals
   b. Professionals describe motivation.
   c. as wanting or intending to do well
   d. frequently

6:B

1. a. land animals
   b. Land animals are linked to their origin in the sea.
   c. a salty stream in our veins
   d. how?
   e. many-celled, circulatory system

3. a. carpet bedding
   b. Carpet bedding is a hideous gardening style.
   c. production and marketing of flowers, Victorian taste, patterns, examples
   d. why? why? what? where?
   e. zinnias, marigolds, etc., patterns of Oriental rugs, mottoes, clocks, etc., examples at Balmoral, Boston, China
   f. production and marketing, Victorian taste, patterns, examples

5. a. the group dynamics approach
   b. Members of policymaking groups have the same pressures as ordinary citizens.
   c. There are social pressures in cohesive groups. There is a need to preserve friendly relations.
   d. platoons; aircrews; heavy smokers

e. display or indication
f. sticking together
g. joint

6:C

1. a. Supporting idea(s)
   b. The television would be fed by an army of inputs.
   c. Level 3
   d. require an entire room

6:D

1. T: Two kinds of logic.
   ST: Inductive inferences and deductive inferences
   a. There are two kinds of logic.
   b. Inductive inferences start with observations and arrive at conclusions.
   c. engine firing
   d. Deductive inferences start with general knowledge and predict something specific.
   e. a horn that doesn't work
3. T: American and Afro-American literature.
   STs: The quest for motion; American and Afro-American literature; the comparison of American and European heroes
   a. American literature and Afro-American literature deal with mobility in the same way.
   b. There are many heroes searching for freedom and independence.
   c. Cooper's West; Melville's ocean; Whitman's open road
   d. American and Afro-American classics view movement and change as being valuable in themselves.
   e. open-ended; a process of becoming
   f. American heroes are unlike European heroes.
   g. Huck Finn, Ellison, Kerouac, the blues, and so forth.

6:E

1. a. knowledge
   b. Why?
   c. Knowledge gives understanding.
   d. How?
   e. relieves loneliness
   f. cries of pain
   g. gives a vision of heaven
   h. hungry children

6:F SA

Chapter 7 Recognizing Basic Structure

7:A

1. Introduction: paragraphs 1 and 2
   Function: provides background information
   Development: paragraphs 3–6
   Conclusion: paragraph 7

Function: summary (last line—commentary)

2. Signal words:

Paragraph 3: three of the major characteristics
First
as opposed to

Paragraph 4: but rather than
yet

Paragraph 5: a second characteristic

Paragraph 6: The third characteristic
rather than

Type of signal words used most frequently: signal words that indicate a shift in direction

7:B IM

Chapter 8 Analyzing Patterns of Organization

8:A IM

8:B

1. neutral (private citizen or member of government agency)
3. issue award
5. persuasion—not definitely settlement

8:C

1. compare/contrast
3. cause and effect
5. compare/contrast
7. problem-solution
9. order (size or place)

8:D

1. For example:
   List: I am taking four courses this semester.
   Order: My courses meet at 9:00, 11:00, 1:00, and 4:00.
   Compare/contrast: The requirements for my English course are different from those for the English course Jane is taking.
   Cause and effect: I did well in my biology course because I studied effectively.
   Problem-solution: If I don't understand the material in a course, I ask the instructor for help.

8:E

1. compare/contrast

8:F IM

8:G

1. Dominant pattern: List
2. Key idea: There are three important forms of *cuatequitl*.
3. Subtopics: village *cuatequitl*
   barrio *cuatequitl*
   cuatequitl of neighbors

8:H IM

Appendix C / Answer Key

8:I

1. The Third World tends to perceive the forest as a perpetual rather than renewable resource.

2. rate of recovery for damaged forests

ratio of deforested areas to replanted ones

deforestation affects the ecosystem

conserving and renewing existing reserves

Chapter 9   Becoming a Critical Reader: Determining the Author's Purpose

9:A

1. inform
3. persuade
5. persuade

9:B

1. a. Key idea: A speaker should distinguish among the attitudes, beliefs, and values of an audience.

b. Subtopic: attitude

c. Supporting idea: Attitude reflects likes or dislikes.

d. Subtopic: belief

e. Supporting idea: Belief is what you hold to be true or false.

f. Subtopic: values

g. Supporting idea: Values are enduring concepts of good and bad, right and wrong.

9:C

1. Teachers' actions have more of an effect upon student performance than teachers' expectations.

3. Children should be allowed to experience a loss.

9:D

a. – gullible + trusting
c. + childlike – childish
e. + aroma – smell
g. + noise – racket
i. – chatter + speak

9:E

1. a. Teachers' expectations have an effect on students' achievement.

b. Cause and effect

c. Subtopics: early studies of teacher expectations and student achievement
Goldenberg's findings
Goldenberg's observations
Goldenberg's conclusion

Chapter 10 Becoming a Critical Reader: Evaluating Evidence and Reasoning

10:A

The reason North America and Latin America are so different lies in their contrasting development as colonies. (They are different societies with different aims.)

10:B

1. F
3. O
5. F
7. F
9. F

10:C

Fact 1: "Democracy is the form of government in which the people have the ultimate power."

Fact 2: "The most important component of a democratic model is that the representatives...are responsive to the wishes of the people."

Fact 3: "The record shows...and the like."

Fact 4: "the basic democratic tenet that the public be informed has also been defied on occasion."

Fact 5: "The executive branch...election campaigns."

Opinion: "This model...the United States is undemocratic in many ways."

Opinion: "The people...are quite powerless."

Opinion: "Congress has shown its contempt for the electorate by the use of secret meetings."

10:D IM

10:E

1. Any criminal justice system like ours conveys a subtle, powerful message in support of established institutions.

2. The system concentrates on individual wrongdoers. Criminal law is put forth as the minimum neutral ground rules for any social living. (The focus on individual criminals diverts attention from the evil of the social order.)

10:F IM

Chapter 11 Putting it Together: Flexible Reading and Active Learning

11:A IM

11:B

1. compare/contrast

3. Underdeveloped countries control a small percentage of the total.

5. Developed countries consume almost all of the metals.

11:C

   1. c and e

   3. b

11:D

   1. Dowsing is using a piece of wood or a rod of a special shape to find underground minerals and water.

   3. Paragraphs 2 to 7

11:E

   1. a. twentieth-century poetry

      b. During the twentieth century, poetry changed from being public or impersonal to being personal.

      c. SA

      d. SA

      e. probably to inform

   3. Allen Ginsberg "dragged poetry into the streets."

11:F

   1. a. dowsing on maps

      b. wartime use

      c. research project

      d. explanation—amplifier

      e. explanation—vibrations

      f. explanation—the rod moves

      g. skeptics

11:G

   1. the battle about smoking in the media

   3. a. par. 10–11 news

      b. par. 12–13 talk shows

      c. par. 14–16 product liability

      d. par. 17–19 new aggressiveness

      e. par. 20–21 events, stunts, and good deeds

      f. par. 22–24 new frontiers

11:H IM

11:I

The breakdown should be under five headings, as follows:

   1. *organization:* topic, key idea, subtopic, supporting idea, supporting details

   3. *basic structure:* introduction, development, conclusion

   5. *author's purpose:* to inform, to persuade

11:J IM

11:K

   1. IM

Chapter 12 Reading the Humanities

12:A

   1. Labels: IM

12:B

   1. a. East Texas furniture

      b. Most of the Texan furniture of the late nineteenth century was built by Germans and has a special character.

      c. list

3. a. function of art

   b. The Realists and the Naturalists believed that the function of art was the betterment of humankind.

   c. cause and effect

12:C

1. a couple who order a picture from a portrait salesman

2. the couple and a portrait salesman

3. as buyers and sellers

4. The couple want a remembrance of their dead son. The salesman wants to make money.

5. The salesman did not keep his promise.

6. The father required the salesman to keep his promise.

7. People will believe what they want or need to believe.

8. Yes (for their setting)

9. to some extent (innocent people and a wartime picture)

10. sympathy for the elderly pair

11. SA

12. SA

12:D

1. a. that Kate Chopin wrote a radical short story about the institution of patriarchal marriage and family

   b. by showing the wife's untraditional response when she heard her husband had died (quotation)

   c. SA

3. a. It is a review of a mathematics book entitled *Archimedes' Revenge*.

   b. *Archimedes' Revenge* is a good introduction to contemporary mathematics.

   c. Yes, because it is a readable, well-informed book, because its author is a journalist who has made effective use of advice and criticism from mathematicians, and because it includes novel, unfamiliar concepts. The reviewer does not, however, think the book will do much to educate the reader.

   d. its strengths and weaknesses

12:E

1. a. Schools should be concerned with art.

   b. by maintaining that, because it deals with the discovery of form, art is an intellectual activity; schools deal with intellectual activity, and so they should include art

   c. triangle example—shows necessity of engaging in the activity of art

12:F

a. It is important for journalists to have a concern for ethics.

b. by offering reasons that ethics should be important to journalists—such reasons as duty, responsibility, and commitment to self and others

c. SA
   d. SA

12:G
   a. to persuade you to finish what you begin writing
   b. Everything you need to finish your writing already exists in you.
   c. cause and effect
   d. to become a better writer
   e. SA

Chapter 13 Reading the Natural Sciences

13:A SA

13:B
   1. The topic is measurement.
   3. SA
   5. There are figures to illustrate the text, new words are in italics (which means there is probably a glossary), there are example of exercises, and there are practice exercises.

13:C
   1. a mutualistic relationship
   3. First Janzen destroyed the ant colony. Second he separated the colony from the tree.
   5. that there is an important mutualistic relationship between the ant and the acacia tree—that is, one can't live without the other.

13:D
   1. a series of examples
   3. SA
   5. both inform and persuade

13:E
   1. c
   3. a and d

13:F SA and IM

13:G
   1. SA
   3. compare and contrast, cause and effect
   5. There is a difference between precision and accuracy.
   7. fact
   9. IM

13:H
   1. animal orientation
   3. problem-solution, compare and contrast
   5. Echo-location is a type of sonar that produces an auditory image of nearby surroundings.
   7. salmon by scent, bats and porpoises by sound, birds by vision, eels and pigeons by magnetic fields

Chapter 14 Reading the Social Sciences and History

14:A

1. alcoholism

3. statistics, facts, research, studies

5. The author wants the reader to know about and understand the problem of alcoholism.

7. The causes of alcoholism, the costs of alcoholism, the effects of alcoholism. Who drinks.

14:B

1. c.

3. e.

   the relationship between price and goods and services

14:C

1. a. the uninsured

   b. Whether or not an individual is insured depends on age, sex, race, income, and employment status.

   c. 85.2 62.0 23.2

   d. an employed Mexican-American between 15 and 44 years old who makes less than $14,000 per year

14:D SA

14:E

1. personal research

1. Daylight saving time should be extended into the winter months.

14:F

1. each other

3. Why? How?

5. inferential

7. methods

9. case studies

14:G

A. 1. world population

   3. inform and persuade

   5. SA

B. 1. IM

Credits (continued)

Page 28. Syllabus for Political Science 101, courtesy of Lois Wasserspring and the Political Science Department, Wellesley College, Wellesley, Mass.

Pages 27–30. Syllabus for "Medical Technology and Critical Decisions," courtesy of Ted Ducas and Alan Shuchat, Wellesley College, Wellesley, Mass.

Pages 33–35, 135–136, 152–153, 183, 364–367, 370, 406, 435–440, Kupchella/Hyland, *Environmental Science*, 3/e, © 1993, pp. xvii–xviii, 48, 135–136, 143, 214–217, 357–359, 438, 478. Reprinted with permission of Prentice Hall, Upper Saddle River, NJ.

Pages 40–42, 137, 254–256. Hoag/Hoag, *Introductory Economics*, © 1991, pp. xix–xx, 5, 8–9. Reprinted with permission of Prentice Hall, Upper Saddle River, NJ.

Pages 48–51, 203–204. Excerpts by Robert A. Baron adapted from *Psychology: The Essential Science*. Copyright © 1989 by Allyn and Bacon. Used with permission.

Pages 52–57. "The Chicanos." Copyright © 1984 by Tino Villaneuva, excerpted from "Introduction," *Imagine: International Chicano Poetry Journal*, Volume I, Number I (Summer 1984). Used by permission of the author.

Pages 90–91, 250–251, 395–399. From Rebecca J. Donatelle and Lorraine G. Davis, *Health, the Basics*. Copyright © 1994 by Allyn and Bacon. Reprinted by permission.

Pages 93, 270–271. From *Basic Concepts of Chemistry* by Alan Sherman, Sharon Sherman, and Leonard Russikoff, copyright © 1984 by Houghton Mifflin Company. Reprinted by permission of the publisher.

Pages 96, 411. Excerpts from Martin Bronfrenbrenner, Werner Sichel, and Wayland Gardner, *Economics*, copyright © 1984 by Houghton Mifflin Company. Reprinted by permission of the publisher.

Pages 113–114, 430–432. Passages by David J. Cherrington excerpted from *Organizational Behavior: The Management of Individual and Organizational Performance*. Copyright © 1989 by Allyn and Bacon. Used with permission.

Pages 117–118. Excerpt by Shelia Tobias reprinted from *Overcoming Math Anxiety* by permission of W. W. Norton & Company, Inc. Copyright © 1993 by Sheila Tobias.

Pages 118–119, 143–144. Excerpt from *Modern Biology* by James H. Otto and Albert Towle, copyright © 1973 by Holt, Rinehart, and Winston, Inc. Reprinted by permission of the publisher.

Page 120. Heinrich Zimmer, excerpt from *The King and the Corpse*, Joseph Campbell, editor, Bollingen Series XI. Copyright 1948, © 1957, 1975, renewed by Princeton University Press.

Pages 123–124. Excerpt from *A Documentary History of the United States*, copyright © 1952, 1956, 1965, 1976, 1985 by Richard D. Heffner. Reprinted by arrangement with New American Library, a Division of Penguin Books USA, Inc., New York, New York.

Pages 148–150. Excerpt from "Making a Way Out of No Way: The Open Journey in Alice Walker's *The Third Life of Grange Copeland,*" by Robert James Butler. Reprinted from Black American Literature Forum (now African American Review), Vol. 22, No. 1 (Spring 1988).

Pages 167, 168, 169–171. Marvin Rosen, selections from *Introduction to Photography,* second edition. Copyright © 1982 by Houghton Mifflin Company. Reprinted by permission of Wadsworth Publishing.

Pages 173–175. Excerpted from *Cognitive Psychology,* copyright © 1983 by Darlene V. Howard. Reprinted by permission of Macmillan Publishing Company.

Pages 176–178. Selection from *Women of America: A History* by Carol Ruth Berkin and Marybeth Norton, copyright © 1979 by Houghton Mifflin Company. Used with permission.

Pages 199–202. Passage by Oscar Lewis is an excerpt from *Life in a Mexican Village: Tepoztlán Restudied,* © 1951 by the Board of Trustees of the University of Illinois. Reprinted by permission of the University of Illinois Press and Ruth M. Lewis.

Pages 203–204, 216–219. Robert A. Baron, *Essentials of Psychology.* Copyright © 1996 by Allyn and Bacon. Reprinted by permission.

Pages 211, 361–362, 385–388. Audesirk/Audesirk, *Biology: Life on Earth,* 3/e, © 1993, pp. 814–815, 845, 982. Reprinted by permission of Prentice Hall, Upper Saddle River, NJ.

Pages 215, 231–233. Passages by Eduardo Galleano are reprinted from *Open Veins of Latin America,* copyright © 1973 by Monthly Review Press. Reprinted by permission of Monthly Review Foundation.

Pages 219–221. Passage by Selma H. Fraiberg reprinted with permission of Charles Scribner's Sons, an imprint of Macmillan Publishing Company, from *Magic Years* by Selma Fraiberg. Copyright © 1959 by Selma H. Fraiberg; copyright renewed.

Pages 237–240. Passage by Jeffrey H. Reiman reprinted from *The Rich Get Richer and the Poor Get Prison,* Second edition. Copyright © 1979, 1984 by Jeffrey H. Reiman. Reprinted by permission of Macmillan Publishing Company.

Pages 242–243. From John E. Conklin, *Criminology,* fifth edition. Copyright © 1995. All rights reserved. Reprinted by permission of Allyn and Bacon.

Pages 251–254. From J. George Bryjak and Michael P. Soroka, *Sociology: Cultural Diversity in a Changing World.* Copyright © 1994 by Allyn and Bacon. Reprinted by permission.

Pages 259–262. Excerpts from *The People's Almanac* by David Wallechinsky and Irving Wallace (Garden City: Doubleday & Co., Inc., 1975). Reprinted by permission.

Pages 263–265. Reprinted from *United States in Literature,* by James E. Miller, Jr., Carlota Gardenas de Dwyer, Robert Hayden, Russell J. Hogan, and Kerry M. Wood. Copyright © 1979 by Scott, Foresman and Company. Reprinted by permission.

Pages 267–269. Excerpt from *Passion for the Piano,* copyright © 1983 by Judith Oringer. Published by Jeremy P. Tarcher, Inc., Los Angeles. Reprinted by permission of St. Martin's Press, Inc.

Pages 273–276. From John Vivian, *The Media of Mass Communication,* third edition. Copyright © 1995 by Allyn and Bacon. Reprinted by permission.

Pages 280–283. Passage by Michele Wallace is an excerpt from *Black Macho and the Myth of the Superwoman,* copyright © 1978, 1979 by Michele Wallace. Reprinted by permission of the author.

Pages 295–300. Howard Zinn, excerpts from *A People's History of the United States.* Copyright © 1980 by Howard Zinn. Reprinted by permission of Harper Collins, Publishers, Inc.

Pages 325–330. Tomás Rivera, "The Portrait," from *Y No Se lo Trago La Tierra,* translated as *And The Earth Did Not Devour Him,* by Evangelina Vigil-Pinon, copyright © 1987 by Tomás Rivera. Reprinted by permission of Arte Publico Press, Houston.

Pages 332–333. Passage by Wendy Martin is reprinted from *New Essays on the Awakening* edited by Wendy Martin. Reprinted by permission of Cambridge University Press, copyright © 1988.

Page 334–335. Passage by Reuben Hersh is from a review of *Archimedes Revenge: The Joys and Perils of Mathematics* by Paul Hoffman, in *American Scientist,* Volume 77, September–October 1989. Reprinted by permission of the Scientific Research Society.

Pages 339–341. Passage by Everett Dean Martin is reprinted from *The Meaning of a Liberal Education* by Everett Dean Martin with permission of W. W. Norton & Company, Inc. Copyright © 1926 by W. W. Norton & Company, Inc. Copyright renewed 1954 by Daphne Mason.

Pages 342–343. Passage by Ralph Smith is from *Aesthetics and the Problems of Education,* © 1971 by the Board of Trustees of the University of Illinois. Reprinted by permission of the University of Illinois Press.

Pages 345–346. Passage by John C. Merrill is reprinted from *The Imperative of Freedom,* copyright © 1974 by Hastings Press. Reprinted by permission of the publisher.

Pages 351–354, 369. W. Kenneth Hamblin, *Introduction to Physical Geology,* 2/e, © 1994, pp. 15, 304–305. Reprinted by permission of Prentice Hall, Upper Saddle River, NJ.

Pages 371–372. Passage by Neil Campbell is an excerpt from *Biology,* Second edition, by Neil Campbell. Copyright © 1990, Benjamin/Cummings Publishing Company, Redwood City, Calif. Reprinted by permission.

Pages 378–384. Stephen Stoker, *Introduction to Chemical Principles,* 4/e, © 1993, pp. 11–16. Reprinted by permission of Prentice Hall, Upper Saddle River, NJ.

Page 402. Excerpt from Elaine M. Blinde, "Female Intercollegiate Athlete," in *Journal of Physical Education, Recreation, & Dance,* March 1989. The *Journal* is a publication of the American Alliance for Health, Physical Education, Recreation, and Dance, 1900 Association Drive, Reston, VA 22091.

Pages 414–417. Selection from "The Partial Reformulation of a Traumatic Memory of a Dental Phobia during Trance: A Case Study," in *International Journal of Clinical and Experimental Hypnosis,* 1983, Volume XXXL, no. 1. Reprinted by permission of Sheldon R. Baker, Ed. D.

Pages 418–426. Susan A. Ferguson et al., "Daylight Saving Time and Motor Vehicle Crashes: The Reduction in Pedestrian and Vehicle Occupant Fatalities," *American Journal of Public Health* 1995, Vol. 85. no. 1, p. 92–95. Reprinted by permission.

Index

Abstracts, 48
Academic language, 72–78
Action, in fiction, 318
Active vocabulary, 66, 78
Aesthetics and the Problems of Education (Smith), 302–303
Allen, Frederick Lewis: *Only Yesterday*, 196–197
American Government, Roots and Reform (O'Connor and Sabato), 94–95, 114–115, 401
American Scientist (Hersh in), 334–335
American Short Stories (Current-Garcia and Patrick), 312–313
Analysis, in problem solving, 373–374
Analytical and critical reading, 5
  of fiction, 318–333
  in the natural sciences, 363–368
  in the social sciences and history, 399–429
Analyze, 101
And The Earth Did Not Devour Him (Rivera), 325–330
Anderson, Bob: *Stretching*, 192
Anderson, Margaret L.: *Thinking About Women*, 198–199
Anthropology, 391, 427
Appendix, 70, 444–467
Application, in natural sciences, 376–377
Archaeology, 391
Argument, in the humanities, 338–344
Art reviews, 332
Articles, previewing, 48–57
Associating, for efficient reading, 10, 13–14
Association clues, 66–69
Astronomy, 349
Audesirk, Gerald and Teresa Audesirk: *Biology—Life on Earth*, 211, 361–362, 385–388
Audesirk, Teresa and Gerald Audesirk: *Biology—Life on Earth*, 211, 361–362, 385–388
Author's purpose
  credibility and bias, 227–233
  determining, 207–225

distinguishing fact from opinion, 233–234
and emotional appeal, 222, 240–244
in the humanities, 307
and reasoning, 237–240
and techniques, 221–223
See also Informational writing; Persuasive writing
The Autobiography of Bertrand Russell (Russell), 151–152

Baker, Sheldon R. and David Boaz: "The Partial Reformulation of a Traumatic Memory of a Dental Phobia during Trance," 414–417
Baron, Robert A.: "Lunar Madness: The 'Transylvanian Effect' Revisited," 121–122
Baron, Robert A.: *Psychology: The Essential Science*, 48–51, 121–122, 193–194
Baron, Robert A.: *Essentials of Psychology*, 203–204, 216–219
Basic Concepts of Chemistry (Sherman et al.), 93, 270–271
Basic Mathematics for College Students (Falstein), 108
Basic structure, 165–178
  and author's purpose, 209–210
  conclusion, 168–169
  introduction, 166–168
  and patterns of organization, 221–222
  signal words for, 171–172
  topic development, 167–168
Beebe, Steven A. and Susan J. Beebe: *Public Speaking*, 112, 213
Beebe, Susan J. and Steven A.: *Public Speaking*, 112, 213
"Beer Ads and Gutter Talk" (Casler), 97
Benedict, Ruth: *Patterns of Culture*, 145–146
Berkin, Carol Ruth and Mary Beth Norton: *Women of America: A History*, 176–178
Bernstein, Douglas A. et al.: *Psychology*, 76, 87

Bias of author, 227–233
Biology, 349
Biology (Campbell), 371–372
Biology—Life on Earth (Audesirk and Audesirk), 211, 361–362, 385–388
The Biology of People (Singer and Hilgard), 109
bird by bird (Lamott), 347–348
Black Macho and the Myth of the Superwoman (Wallace), 280–283
"Blame Negligent Doctors, Not Insurance" (Sargent), 99
Blinde, Elaine M.: "Female Intercollegiate Athletes," 402
Blum, John M., 83, 101
Boaz, David and Sheldon R. Baker: "The Partial Reformulation of Traumatic Memory of a Dental Phobia during Trance," 414–417
Book reviews, 331
Bowie, Henry P.: *On the Laws of Japanese Painting*, 209–210
A Brief History of Time (Hawking), 89–90
Broadcasting in America (Head and Sterling), 98, 140
Broadcast review, 336
Bronfenbrenner, Martin, Werner Sichel, and Wayland Gardner: *Economics*, 96, 411
Brue, Stanley L. and Campbell R. McConnell: *Economics: Principles, Problems, and Policies*, 214
Bryjak, George J. and Michael P. Soroka: *Sociology: Cultural Diversity in a Changing World*, 251–254
Butler, Robert James: "Making a Way Out of No Way: The Open Journey in Alice Walker's The Third Life of Grange Copeland," 148–150

Cameron, Kenneth M. and Patti P. Gillespie: *The Enjoyment of Theatre*, 315
Campbell, Neil A.: *Biology*, 371–372
Career choice
 and the humanities, 345–348
 in natural sciences, 376–377
 in social sciences and history, 429–431
Carson, Rachel: *The Sea Around Us*, 135
Case studies, 412, 431–432
Casler, Lawrence: "Beer Ads and Gutter Talk," 97
Catch a Fire: The Life of Bob Marley (White), 311–312
Causal relationship, 190
Cause and effect
 as pattern of organization, 190–192
 signal words for, 191–192
Chaffee, John, *Thinking Critically*, 109
Chapsel, Madeleine: *Reporter*, 332
Chapters of textbooks
 previewing, 44
 titles, 96
Characters, in fiction, 318–319
Chemistry, 349
Cherrington, David J.: *Organizational Behavior: The Management of Individual and Organizational Performance*, 114, 430, 432
The Chicanos (Villaneuva), 52–57
Chopin, Kate: "The Story of an Hour," 321–323
Chronological order, as pattern of organization, 183
Cicero, 101
Civilisation (Clark), 140–141
Clark, Kenneth: *Civilisation*, 140–141
Classroom aids, 75
Clouse, Barbara Fine, 172
Cognitive Psychology (Howard), 173–175
Compare and contrast
 as pattern of organization, 186–190
 signal words for, 188–189
Concentration, 9, 10, 12
Conclusion, 168–169
 in problem solving, 374
Conflict resolution, 318
Conklin, John E., *Criminology: The Study of Criminal Behavior*, 242–243
Connections, making, 3–10
Connotative language, 222–223
Contextual clues, for vocabulary, 61–66
Contrast
 as contextual clue, 63
 See also Compare and contrast
Cornell method, 285–287
Credibility of author, 227–233
Criminology: The Study of Criminal Behavior (Conklin), 242–243
Critical reading, 5, 207–225, 226–244
 approaches to, 207–244
 and author's credibility and bias, 227–233
 determining author's purpose, 207–225
 and emotional appeal, 240–244
 evidence and reasoning, 226
 of fiction, 318–333
 in the humanities, 307–348
 in the natural sciences, 363–368
 and problem solving, 373
 in social sciences and history, 399, 427–429

See also Informational writing; Persuasive writing; Reading
Critical thinking, 4, 207–225, 226–244, 373–376, 432
Criticism, in the humanities, 331–337
Crowder, Michael and LaRay Denzer: *Protest and Power in Black Africa*, 428–429
Curran, Daniel J. and Claire M. Renzetti: *Social Problems: Society in Crisis*, 197–198, 204–205, 228–231, 405
Current-Garcia, Eugene and Walton R. Patrick: *American Short Stories*, 312, 313

Dabaghian, Jane: *Mirror of Man*, 182
Dance reviews, 331
Davis, Lorraine G. and Rebecca J. Donatelle: *Health, the Basics*, 90–91, 250–251, 395–399
"Daylight Saving Time and Motor Vehicle Crashes" (Ferguson et al.), 418–426
Definition
  as contextual clue, 62
  in problem solving, 373
"A Delicate Operation" (Selby), 112–113
Denzer, LaRay and Michael Crowder: *Protest and Power in Black Africa*, 428–429
Descriptive writing, in the humanities, 309
Designing and Painting for the Theatre (Pecktal), 310
Details
  in natural sciences, 363
  supporting, 128–153
Dethier, Vincent C.: *To Know a Fly*, 184
Development of the topic, 167–168
Diacritical marks, 74
Diagraming, 278, 289–294
  in fiction, 325
Diagrams, 291, 406
Dictionary, using a, 74
A Documentary History of the United States (Hefffner), 123–124
Donatelle, Rebecca J. and Lorraine G. Davis: *Health, the Basics*, 90–91, 250–251, 395–399
Drugs, Crime, and Social Policy (Mieczkowski), 112
Ducas, Ted, 27–30
Duncan, Frederick J., Jr., and Barbara Rockett: "Malpractice Costs Hurt All," 99

Economics, 391, 427
Economics (Bronfenbrenner, Sichel, and Gardner), 96, 411

Economics: Principles, Problems and Policies (McConnell and Brue), 214
Eitzen, D. Stanley and Maxine Baca Zinn: *In Conflict and Order: Understanding Society*, 235
Ellison, Ralph, 102
Emotional appeal, 240–244
The Enjoyment of Theatre (Cameron and Gillespie), 315
Environmental Science (Kupchella and Hyland), 32–38, 135–136, 152–153, 183, 364–367, 370, 406, 435, 440
Escape from Childhood (Holt), 92
Eshleman, J. Ross: *The Family*, 106–107
Essentials of Psychology (Baron), 203–204, 216–219
Etymology, 74
Evaluation, steps to making an, 226–244, 432
Evidence, evaluation of, 233–244, 375–376, 427–429
Examples
  as contextual clue, 62
  textbook, 355–356
Exercises, textbook, 356
Experiments, in social sciences, 412
Explanations
  as contextual clue, 62
  textbook, 355

Facts
  evaluating, 236
  opinion distinguished from, 233–235
Factual writing, in the humanities, 308–309
Falstein, Linda: *Basic Mathematics for College Students*, 108
The Family (Eshleman), 107
Faulkner, William, 102
"Female Intercollegiate Athletes" (Blinde), 402
Ferguson, et al.: "Daylight Saving Time and Motor Vehicle Crashes," 418–426
Fessenden, Joan S. and Ralph J. Fessenden, 77
Fessenden, Ralph J. and Joan S. Fessenden, 77
Fiction, 316–333
  evaluating, 320–333
  previewing, 316–318
  skimming, 325
  See also Imaginative writing; Literature
Figurative language, 222–223
Figures, 407
Film: Form and Function (Wead and Lellis), 106, 311
Fisher, Dexter: *The Third Woman: Minority Women Writers of the United States*, 110

Fleisher, Belton M. et al.: *Principles of Economics*, 76, 403
Flexible reading, 245–294
  approaches to, 245–294
  definition of, 246
  sectioning and, 266–277
  skimming in, 247–266
  studying and organizing in, 277–294
Flitcraft, Anne, 105
Flowcharts, 290
"Flu/Cold—Never the Strain Shall Meet" (Larkin), 110
"For Liberal Arts Students Seeking Business Careers, Curriculum Counts" (Garis, Hess, and Marron), 16
Fraiberg, Selma: *Magic Years*, 219–221
Fry, Edward: *Skimming and Scanning*, 247

Galbraith, J.K.: *The New Industrial State*, 139–140
Galeano, Eduardo: *Open Veins of Latin America*, 215, 231–233
Gardner, Wayland, Martin Bronfenbrenner, and Werner Sichel: *Economics*, 96, 411
Garis, Jeff W., H. Richard Hess, and Deborah J. Marron: "For Liberal Arts Students Seeking Business Careers, Curriculum Counts," 16
Gaylin, Willard: "Still, a Prisoner Owns Himself," 210
General words, 73
Geology, 349
Ghai Dharam P.: *Protest and Power in Black Africa*, 97–98
Gillespie, Patti P., and Kenneth M. Cameron: *The Enjoyment of Theatre*, 315
Glossaries, 73, 449–454
Gombrich, E.H.: *The Story of Art*, 309
Government, 391
Graphics
  in natural science textbooks, 358
  previewing, 404
  in social sciences and history, 404–411
Graphs, 291, 406–408
Green Thoughts (Perenyi), 136–137
Groupthink (Janis), 138

Hamblin, Kenneth: *Introduction to Physical Geography*, 351–354, 369
Hare, Richard Mervyn: *Men of Ideas*, 338–339
Hawking, Stephen W.: *A Brief History of Time*, 89–90
Head, Sydney and Christopher Sterling: *Broadcasting in America*, 98, 140

Health, the Basics (Donnatelle and Davis), 90–91, 250–251, 395–399
Heffner, Richard D.: *Documentary History of the United States*, 123–124
Hersh, Reuben, 334–335
Hess, H. Richard, Jeff W. Garis, and Deborah J. Marron, "For Liberal Arts Students Seeking Business Careers, Curriculum Counts," 16
Highlighting, 278
Hilgard, Henry and Sam Singer: *The Biology of People*, 109
History, 390–441
  analytical and critical reading in, 399–429
  career choices in, 429–431
  definition of, 392
  evaluation of evidence in, 427–429
  graphics in, 404–411
  nontextbook material, 393–394
  patterns of organization in, 400–404
  reading, 390–441
  textbooks, 393
  vocabulary of, 400
  See also Social sciences
History of Art (Janson), 310
Hoag, Arleen J. and John H. Hoag: *Introductory Economics*, 40–42, 137, 254–256
Hoag, John H. and Arleen J. Hoag: *Introductory Economics*, 40–42, 137, 254–256
Holt, John: *Escape from Childhood*, 92
"Horror of Horrors" (Wood), 89
Howard, Darlene: *Cognitive Psychology*, 173–175
How to Study in College (Pauk), 92
Human Development (Ripple et al.), 107
Humanities, 307–348
  and career choices, 345–348
  critical reading in the, 330–344
  definition of, 307
  descriptive writing in the, 309
  factual writing in the, 308–309
  imaginative writing in the, 316–330
  informational writing in the, 308–316
  patterns of organization in the, 312–316
  persuasive writing in the, 330–344
  process writing in the, 309–310
  reading the, 307–348
Hume, David: "Of the Delicacy of Taste and Passion," 343–344
Hyland, Margaret C. and Charles E. Kupchella: *Environmental Science*, 32–38, 135–136, 152–153, 183, 364–367, 370, 406, 435–440
Hypothesis, 350

Ideas, reading for, 3–24
supporting, 128–153, 284–286
Illustration, as contextual clue, 62
Imaginative writing
fiction, 316–330
See also Literature
The Imperative of Freedom (Merrill), 345–346
Importance, as pattern of organization, 185–186
In Conflict and Order: Understanding Society (Eitzen and Zinn), 235
In Search of History (Tuchman), 314–315
Inferential reading, 5
and context clues, 61
key ideas, 110–111
topics from clues, 95–97
Informational writing, 208–214
contained in persuasive writing, 227–228
distinguished from persuasive writing, 208–210
in the humanities, 308–311
patterns of organization in, 210–211
See also Author's purpose; Persuasive writing
Introduction, reading the, 166–168
Introduction to Chemical Principles (Stoker), 378–384
Introduction to the Foundations of American Education (Johnson et al.), 216
Introduction to Photography (Rosen), 167, 168, 169–171
Introduction to Physical Geography (Hamblin), 351–354, 369
Introductory Economics (Hoag and Hoag), 40–42, 137, 254–256
Irvings, Mark, 189–190

Janis, Irving L.: *Groupthink*, 138
Janson, H.W.: *History of Art*, 310
Johnson, James A. et al.: *Introduction to the Foundations of American Education*, 216

Kaye, Marvin: *The Story of Monopoly, Silly Putty, Bingo, Twister, Frisbee, Scrabble, Etc.*, 91
Key idea, 100–127
of articles, 48
Cornell Method and, 285
definition of, 100
inferring the, 110–113
of longer readings, 113–124
outlining for, 323–324
in paragraphs, 103–110

and persuasive writing, 214
placement of, 105–110
in science textbooks, 351
sectioning and, 266–271
of a sentence, 100–102
skimming for, 248
supporting words and, 129–130
Key words, supporting words and, 129–130
Kidder, Tracy: *Soul of a New Machine*, 196
The King and the Corpse (Zimmer), 120
Koffman, Elliot B.: *Problem Solving and Structured Programming in Pascal*, 110
Kupchella, Charles E. and Margaret C. Hyland: *Environmental Science*, 32–38, 135–136, 152–153, 186, 364–367, 370, 406, 435–440

Laboratory manuals, 350
Lamott, Anne: *bird by bird*, 347–348
Language, in fiction, 320
Larkin, Tim: "Flu/Cold—Never the Strain Shall Meet," 110
Learning, definition of, 3
Learning and Memory (Norman), 113
Lecos, Chris W.: "Sugar: How Sweet It Is—and Isn't," 109
Lellis, George, and George Wead: *Film: Form and Function*, 106, 311
Lewis, Oscar: *Life in a Mexican Village: Tepoztlan Restudied*, 199–202
Life in a Mexican Village: Tepoztlan Restudied (Lewis), 199–202
Lincoln, Abraham, 131
List pattern
as pattern of organization, 181–182
signal words for, 181–182
Literal reading, 5
Literature, 309
See also Fiction; Imaginative writing
The Lives of a Cell (Thomas), 147–148
Lochhead, Jack: "Teaching Analytical Reasoning Skills Through Pair Problem Solving," 107
Locke, John, 4
Logic, as contextual clue, 62–63
Longer readings
and key idea, 113–124
supporting ideas and details in, 141–153
"Lunar Madness: The 'Transylvanian Effect' Revisited" (Baron), 121–122

The Magic World of Orson Welles (Naremore), 336–337
Magic Years (Fraiberg), 219–221
"Making a Way Out of No Way: The Open Journey in Alice Walker's *The Third*

Life of Grange Copeland" (Butler), 148–150
"Malpractice Costs Hurt All" (Duncan and Rockett), 99
Manwatching (Morris), 89
Mapping, 278, 289–294
Marking up
  for active studying, 278–283
  fiction, 325
  in the natural sciences, 370–372
Marron, Deborah J., Jeff W. Garis, and H. Richard Hess: "For Liberal Arts Students Seeking Business Careers, Curriculum Counts," 16
Martin, Everett Dean: *The Meaning of a Liberal Education*, 339–341
Martin, Wendy: *New Essays on the Awakening*, 332–333
Massachusetts Bay Community College, 430–431
Mathematics, 350–358
  textbooks for, 350–358
  See also Natural sciences; Social sciences
Math reviews, 351
McConnell, Campbell R. and Stanley L. Brue: *Economics: Principles, Problems, and Policies*, 214
McNerney, Kathleen: *Understanding Gabriel Garcia Marquez*, 333–334
The Meaning of Liberal Education (Martin), 339–341
The Media of Mass Communication (Vivian), 273–276
Men of Ideas (Hare), 338–339
Merrill, John C.: *The Imperative of Freedom*, 345–346
Meteorology (Weisberg), 368–369
Mieczkowski, Thomaas: *Drugs, Crime, and Social Policy*, 112
Mill, John Stuart, 13
Miller, James E., Jr. et al.: *United States in Literature*, 263–265
Mirror of Man (Dabaghian), 182
Modern Biology (Otto and Towle), 119, 143–144
Morris, Desmoong: *Manwatching*, 89
Morton, Robert: *Southern Antiques and Folk Art*, 314
Movie reviews, 331
Mursell, James: *Using Your Mind Effectively*, 105–106
Music reviews, 331–332

Naremore, James: *The Magic World of Orson Welles*, 336–337
Natural sciences, 349–389
  analytical and critical reading in the, 363–368
  career choices in the, 376–377, 429
  characteristics of the, 349–350
  evaluation of evidence, 375–376, 427–429
  organizing for study in, 370–372
  patterns of organization in the, 368–370
  previewing in the, 351–355
  problem solving in the, 372–375
  skimming in the, 363
  textbooks for, 350–359
  vocabulary of, 356–357
New Essays on the Awakening (Martin), 332–333
The New Industrial State (Galbraith), 139–140
Nonfiction, 61
Norman, Donald A.: *Learning and Memory*, 113
Norton, Mary Beth et al.: *A People and a Nation*, 184–185
Norton, Mary Beth and Carol Ruth Berkin: *Women of America: A History*, 176–178
Note taking, 278, 284–289, 371
Novels. *See* Fiction; Imaginative writing; Literature

Observation, in social sciences, 413
O'Connor, Karen and Larry J. Sabato, *American Government, Roots and Reform*, 94–95, 114–115, 401
Of the Delicacy of Taste and Passion (Hume), 343–344
On the Laws of Japanese Painting (Bowie), 209–210
Only Yesterday (Allen), 196–197
Open Veins of Latin America (Galeano), 215, 231–233
Opinion, fact distinguished from, 233–235
Order pattern
  as pattern of organization, 183–186
  chronological, 183
  importance, 185–186
  process, 183–184
  signal words for, 186
  size or place, 184–185
Organization patterns. *See* Patterns of organization
Organizational Behavior: The Management of Individual and Organizational Performance (Cherrington), 114, 430, 432
Organizing, 277–294, 370–372
Oringer, Judith: *Passion for the Piano*, 267–269

Orlich, Donald C.: *Teaching Strategies*, 116
Orlik, Peter B., 130
Otto, James H. and A. Towle: *Modern Biology*, 118–119, 143–144
Outlining, 27, 278, 284–289
    fiction, 325
Overcoming Math Anxiety (Tobias), 117–118
Overview, skimming to gain, 248–257

Paragraphs
    finding the topic in, 86–90
    key idea of, 103–110
    supporting ideas and details in, 132–141
"The Partial Reformulation of a Traumatic Memory of a Dental Phobia during Trance" (Baker and Boaz), 414–417
Passion for the Piano (Oringer), 267–269
Passive vocabulary, 66, 78
Patrick, Walton R. and Eugene Current-Garcia: *American Short Stories*, 312, 313
Patterns of Culture (Benedict), 145–146
Patterns of organization, 5, 179–206
    and author's purpose, 221–222
    cause and effect, 190–192
    chronological order, 183
    compare and contrast, 186–190
    in fiction, 318
    in the humanities, 312–316
    importance as, 185–186
    and informational writing, 210–214
    list pattern, 181–182
    in the natural sciences, 368–370
    order pattern, 183–186
    and persuasive writing, 221–222
    problem-solution, 192–194
    process pattern, 183–184
    in scientific writing, 368–370
    sectioning and, 266
    size or place, 184–185
    skimming for, 248–249
    in social sciences and history, 400–404
Pauk, Walter, 92, 285
Pecktal, Lynn: *Designing and Painting for the Theatre*, 310
A People and a Nation (Norton et al.), 184–185
The People's Almanac (Wallechinsky and Wallace), 259–262
A People's History of the United States (Zinn), 295–300
Perenyi, Eleanor: *Green Thoughts*, 137
Persuasive writing, 203–210, 214–221
    and author's credibility and bias, 227–233

connotative and figurative language, 222–223
distinguished from informational writing, 208–210
distinguishing fact from opinion, 233–235
and emotional appeal, 240–244
in the humanities, 330–344
informational writing contained in, 227–231
and patterns of organization, 221–222
propaganda, 241
reasoning, 237–240
and scientific reports, 360
See also Author's purpose; Informational writing
Philosophy, argument used in, 338–344
Physics, 349
Pirsig, Robert: *Zen and the Art of Motorcycle Maintenance*, 146–147
Place or size, as pattern of organization, 184–185
Play reviews, 331
Plot, in fiction, 319–320
Political science, 391, 427
Postman, Neil: *Teaching as a Conserving Activity*, 88
"The Poverty of Criminals and the Crime of Poverty" (Reiman), 237–240
Precision, in natural sciences, 363
Predicting, for efficient reading, 10, 14–16
Preface, of textbooks, 31–37
Prefixes, 70–73, 445–446
Previewing, 10, 26–58, 84
    an article, 48–57
    chapters, 44–48
    course syllabus, 26–31
    definition of, 26
    fiction, 316–318
    graphics, 404
    natural science textbooks, 351–355
    questions and questioning, 31–33
    social science textbooks, 393–394
    table of contents, 36–37
    textbooks, 31–44
    See also Skimming
Preview Questions, 58, 99, 127, and inside front cover
Principles of Economics (Fleisher et al.), 403
Problem-solution
    in the natural sciences, 372–375
    as pattern of organization, 192–194
Problem solving, 372–375, 431
Problem Solving and Structured Programming in Pascal (Koffman), 110

Process, as pattern of organization, 183–184
Process writing, in the humanities, 309–310
Propaganda, 241
  See also Persuasive writing
Protest and Power in Black Africa (Ghai), 97–98, 428–429
Psychology, 391, 427
Psychology: The Essential Science (Baron), 48–51, 121–122, 193–194
Psychology (Bernstein et al.), 76
Public Speaking (Beebe and Beebe), 112, 213
Punctuation, and context clues, 61–66
Purpose, defining a, 11–12
Pyramids, 291

Questions and questioning
  and basic reading, 10–11
  fiction, 317
  and finding the topic, 83–87
  and key ideas, 100–105
  and previewing, 31–33
  and problem solving, 372
  scientific reports, 360
  sectioning and, 266
  in social sciences and history, 399–400, 427–428
  and supporting ideas and details, 128–131
Quinn, Andrew, 86

Raven, Peter H.: "Third World in the Global Future," 77, 256
Reading
  approaches to, 246–294
  definition of, 3, 4–6
  graphics, 358, 404–411
  and the reader, 6–9
  See also Analytical reading; Critical reading; Flexible reading; Inferential reading; Literal reading
Reading rates, 247
Reasoned argument, 428
Reasoning
  and critical reading, 237–240
  and evidence, 237–240
Reiman, Jeffrey: "The Poverty of Criminals and the Crime of Poverty," 237–240
Remembering and forgetting, 155–159
Renzetti, Claire M. and Daniel J. Curran: *Social Problems: Society in Crisis*, 192–198, 204–205, 228–231, 405
Report form, 412–426
Reporter (Chapsel), 332
Reports, 412–426, 431

Research papers
  note taking for, 287
  in social sciences, 412–426
Retention, 9
Reviewing
  skimming and, 262
  textbooks, 351
Reviews. *See* Persuasive writing, in the humanities
Ripple, Richard A. et al.: *Human Development*, 107
Rivera, Tomas: *And The Earth Did Not Devour Him*, 325–330
Rock of Ages: The Rolling Stone History of Rock and Roll (Wenner), 308–309
Rockett, Barbara and Frederick J. Duncan, Jr.: "Malpractice Costs Hurt All," 99
Roots, 70–72, 446–447
Rosen, Marvin J.: *Introduction to Photography*, 167, 168, 169–171
Russell, Bertrand: *The Autobiography of Bertrand Russell*, 150–152

Sabato, Larry J. and Karen O'Connor: *American Government, Roots and Reform*, 94–95, 114–115, 401
Sargent, David J.: "Blame Negligent Doctors, Not Insurance," 99
Scanning, 257–262
  See also Skimming
Scarr, Sandra, and James Vander Zanden: *Understanding Psychology*, 19–22
Sciences. *See* History: Natural sciences; Social sciences
Scientific knowledge, 350
Scientific method, 360
Scientific reports, 359–362
The Sea Around Us (Carson), 135
Sectioning
  and flexible reading, 266–277
  scientific reports, 360
  textbooks, 351–354
Selby, Roy C., Jr.: "A Delicate Operation," 112–113
Sentences
  finding the topic in, 84–86
  key idea of, 100–102
  supporting words and phrases in, 129–131
Setting, in fiction, 319
Sherman, Alan: *Basic Concepts of Chemistry*, 93, 270–271
Shuchat Alan, 27–30
Sichel, Werner, Martin Bronfenbrenner, and Wayland Gardner: *Economics*, 96, 411

Signal words
　for basic structure, 171–172
　for cause and effect pattern, 191–192
　for compare and contrast pattern, 188–189
　for list pattern, 181–182
　for order pattern, 186
　skimming for, 248
Singer, Sam and Henry Hilgard: *The Biology of People*, 109
Size or place, as pattern of organization, 184–185
Skimming, 12, 247–265
　fiction, 325
　in flexible reading, 247–265
　in natural sciences, 363
　in social sciences and history, 399
　See also Previewing; Scanning
Skimming and Scanning (Fry), 247
Smith, Frank: *Understanding Reading*, 249
Smith, Ralph: *Aesthetics and the Problems of Education*, 342–343
Social Problems: *Society in Crisis* (Curran and Renzetti), 197–198, 204–205, 223–231, 405
Social sciences, 390–441
　analytical and critical reading in, 399–429
　career choices in the, 429–433
　definition of, 390–392
　evaluation of evidence in the, 427–429
　graphics in, 404–411
　nontextbook material, 393–394
　patterns of organization in, 400–404
　previewing, 393–394
　reading the, 390–441
　research report in, 412–426
　skimming in the, 399
　textbooks, 393
　vocabulary of, 400
　See also History
Sociology, 391, 427
Sociology: Cultural Diversity in a Changing World (Bryjak and Soroka), 251–254
Soroka, Michael P. and George J. Bryjak: *Sociology: Cultural Diversity in a Changing World*, 251–254
Soul of a New Machine (Kidder), 196
Southern Antiques and Folk Art (Morton), 314
Stark, Evan, 105
Steinbeck, John, 102
Sterling, Christopher and Sydney Head: *Broadcasting in America*, 98, 140

"Still, a Prisoner Owns Himself" (Gaylin), 210
Stoker, H. Stephen: *Introduction to Chemical Principles*, 378–384
"The Story of an Hour" (Chopin), 321–323
The Story of Art (Gombrich), 309
The Story of Monopoly, Silly Putty, Bingo, Twister, Frisbee, Scrabble, Etc. (Kaye), 91
Stretching (Anderson), 192
Structure. *See* Basic structure
Study guides, 350
Studying, 247, 277–294
Study questions, 351
Style guides, in the social sciences, 413
Subtopics, 90–95
　sectioning and, 266–277
　skimming for, 242–266
　and supporting ideas and details, 142–144
Suffixes, 70–72, 447–448
"Sugar: How Sweet It Is—And Isn't" (Lecos), 109
Summaries, 124–126
Summary exercises, 58, 99, 127, 178, 206, 225, 244, 294, 348, 389, 441
Supporting details, 128–153
　Cornell Method and, 285–287
　definition of, 132–134
　in longer readings, 141–153
　outlining for, 284–285
　in paragraphs, 132–141
　and skimming, 249
Supporting ideas, 128–153
　Cornell Method and, 285–287
　definition of, 132–134
　in longer readings, 141–153
　outlining for, 284–287
　in paragraphs, 132–141
Surveys, 412
Syllabus
　definition of, 26
　previewing a, 26–31
Symbols, in textbooks, 357

Table of contents, 36–37
Tables, 291, 405–406
"Teaching Analytical Reasoning Skills Through Pair Problem Solving" (Lochhead), 107
Teaching as a Conserving Activity (Postman), 88
Teaching Strategies (Orlich et al.), 116
Technical words, 73–74
Terms, in textbooks, 356–357
Textbooks
　in history, 393

for natural sciences, 350–359
and nontextbook material, 393–394
organization of, 355–358
preface of, 33–37
previewing, 31–37
in the social sciences, 393, 431
Textbook aids, 75
Theme, in fiction, 319–320
Theses, of textbooks, 32
Thinking about Women (Andersen), 198–199
Thinking and words, 60
Thinking, critical, 4, 207–225, 226–244, 373–376, 432
Thinking Critically (Chaffee), 109
Thinking, definition of, 3, 4
The Third Woman: Minority Women Writers of the United States (Fisher), 110
"Third World in the Global Future" (Raven), 77, 256
Thomas, Lewis: *The Lives of a Cell*, 147–148
Thorndike, 4
Thought, 19–22
Time lines, 290
Tobias, Sheila: *Overcoming Math Anxiety*, 117–118
To Know a Fly (Dethier), 184
Topic(s), 83–99
　definition of, 83
　development of, 167–168
　inferring, from clues, 95–98
　in longer readings, 90–95
　in paragraphs, 86–90
　in sentences, 84–86
　skimming for, 246–251
　and subtopics, 90–95
　and supporting ideas and details, 142–144
Towle, A. and James H. Otto: *Modern Biology*, 118–119, 143–144
Tuchman, Barbara: *In Search of History*, 314–315

Underlining, 274–275
Understanding Gabriel Garcia Marquez (McNerney), 333–334
Understanding Psychology (Scarr and Zanden), 19–22
Understanding Reading (Smith), 249
United States in Literature (Miller et al.), 263–265
Using Your Mind Effectively (Mursell), 105–106

Vertical diagrams, 291
Villanueva, Tino: *The Chicanos*, 52–57
Vivian, John, *The Media of Mass Communication*, 273–276

Vocabulary, 59–79
　and academic language, 72–78
　general, 60–72
　of natural sciences, 356–357
　passive and active, 66, 78–79
　of philosophy, 338
　in social sciences and history, 400
　using association clues, 66–69
　using context clues, 61–66
　word-part clues, 69–72
　See also Words

Wallace, Irving and David Wallechinsky: *The People's Almanac*, 259–262
Wallace, Michele: *Black Macho and the Myth of the Superwoman*, 280–283
Wallechinsky, David and Irving Wallace: *The People's Almanac*, 259–262
Wasserspring, Lois, 28
Wead, George and George Lellis: *Film: Form and Function*, 106, 311
Webster's New World Dictionary, 74, 449
Weisberg, Joseph S.: *Meteorology*, 368–369
Wenner, Jann S.: *Rock of Ages: The Rolling Stone History of Rock and Roll*, 308–309
White, Timothy: *Catch a Fire: The Life of Bob Marley*, 311–312
Women of America: A History (Berkin and Norton), 176–178
Wood, Michael: "Horror of Horrors," 89
Word-part clues, 69–72
Words
　and academic language, 72–74
　connotative and figurative language, 222–223
　and meaning, 59
　prefixes and suffixes, 69–72, 445–448
　supporting, 129–130
　See also Signal words; Vocabulary

Zanden, James Vanden and Sandra Scarr: *Understanding Psychology*, 19–22
Zen and the Art of Motorcycle Maintenance (Pirsig), 146–147
Zimmer, Heinrich: *The King and the Corpse*, 120
Zinn, Howard, *A People's History of the United States*, 295–300
Zinn, Maxine Baca and Stanley D. Eitzen, *In Conflict and Order: Understanding Society*, 235